D1380486

Fauna Scotica

Fauna Scotica

ANIMALS AND PEOPLE IN SCOTLAND

Polly Pullar and *Mary Low*

BIRLINN

First published in 2012 by
Birlinn Limited
West Newington House
10 Newington Road
Edinburgh
EH9 1QS

www.birlinn.co.uk

Copyright © Polly Pullar and Mary Low 2012

The moral right of Polly Pullar and Mary Low
to be identified as the authors of this work has
been asserted by them in accordance with the
Copyright, Designs and Patents Act 1988

All rights reserved. No part of this
publication may be reproduced, stored or
transmitted in any form without the express
written permission of the publisher.

ISBN: 978 1 84158 561 1

British Library Cataloguing-in-Publication Data
A catalogue record for this book is available
from the British Library

Designed and typeset by Mark Blackadder

p. ii Polly Pullar's dog Kim on
Kenmore Hill, Perthshire (Polly Pullar)

p. 304 Robert Harrison, Glen Artney, with Blackface
and North Country Cheviot tups (Polly Pullar)

Printed and bound in Europe

Am fear bhitheas trocaireach ri anam,
cha bhi e mi-throcaireach ri bhruid

(He who is merciful to his soul will
not be unmerciful to a beast)

*

For

Freddy, Iomhair, Mum and Susie
(Polly Pullar)

and

Emil, Oscar and Theo
(Mary Low)

ACKNOWLEDGEMENTS

Many people have helped me with this book but without my mentor and guide, Fergus Crystal, it would have been a hard task indeed. I would like to specially thank Iomhair Fletcher, and my son Freddy, both of whom have provided support, advice and eternal help. Mervyn Browne deserves special thanks for his invaluable input. Thanks are also due to my writer friends Linda Cracknell, Jamie Grant and Ruary McKenzie Dodds. Sadly, photographer Malcolm Gosling is no longer here to see his wonderful images in print. I am most grateful to his widow, Margaret.

I would also like to thank: Les and Chris Humphreys; Paul and Louise Ramsay – Viva La Beaver!; Beryl and the late Russell Coope; Patrick Steuart Fothringham; Tim and Ruth Fison, whose wildlife knowledge is second to none; Alex Murray (of Loch Earn); Donald Houston; Jim Crumley; Clare Mackie; Kenneth Steven; Donald and Sally Crystal; Pete Small; Aonghus MacKechnie; Alan Stewart; George Jamieson; Kate Macpherson; Andy and Gay Christie; Cameron Thomson; Nancy Lavering; Neil McIntyre and Laurie Campbell.

Polly Pullar

Many people who have shared their time and expertise with me. The following deserve a special mention: Bruce for his unstinting support, Phyllis Ashburn; Ronald Black; Joe Brown; Rupachitta; Chris Cameron; Tony Dilworth; Walter Eliot; Bob and Wilma Hewit; Calum Laing; Cathlin Macaulay; Donald MacLennan; Kenna Moffat; Dòmhnall Uilleam Stiùbhart; the late Brian Wain; the library and IT staff at Sabhal Mòr Ostaig and the special collections department of Edinburgh University Library. None of these are at all responsible for any errors of fact or dubious opinions expressed here. A huge thank you to all concerned.

Mary Low

CONTENTS

INTRODUCTION

You have to be really passionate about wildlife to take a rotting bird to bed with you, or dress as a pantomime horse to photograph owls. Such was Shetlander Bobby Tulloch's love of the natural world that, as a very small child, his mother found him asleep locked in embrace with a putrefying puffin, the fishy aroma of which pervaded the entire room. No Scotsman fuelled my own passion in natural history more than Bobby Tulloch because he epitomised all that I love about nature.

Wildlife enthusiasts come in various guises. Some adopt a scientific approach and have an encyclopaedic knowledge gained from text books and hours of study. Some travel the length and breadth of the country in search of particularly rare birds, adding a tick to their extensive lists before departing hurriedly to find another. Others have a cursory interest and only require a little inspiration to light the spark of a lasting passion. And then there are field naturalists, who observe nature everywhere, lying for hours in cold, wet conditions, waiting patiently in the hope of catching the tiniest glimpses in order to learn a little more. Bobby Tulloch was one such person, a student of nature.

He forged a vital link between man and animals, and the impact that both had on one another's lives. With unsurpassed field knowledge, he also understood the lore and beliefs that surrounds creatures; how the struggling Shetlanders endeavouring to eke out an existence in the harshest of environments, once killed the otter, or *dratsie*, for its luxuriant pelt. How they gathered the eggs of seabirds including those of the *bonxie*, or great skua, to add to their frugal fare; how fishing and collecting shellfish were activities of vital importance to their survival. When it was necessary to take creatures in order to live, the islanders did as people did elsewhere. During the war years shags and gannets were regularly sent to London from Scotland's islands and marketed under the guise of Highland geese and ducks.

Bobby was made Shetland's first full-time RSPB representative in 1964. His anecdotes delighted thousands of visitors; he spoke to people about wildlife and its conservation on a level where they felt totally comfortable, thus bridging the gap between science and ignorance. It is this very approach that has provided much of my inspiration for *Fauna Scotica.*

Despite its small area, Scotland is surprisingly diverse, and it is due to this diversity that *Fauna Scotica* has been divided into habitats, and the creatures herein are not organised taxonomically. It is important to appreciate the wealth of beautiful habitats found here, from seashore to Alpine montane terrain, from the rare machair of the Western seaboard to the rich farming lands of the east. While many of the animals and birds could be found in most, or indeed all, of these habitats, they have been placed where

Opposite. Puffin carrying nest material (Polly Pullar)

they are most likely to be found, and grouped with others that are similar because we hope to bring a fresh approach to this book.

Fauna Scotica does not set out to be the definitive guide to all Scotland's wildlife, and due to limitations of the book's size, not all of our fauna could be included. However, it is a celebration of our extraordinary biodiversity, including our native farm animals, a taster to whet the enthusiast's appetite. It seeks to portray through anecdote, natural history fact, superstition, myth and legend, the importance of the interaction between humans, birds and beasts in a bid to light the fire of a lifetime interest. It also highlights the power of observation, and the oft-underestimated value of the oral tradition in encouraging the young naturalist. A scientist's take on a particular beast may be far removed from that of a countryman who spends all his days out on the hill or amongst his livestock, and often wildlife facts can never be set in stone. To this end we have endeavoured to relate it the way we have best understood it.

Sadly, few children now have their roots in the country, and many know little or nothing of country matters, and even less about natural history and farming. My parents and grandparents were all true countrymen. My mother frequently played with passing gypsy children, and my grandmother was once fed baked hedgehog at a gypsy encampment. We hand-reared orphan birds and mammals, usually had pet lambs and a house full of other animals. Much of my childhood was spent on Britain's most westerly mainland peninsula, Ardnamurchan, where time was spent with shepherds, stalkers, crofters and fishermen. I understood from an early age that crows, ravens and black-backed gulls would peck out the eyes of our sheep when they were having lambing difficulties, and that lambs and hens were fair game for foxes. I knew that rogues had to be removed. I also knew that a good bullock caught in a bog, or with a broken leg, would be culled and eventually served up for dinner. My parents often went out with a gun to shoot something for the pot.

Our primary schoolteacher, Mary Cameron, was keen to encourage nature education. We whiled away hours in rock pools, and had tanks of tadpoles in the classroom. My son Freddy had a very similar upbringing and was always collecting items to take to his school's nature table. However, the sheer weight of a piece of minke whale bone he lugged in, found on a remote Hebridean beach, made it almost collapse. Today health and safety laws would prevent this. Children do not have the opportunities that they need to understand the importance of respect and understanding for nature, and the wealth of tales, both fact and fiction, passed from generation to generation, is diminishing.

We have come a long way since the Victorian era and the days when lark pie might have been served up at a celebration dinner. However, it was not until the 20th century that the conservation movement really began to grow apace. There is much good and bad: though we are still losing species, we have also gained others. The osprey has made a spectacular comeback; sea eagles, and red kites have been reintroduced, and we now have beavers on some of our rivers.

Wildlife is vital to our wellbeing. Bobby Tulloch's extraordinary discovery of Scotland's first breeding snowy owls on the Shetland island of Fetlar in 1967 caused enormous excitement, and was testimony to the importance of interaction between man and the natural world. Once the press had been informed, the reaction was explosive and immediately a 24-hour guard was put on the nest. Bobby and the owls found themselves in the limelight of a countrywide stage. The owls in his care went on to breed for nine years, rearing a total of twenty owlets.

In February 1989, an oiled snowy owl was found on a BP tanker crossing the Atlantic from Canada. The vessel docked at a Forth port and the bird was given to me to look after by the SSPCA. It too caused a flurry of media interest.

Eventually, after it had been cleaned and rehabilitated, it was agreed that the young male owl should be flown to Shetland and released on Fetlar. At the time there were two elderly female snowy owls on the island – the last male had died in 1974.

Prior to the flight, I waited with the owl and SSPCA officer Martin Love in the VIP lounge at Aberdeen airport where there was intense press activity; excitement was mounting.

Prior to release we took the owl into Fetlar's primary school. The delighted children told us tales of the birds on their island and said that they frequently saw the two lone female owls sitting on the dry stone dykes from their window. RSPB warden of the time, Pete Ellis, was adamant that allowing children to become close to wildlife, and explaining things to them was the way forward. Having taken owls, raptors, hedgehogs and lambs for school visits around Scotland, I had witnessed these benefits.

The release was dramatic. Through damp-fogged binoculars, we watched, silently oblivious to the icy weather and the rain seeping down our necks, as the owl was freed. The female sitting atop the dyke bobbed her head back and forth, eager to have a better look at the new arrival. Magnificent with his daffodil-yellow eyes, the male, unperturbed, largely ignored her. He did not bide long. Like many young males, he had wanderlust and was later seen on Fair Isle. Though there have been other records of vagrant snowy owls in Scotland, none have bred here since.

The correspondence and paintings that children from all over Scotland sent me afterwards were testimony to the importance of raising awareness of our fauna with each new generation. Fetlar, previously just a tiny dot on the map of Scotland, was now a noteworthy location; and on a personal level, it forged a link for me with Bobby Tulloch, a man whose approach helped fuel my own all-consuming wildlife passion, and subsequently provided much of my inspiration for *Fauna Scotica.*

Polly Pullar
Aberfeldy, July 2012

Fauna Scotica explores how human beings observe and interact with other animals, not just physically and economically, but also at the level of feeling, imagination and belief. These powerful but less visible motivators have been my remit. Beliefs are notoriously difficult to pin down, not least because people have a disconcerting way of inhabiting more than one worldview at a time, often without knowing it. We can be nature-lovers and consumers, vegetarians and pragmatists, hard-nosed about some things, sensitive about others. The traces we leave behind in images can be just as ambiguous as what we say. Pictish carved stones, for example, provide ample evidence that animals were hugely significant to the people who made them, but there is no consensus as to what these images meant. Shamanism, as it exists in other cultures, may shed some light on stories of animal helpers and flights or journeys to strange countries. Durkheim's classic description of totemism finds an echo in animal kinship stories like that of Oisìn and his deer-mother. An unwilling affinity is found in the Border ballad 'Tam Lin', in which Tam is changed successively into a newt, an adder, a bear, a lion, and so on. It is too lengthy to be included here, but stories about people turning into birds, seals, deer, hares and back again are common, here as in other cultures. Superstition was once the catch-all term for such beliefs. There undoubtedly is such a thing. You only have to spend half an hour with some of the Victorian folklore collectors, to feel its jittery cobwebby influence, but a closer look may reveal art, psychological strategy, prayer, and metaphors for things that cannot be spoken of directly.

The churches have also had a powerful influence on how Scots have looked upon their non-human neighbours. The uselessness of animal sacrifice, for example, and the acceptability of eating meat in moderation, are both biblical ideas.

The belief that animals exist *only* for human use found its way into Christian theology from Artistotle during the thirteenth century, along with the argument that they have no moral sense and therefore no immortal soul. Even the austere John Calvin had difficulty with this one, but it is still the prevailing view. Even so, visitors to the pet cemetery in Cullen will notice a few crosses among the memorials there and a simple plaque of a horse's head, set into the wall of a roofless chapel in Arran, points to a similar dissident streak in our nature. Prayers for animals have been preserved, especially in the Gaelic tradition. Probably these were once widespread throughout Scotland. These are mostly for domestic animals, especially cattle. Some address the creature by name, with evident compassion ('*beo bhith d'ire-sa, bheothaich bhoch*' / life be near you, poor beast') but an interest in animals for their own sake, independent of their usefulness, was limited. Bestiary animals always stand for something other than themselves, as do many animals in early Scottish literature. Our finest and funniest fable-writer, Robert Henryson, was so brilliant at caricaturing human foibles through other animals that we can only sit back and enjoy it. Michael Scot was an exception. Interested in all kinds of natural phenomena, this Scots-born thirteenth-century Franciscan was the first translator of Aristotle's *De Animalia.* The Chronicle of Melrose quotes from this work, so someone in the Tweed valley shared his interests before the dissolution of the monasteries.

It could be tough combining animals with spirituality. Henryson gives us a rare glimpse of a ploughman starting his day 'with Benedicite'. This was the first word of the Canticle 'Bless the Lord, all created things' and includes the line 'Bless the Lord all birds of the air, bless the Lord all beasts and cattle …'. So we would seem to be looking at a custom of starting work by calling on your fellow-creatures to give thanks for the simple joy of being alive. But Henryson knows all about human frailty. Soon the ox-team are trying the ploughman's patience and he starts cursing them instead: the wolf may have you by nightfall, he shouts, his equanimity in tatters.

By and large, animals have been peripheral to theology. During the eigheenth century however, a new kind of clergyman began to emerge. The Anglican divine, John Lightfoot travelled with Thomas Pennant on his tour of the Hebrides in 1772 and included a section on mammals in the resulting *Flora Scotica*. In 1822, a Church of Scotland minister, John Fleming, published a *Philosophy of Zoology* before embarking on a *History of British Animals*, six years later. His inclusion of fossil species rejected literalist readings of the creation story and came as something of a bomb-shell at the time. Fleming went on to become Professor of Natural History at the Free Church College in Edinburgh, challenging trainee ministers to engage with science. When the *Berwickshire Naturalists' Club* was founded in 1831, fully a quarter of its members were clergymen, while beyond the Highland line, Rev. Alexander Stewart, ('Nether Lochaber') contributed nature notes to the *Inverness Courier* throughout the 1860s and 70s and dreamed of writing a 'Celtic natural history'.

William MacGillivray, arguably the first professional naturalist in Britain, was born in Aberdeen in 1796 and brought up on Harris. He pursued his interests with unprecedented vigour, insisting that his students actually observe animals in the field. He was also a keen shot, and it was around this time that taxidermy collections began to appear in the newly-built city museums. Now anyone could get up close and personal with an eagle or a wild cat – or what remained of them. We began to know more about other animals physically than ever before. Scotland's first vet came to Kelso in 1816. Six years later, the Royal School of Veterinary Studies (the 'Dick Vet') opened in Edinburgh, offering a scientific training in animal medicine for the first time.

Some animals ambush us from a place beyond reason or religion. How else could the poet have imagined Finn's grief for his hound – as being like 'a parting of soul and body'? On a lighter note, the tenant of Fladda Chuain, off Skye, had a soft spot for plovers. A flock of about 2,000 of them used to arrive on the island each year in September, while the sportsmen were blasting away across the water. The tenant looked forward to their arrival, and when

Martin Martin suggested that he have two for every meal throughout the winter, the response was not what we have come to expect from an eighteenth-century Gael:

> My notion seemed very disagreeable to him; for he declared that he had never once attempted to take any of them, though he might if he would: and at the same time he told me, he wondered how I could imagine, that he would be so barbarous as to take the lives of such innocent creatures as came to him only for self-preservation.

The philosopher David Hume believed that 'the laws of humanity' bind us to treat other animals with kindness and compassion. This drew strong opposition, even ridicule at the time, but by 1839 the Scottish Society for the Prevention of Cruelty to Animals (SSPCA) had lobbied successfully to put the humane treatment of animals a firm footing in law. Its first patron was a Mrs Martha Gibson, about whom more deserves to be known.

New Scots bring their own beliefs and traditions. A few winters ago I saw, from a tenement window in Glasgow, trays loaded with rice and chapattis in the back green below. Food for the birds, I was told. A Gaelic-speaking Buddhist corresponded with me about hares. There is so much more to be explored here. The churches have moved on as well. There are now nearly 300 'eco-congregations' in Scotland, some of them directly involved in wildlife projects. There are still two views, however. One holds that people care for animals best when it is in their own interests to do so. Others believe that in the great scheme of things, animals have their own intrinsic value. Meanwhile, in the global market, animals are defined as natural resources, nothing more. This too is a belief.

Ideally, *Fauna Scotica* would have presented an even spread of traditions across Scotland, but the sources are notoriously patchy. There is not – nor could there ever be – a map of who believed what, where, when and why. When I describe a tradition as being 'from Argyll' or 'from the North-east' this should not be taken to mean that it was only ever to be found there. It simply means that an instance was recorded there. It might have been more widespread, even with parallels abroad or in other parts of the British Isles. As for common names, there are so many that we have had to be selective. They can also vary, even along one short stretch of coastline. There is no formal classification system for bird and animal names in Scots or Gaelic. Our main sources for common names have been Polly's extensive knowledge of local usage, the *Scots Thesaurus*, the *Dictionary of the Scots Language*, Dwelly's *Gaelic Dictionary* and Ellen Garvie's *Gaelic Names of Plants, Fungi and Animals*. Alexander Forbes's classic *Gaelic Names of Beasts* has been used with caution since the day I encountered nightjar and dotterel under the same heading as snipe.

Mary Low
Melrose, July 2012

CHAPTER ONE

MOUNTAIN

INTRODUCTION

You seldom hear a hill shepherd or stalker mention a mountain, for in Scotland the word is generally used by tourists, even though it is perfectly correct. To those living and working in this harsh environment, even the highest peak is referred to as 'the hill'.

The rugged mountain terrain stretches from the vertiginous scree-covered peaks of the Isle of Skye with its infamous Cuillin Ridge, to the sweeping majesty of the Cairngorm Massif, the rounder hills of Galloway, and the grassy knolls of the Angus Glens. Hugely varied, all are blessed with a savage beauty, enhanced by wild weather systems and a complex geological history. In 1901 the geologist and writer Sir Archibald Geikie highlighted this: 'The records of the Ice Age are so abundant, so clear, and so indisputable – everywhere the trail of the ice meets our eye.'

Due to the inaccessibility and ruggedness of the terrain, it is the mountain landscape that has been least interfered with by man. Experts predict that fauna such as mountain hare and ptarmigan may soon vanish altogether if the climate warms even a few degrees. The deforestation of huge tracts of hill land has totally altered mountain ecology over the centuries, leading to large areas of blanket bog replacing richer habitat. Animals and birds that previously lived in the forests were either lost altogether, as in the case of bear, lynx, wolf, auroch (wild cattle) and wild boar, or they had to adapt, in the case of red deer.

There was one other major event that was to have far-reaching consequences after the Jacobite Rising of 1745 – the Highland Clearances. This devastating project was initiated in 1762 and continued until the Crofting Act of 1886. Highland lairds brought in huge numbers of a new breed of sheep, the Cheviot, together with the Scottish Blackface. Local crofters were driven out of their crofts and sheilings, hounded from the land because it was thought sheep would provide easy money for the gentry. In a cruel twist, this proved to be far from the case. Perhaps the subsequent 'glens of silence' afforded wild creatures more peace, but the loss of habitat ruined any benefits this newfound peace might have brought.

It is the vegetation clothing the hills and mountains that provides the key to the species of fauna living there. Shrubby plants, heather, lichen, moss and native trees grow in surprising places. The influx of large numbers of sheep led to the depletion of vegetation from over-grazing. They devoured even the tiniest saplings, preventing any natural regeneration of the magnificent Scots pine forest that once covered much of the high ground. Mountainous regions began to alter, with only the highest tops safe from the inva-

Opposite. Loch Baa and Meall à Bhuird (Polly Pullar)

sion, retaining their own particular character of tundra-type vegetation above the tree line.

Natural changes constantly occur but are harder to gauge; we are perhaps unaware that even mountains are altering by degrees. Closer to the clouds and fluctuations in extremes of temperature, the onslaught from icy gales, and periods of drought, allow nature to ceaselessly hone and sculpt the high ground.

Stalkers and shepherds say that the increased activity of thousands of hillwalkers and mountain bikers is altering the landscape, causing disturbance and erosion of old stalker's paths. Ironically, during the Victorian era of the great Scottish sporting estates, it was keepers and shepherds who brought about devastation as they massacred birds of prey and mammals in thousands, in favour of maintaining unnaturally high populations of grouse and sheep. They in turn played a part in ecological destruction.

Many organisations are now trying to protect our mountains by building paths and attempting to heighten awareness and respect for the natural history of the area. Trees are being replanted, with grant schemes set up for the re-establishment of native woodland: the landscape is set to change once again.

In 1875 John Muir wrote, 'Thousands of tired, nerve-shaken, over-civilized people are beginning to find out that going to the mountains is going home. That wildness is a necessity.' We need to ensure we retain the greatest respect for this wild land. This is surely the key to safeguarding the future of some of the finest landscape in the British Isles, and it is vital to the survival of its wildlife.

RED DEER AND THEIR FOLLOWERS

Red Deer

Cervus elaphus
S: reid deir, rede deer
G: *fiadh*

In 1851 Sir Edwin Landseer's famous painting *Monarch of the Glen* epitomised all that we revere about wild red deer. Even now, people may view a magnificent stag silhouetted against a stormy sky and mention this work of art. Although there is probably no native species that has caused more controversy over the decades, the red deer is without doubt one of the most beautiful animals we have, and its life cycle and natural history is a source of fascination.

Deer specialist and vet John Fletcher has spent a lifetime working with red deer and writes in his autobiography, *A Life for Deer*, of the importance of the earliest deer parks to the Scottish economy. Close to his own pioneering deer farm at Reediehill, Auchtermuchty, a huge deer park at Falkland Park had been the source of venison for the King's wedding in 1503. Earlier records show payments made for hay for deer in 1288 at a deer park at Stirling, and there are records of cows being bought for milk for rearing deer calves in Falkland in 1479.

Red deer have had to adapt to major habitat change. Once a strict woodland species living freely in the ancient wood of Caledon, many now live on open moor. From there, they ascend to high plateaux in summer to avoid the onslaught from flies. The cover of the ancient forest is no longer available – by the start of the nineteenth century nearly all of it had been felled. Conflicts of interest between stalkers, shepherds, foresters, hillwalkers and naturalists mean that there will always be challenges for the conservation or control of deer populations. Landowners face a difficult task reconciling the situation while sustaining economic viability.

Deer thrived during the Victorian era with the evolution of large Highland sporting estates. Paying sportsmen

A typical 'batchelor' herd of stags in Glen Lyon (Polly Pullar)

came in large numbers to Scotland to shoot a stag, and many fine heads with beautiful antlers were lost. Today the practice has altered and there is a trend not to shoot trophy animals, but to eradicate the poorest members of the herd. Carefully managed by keepers and stalkers, the deer are culled annually to try to keep numbers under control. Without this they become weaker and succumb to starvation, as was witnessed in the recent severe Scottish winters. Exceedingly wet winters also take a heavy toll but high deer numbers further damage the natural habitat. Many parts of the hills are still referred to as deer forests, although they are largely treeless today.

The red deer rut is one of the most exciting highlights of the Scottish natural calendar, and takes place each autumn as the days shorten and the hinds come into oestrus. The stags that have been living in large bachelor herds for the rest of the year try to establish a harem – only the biggest and best stags are strong enough to hold a group of hinds, and most small males never have the chance to mate. During the rut their primeval roaring echoes round the glens. At all other times of the year stags are largely silent, although hinds and calves constantly emit their yelping contact calls.

While rutting, the stags use peat hags, stirring them up frantically as they wallow and urinate in them, throwing the dark substance up over their bodies with feet and antlers, or simply rolling in it. They emerge blackened with peat, and their darker colour makes them appear larger and more imposing. With its strong aroma, the mixture of peat and urine is a stag's equivalent of aftershave and is used to impress the ladies. Fierce battles and the sound of clashing antlers often end in serious puncture wounds, and the subsequent death of a stag. John Colquhoun writes in *The Moor and the Loch*: 'In former times poachers used to fasten spears with the points upwards in these places, and when the stag threw himself into the hole, he was impaled.'

Calves are born in June when the hills have turned green. By this time most adult deer have moulted their dull grey-brown coats in favour of the rich red ones that give them their vernacular name. Antlers are cast annually. The new antler comes coated in protective 'velvet'. Deer antler is the fastest-growing mammalian tissue of all and can grow at a rate of up to two or three centimetres per day. Pregnant hinds often chew discarded antlers at a time of year when they need a calcium boost for their developing calves.

The Nature Conservancy Council created a special reserve for red deer in 1958, when it procured the whole island of Rum. Much has since been learned about the breeding ecology of this species. There is also a Manx shearwater colony on the island and researchers were surprised to find the deer eating bird carcasses there. With Rum's impoverished hilly ground lacking essential minerals, the calcium from the birds' bones provides the island's deer with a valuable source of minerals.

Red deer hind with calf (Polly Pullar)

Much energy goes into antler production each year. A small percentage of stags lack antlers and are known as 'hummels'. Once thought to be a genetic defect, this is not the case. Due to their weight and strength, hummels may often hold a harem of hinds and their male offspring grow normal antlers.

Stalkers who have been on the same estates for years know many of their animals individually. Most have fascinating tales of the deer on their ground, and collect the stags' shed antlers annually, often matching a pair from a particular animal. One stalker in Glenartney has pairs of antlers from the same stag from consecutive seasons. Traditionally stalkers sold the antlers, and other body parts, as perks of their jobs. They also sell the pizzle (penis), velvet, sinews, and tail. All are prized in Chinese medicine, the first two as aphrodisiacs. One stalker from Islay commented that a pizzle would need to simmer for a fortnight at gas mark 4 just to allow the fork to go in due to its terrible toughness.

In 1967 Willie Munro, the head stalker on the Wyvis Estate in Sutherland, hand-reared a hind calf. She was seen travelling in the passenger seat of his car, even when she was almost fully grown. The calf followed him everywhere, even out stalking. She gave birth to a hind calf of her own, and eventually the two beasts were to be seen setting off on stalking expeditions with their owner. They lay quietly chewing the cud while a stag was shot, and remained unperturbed when the animal fell to the ground, or when it was bled and disembowelled, before following their owner home again.

Deer have long been poached. In the past the odd deer, cleanly culled for the pot of a needy family, was often overlooked. Today's poachers, however, are unskilled and use totally unsuitable weapons, all too often leaving a trail of wounded animals in their wake. Venison is succulent meat – low in fat, rich in iron, it is claimed by many to be far superior to beef. Much of Scotland's venison is exported to Europe. At the time of the Chernobyl catastrophe in 1986, demands for venison plummeted due to the fact that traces of radioactivity were found in animals as far away as Scotland. Today it has once again gained in popularity and

The deer in Gaelic literature

Deer were to hunter-gatherers what cattle were to the early farmers: they made it possible for people to live well rather than simply survive. Skill and muscle were needed to bring home a deer, so deer hunting appears early in Gaelic literature as the work of heroes and men in their prime; men like the legendary Finn Mac Cumhaill and his companions, known in Ireland as the *Fíana* and in Scotland as the *Féinne* or Fingalians. The twelfth-century poem 'Arran of the Stags' imagines one of their hunting expeditions.

> Arran of the many stags,
> The sea strikes against its shoulder,
> Isle where companies are fed,
> Ridge on which blue spears are reddened.
> Skittish deer are on her peaks,
> Delicious berries are on her manes,
> Cool water in her rivers,
> Mast upon her dun oaks.
> Greyhounds are there and beagles,
> Blackberries and sloes of the dark blackthorn,
> Her dwellings close against the woods,
> Deer scattered about her oak-woods.
> Gleaning of purple upon her rocks,
> Faultless grass upon her slopes,
> Over her fair shapely crags
> Noise of dappled fawns a-skipping.
> Smooth is her level land, fat are her swine,
> Bright are her fields,
> Her nuts upon the tops of her hazel-wood,
> Long galleys sailing past her.
> Delightful it is when the fair season comes:
> Trout under the brinks of her rivers,
> Seagulls answer each other round her white cliff,
> Delightful at all times is Arran!
>
> *Anon.*

Finn's son, Oisín, or Ossian, had a taboo against killing deer. His name means 'little fawn' and his mother is said to have been a woman who had been turned into a hind by a jealous rival. Poets liked to imagine their meeting, years later, when Oisín was taking part in a hunt: he urges her to escape, gives up hunting and never eats venison again. This story goes back a thousand years or more in the Irish/Gaelic tradition and was still being told in the Western Isles in the nineteenth century or later. The image of the deer-woman may derive ultimately from ancient beliefs about a deer spirit or deity. Cave-paintings of deer and antlered figures are among the oldest religious art in Europe, so it would not be at all surprising if there were once similar beliefs in Scotland. A hind's head is one of the commonest images on Pictish carved stones.

Red deer calf (Polly Pullar)

In the Highlands, nurses sang lullabies about hunting to the baby sons of chieftains. When the day came for their 'first specimen of manly exercise' they would be accompanied by a retinue of other gentlemen and by 'foresters' – men who worked in the deer forest and knew the deer as a shepherd knows sheep. The great Gaelic poet Duncan Bàn McIntyre was a forester in Breadalbane in the 1750s and loved being out in the hills watching the 'light-hooved, quick-limbed' animals. This bond between the hunter and hunted is particularly strong in the story of the white hind that is said to have followed the Earl of Argyll's army in 1644. In happier times, she had had a special bond with one of the foot soldiers, a forester from Coire an Tee (the fairy corry) in the Cowal peninsula. In storytelling terms, she was his 'fairy lover'. She follows him all the way to Badenoch, much to the irritation of the Earl, who eventually orders his men to shoot her. Every one of them misses. Finally, the forester is ordered to shoot. He says it will be the last thing on earth he does, obeys the order and falls dead on the spot. The hind screams and springs off up the hillside, never to be seen again. This story is still loved by the forester's descendents at the beginning of the twenty-first century. It has survived radical Presbyterianism, atheism and relegation to the realms of folklore and superstition. Long may it continue to make sensible men feel proud, and a little confused.

should be viewed as one of the finest natural resources we have, and one of the healthiest meats of all. Red deer management also provides vital jobs for those living and working in the hills.

Deerhound

The distant relatives of the Scottish deerhound might have helped early settlers in their pursuit of hoofed quarry. Certainly there are records of rough-coated hound-like animals in many early pictures of the hunt. Once referred to as the Scotch greyhound, the rough greyhound, and the Highland deerhound, it became a breed during the sixteenth century. Deerhounds frequently accompanied Highland lairds. In earlier times, generally, they were viewed as the Royal Dog of Scotland, and no one below the rank of earl was permitted to own one. Later on, this rule was changed. Both Queen Victoria and Sir Walter Scott had deerhounds.

Hounds were often badly gored by stags, yet proved courageous, seldom giving up the chase. Surprisingly, deerhounds in a domestic situation have always had the repu-

Donald Houston of Ardnamurchan with his deerhound (Polly Pullar)

Finn Mac Cumhaill's Bran

Pride of place among deerhound ancestors goes to Finn Mac Cumhaill's legendary dog Bran, who went with him everywhere, even into the jaws of death. He or she (male in some stories, female in others) first appears in Irish/Gaelic poetry of the twelfth century where Bran is described as 'a hound but not a hound'. Indeed, in the language of myth, Bran is a blood relative, a cousin, Finn's aunt having been turned into a deerhound by a jealous rival. Finn treats Bran with enormous respect, reciting her exploits and triumphs to her before slipping her leash on the hill. She catches deer, hares, boar, fish and supernatural enemies for him. When she dies, Finn is inconsolable: it is like 'the parting of soul and body' for him. In South Uist, Bran was definitely male and stories were still being recited about him in the twentieth century. In one, Finn is swallowed by a monster and Bran dives down its throat after him. They fight their way out, but both emerge hairless and covered in sores. Finn insists that the doctors treat his hound as well as himself but poor Bran ends up looking like a white hairy mop, more poodle than self-respecting hound. Finn insists they can do better:

> Yellow legs on Bran,
> White belly, two black sides;
> A green back for the hunt,
> Two pointed blood-red ears.

Finn's companions are astonished at the result. 'Isn't that dog like Bran?' they say. 'But that's not the colour he was at all.'

tation for being placid, and are said to be far more likely to lead an intruder to the valuables than chase them away.

With the arrival of the gun, their use as sight hounds was no longer required. Deerhounds dwindled to the brink of extinction, only saved by the dedication of a few breeders. Today, like many other breeds, the deerhound is predominantly a pet or show animal.

Highland Pony

The hardy Highland pony has a long history. Its ancestry dates back to the last Ice Age. During the Spanish Armada, the Highland pony was thought to have received an infusion of blood from fine, strong-muscled Andalusian horses. A local legend on the Isle of Mull states that a Spanish galleon sheltering in Tobermory harbour sank in the bay. A beautiful Andalusian stallion swam ashore from the wreck, and was captured and used to improve the ponies on the island and elsewhere.

Highland ponies have always been highly valued and although they may have altered greatly over the centuries, they have held their own as garrons. (The name 'garron' originates from the Gaelic for a castrated male. During the 1800s, however, it became the recognised term used for any Highland ponies, mares or geldings.) The ponies carried deer carcasses off the hills, and worked as pack and draft animals, ferrying goods to and from remote parts of the Highlands. On the crofts they carried peat and were used for ploughing and other work, while on the islands they could be seen laden with panniers of seaweed. They were also employed extensively in cattle droving.

Highland ponies have been used as mounts for numerous battles and skirmishes, and during the time of the Jacobite Rising were captured and taken away from their owners and sold to English buyers. They were highly valued, not only for working the land, but also for riding and carriage driving, much as they are today. When the Lovat Scouts left Scotland for the Boer War at the end of the nineteenth century, they took a large consignment of trusted Highland ponies with them.

Although mostly used as riding ponies now, they are one of the few animals left in Scotland that still fulfil the role they have had for generations. Breaking them to carry deer is not hard, although it is important to familiarise them with the smell of blood. Once they are used to a beast without antlers, a calf or hind, then the first dead stag is shown to them. Able to carry large weights across the roughest terrain, ponies often manage to go where a tracked vehicle cannot. Most Highland ponies have an inbuilt awareness of the dangers of deep peat hags and are sure-footed. They are a vital part of the continuation of the long association of man with red deer.

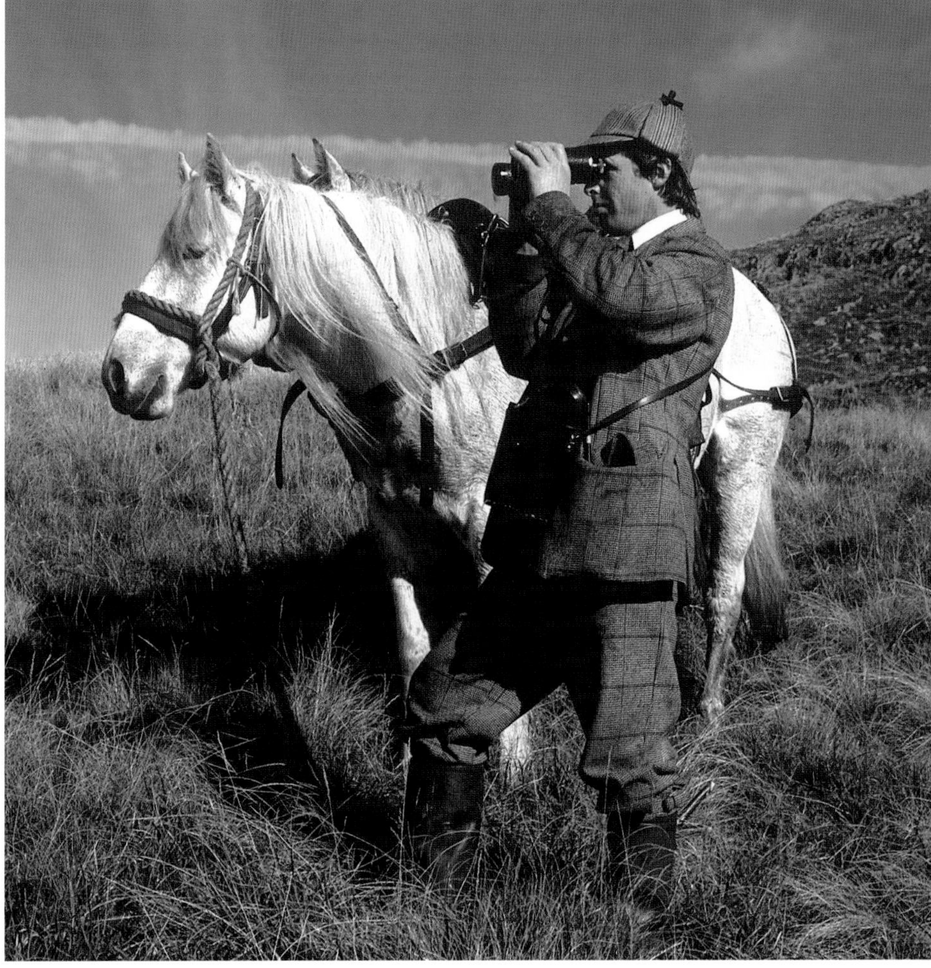

Glen Artney stalker Jock MacDonald with garrons (Polly Pullar)

THE OVERLORD

Golden Eagle

Aquila chrysaetos
S: erne, yirn (both also used of white-tailed eagle)
G: *iolair dhubh, iolair bhuidhe*

It is impossible to write about the golden eagle without mention of the great Highland kilted gentleman, Seton Gordon (1886–1977), whose groundbreaking observations of this symbol of the Scottish wilderness spawned generations of eagle watchers. His book *Days with the Golden Eagle*, and many other superb Scottish nature books, brought the birds into the heart of people's lives, conveying the joy of viewing fauna with the eye of a naturalist instead of, as had become the norm, down the barrel of a gun.

In earlier times, no Highlander was considered a true sportsman until he had shot the three monarchs: a royal stag of the earth, the wild swan of the water, and the eagle of the air, all with bow and arrow. Following the Victorian era when the hills and glens witnessed mass slaughter of wildlife, Seton Gordon and his wife Audrey stood against the horror of the killing fields, inspiring and educating instead. His observations helped turn the tide of terrible destruction, leading to the current public perception of the eagle as an almost mythical creature.

Many visitors to Scotland are keen to see an eagle – it is often top of their list. However, this is not a bird that can be easily found. Although widespread, it is far from common, and a sighting demands sharp eyes, patience and local knowledge.

In 2009 a ringed eagle was found dead on the island of Jura. An eagle may live in captivity for up to 40 years, but the wild is fraught with natural and man-made hazards. It had died at the ripe old age of 22, a record for a wild eagle.

A pair require a large home range with abundant prey in order to rear young. They make several vast eyries of sticks high on cliff ledges, or in trees, and tend to use a different one each year, returning to the same sites for generations. Many types of prey have been found at the nest. Eagles readily take advantage of carrion, gorging on

Eagle myths

A Skyeman known as 'Iolair' was said to have been carried off by an eagle as a baby. This is probably fanciful, but there was a similar story on Yell, and eagles were among the predators placated on Quarter Days with offerings of food. There was also a Hogmanany curse wishing eagles and other raptors on households which failed to give the guisers a good welcome. On St Kilda, however, the Skye-born writer Martin Martin (d.1719) was told that eagles 'never take so much as a lamb or hen' but always seek their prey on other islands. There is a protectiveness here. Eagles, when not perceived as rivals, have been admired and wondered at. The Pictish nobility commissioned carvings of them – two or three different species, including the golden eagle, appear on Pictish stones; impressive big-bodied birds, probably drawn from life.

An eagle is one of the helpful creatures in the Gaelic tale '*Math-ghamhainn Donn a' Ghlinn Uaine*' (The Brown Bear of the Green Glen). She carries the hero on her back to the healing well on the Green Isle, in return for an act of kindness: cutting a wart from her ear without drawing blood. 'Och! Is that not a fearful lie,' exclaims the storyteller in English – caught between art and science. Natural History professor William MacGillivray (1796–1852) was firmly on the side of science, but recorded that in Harris 'the vulgar commonly believe that the eagle renews its age – but what idea they attach to the word renew I cannot gulp. However, the shepherd says it casts its bill and claws etc three times during its life.' The shepherd was in touch with an old mythology: deer live three times longer than humans, he said, ravens three times longer than deer, eagles three times longer than ravens, and the world three times longer than the eagle. This is a version of the international 'legend of the oldest animals', although salmon and certain trees are older in other versions.

Golden eagle with impressive wingspan of between 6½–7½ feet (over 2 metres) (Neil McIntyre)

it until they can barely take off. Keepers tell of eagles accidentally caught in their Larsen (crow) traps (see page 34), having killed and devoured the captive birds caught in them. They have also been seen tearing at foxes trapped in snares. There are tales too of eagles riding on the backs of deer, usually hinds or calves. With talons deeply embedded in the animal's flesh, the birds hang on, driving the hapless creatures over cliffs. Adult red deer would be otherwise impossible for an eagle to kill. They have also been seen harrying weaker animals over precipices by repeatedly dive-bombing them until they plummet to their deaths. Domestic cats will sometimes end up on the menu too.

Eagle feathers have long been prized – their primary feathers were worn by Highland chiefs as a mark of rank;

three were worn in the bonnet of a chieftain, while a gentleman wore a single one. Feathers were used as arrows, with the best plumes thought to have come from the eagles of Loch Treig, in Lochaber.

The eagle, like the peregrine falcon at the top of the food chain, has battled with the horrors of man-made chemicals and suffered as a result of reduced fertility, clutch loss and brood failure. They have been popular subjects for taxidermy and were often stuffed to decorate Victorian country retreats. Eagles have also been the victims of egg collectors, and 24-hour watches are frequently put on their nests nowadays. The eggs are worthless to thieves, while in the wild they are beyond value. The stolen booty may simply end up in a collection maintained by vanity and a smug bravado on the part of the collector. This is a pastime that is, at last, viewed as a serious crime.

'The whole air is a thoroughfare for the eagle,' wrote Euripides. Anyone who has been lucky enough to spend time eagle watching will appreciate this statement. Eagle flight is dramatic and their courtship display is an almost unbelievable feat of aerial acrobatics. Skydiving with talons locked in mid-air must surely be one of the greatest wildlife sights. This spectacle can be seen in January and February, with birds rising and falling, their great wings swept back. On a snow-capped mountain, the great shadow of an eagle may appear over a ridge, sending a covey of grouse scattering in panic. Many claim that their first sighting of an eagle changes their lives. From a tourist's point of view, the golden eagle has a powerful draw. If sightings could be guaranteed, together with perfect sunshine, then Scotland would probably end up being as popular with tourists as famous foreign resorts. Yet many fabulous views of eagles are had when the weather is far from clement, which brings its own rewards.

Opposite. Peregrine falcon, once the chosen hunting bird of royalty (Malcolm Gosling)

THE SENTINEL

Peregrine Falcon

Falco peregrinus
S: falcoun, fawcown, hunting hawk
G: *seabhag-ghorm, clamhan*

Although the eagle is perhaps seen as the most majestic of Scottish birds, many also hold the peregrine falcon in the highest esteem too. It is found on high mountain ranges and remote sea cliffs, where it feeds on grouse, waterfowl, waders, auks and other seabirds.

The peregrine is one of the most beautiful Scottish birds, with its dramatic facial moustache, dark eyes and bold plumage. In his book *British Birds of Prey*, Leslie Brown named the peregrine falcon a 'hot contender for the world's most successful bird of prey'. This is because it is highly adaptable and occurs on all continents, even on many oceanic islands.

Despite its success, the peregrine faced near-extinction in Britain and has always been unpopular with pigeon fanciers, who claimed during the 1950s that numbers were too high. Following a national survey this was found to be far from the case. Indeed, peregrine numbers were falling drastically, and surviving birds were not managing to rear

The falcon, the dog and the otter

For all the connections with royalty, stories about falcons survived best among the tradition-bearers of the Gaelic-speaking world – people like James Wilson, a blind fiddler on Islay. His story about the young king of Easaidh Ruagh ('*Righ Og Easaidh Ruagh*') tells how a trio of helpful animals – a dog, an otter and a falcon – help the young man to recover his wife and horses. This kind of story (a loss, a quest, animal helpers) is extremely old and belongs to the world of myth and primal imagination. Falcons appear in several such tales collected at around the same time, from Argyll to Wester Ross. 'Easaidh Ruagh' is probably Assaroe in Donegal.

chicks. The survey revealed a dramatic thinning of their eggshells, infertility, and unusual behaviour – the cause of this was the use of organo-chlorine pesticides entering the food chain and causing damage to the peregrine, a predator at the top of the chain. The toxic substances Dieldrin and DDT were thought to be the most serious offenders, and a ban was imposed.

Eventually peregrines recovered, but there will always be conflict between them and pigeon fanciers. A passing flock of brightly patterned racing pigeons is often too tempting to resist. The peregrine's varied diet includes waders, waterfowl, game birds, small songbirds, and even other birds of prey. The fulmar, a seabird frequently taken as prey, can be a threat to hunting and nesting peregrines. When nesting or roosting fulmars are disturbed or cornered, they back away, lining themselves up ready to spit a quantity of viscous fishy oil from their crops. If the gob of oil lands on the wings of an attacking peregrine, it will render its flight feathers useless. No amount of cleaning will remove the substance. A peregrine rescued in such a state will have to wait in captivity until after its moult to be rid of the dreaded potion. It then has to be passed to a falconer to be trained, to ensure it has built up its strength again prior to release.

For generations, this master of the air has been highly prized and, due to its brilliant ability to catch other birds in mid-air, has had a long association with man. Since medieval times it has been the chosen falconry bird for kings. Mary, Queen of Scots was said to enjoy the sport, favouring the peregrine falcon as well as the diminutive merlin. The male peregrine is known as a 'tiercel' (from the French *la tierce* – a third), and like many birds of prey he is smaller than his mate. Their Latin name originates from the verb 'to peregrinate', or go on a pilgrimage or travel abroad – when birds are not breeding, they migrate large distances to find food. The Germans call the bird *wanderfalke.*

Peregrines use traditional nest sites and young chicks and eggs were often stolen and smuggled out of the country. The large dark-coloured peregrines typically found in

The young king of Assaroe

The young king decided to gather firewood and make a fire. He began to warm himself and he had not been at it long when the grey falcon of the green rock came to him. 'Dear me,' she said, 'that was an evil fate for your wife and your two horses last night, with the big giant.'

'There's nothing can be done about it,' he said, 'plenty trouble and little pleasure I got from them.'

'Have courage,' she said, 'you will get some pleasure yet. You should not be without food here,' says she.

'There is no way of getting food,' says he.

'We'll get food before long.' Off she went and she wasn't away long when she was back with three ducks and eight blackcocks in her mouth. They prepared the food and ate it. 'You shouldn't go without sleep,' says the falcon.

'How can I sleep with no one to ensure my safety from the same evil?'

'Sleep, king, and I will ensure your safety.' He lay down, stretched out and fell asleep. In the morning the falcon got him up. 'Whatever hardship or difficulty you meet with, remember, at any time, you will get help from me.' Off he went, keenly and valiantly, quick and strong.

the Highlands are viewed by Arab falconers as among the best falconry birds. Now with captive breeding programmes, birds are seldom stolen from the nest, and this has improved wild peregrine numbers. During the war years, trained peregrines were frequently used to help clear airfields of other birds, as they still are today – strikes with planes can have catastrophic results.

To watch a peregrine scatter a large flock of waders at an estuary, sending them skywards, is memorable. Rising higher and higher in the air, the peregrine will then stoop with great speed as it strikes its chosen victim, flying off with it to a favourite plucking post. It is this incredible speed that makes them unique; the ultimate boy racers of the avian world.

THE SPY

Raven

Corvus corax
S: corbie (also used for hooded crow and rook), croupie
G: *fitheach, biadhtach*

The collective noun for ravens, an unkindness, paints an ominous picture. Indeed, they have been seen as birds of ill omen for centuries, and have more folklore surrounding them than most other Scottish birds. Raven symbols have been used as emblems and on family crests; in many cases, the birds were revered as seers or harbingers.

Said to be able to smell death from great distances, large numbers appeared at battlefields and swiftly set to work picking at corpses – little wonder then that they were viewed in the pagan world as a bird of doom. Early Christians had a different view and recognised their helpfulness to man, particularly in cleaning up, but to this day there is something eerily intelligent about their behaviour, and ravens retain a special aura of their own.

Many stalkers will tell you that ravens are supremely clever. The birds follow them up the hill during the stalking season, keeping a safe distance, but as soon as a shot has been fired and its harsh retort ricochets round the glen, the ravens re-appear to clear up the 'gralloch' – excised deer innards. During the stalking season, ravens, buzzards, crows and eagles take advantage of this easy meal. Stringent new laws to impose restrictions on keepers may mean they have to carry a spade, and bury this natural waste instead. This would have a detrimental effect on carrion-feeding birds. The rich pickings never lie long and come at a time of the autumn and winter when there is great need for extra nutrition.

Ravens once lived closely alongside man. They were a useful addition to the wildlife of Edinburgh's heart, clearing up rubbish thrown out onto the streets. This refuse collection made them highly popular. For many years ravens nested on Arthur's Seat – the craggy hill dominating the city. However, as they came into conflict with sheep and game birds, they suffered relentless persecution. Numbers dwindled drastically and the birds fled to safer places to avoid man, preferring remote mountainous areas where they nested on crags or wind-sculpted trees.

Happily, numbers have now increased again and ravens are moving back into some of their old haunts. From a naturalist's viewpoint the raven is a fabulous bird – intelligent, clever, and acrobatic. They gather in large communal roost sites, and frequently their aerial displays delight as they tumble, filling the air with a repertoire of calls, some almost melodic in tone. Ravens at roost sites seem to have a vast vocabulary of croaks and clunks, and even imitate shepherd's whistles or dog barks. Some regular observers of roosts say they feel they are recognised by the birds in the roost. The birds also love to play in the snow and in the Highlands have been seen sledging down a snow chute on their backs, then flying back up again to repeat the process. It is hard to describe this behaviour as anything other than play.

Frequently an eagle may be seen in the sky close by as it dwarves the largest of the crow family. Most wildlife watchers will have had the joy of witnessing ravens mobbing an eagle and harrying it as it glides effortlessly through the airspace.

Ravens devour large amounts of carrion – they nest early in the season and chicks are hatched to coincide with lambing time when casualties and afterbirths, together with the weak and sickly, feature heavily in their diet. With the hooded crow and the greater black-backed gull, their reputation for pecking out the eyes of lambs and sheep is well documented, and one of the main reasons for the intense persecution they suffer. With their penchant for mutton, they have always had enemies. During the 1800s, bounties were paid for dead ravens. On various estates in Sutherland, including that of the Duchess of Sutherland, two shillings was paid for each raven killed.

Ravens have eclectic tastes. As someone once commented, 'from a worm to a whale'. Other than carrion and refuse, their diet includes berries, roots, nuts, seeds, worms, insects, eggs and shellfish. Vast numbers were witnessed in Shetland in the year 1900 when 500 birds were seen cleaning up the remains of a pod of stranded killer whales. There are reports of them feeding on other carcasses washed ashore – a bloated cow or sheep, a large fish, dead seal or even a turtle; almost anything will be devoured with tenacity, using their can-opener-like bill to rip apart the putrefying flesh. Large unkindnesses have also been recorded on rubbish tips.

The perjorative term 'bird-brain' could not be applied to the raven. Pet ravens have proved to be amongst the most intelligent of birds, and they have an ingenious ability to adapt. Orkney, for example, is largely treeless and nesting materials are scarce. One pair of ravens there built an enormous cliff nest high on a ledge in the Hole of Ro – a *geo* (large gully) on the mainland's west side. The vast structure was entirely constructed from small pieces of rusted barbed wire topped with seaweed and sheep's wool as padding, with not a twig in sight.

Raven knowledge

Ravens were often associated with knowledge, especially arcane knowledge. One medieval Gaelic text provides an elaborate key to their language: if a raven settled above the centre of the house, saying '*gràd, gràd*' ('orders, orders', as in 'holy orders'), a priest was coming; if one called from the direction of the sheepfold, saying '*carna carna, grob grob, coin coin*' ('meat meat, distress distress, dogs, dogs'), wolves were approaching. Raven lore in Britain and Ireland probably owes more than a little to the Vikings. In Norse mythology, two ravens known as Hugin (thought) and Munin (memory) travel daily between the earth and Valhalla, bringing Odin the latest news about what humans are doing.

Father Allan MacDonald (1859–1905), of South Uist and Eriskay, was told that 'raven knowledge' refers to their ability to find carrion. This was why the raven did not return to Noah's ark after the flood. He was gorging himself on carcasses and became so adept at finding them that his descendents could ever afterwards do the same. There are still proverbs about 'raven knowledge' in Gaelic: '*Tha gliocas an ceann an fhithich*' (There is wisdom in the raven's head), but the sceptics took a different view: '*Na creid feannag na fitheach, is ann mar is toil le Dia a bhios an la*' (Do not believe crow or raven, the day will be as God wills).

MUNRO BAGGERS

Mountain Goat

Capra hircus
S: gait
G: *gobhar fhiadhaich*

Wild billy, nanny and kid, Kingairloch (Polly Pullar)

A few herds of feral goats exist in some of the wildest areas of Scotland. They were introduced from Persian domesticated stock over 3,000 years ago. Others have more recently been released and have gradually naturalised. Due to the inaccessibility of their chosen habitat, they are hard to control: considerably more agile than sheep, they are adept at skipping across the most perilous cliffs. In Gaelic the phrase '*Miann goibhre: gaoth 's dol 'an aodann creag*' is translated as 'the goat's desire: wind and climbing up a crag'.

The horns of a wild billy goat may grow huge, frequently becoming gnarled and twisted, showing growth rings and ridges reminiscent of age rings on felled trees. During the autumn when the blood is up, and the air even more pungent with the smell of rampant males, there may be many heated battles, with the loser ending up tumbling over a sea-girt cliff. The life cycle of the feral goat is very similar to that of the red deer and an annual rut brings excitement during a few frenzied weeks of mating activity. The kids are usually born in March or April.

Wild goats are varied in colour and appearance; a patchwork of hues ranging from brown, tan, black, to grey. They may have long shaggy coats, vast beards and neck ruffs and be impressive indeed. They frequently give birth to twins although one of a pair may become prey for a passing eagle, or in mainland herds, dinner for a fox. Only the fittest survive.

Wild goats are shy and wary, snorting loudly and stamping their hooves on sight of humans and dogs. They flee as fast as the wind that sweeps the cliff tops, their long woolly coats flapping like scruffy sackcloth. Even outwith the breeding season, their sickly sweet smell lingers long after they have left the area.

One large wild goat head, complete with flowing beard, is in the Natural History Museum. Shot in Scotland in 1894, the specimen was presented to the museum by the shipping magnate Sir Donald Currie. This beast came from Schiehallion, where until the late 1990s a herd of naturalised goats still existed. Some placenames reveal a more widespread presence. The wild and beautiful Mull of Oa, on Islay, remains a stronghold, its cliffs and untamed moor providing ideal terrain for them. There are also small herds of wild goats in other craggy, wild areas, including the Grey Mare's Tail in Dumfries and Galloway. Another wild herd on the slopes of Ben Lomond is thought to have originated from stock that has been there since the time of Robert the Bruce.

Goat place names

Some place names reveal a more widespread presence of goat, although surprisingly this does not include the famous Goat Fell on Arran. It is probably the windy hill, not goat hill; but Ardgour, south west of Fort William, is very likely taken from '*aird ghobhar*' (goat height). We also find mention of goats in the pass of Bochan Ubhaidh, near Kingussie, with the complaint that there is no grass there, just wild strawberries and blaeberries – and goats. Poor country for cattle then, but not without its attractions.

Reindeer

Rangifer tarandus
G: *fast, bràc*

Many people are unaware that reindeer were native to Scotland in previous centuries and herds continue to exist here today. For millennia, in the Arctic regions of the far north, reindeer have lived closely alongside man. Domesticated herds provide meat, skins, milk and antlers for tribal people. However, reindeer ceased to be present in Scotland sometime during the Mesolithic period. Attempts to bring them back by the Duke of Atholl during the eighteenth century were unsuccessful.

After visiting Scotland in the early 1950s, a Swedish reindeer herder, Mikel Utsi, returned home with the idea of reintroducing reindeer to the Cairngorms. He had been in a remote area of the Cairngorms, overlooking extensive country that he recognised as perfect reindeer ground. The vegetation he saw was of little use to other mammals, and there was a richness of varied lichens. He began ambitious plans to import a herd of his beloved reindeer, and the first animals arrived in 1952.

Together with his wife, Ethel Lindgren, he founded the Reindeer Company and the Reindeer Council of Great Britain. The venture was a great success and the animals proved that, unlike red deer, they did not damage forestry, and were therefore afforded a larger area to roam.

Today reindeer flourish, and through a controlled breeding programme they are kept to approximately 150 animals in two separate herds. There is a small one on the Glenlivet Estate, and another at Glenmore's Reindeer Centre, where visitors may see at first hand wild reindeer in natural surroundings. Some are trained and used for highly popular Christmas outings to local towns and shopping malls, and also for filming.

Reindeer perfectly at home in the Cairngorms (Laurie Campbell)

Mountain Hare

Lepus timidus
S: whiddie baudrons, bawtie, cutty, donie, fuddie, lang lugs, maukin, pussy
G: maigheach bhàn, bocaire fasaich

Early depictions of hares found in cave art are thought to be of the mountain hare and not its close relative, the larger brown hare. It is frequently referred to as the blue hare due to the smoky tinge of its summer pelt. Together with the stoat and ptarmigan, it makes up a trio of creatures that turn completely white in winter. Although this helps to give them excellent camouflage, it may also put them at high risk of predation from foxes and golden eagles. With the climate proving more and more erratic, snow can vanish overnight, leaving the hare blatantly obvious. Much less timid than the brown hare, it is sometimes possible to approach a group of mountain hares huddled in deep snow. At a barytes mine (a dense mineral used as a lubricant for drilling on North Sea oil rigs) high in the Perthshire hills, hares are often seen near the mine workings, where they appear unperturbed by the vast machinery operating noisily beside them.

Mountain hare numbers are subject to fluctuations, sometimes increasing ten-fold with ten-year peaks, and they may be locally common, while other places with apparently suitable habitat hold none. They appear to thrive on well-managed grouse moors where the heather is regularly burnt in patches to produce plenty of young shoots among a patchwork of different-aged plants.

During severe blizzards, hares sit tucked up tight, seemingly oblivious to the harsh onslaught. Unfortunately, they are often killed on the road. Headlights cause mad confusion and the hare runs straight into the oncoming vehicle, perhaps due to the fact that it has paler irides than the rabbit and is more easily dazzled. Foxes, buzzards, crows or ravens soon eat casualties.

Shooting hares

In some areas of Scotland mountain hares were once shot in large numbers – records from a Perthshire estate at Logiealmond from November 1889 tell of six guns accounting for a bag of 1,280 hares. English sportsmen coming to Balmoral to shoot during the reign of Queen Victoria commented 'the blue hare cannot run fast and they look like starved cats, scraggy, ungainly and mean', an unfair description for one of Scotland's most elegant mammals. In favourable conditions, they may breed several times in a season, and even after a devastating cull, the local population can recover quickly.

Mountain hare in white winter pelage (Neil McIntyre)

A TRIO OF AVIAN ALPINISTS

Ptarmigan

Lagopus muta
S: termigan
G: *tàrmachan*, *gealag-bheinne*, *sneachdaire*

Three birds may be viewed as the ultimate alpine specialists. The best known of these is the ptarmigan.

Two Gaelic words for ptarmigan refer to its winter plumage: *gealag bheinne* (the little white one of the mountain) and *sneachdaire* (the snowy one). Other names include 'white grouse', 'cairn bird', 'snow chick' and 'rock grouse'. Many mountains have Gaelic names that derive from the word ptarmigan, the perfect example being Meall nan Tàrmachan in Perthshire, which translates as 'Hill of the Ptarmigans'.

Increasingly rare, it was once a favoured target for sportsmen. Only the fittest could bag this lovely member of the grouse family for it is usually found on high, inaccessible summits above 1,000 metres.

In 1621 you could buy the 'best termigant' in the poultry market for five shillings, six shillings and eightpence dressed.

That doyenne of culinary skills, Mrs Isabella Beeton (1836–65), claimed in her cookery book that these most challenging wild game birds were 'exceedingly fine eating, and should be kept as long as possible to be good'. Others say that they are horribly bitter, but most find there is little difference in taste to the red grouse – a bird that retains a popular culinary niche in the market today. Sadly, reintroduction attempts have failed, particularly in areas such as the Outer Hebrides where the last pair of ptarmigan bred at the end of the 1930s.

Ptarmigan, a bird that may dwindle with global warming (Neil McIntyre)

Blending in

There are few creatures that provide such a good example of camouflage: three annual temperature-triggered moults transform ptarmigan, each providing a seasonal dress change that blends them with the background. Often choosing boulder fields to nest in, their gold-dappled summer plumage perfectly replicates the lichen-encrusted surroundings; in autumn, the white wings against a colder, greyer mottling resemble patches of snow appearing among the rock forms along a ridge; in the depths of winter their pristine white feathers afford them secrecy on the snowiest days. Ptarmigan love to bask in the lee of the wind as stray rays of winter sunshine penetrate the cold tops, and chilling spindrift blusters overhead.

Their spring camouflage is so effective that despite a lack of nest material, a female may sit tight on her clutch of eggs and perfectly resemble a large oval stone. Only one brood is reared due to the climate, and it is vulnerable to predators such as the eagle, fox, stoat and raven. Sometimes it is the call which reveals a ptarmigan's location. Or perhaps they show themselves disturbed by an ominous shadow overhead, as an eagle sends a covey bursting forth from the edge of the mountain.

Dotterel

Charadrius morinellus
S: foolish dotterel
G: *amadan-mòintich*

An extraordinary mountain plover, another true alpine bird, the rare dotterel returns north to Scotland from sun-baked low ground in Africa each spring to the same places where it bred the previous year. Unlike the ptarmigan, it favours different mountain habitat, preferring grassier, whale-backed hills and low-growing, tundra-like vegetation. Set apart from other birds by its extraordinary tameness, it can be approached, seeming almost stupid in its lack of concern at the proximity of a human. Its Gaelic name, *amadan-mòintich*, means 'fool of the peat moss', referring to its apparent nonchalance when faced with a passing human. In the past, this behaviour made the work of illicit egg collectors too easy, and contributed to the bird's decline. Groups of dotterel, called 'trips', were shot on passage. Not only were they valued as a delicacy, but their feathers were used in flies for fly-fishing.

During the breeding season it is the female that wears the trousers, courting her mate in brighter breeding plumage and generally dominating the scene with her display flight. Unusually, once she has laid her eggs in a mossy scrape on the ground, she retreats to form groups with other females. Together they roam nearby hills and take little further interest in the rearing of offspring, leaving their mates in charge of the brood. Females have only occasionally been found incubating. Like the golden plover, the call of the dotterel is plaintive and melancholy, particularly when heard breaking the silence of the high tops, carried on the wind across a desolate horizon. Records show that although the bird is now scarce, there were never large numbers in the Scottish hills.

Dotterel, often seen as foolish due to its tameness (Polly Pullar)

Snow bunting, a delightful winter visitor (Laurie Campbell)

Snow Bunting

Calcarius nivalis
S: snawflake, gwalock
G: *gealag an t-sneachda*

This little bird is a true tundra species which has very occasionally been seen at garden feeders in winter. It seems to blow in on a gale, particularly in remote parts of the Hebrides, where it may be seen in flocks picking at the tide line in search of insects and stray seeds. It is also the most northerly breeding land bird, and has been nicknamed the Arctic sparrow due to the close proximity in which it lives with Inuit tribes in the far north. It is a rare breeder in Scotland, where it chooses the highest sites hidden in rock crevices, out of the savage blast of the wind. Snow buntings tend to stay close to the last vestiges of winter snow which harbour an abundance of insects. The naturalist Desmond Nethersole-Thompson, who compiled a ground-breaking work on the snow bunting, concluded that the patches of melt nearby are wet all year round, and provide moist breeding grounds for succulent craneflies.

Nicknamed 'snowflakes', on occasions snow buntings are found at Scottish ski resorts, and there take advantage of tiny crumbs of food left in the car parks, although they are chiefly insectivorous. Their presence is always a delight. In some winters, vast flocks may appear as if from nowhere, probably as a direct result of a particularly hard winter further north. Wildlife artist and naturalist Donald Watson witnessed one such impressive invasion during the winter of 1932 when the birds appeared in great numbers, even landing on the playing field at Murrayfield in Edinburgh during a rugby international.

EARLY BIRD

Ring Ouzel

Turdus torquatus
S: heather/hedder blackie, osill, chack
G: dubh-chreige, lon-monaidh, druid-mhonaidh

The spring arrival of the ring ouzel, or mountain blackbird, is a great joy. It appears early in the season and leaves later than some other migrants. Largely resembling a paler-coloured blackbird, with a dapper white bib, it is more shy and slightly larger, with more elongated wings than that species. Many hillwalkers may overlook the ring ouzel in their hurry to reach their goal of a particular mountain summit. But sitting a while in silence, listening, may reap rewards. The birds favour rocky places with safe nooks and crannies for nesting. Even as early as mid March a first sighting may be possible, particularly on days when primroses dot the wizened moor grasses and the warmth of the sun lulls the optimistic into proclaiming spring has arrived – it is then you may hear the distinctive sound. A *chack* call – it often echoes around, and is hard to place. Then with a flurry of wings a ring ouzel makes a brief appearance. The call has given rise to another country nickname – the 'mountain blacksmith'. Its fluting song is also distinctive and hard to confuse with other birdsong.

Despite their shyness, ring ouzels often nest in old buildings. One elderly shepherd said that there was a nest every year in a remote hill bothy where he stayed while gathering sheep. The birds appeared to be unperturbed by his presence.

The decline of the ring ouzel

Early naturalists noted that the ring ouzel often favoured areas of abundant juniper which provided food and shelter. Once a prolific shrub covering hillsides with its gnarled and twisted forms, juniper has since become scarce. It burns with little smoke and was frequently collected to fuel the fires of illicit stills in the mountains. This is thought to have contributed to the decline of the ring ouzel.

Ring ouzel, with distinctive white collar (Laurie Campbell)

CHAPTER TWO

MOOR AND BOG

INTRODUCTION

Moors and bogs form a vital part of the Scottish ecosystem. Both habitats are highly sensitive and botanically diverse. In Scotland there are many important tracts of country covered by these areas – in the far north in Caithness and Sutherland, the Flow Country is the largest wetland area in Britain, consisting of over 4,000 square miles of expansive peat land. It offers ideal breeding grounds for birds such as black-throated diver, hen harrier, merlin, golden plover, greenshank, dunlin, snipe and curlew. This landscape has remained unchanged since prehistory, but was severely threatened by efforts to drain vast areas and introduce non-native conifers between 1979 and 1987. The RSPB now owns a large part of the Flow Country, and at Forsinard has an important nature reserve where work continues to reinstate natural blanket bog.

Flanders Moss, a national nature reserve belonging to Scottish Natural Heritage in Stirlingshire, reveals the extraordinary riches of this type of raised bog; it is the largest of its kind left in Britain. Constant water flow keeps the bog healthy, allowing natural decomposition of plant material to form a dense layering of peat, with thick sphagnum mosses and other plants living on the surface. Visitors to the site can witness the flush of colours throughout the changing seasons with the vivid greens, rich-brown and orange hues of mosses. During the eighteenth and nineteenth centuries, areas of Flanders Moss were drained to make it viable for agriculture, with resulting damage. Here too, work continues to restore the precious habitat to its natural state.

Moors are typically found in upland areas, and are characterised by scrub vegetation, and in some cases a dense covering of heather. We have long celebrated heather in all its glory: in song, painting and prose. In July and August, the sight of a hillside swathed in pinkish-purple is something that many visitors travel a great distance to see.

In the east of Scotland, lower rainfall and drier conditions than those on the west side of the country encourage a different shrub layer. All moors are sensitive, and benefit from careful management. Small creeping plants like blaeberry, crowberry and cowberry form part of a nutritious understorey: their shoots, leaves and berries all provide a valuable food source. Foxes and birds, including grouse, feast on large quantities of the berries in summer, when their droppings are stained purple with the telltale signs of gluttony.

Butterwort and sundews trap midges and other tiny insects in their sticky leaves, absorbing protein from them in otherwise nutrient-poor ground. These plants are exquisite inhabitants of bog and moorland. Many people are

Opposite. Glen Lyon, Perthshire (Polly Pullar)

unaware of their existence. Other small treasures that thrive on acidic soils include milkwort, lousewort, bog asphodel, chickweed wintergreen, harebell, tormentil and many varieties of orchid.

Rannoch Moor, an important area of moorland bog, is designated as a Natural Heritage site. It lies to the west of Loch Rannoch, and sweeps through to Glencoe. Making a road east and west across this vast stretch of ground has always proved impossible: dense peat deposits do not provide a stable base. Many parts of the moor remain largely undiscovered and could prove to host some rare nesting birds and plants.

Much of Scotland is covered by bogs and moors often viewed as commercially unproductive land. Although these areas may in some cases be drained and altered, retaining them in their natural state allows a wealth of fauna to thrive. Overgrazing and forestry have brought new issues to the fore but gradually we are becoming enlightened – a bog is simply never just a bog – even the tiniest can be of vital importance biologically, and supports a huge abundance of life within its parameters.

THE SPECIALISTS

Red Grouse

Lagopus lagopus scotica
S: groose, gorcock, mure cock, mure hen
G: *coileach-fraoich, cearc-fhraoich*

> There is not a more beautiful bird in our island, and in January a cock grouse is one of the most superb fellows in the world, as he struts about fearlessly with his mate, his bright red comb erected above his eyes, with his rich dark plumage shining in the sun.
>
> Charles St. John, 1863

Even today many people would agree with the above sentiment, and it is with good reason that one of Scotland's most famous brands of whisky uses a red grouse for its name and logo.

The red grouse has probably had more indirect impact

Song: Composed in August

Robert Burns disliked the 'Glorious Twelfth'. His bitter-sweet 'Song: Composed in August' (1784) contrasts the 'slaughtering guns' with the loveliness of the season and the quiet contentment of the birds. Was he simply telling his sweetheart of the moment, Peggy Thomson, what he thought she might like to hear? Perhaps, but I doubt it. This was, after all, the same man who would feel wretched the following year about turning up a mouse's nest with the plough.

Now westlin' winds and slaught'ring guns
Bring Autumn's pleasant weather;
The gorcock springs on whirring wings
Among the blooming heather:
Now waving grain, wide o'er the plain,
Delights the weary farmer;
The moon shines bright, as I rove by night
To muse upon my charmer.
The paitrick lo'es the fruitfu' fells,
The plover lo'es the mountains;
The woodcock haunts the lonely dells,
The soaring hern the fountains;
Thro' lofty groves the cushat roves,
The path o' man to shun it;
The hazel bush o'erhangs the thrush,
The spreading thorn the linnet.
Thus every kind their pleasure find,
The savage and the tender;
Some social join, and leagues combine,
Some solitary wander:
Avaunt, away, the cruel sway!
Tyrannic man's dominion!
The sportsman's joy, the murdering cry,
The flutt'ring, gory pinion!
But, Peggy, dear, the evening's clear,
Thick flies the skimming swallow,
The sky is blue, the fields in view
All fading green and yellow:
Come let us stray our gladsome way,
And view the charms of Nature;
The rustling corn, the fruited thorn,
And ilka happy creature.
We'll gently walk, and sweetly talk,
While the silent moon shines clearly;
I'll clasp thy waist, and, fondly prest,
Swear how I lo'e thee dearly:
Not vernal show'rs to budding flow'rs,
Not Autumn to the farmer
So dear can be as thou to me,
My fair, my lovely charmer!

on the environment than any other bird, for its habitat has long been managed in a specific way to ensure that numbers flourish. At the peak of their popularity during the time of the Victorian sporting estate, grouse were seen as the most exclusive sporting bird of all. Approximately three million acres of moorland were intensively managed to accommodate them. Both economically and socially, this meant that grouse were for a time more important than either deer or sheep. Such was the esteem in which this bird was held, that a great many other creatures – raptors, corvids, foxes, stoats and weasels – were slaughtered annually in order to protect them.

Grouse peaked, with vast numbers shot, and many Scottish grouse moors let to foreign sportsmen during the shooting season. The completion in 1863 of the London–Inverness railway line enabled rich businessmen and their families to migrate north for the season which began with the opening of grouse shooting – on the Glorious Twelfth of August. They brought with them a huge entourage of staff and gundogs. As well as grouse shooting, they could go stalking in pursuit of red deer stags.

In 1872 on the Grandtully Estate in Perthshire, Maharajah Duleep Singh had the grouse shooting rights, and is reputed to have shot 250 brace himself in a single day from pony-back. The birds were usually driven towards the guns by beaters, while loaders helped guns to shoot the large numbers of grouse flying over each peg or butt. Most birds have lice, and it is said that on some estates, so many birds were shot that heaps of dead birds used to swarm with these parasites.

There has always been a race to send the first shot birds of the new season to London to some of its top restaurants. Grouse are still specially packed and flown by plane or helicopter, ending up as a gourmet main course. Young birds are usually favoured, but Mrs Beeton gives a recipe for a grouse pudding in her famous cookery book, and suggests that mixing it with stewing steak is an excellent method of using a tough bird.

The highly esteemed red grouse (Polly Pullar)

Grouse shooting has long been seen as the sport of kings, the most exclusive shooting in the British Isles, but much has changed since its zenith. Disease appeared with a vengeance, and birds became badly infested with parasites, large worm burdens, and numerous other health issues. Compared to many other birds, grouse biology has been well researched. Grouse were so important to the country that in 1904, following a Parliamentary Committee of Enquiry, Lord Lovat produced *The Grouse in Health and Disease,* one of the earliest in-depth studies of the species. Since then, many organisations have further surveyed and studied grouse. Medicated grit has helped with parasites, and is readily taken as grouse need grit daily to help them digest the food in their gizzards, or crops.

During the war years, most active keepers were called up to fight, and there was less predator control on the moorland. The rotational burning that had kept the heather in good condition largely stopped, and together with pressure from too many grazing animals, heather began to seriously decline.

Today, although red grouse are still shot, numbers have dwindled and large bags are no longer obtainable; most estates have cut down to only a few days' grouse shooting each season. Grouse are dependent on young heather shoots, but the spread of bracken has also added to the demise of its mainstay.

The Latin name *lagopus* means hare-footed, and refers to the densely feathered feet of the grouse. Viewed up close, each toe has an extraordinary horny, comb-like outer fringe that increases the surface area of their tread, enabling them to walk on fresh snow, as well as protecting their feet from becoming frozen and fused to the ice at night.

Grouse do not seasonally migrate: they spend the entire year on the moor, moving lower down in the most severe weather. In December 1917, however, a small covey of grouse landed on the deck of the destroyer HMS *Ophelia* as it was moored just off the coast of Shetland. They have also been seen flying between the mainland and Orkney on various occasions.

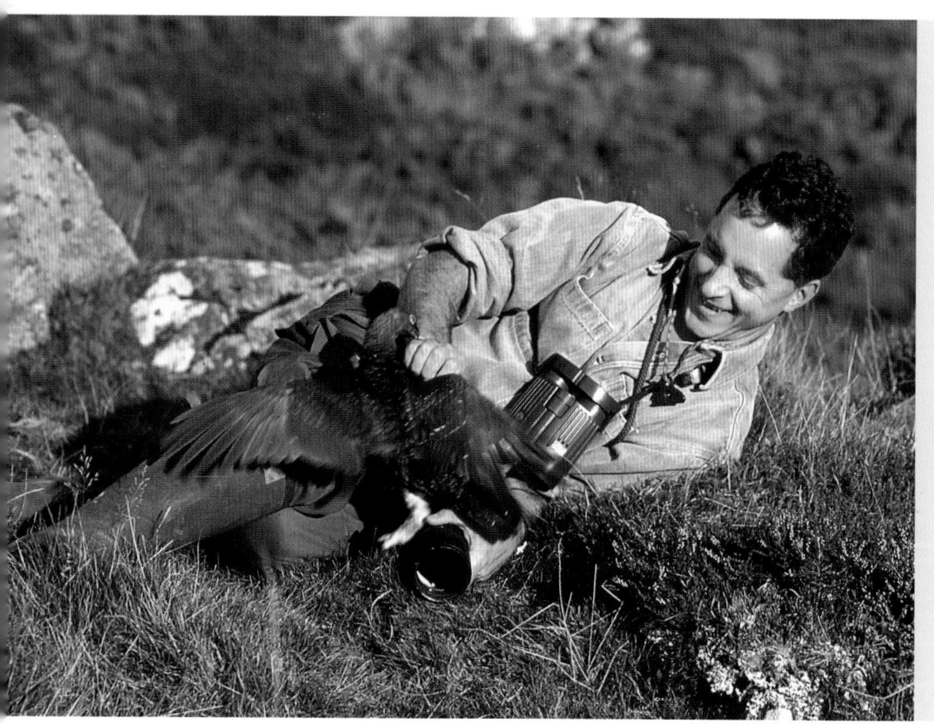

Artist Keith Brockie witnesses the wrath of a territorial cock grouse (Polly Pullar)

Grouse aggression

During the breeding season, cock grouse can be surprisingly aggressive, and are fiercely territorial. Some become almost psychopathic in their behaviour. With engorged red wattles and a belligerent stance they stand their ground, proclaiming their importance with their easily recognised, *go back, go back, go back* call. The colour of the wattles and general defensive behaviour are indicative of a bird's bodily condition.

Walkers and tourists may come across aggressive cock grouse in remote Highland glens, and there witness their extraordinary behaviour. One such bird spent much of its time waiting beside a narrow hill road. Walkers and visitors admiring the view were prime targets for the ire of this particular cock, and most hastily fled back to the safety of their cars as a brown missile came hurtling in their direction with sharp claws at the ready. Cyclists clad in lurid lycra seemed to provoke the severest reaction. Grouse can inflict quite a wound, and rogue cock grouse are not unusual.

Black Grouse

Tetrao tetrix
S: groose, black game, greyhen
G: *coileach-dubh, liath-chearc*

Dawn breaks over moorland, the cries of the curlew fill the air. A bubbling, hissing sound drifts through the mist as the ground begins to warm. This is the time when black game gather on their traditional lek sites (from the Swedish *leka* meaning to play).

The male black grouse is a stunning bird. Smart with almost blue-black feathers resembling shot silk, and sporting brilliant-red wattles above their eyes, their breeding display is a dramatic spectacle and takes place for an hour or so in the early mornings and evenings in spring. With lyre-shaped tails fanned out, flashing as the white underfeathers are exposed in a puff, the male black grouse gather together to show off their finery, backing and advancing on one another in a series of sham fights, trying to impress the females, known as 'greyhens'. The black grouse (black game) use the same lek sites every year. Their lovely tail feathers were once used to adorn Glengarry bonnets, the boat-shaped caps worn by Scottish regiments excluding the Black Watch. While some bonnets had a red and white diced or chequered border and ribbons, others had the addition of cock plumes. Alasdair Ranaldson MacDonell, 1st Chief of the Clan MacDonell, first introduced the hats. Similar bonnets are still worn by pipers today, although it is rare for them to have authentic black cock feathers.

Although a sporting bird, black game are now seldom shot and an unspoken agreement with many landowners protects them. From a sporting perspective, they were never as popular as their close relation, the red grouse, as they do not fly with any pattern and cannot be driven by dogs. Following a drastic drop in number due to habitat loss, important steps have been taken in many areas to re-introduce native pinewoods. During the 1980s and 1990s new fences were erected to keep deer out of plantations, but this had disastrous consequences as black grouse and capercaillie flew into the fences, often breaking their necks or wings. Ironically, the fences were there to help the establishment of new habitat for black game, and the project ended with many casualties instead. Now fences are marked with either bamboo canes or colourful plastic banners so that the birds can see them clearly.

Black grouse are almost entirely vegetarian and thrive on blaeberry, alder and Scots pine. They are sometimes seen feeding on farmland, gleaning stubble fields, or in fields of Brassica. During hard weather they fly to the top of conifers and feed on their soft new shoots. In spring, larch buds are also popular and it is not unusual to see birds, round like puddings, feasting in the trees.

Black grouse at lek site (Neil McIntyre)

TICKS AND MOORLAND MANAGEMENT

The management of a grouse moor has always been a sensitive issue. Sheep farmer and conservationist Mervyn Browne has long been interested in heather management and says that it is the vegetation which covers the moor that dictates the species that live there. For a healthy grouse population it is necessary to have short springy heather which is burnt in a ten-year rotation showing a mosaic of blacker areas, mixed with new growth across the upland. Providing grazing for hill sheep, and the right kind of heather for grouse, is not an easy matter. In 1984 the Heather Trust was established to try to reconcile grazing and grouse and since then Mervyn has worked with them and been key to raising awareness of the importance of heather for various species.

Below. Mervyn Browne with Queen (Polly Pullar)

Opposite. Tick infestation around cock pheasant's eye (Polly Pullar)

Heather burning, or *muirburn*, as it is referred to, can take place between 1 October and 15 April below 1,500 feet, and between 1 October and 30 April on higher ground. This ensures that it does not interfere with breeding species returning to the moor. In the days when farms and estates had numerous keepers and shepherds working there, burning involved a large squad, and strict control of fires was easier. Mervyn explains: 'People burn their hill for different reasons, some want a quick flush of grass for sheep and burn in a gung-ho fashion which will encourage moor grass such as *molinia*, while others plan it to ensure there is young heather to provide grouse with the right food. In my lifetime the heather has receded drastically on most hills all over Scotland, and the Trust tries to advise people on ways to encourage regeneration.' Heather beetle *Lochmaea suturalis* has also affected the situation. This small insidious pest is hard to see and little is known about it. Its larvae, however, feed exclusively on heather plants and cause much damage, as the heather is gradually defoliated, allowing stronger plants such as grasses and bracken to take over.

The spread of highly invasive bracken in recent times has altered the moorland ecology too. Not only does it

Ticks and disease

Ticks carry a wide range of diseases. For humans, Lyme disease has become a serious concern, with far-reaching long-term effects for hillwalkers and those working outside. Awareness of the possible dangers, however, along with careful observation of reactions after a tick bite, can avert disaster. Not all ticks carry this disease, but for humans if there are flu-like symptoms following a reaction around a bite, then medical help should be sought. A course of antibiotics will prevent more serious symptoms from developing.

compete directly with heather but it also provides excellent cover for one of the smallest, yet most dangerous creatures found in Scotland today – the blood-sucking sheep tick *Ixodes ricinus.* With a complex life cycle, the tiny tick transmits many fatal diseases for grouse and other fauna, including sheep and cattle. It was originally thought that disease was only spread when birds had ticks attached to them, but now it is thought that ingesting them also causes infection.

One red deer calf was recently found to have over 200 ticks and serious paralysis caused by tick-carried toxins. This also affects many farm animals every year, causing huge financial loss. Following an intensive course of antibiotics and other treatment, the calf made a full recovery. Not many animals are so lucky and it is likely that this will become a more common occurrence all over Scotland.

Since 1997 Mervyn Browne has been the Scottish agent for a bracken-spraying company that uses helicopters. He believes that controlling this member of the fern family can help improve the tick situation. They hope to obtain a 95-per-cent bracken kill using weedkiller, thus improving the productivity of the ground for grouse conservation and farming interests.

ONCE BITTEN, NEVER FORGOTTEN

Midge

Culicoides impunctatus
S: midgeck, mudgeick, midgie, mudge
G: *meanbh-chuileag*

If it were not for our inclement climate and the infamous Highland midge, then Scotland would probably be an even more popular holiday destination. There is little doubt that both are a huge deterrent to visitors.

Despite its tiny size, the midge is the most irritating insect of all. There are 37 species of midge in Scotland and each type favours a slightly different habitat. Not all are a major problem and it is generally recognised that the Highland midge *Culcoides impunctatus,* nicknamed 'midgie', causes the most bother. During warm, humid conditions, bogs, moors and woods may be swarming with these exasperating creatures, and they can turn a beautiful outdoor experience into a living hell. One irate tourist to the High-

Midge control

In the 1940s government-funded investigations into ways of controlling the midge drew a blank, and continue to do so today. Various lotions and potions have been manufactured to keep them at bay but few seem to have foolproof results. Some even appear to lure them in from afar. There are midge nets to be worn over the face and head, and entire anti-midge body suits. But it only needs one or two to find a way in and the misery persists. In recent years, highly effective machines that attract midges with carbon dioxide and then destroy them have proved their worth, although they are expensive and only clear the immediate area. Some conservationists are concerned about the impact of such machines for bats and birds which need midges to survive. Anyone who manages to find the solution to the greatest aggravation in Scotland, however, will certainly have no need to buy a lottery ticket each week.

land hills commented recently, 'It should be your choice to give blood, but these blighters have put paid to that. They are going to bleed me dry.'

Midges do not bite, but suck blood, and it is the females that are the culprits, as they require high protein (warm blood) to provide nutrients for their eggs. It is the chemical reaction to the anticoagulant the female injects prior to sucking that causes all the skin reactions. In some cases people's bodies react badly, with welts and lumps appearing wherever the midges have been, and there may also be persistent irritation that returns with a vengeance 24 hours after the original bite, and for days later.

Midges lay their eggs in wet, boggy areas and after the larval stage newly fledged adults emerge in April's warm weather. They are dependent on areas of high rainfall. During constant clan skirmishes that broke out all over the Highlands (usually over cattle or women), midges were said to have been the best weapon – they drove enemies away post-haste. Few can tolerate a really bad onslaught and certain places are renowned for being no-go areas when the midges are out.

Meadow pipit

THE STAPLES

Meadow Pipit

Anthus pratensis
S: gray cheeper, moss cheeper, muir cheeper, titlin
G: *snathag*

The 'moss cheeper', as it is often called, arrives back on the hill from the low ground in large flocks. The arrival occurs as early as February, depending on the temperature. Their thin squeaky calls are often all that can be heard on an otherwise desolate moor. Although it may seem frail and nondescript, the meadow pipit is a beautiful and hardy little bird, well able to stand the rigours of life in upland Scotland. Frequently overlooked, they are in fact the building blocks of the moorland ecosystem, providing vital food for many species including the short-eared owl, hen harrier, merlin, peregrine, buzzard and raven, while they in turn take advantage of the copious hatchings of craneflies in the heather.

During the pipit's breeding display the male rises high into the air, giving a steady pulse of call notes that quickens as it reaches the highest point. Then with outstretched wings, he falls down in stalling spirals while emitting a trilling crescendo that finally falls away as the bird alights on a tussock. This is called 'parachuting'.

You may frequently see meadow pipits and other small birds mobbing cuckoos, and with good reason. In a 1950s survey, one in five nesting meadow pipit pairs was found to be the victim of the cuckoo's dubious breeding activities, and was playing host to a fledgling cuckoo. Together with the dunnock, they are the birds most frequently chosen for brood parasitism by the cuckoo.

Short-tailed field vole

Short-tailed Field Vole

Microtus agrestis
S: land mouse
G: *famhalan feòir*

Voles are widespread throughout Scotland. For one so small, the damage a vole can inflict on young trees and hedge plants is astonishing. It can gnaw its way through surprisingly thick stems and ruin any chance of a hedge or wood being established without the use of special vole-guards. An adult vole may eat as much as 30 grams of vegetation per day, which for a mammal only weighing approximately 14–50 grams is quite a feat.

Moorland with old grasses may be thickly latticed with a maze of vole tunnels and wellworn runs, each with tiny dark-coloured droppings showing signs of intense activity. There may also be a constant shrill piping noise, and a scurrying flash of grey indicating that the inmates are also active by day as well as by night.

Voles, like meadow pipits, form a vital part of the food chain. Their populations are subject to major peaks and troughs over a cycle of four or five years. This directly affects the breeding success of certain birds of prey including short-eared owls. Foxes also eat large quantities of voles and listen patiently for signs of activity in the mat of grasses, leaping up and then quickly diving down to grab the unsuspecting vole. Like owl pellets, fox droppings are predominantly grey with vole fur.

THE PREDATORS

Hen Harrier

Circus cyaneus
S: gled, grey gled (male), ringle-tailed gled (female), 'Sanct Martynis fowle'
G: *brèid-air-tòin, clamhan nan cearc*

The hen harrier is something of a paradox. Not only is it one of the most beautiful birds on the moors, it is also probably the most loathed. While naturalists and conservationists would walk a long way in the hope of seeing a harrier, gamekeepers and landowners hope they will not come across them. Harriers take grouse, especially when feeding a voracious brood of young. Although they also feed on a variety of other prey including pipits, skylarks, small mammals, and waders and their chicks, it is their close proximity to nesting grouse that has raised keepers' hackles for generations.

The hen harrier has been more persecuted than most other birds of prey. During the Victorian era it was

The Langholm Project

In the 1990s the relationship between harriers and grouse gave rise to the Langholm Project, in which the Duke of Buccleuch allowed 12,000 acres of grouse moor to be studied for the effects of raptors on red grouse populations. Several phases of this large and ambitious operation involved many conservation organisations including the RSPB, SNH, the Game Conservancy Trust, Buccleuch Estates, and Natural England.

Numbers of grouse had been dropping dramatically, and the aim was to find out the affect of the raptors. By the end of the first stage of the project, harrier numbers had risen and grouse numbers had dropped even further. Food was put out for the harriers by the gamekeepers to supplement their diets in the hope of keeping them away from grouse. The estate ceased all grouse shooting, and removed keepers. Interestingly, since the keepers stopped maintaining the moors, it has been found that all bird species have declined. The intensely complex study is ongoing, and sets out to try to resolve conflicts between moorland management for raptors and red grouse. It also aims to extend and improve the moor for conservation in general, helping it become financially viable with healthy numbers of grouse maintained for limited shooting interests.

Hen harrier, loved and loathed in equal measure (Laurie Campbell)

frequently shot. It is a ground nester, and eggs or chicks were routinely destroyed. This practice continues despite their protection by law. As one keeper was quoted, 'If the slugs are eating your lettuces, you will put pellets out to get rid of them. The grouse are my harvest ….' Keepers were once paid a bounty to ensure their moors were free of these elegant raptors. During the two world wars, when many keepers went away, the harrier had a brief respite and numbers recovered. Even today, you only have to mention them to owners of a grouse moor to invoke a reaction and intense debate.

The courtship display of the hen harrier is elaborate and sometimes involves a food pass in midair. The sexes are very different – the brown female and juvenile are often referred to as a ringtail due to the defined white band at the top of the tail. The male is conspicuous, a bright, shining pale grey, and is sometimes mistaken for a gull. He is easy to see flying across heather or bog. Harriers are graceful in flight, and have an almost owl-like, rounded face, and brilliant-yellow eyes. Hen harriers are polygamous – one male in Orkney was recorded with seven females. There have also been records of communal nesting, with two or even three females in the same nest. During the winter, birds may also use a communal roost site.

The name 'hen harrier' dates as far back as 1544 when they made themselves unpopular for 'butchering' domestic poultry, yet you seldom hear of this today. In the Highlands, seeing a hen harrier was taken as a sign that you had enjoyed a good day, indicating that they were, perhaps, not always disliked.

On Islay, the RSPB reserve at Loch Gruinart is an excellent place to see harriers hunting over the marsh. Indeed most of Islay is a stronghold for the birds, and they are also easy to see on the nearby island of Jura.

Merlin

Falco columbarius
S: merlzeoun, maalin
G: *mèirneal, seabhag ghorm an fhraoich*

Small although the merlin may be, it has incredible energy and has long been revered as a traditional falconry bird. It was seen as the ideal bird of prey for a lady – Mary, Queen of Scots was a keen falconer, and regularly used merlins as well as peregrines. The name is thought to originate from the Latin *merula,* for blackbird, a bird the same size as the male, or jack merlin. Merlins are largely bird-eating falcons – meadow pipits form the largest part of their diet, along with emperor moths and beetles. They occasionally take small mammals. There is a tale of one falconer who kept a merlin, and let it spend some of its time with his gardener while he was out digging. Apparently the little bird would perch, waiting patiently for worms to appear, before immediately diving down to feed on them.

Merlins were once trained to hunt larks. In *Falconry in the British Isles*, written in 1855, Francis Henry Salvin and William Brodick suggested keeping larks in an aviary to help train the merlins on them when they were released. Merlins trained for lark hunting were also adept at taking snipe, giving rise to one of their nicknames, the snipe or bog hawk. Some falconers in the past claimed that they had very good sport with this dapper little falcon, hunting blackbirds and thrushes out of turnip fields.

The bold and dashing merlin (Neil McIntyre)

Merlins winter on low ground nearer the coast, returning to the uplands in spring to breed. They can occasionally be seen in hurried flight, or perhaps perching on a rock or fence post, eyeing the situation in readiness for a hunt. During the Victorian era, pole traps were set on fence posts regularly used as perches. Merlins, along with many other birds of prey, were frequently the unfortunate victims. They have also suffered as a result of organo-phosphate residue in their prey, and on occasions this quicksilver bird has been known to inadvertently kill itself flying at high speed into windows or wires.

Bold and dashing in flight, the plumage of females and juveniles is a darker brown than the kestrel, but like the kestrel and peregrine, they also have the dark-brown eyes typical of falcons. At the beginning of the 1900s merlins were frequently seen on the chimneypots in Glasgow, waiting for pigeons. In 1983 a merlin was recorded flying down the streets of Stornoway in pursuit of its quarry.

Jock o' Hazeldean

The 'managed hawk' in the Border ballad 'Jock o' Hazeldean' was probably a merlin. It appears in a list of luxuries proferred to a reluctant bride. Her would-be father-in-law tries everything:

A chain of gold ye shall not lack,
    nor braid to bind your hair,
Nor mettled hound nor managed hawk,
    nor palfrey fresh and fair,
And you the formost o' them a',
    shall ride our forest queen,
But aye she loot the tears doon fa' –
    for Jock o' Hazeldean.

Sir Walter Scott, 1816

Newly fledged short-eared owl in typical heathery habitat (Polly Pullar)

Short-eared Owl

Asio flammeus
S: cataface, short-horned hoolet
G: *comhachag chluasach*

There are records from the 1890s of plagues of short-tailed field voles causing heavy damage to forestry. Coinciding with this, large numbers of short-eared owls were recorded feasting on the voles. At this time, one farmer witnessed more than 36 owls on a small hillside in southern Scotland. He claimed that the owls were active far into the night, quartering the ground with their almost casual way of hunting, belying their power and intent. The relationship of short-eared owls with voles is similar to that of the snowy owl with the Arctic lemming in the tundra – a cyclical boom-and-bust situation. Although voles form the largest part of a short-eared owl's diet, owls also eat small birds and rabbits. Young plantation edges with tussock grasses provide excellent hunting ground. Once the trees start to mature, the habitat alters and becomes too dense and the owls move on.

The short-eared owl is diurnal: it is as likely to be seen by day as by night. It frequently perches on a rocky outcrop or roadside post, keeping a watchful eye for both prey and dangers. Its dramatic unblinking yellow eyes and heart-shaped facial disc are remarkable: the so-called ears, like those of its close relative the long-eared owl, are made up of tufts of feathers and are not ears at all. These feathers provide extra camouflage. They can be extended when the bird is alarmed and may also make it seem threatening. Owls have huge ears compared to other birds – large sensitive openings situated in almost the same position on their heads as those of humans, these may easily be seen when the feathers are parted.

Short-eared owls nest on the ground; chicks hatch at intervals giving rise to a variation in brood size. In years of low vole numbers, not all owlets survive, and their parents or siblings may eat some. The adult birds are very protective over their grey down-covered owlets, and will readily feign a broken wing to lure a human away. Short-eared owls have a harsh, almost barking alarm call, and during the breeding season they perform dramatic wing-clapping displays to one another in midair.

THE GLEANERS

Carrion Crow

Corvus corone
G: *feannag, feannag dhubh*

Hooded Crow

Corvus cornix
S: craw, corbie (also used for raven and rook), hoodie, hiddie, gray back
G: *feannag ghlas, starrag*

Two corvids that were long seen as different races of the same bird now have their own separate status although their behaviour and characteristics are similar. The hooded crow has a smart grey mantle and hood and is usually referred to in the hills as the hoodie. It tends to be seen more to the west and north of Scotland and is usually the crow found at higher altitudes. Confusingly, some keepers on low ground also refer to the plainer carrion crow as the hoodie. On occasions the two types interbreed. Once referred to as Satan's messengers, both types are viewed as robbers and regarded as the ultimate pest, and to this end have been much persecuted.

Crows are highly intelligent. They rise early and do not roost till late and are therefore able to take advantage of any situation that may arise. On the seashore they gather dog whelks, crabs and other delicacies then rise into the air and drop them onto the rocks to smash them open. They have also been seen pulling the tail of an otter quietly eating a butterfish and annoying it so much that it slipped away, leaving the fish on the rocks. Crows are skilful. The term crow-bar for a metal bar used to force and prise things apart is probably a reference to a crow's powerful, destructive bill.

Hand-reared crows make amusing pets although they test the patience of their handlers and any other household pets with their antics and devilry. They are opportunists – countrymen, shepherds, farmers and keepers will frequently refer to them with a string of oaths. Scarecrows have long been made to keep them and other corvids off

Twa Corbies

The Border ballad 'Twa Corbies' gives us a glimpse of one of their more gruesome feeding habits. Here, their dinner is the body of a new-slain knight, with no detail spared:

> Ye'll sit on his white hause-bane,
> And I'll pike out his bonny blue een;
> Wi ae lock o his gowden hair-o
> We'll theek our nest when it grows bare.

No wonder people disliked them. Further back, in the Irish tradition, crows had been associated with the 'war goddesses' Badb and the Morrïgan who were imagined flying in the sky above battles, terrifying figures, attracted by the fray.

Even the sensible John Hewit, blacksmith bird-watcher form Heiton, Roxburghshire, speaking in 1956, found something mysterious about the crows that habitually gathered on a certain ash tree near Kelso. 'On different mornings,' he says, 'the hiddies congregate there, caw away and make circular flights and come back a' thegither again, and have a confab for a quarter of an hour or so and then disperse.' He'd noticed this over and over again. The location ('where three lairds' lands meet') seemed significant too. In the Highlands, 'where three streams meet' could be a place of power. Hewit's testimony and tone of voice hint at something similar in the Lowlands, although he returns quickly to natural history and observation: 'they change their voice every month,' he says, 'and as the season comes roond, you can tell aforehand wi' the cry o' the cra's. You can notice the change. And it's a funny thing – I've studied that up since I was a laddie – and you can notice the different behaviour o' the different birds.'

crops, but after a time, a savvy crow will find this a convenient place to perch, preen and rest, in between its grain-pillaging forays.

Crow nests are messy affairs largely made of twigs, sometimes lined with sheep's wool or old baler twine. They often use the same nests each year, choosing trees or crags. Frequently the bottoms of the nests were shot through by shepherds to ensure that the sitters did not rear another brood, and this practice still continues where crows are unpopular.

The Larsen trap was introduced in the 1950s. Crows are very territorial, and will angrily mob another crow on their patch. A live crow is placed in the trap as a decoy and the clever funnel system allows other crows to literally drop in, but not get out. The decoy crows should have food and water available at all times. Sometimes many crows are caught in this way. The Larsen trap is still legally used, although it often causes controversy, as rarer birds can sometimes be caught, and there is concern that traps in more remote areas of hill are not checked as often, and the food and water supplies are not regularly replenished. Protected carrion eaters such as buzzards, golden eagles or red kites die of starvation in unchecked traps.

Conflict with sheep at lambing time is probably the crow's biggest crime and many become adept at pecking out the eyes and tongues of weak ewes and lambs. They also steal eggs from other birds. The naturalist and writer Seton Gordon came across an egg dump left by crows on seabird cliffs which contained no less than 150 eggs. On one grouse moor where research was being carried out, grouse nests were marked with canes. The local crow population soon learned why the markers were there, and took advantage.

Crows are bold birds. However, in some areas where they are persecuted, they stay away from humans as much as possible. They are frequently seen mobbing eagles, ravens and buzzards, and readily share a deer or sheep carcass with a fox, cheekily pulling at its brush to annoy it, ensuring that they get enough of a chance to feed too. It is hard not to be impressed by a bird that is not only intelligent, but almost seems to have a sense of humour.

The hooded crow, like its relative the carrion crow, is extremely clever (Malcolm Gosling)

THE WILY

Cuckoo

Cuculus canorus
S: gowk, gokk
G: *cuthag*

There has been a great deal of speculation surrounding the cuckoo – the only British bird to use 'obligate brood parasitism' as its means of breeding: it uses other birds to brood its eggs and rear its young. For years people believed that in autumn the cuckoo turned into a hawk. Cuckoos are often misidentified as sparrowhawks; not surprising given their similarity in colour and silhouette. It was also believed that the female cuckoo laid her egg, swallowed it, and then regurgitated it into the nests of small birds: meadow pipit, dunnock, reed warbler, and other unfortunate victims. Following dedicated study between 1918 and 1925, two naturalists, Edgar Chance and wildlife photographer Oliver Pike, proved otherwise.

The female cuckoo waits patiently till her chosen host leaves the nest, and flies swiftly to it, depositing her own egg neatly into even the tiniest domed nests. This is done at exactly the right time, when her egg will stand the best chance of hatching out before that of the host bird. Female cuckoos almost shoot their eggs from out of a specially adapted cloaca – some may lay as many as 25 eggs in a season, leaving them in nests all over a small area.

Each cuckoo favours a particular species of small bird, and in a brilliant quirk of nature adapts her own egg to a similar size and colouration as that of the chosen victim. If the hosts' eggs have hatched out earlier than the baby cuckoo, then despite its age difference, when it hatches it will quickly oust the unfortunate chicks until it is the only one remaining in the nest. A tiny cuckoo nestling can even cleverly manoeuvre whole eggs from the nest, pushing them out on its broad back.

It is only the male cuckoo that makes the *cu-koo* sound. The female makes a laughing call, almost like chuckling.

A juvenile cuckoo awaits the attention of its unfortunate songster parent (Laurie Campbell)

Each year all over Scotland, we await the sound with impatience – it has long been seen as the harbinger of spring. Depending on the area and the weather, the cuckoo arrives between mid April and mid May. A recent dramatic drop in cuckoo numbers, however, has become cause for serious concern.

Lack of suitable food appears to be the problem: climate changes have reduced their favourite food – hairy caterpillars – at a time when they are most needed. Cuckoos are also struggling to find enough food as they migrate back from Africa. Experts are worried. Although we can help many birds by supplementing their food in our gardens, cuckoos will not come to feeders, and cannot adapt in this way. Within the foreseeable future, the cuckoo could become a very rare bird in Scotland and its demise would be much mourned. Its extraordinary behaviour has always been the subject of mysterious conjecture, and its call is loved by many.

Fox

Vulpes vulpes
S: tod, Lowrence, Lowrie
G: *sionnach, balgair, madadh-ruadh*

You cannot but admire the fox. Through the centuries it has been hunted, shot, chased, trapped, and poisoned, but still remains a wily survivor, skilled hunter, voracious predator and a secretive beast that can outwit man's most determined efforts to exterminate it. Bounties have long been paid for a fox's brush, and even in the late 1960s a £5 sum was being paid for it. At one time, those who could afford it lined their clothes with fox fur, hence the curious entry in the royal accounts of 1538, that a furrier had been paid 'for ane lynyng of toddis to the bak quarteris of the kingis nycht goune'.

Foxes survive almost anywhere despite relentless perse-

Cuckoo proverbs

There are many proverbs relating to the cuckoo, such as, 'Heard in September, a thing to remember, heard in October, you're not sober!'

> The cuckoo comes on Donald's day
> An' with a shoor o' rain,
> An' when she sees a stalk o' bere
> She flies awa again.'

It was unlucky in parts of Scotland to hear a cuckoo on an empty stomach. Indeed, some people kept a piece of oatcake under their pillow in spring, so that they could eat it on waking and avoid misfortune as the year unfolded. There are hints of these darker associations in one of William Ross's great Gaelic love songs, when he tells his femme fatale that her voice is sweeter to him than the voice of the cuckoo on a May morning, although cuckoos also appear in Gaelic poetry simply as harbingers of spring. Indeed, children in Highland townships used to enjoy making cuckoo imitations on the first of May, simply for fun: '*Gug-ùg!' ars a' chuthag Latha Buidhe Bealltainn*' (Cuckoo, said the gowk on yellow Beltane morning). John Hewit, the blacksmith, dismissed a question about the ominousness of cuckoos – maybe it was unknown in the Borders – and many Scots have shared his straightforward pleasure in the arrival of the spring migrants.

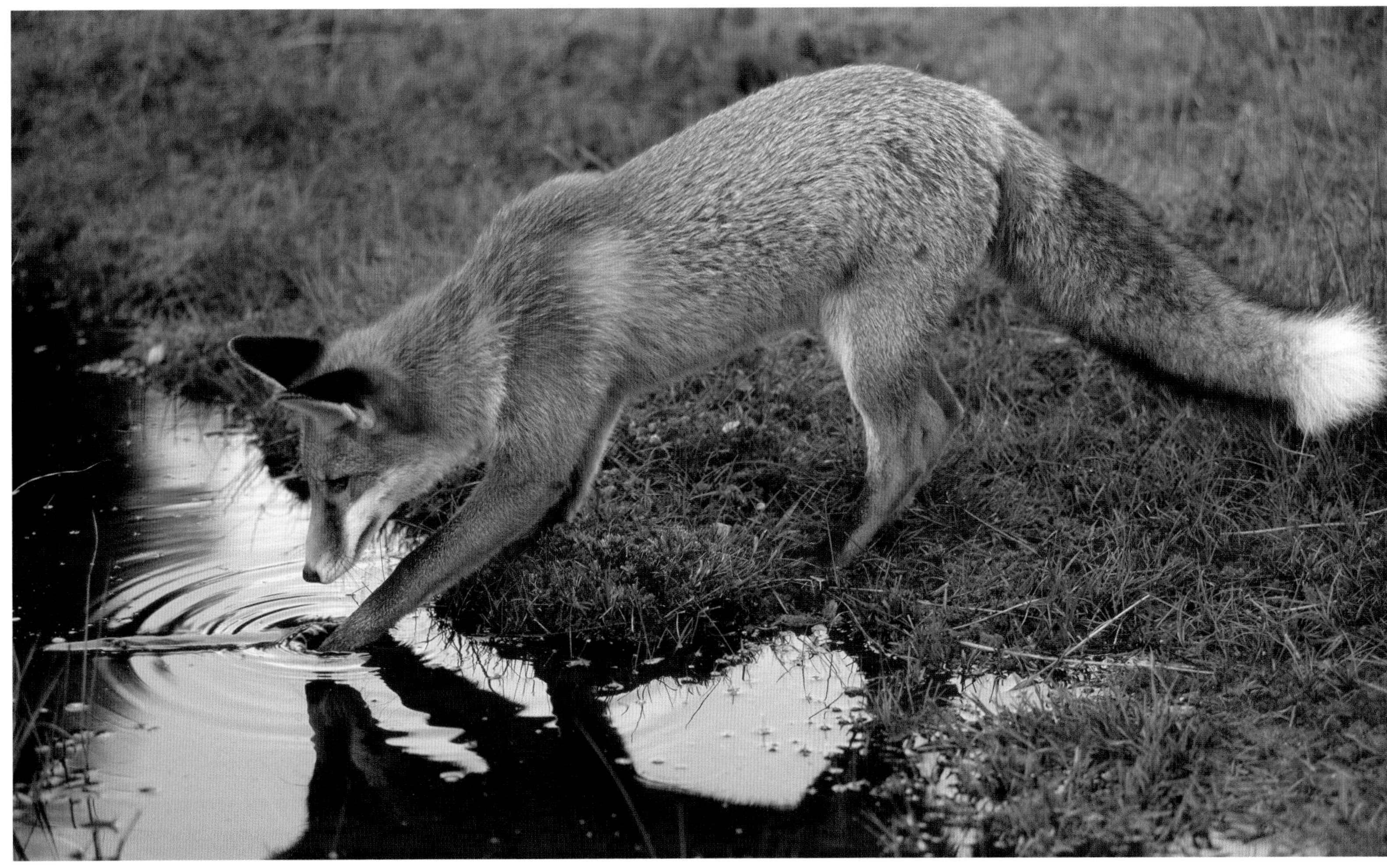

The fox, like the dog, is highly inquisitive (Laurie Campbell)

cution, and are as at home living on wild moorland as they are in woodland, farmland, coastal areas and even urban environments. The hill fox tends to be large and rangy, and exists on a diet of ground-nesting birds, rabbits, hares and voles, and frequently takes advantage of deer carcasses and other carrion. A nearby lambing field may also provide further temptation. Foxes adapt their menu to food availability and are seldom short of provisions. It is not without reason that fox cubs are born to coincide with the lambing season, and at the start of the year, a new war is waged to endeavour to clear them from sheep areas. When humans disturb a den, a vixen quickly moves her cubs to safety.

During a few short days of the breeding season, the vixen emits one of the eeriest and most unearthly sounds of all. For any that have not heard this before and do not know what it is, it can be spine-chilling. The sound is enough to make a dog's hair bristle, or set it off howling madly. The noise, often heard on moonlit nights in December and January, attracts the attentions of a nearby dog fox, and cubs are then born after a gestation period of 52 days.

While the cubs are still blind, and their fur is dark brown, the dog provides food for the vixen, although she may not let him enter the den. A fox abroad in daylight on nefarious business is furiously mobbed by jays, crows and songsters, and cannot move far unnoticed. Although they usually tend to hunt under cover of darkness, when under

Fox and fable

The fox often stands for temptation, wordliness and the wiles of the devil in *The Morall Fabillis of Esope the Phrygian* by Robert Henryson (c.1460–1500). He is always a dog fox and can be a smarter, more likeable character than the aristocratic wolf. He belongs to the middle rank of society, above farm animals (representing the peasantry) and below wolves and lions (voracious or noble rulers). He has an international reputation, cropping up in folk tales all over the world, and can be successful or come to a bad end, depending on the perspective of the storyteller, but very often he is a metaphor for human deviousness, as in the proverb, 'When the tod preaches, beware the hens'. In Scotland, self-seeking churchmen were sometimes characterised as foxes, but the slur could be applied to secular authorities as well. Colin Campbell of Glenure, famously, was known to his enemies as 'the red fox'. A Hanoverian factor on a forfeited Jacobite estate, he was murdered near Ballachullish in 1752. Fox stories allowed people to comment covertly, not just on human nature, but also on politics and current affairs. The Islay-born collector John Francis Campbell (1821–1885) came across fragments of a story about a fox who killed and ate the kids of an impoverished nanny goat, then resolutely denied it, even when she came to his house and sat on the roof, blocking the smoke hole and demanding justice. The story was familiar in Barra, Skye and on the shores of Loch Hourn, but people were very reluctant to tell it, although everybody knew it. Was it perhaps a parable about some dastardly event?

'*Cho carrach ri sionnach na Maoile*' (as cunning as the fox of the Mull) refers to a legendary fox who was said never to hunt near his home in Kintyre, but always ten or twenty miles away. His main cunning was as an escape artist – a hunter swore that he deliberately led dogs to their deaths by leaping off a cliff and seizing a rowan sapling in his teeth on the way down.

It was also widely believed that foxes could rid themselves of fleas. Several people claimed to have seen them lying down tail-first in water, with a piece of straw or wool in their mouths. The fleas hopped onto the wool and the fox let go. So there was a sneaking admiration for foxes, in spite of everything.

Children in particular could enjoy foxes and even identify with them – in Lanarkshire and Ayrshire, the 'den' (safe house) in the game of tig was called 'toddie's grund'.

But people of all ages can chuckle at the image of the fox who made off with a sheep's stomach that came with hidden extras: '*Tha biadh is ceòl an seo', mun duirt am madadh-ruadh 's e ruith air falbh leis a' phìob.*' (There's meat and music here, as the fox said when he ran away with the bagpipes.)

pressure to feed growing cubs they may visit a pheasant pen or hen run during the daytime, returning with a chicken takeaway. Hens are always vulnerable to fox predation. It seems extraordinary that, given a fox's reputation, new poultry keepers are often blissfully unaware that birds not shut in securely at night are fair game, and are shocked to find carnage in the morning. But as the renowned Scottish naturalist David Stephen commented, 'I've never yet found a fox carrying a key to get into the henhouse.' Once inside they are fuelled by the excitement of flapping fowls, and spurred into a killing frenzy.

In 2000 the Game Conservancy Trust carried out a survey of foxes killed: 16,000 were accounted for by hunts, 80,000 by gamekeepers, and natural causes and traffic accidents accounted for a further 300,000. Despite this there is little impact on fox numbers, and it would seem that the more they are persecuted the more they thrive.

Foxes are frequently caught in snares; there are many records of them having gnawed off their own leg in order to escape, and managing to exist perfectly well for many years afterwards. Like well-honed poachers, they are quick to take advantage of other snare victims, and will readily steal a warm rabbit or pheasant when the chance arises. They may also be seen leaping acrobatically into the air to catch a pheasant as it takes off.

The fox's reputation for guile and stealth is famous. They will run over the backs of sheep, enter water or hide in an outbuilding to evade a hunt. They are also one of the few animals that have learned to get into the prickly armour of a hedgehog. Indeed some foxes become hedgehog specialists, and push the tightly rolled-up animals to water, forcing them to open up so that they can be quickly killed and eaten. Foxes are also great ratters. They have been seen killing them in a farmyard almost for the sheer love of it. Like the badger, foxes may dig out a wild bees' nest, although are not as tenacious when it comes to coping with the ensuing stings. They are also seen on the seashore sometimes, searching rock pools for shellfish and small crabs.

Grey furry scats are clear signs that a fox is in the vicinity, and their distinctive pungent aroma is much stronger during the breeding season when foxes scent mark wherever they go. During the day they choose a suitable place to lie up and sleep until nightfall, and may be spotted dozing on a bracken bed on a south-facing hillside enjoying the sun. A farmer friend told me of a most unusual choice of sleeping place and although he knew the fox was there, took great care not to disturb it. Being the ultimate opportunist, it had chosen a well-heated spot, securely hidden curled in a large tractor tyre used to hold down the cover on the silage pit. The warmth of the fermenting process underneath must have been akin to the best possible under-floor heating.

Although foxes are widespread in Scotland, there are a few places that remain devoid of them. There are none in Islay, Mull, or many other Hebridean Islands, and none in Orkney and Shetland, although there were efforts to introduce them to Orkney in 1930. A dog fox was found dead on the road there in 2007, but it is thought it had been brought in as a pet. Needless to say, conservationists would not be pleased to have Old Charlie on the island due to the havoc he would wreak with ground-nesting bird species.

In literature, the fox is often portrayed as a Jack the lad, cunning rogue, or a cad. And in everyday parlance, the term 'foxy lady' refers to someone who is sexy. A woman described as 'an old vixen', however, is none too flattered. Despite the constant war waged on one of the most beautiful and wily creatures in Scotland, the fox is thriving, and what is more, there is probably not a single gamekeeper in Scotland who is not secretly glad of that fact.

Stoat

Mustela erminus
S: whitrat, futrat, whitterick, whittret
(also apply to weasel)
G: *neas, neas mhòr, neas gheal*

Stoats are extraordinary: they have strange sexual habits, and immense strength for their size – they have been known to kill fully grown rabbits. They are also determined swimmers. In 1902 *The Scotsman*'s correspondent for Drumnadrochit reported that a local gamekeeper had seen a 'stoat weasel' attempting to cross Loch Ness. She nearly made it, apparently. One wonders whether she might have made it if the observer had been of a different profession.

An orphaned female stoat, less than a couple of weeks old, was handed to a wildlife hospital and successfully hand-reared. It was a delightful and fascinating creature, but being too tame was not fit for release. Months later, having never been with any other stoats, while in captivity she gave birth.

Stoats are incestuous and the males sometimes mate with their own kits in the nest. They have a complex system of delayed implantation. Although eggs are released from the ovary during the breeding season and after mating are

Shetland stoats

There is an old folk tale which claims that the king's falconer introduced the stoat to Shetland. He went to the islands every year to catch highly sought dark-coloured peregrine falcons, and each islander was asked to give a hen to feed the birds on the journey south. People in one area decided that this was unreasonable and refused to give up their precious fowls. The next time the falconer came north, he brought with him a pair of 'whittrets', a Scots name for the stoat, and set them free in the hope that they in turn would kill the hens and pay the islanders back for their meanness. Stoats are still prolific on Shetland.

fertilised, they remain dormant and do not start to develop into young immediately but remain as a 'blastocyst'; a tiny pinhead surrounded by fluid. The blastocyst, or in the case of a litter, several blastocysts, do not attach to the uterus wall for some time. In the case of the stoat, after about nine months, foetuses begin to grow and from the start of gestation take just 25 days to fully develop. Up to 13 kits may be born.

Stoats, like most mustelids, are extremely playful. Without doubt they are the most lithe, sinuous and acrobatic creatures of all, as they leap and dance sometimes high in the air. Stoats are also reputed to do a death dance, mesmerising their victims with their high jinks. Rabbits often fall under this spell.

In a moorland habitat, they may live in old walls or shielings, and take a wide range of prey including eggs and nestlings of game birds and waders, and mammals including rabbits. Mother stoats will frequently move young kits if their nests are disturbed and have often been seen ferrying the babies hurriedly to a new location, clutching them by the scruff of their necks. They are ruthless killers; a stoat is not welcome in a hen house and will murder for the sake of it.

Rabbits form an important part of a stoat's diet. During the 1970s and early 1980s, when myxomatosis wiped out many rabbits, stoat numbers fell accordingly. They are also skilled ratters and in the days when most farms had corn stooks, stoats were often seen hunting almost joyously round them, quickly dispatching emerging rats. They are now sometimes seen where rats reach plague proportions, at landfill sites and other unsavoury locations. With the increasing use of rat killer, secondary poisoning can be lethal to stoats, as it is to birds of prey, foxes, and domestic animals.

In winter, the stoat's fur turns pure white with only the black tip of its tail remaining unchanged. Referred to as ermine, this smart winter dress was once highly sought and was used as far back as 1138 to decorate ceremonial robes. At that time only the royal family were permitted to use ermine for trimming robes, but later it was used for other nobility too. Today, a substitute is still used to trim robes for members of the House of Lords, and for garments worn at coronations or affairs of state. The black dots on the fur collars represent the stoat's black tail tips.

Weasel

Mustela nivalis
S: whitrat, futrat (also apply to stoat)
G: *easag* (female), *coinneas* (male)

The weasel is our smallest carnivore and, like its close relation the stoat, is astonishingly strong for its diminutive size. It is an aggressive and successful hunter and also highly protective of its young. Unlike the stoat however, weasels may breed twice a year and have a longer gestation period of approximately 36 days, without delayed implantation. Young female weasels are ready to breed in their first summer. Litters may be up to eight in number although mortality rates are high. Sometimes nests are lined with the fur from their prey – rabbit wool, mouse and vole fur, or feathers.

Weasels do not change colour in winter but remain gingery-brown and have no black tip to their tails. Despite this, there is still frequent confusion between stoats and weasels.

Gypsy lore

Gypsies always thought that it was bad luck to meet a weasel, and another old country saying, 'catch a weasel asleep if you can', pointed to their supreme alertness. A 'weasely person' is thought to be devious and scheming, sharp-featured and untrustworthy. Perhaps the most amusing use of the word is when describing someone as being 'as cross as a bag of weasels'.

Left. The call of the curlew is hauntingly beautiful (Malcolm Gosling)

Below. Nesting dunlin suffered as a result of foraging hedgehogs (Malcolm Gosling)

THE CHORISTERS

Curlew

Numenius arquata
S: whaup, whitterick
G: *guilbneach*

Robert Burns described curlews as 'lang leggity beasties'. They are indeed the largest wader in Britain. They seem to epitomise the wild with their distinctive, haunting sound. Lord Grey wrote in *The Charm of Birds*, 'Of all the bird songs or sounds known to me, there is none that I would prefer to the spring notes of the curlew'. Farmers and hill shepherds look forward to the return of the curlew, or 'whaup', to the high moors and lament the recent drop in number. The 'wheeple of the whaup' is a well-known Scots expression describing the curlew's cry.

The female is larger, with a thicker, longer bill, a clear distinguishing feature when seen alongside a male. Like the golden plover, curlews join together in large winter flocks, feeding on the shore or on stubble fields.

Curlews can live for a considerable time. One ringed in Sweden in 1936 was shot in Norfolk at the age of 32. Sir Hugh Gladstone recorded an albino curlew on a Dumfriesshire moor. It returned to breed there for 22 consecutive years.

Internationally acclaimed falconer and writer Philip Glasier of Selkirk wrote me a letter in the 1990s in which he perfectly summed the curlew up: 'The curlews are back on the hill, also the sea pies (oyster-catchers). The curlew's song is far better than any old nightingale, I reckon.'

Dunlin

Calidris alpina
S: horse-cock, pickerel, sleeper, ebb-sleeper, pliver's page, sea lark
G: *gille-feadaig, pollaran, grailleag*

The diminutive dunlin is the smallest wader to visit the moors in spring and summer. Once the breeding season is over, large flocks are seen on the shore running over a mudflat. Nicknamed the sea mouse, they have also been fondly referred to as the plover's page, due to their habit of staying close to golden plover. This odd behaviour is

Golden plover, spectacular in flight (Laurie Campbell)

thought to help protect the smaller wader from predators, benefiting from the alarm raised by the plovers.

Dunlin breed in many moorland areas, and favour the ideal habitat of parts of the Flow Country, and the Hebrides. In the Uists they have come into conflict with introduced hedgehogs. These unfortunate animals were brought to the Hebrides to help with garden slug control. Their rapid population explosion has caused mayhem among ground-nesting birds. Hedgehogs adore eggs. During nocturnal forays they quickly snuffle out nests. Large quantities of eggs may be devoured over a short period, and this has raised grave concerns for wader numbers, in particular the dunlin. SNH organised a scheme to trap the animals, with a bounty paid for each. Suggestion of an outright cull of the misplaced culprits caused outrage – instead the hedgehogs are now harmlessly caught and removed from the island to be taken to a more suitable habitat. The local dunlin population can now nest in peace.

Golden Plover

Pluvialis apricaria
S: yellow pliver
G: *feadag bhuidhe*

Together with the snipe and woodcock, the beautiful dappled golden plover is one of only three waders on the quarry list: it can legally be shot within a specific season. Due to its excellent camouflage, its plaintive cry may be the only indication of its presence on a remote moor in spring and early summer, for this is usually where the birds come to breed. In Aberdeenshire the cry of the golden plover was thought to offer advice to ploughmen: 'Plough weel, tyauve [sow; work] weel, harrow weel,' and the birds were also seen as lost souls – a reference to the melancholy tone of their call. The Skye minister Alexander Forbes was told that it was an omen of death to hear plovers calling at night, but thought the story was put about to discourage people from frequenting lonely places at night, places where there might be smugglers or illicit stills.

In the breeding season the plumage of the golden plover makes it an easy bird to identify. Its large, dark chest patch and spangled golden-ochre markings are gloriously eye-catching. They lay approximately four eggs, and once the young are hatched, sometimes divide a brood between the two parent birds. Chicks are very susceptible to heavy rain, and predation. The adult birds often feign injury to lead a human or other threat away from their young.

Large flocks of golden plover winter together with lapwing, and favour open farmland close to the coast. Dedicated sportsmen still travel to the Hebrides to shoot them, and say that shooting the initial bird is fairly easy, but to secure a second is a real challenge. Apparently once a shot has been fired, the group will quickly employ evasive action and fall low to the ground, keeping together in a tight group.

Golden plover numbers have fallen dramatically as a result of habitat loss and increased forestry, but in high summer healthy numbers continue to breed in such places as Unst in Shetland, at the reserve at Hermaness, ideal moorland habitat providing suitable short turf, and tundra-type vegetation. They seem perfectly at one on the summer moor surrounded by wavering bog cotton as they dash back and forth with their chicks, a glorious wader evocative of lonely places.

Greenshank

Tringa nebularia
S: green-legged horseman, long shank
G: glaisean-daraich

'The sound of the greenshank echoing among the hills in the summer evenings or very early mornings is one of those nostalgic sounds which brings back to the mind in swift pageant the whole wild complex of the deer country,' wrote Frank Fraser Darling, in his widely acclaimed book, *The Natural History of the Highlands and Islands.*

The call of the greenshank is a ringing triple cry that haunts the listener as it echoes out over a lonely river mouth or open moor. Another well-known and influential naturalist, Desmond Nethersole-Thompson, described the greenshank as 'the most wonderful bird that flies,' and became so entranced by them that he wrote the monograph *The Greenshank* in 1951, and followed this ground-breaking work with three other notable monographs on other rare and difficult-to-study Highland birds: the snow bunting, crossbill, and dotterel.

The intrepid egg collector Norman Gilroy claimed that the nest of the greenshank was the hardest to find. Its nest is no more than a mere scrape on the ground, out on the treeless moors. Breeding greenshank are highly secretive, but Nethersole-Thompson became adept at finding nests, and he even had pet names for many of the sitters.

The greenshank has a distinctive triple-note call (Laurie Campbell)

Snipe

Gallinago gallinago
S: mire-snipe, snippie, snippock, horse-gook, bog-bleater, moss bluiter, earn-bleater, hedder-bleater, hawk-fit
G: *naosg, gobhar-adhair, eun-ghòbhrag, eunarag, budagoc*

Thomas Bewick wrote, '[the snipe is] a very fat bird, but its fat does not cloy, and very rarely disagrees even with the weakest stomach, it is much esteemed as a delicious and well-flavoured dish, and is cooked in the same manner as the woodcock'. It seems an odd description for this tiny bird whose culinary qualities must be minimal. Some still value its meat, barely an ounce from each breast. Unlike other birds, the snipe is not eviscerated, and is roasted in its entirety before being eaten on a slice of toast. It's hard to imagine getting fat on such a repast.

Snipe often use fence posts as perches (Polly Pullar)

For sportsmen, the snipe is seen as the most testing game bird of all due to the speed and height at which it flies. Once far more common over much of the British Isles, sportsmen have hunted the snipe since as early as the thirteenth century, and have always seemed keen to pay for the rent of a bog over which to shoot them.

Robert Burns called them the 'blitter from the boggie,' and other names include 'snippack' and 'heather bleater'. The names all relate to the extraordinary drumming sound that the birds make, thought of by many as one of nature's most evocative sounds in the hills. For a long time this noise caused speculation about how the birds make it. Drumming has an eerie, mysterious quality. During the breeding season, the male snipe rises high into the air, then descends in sharp swoops, rising and falling, dipping through the air, with two specially stiffened tail feathers outstretched. These catch the wind and make a tremulous, winnowing sound, completing this elaborate breeding display. Some used to think the sound was made by bats, as in some areas it may be heard right through the stillness of a clear night in spring and summer.

On Hirta, St Kilda, in late May, I once stood in the *cleits*, (stone structures made by the St Kildans for storing seabirds and sheep) and by the light of a full moon rising over Village Bay, listened to the magical sound – more than 30 snipe drumming in unison, a resonant hum filling the sharp night air. It is without doubt for me the most beautiful sound of all. Campers in remote moorland areas often lie awake listening to the noise. It is very much an integral part of wild places in spring.

Relative to its body size, the snipe has the longest bill of any Scottish bird, used to great effect for probing in wet muddy ground. It may burst forth from a bog, flying into the air with a hoarse call before quickly disappearing from view with high, fast, jinking movement.

Snipe proverb

In parts of the Highlands, the snipe was associated with 'flitting' or moving house. The Gaelic proverb 'It's before you the snipe rose' used to mean 'you're lucky' and reflected the cheerful mood on the day when people and animals were setting off for the shielings and the summer pastures. But a snipe was a terrible thing to see if you felt in imminent danger of eviction. A poem from South Uist captures that feeling of desolation and inevitability:

Chuala mi Di-mart
Eunarag nan trath

Meannanaich 's an àrd
'S ag èigheach.

(On Tuesday, I heard the snipe of the seasons, bleating on high and calling.)

THE HIDDEN

Adder

Vipera beris
S: edir, veeper
G: *nathair-nimhe*

The adder is our only poisonous snake; indeed it is the only snake in Scotland, for the slow worm is in fact a legless lizard. During the 1990s, a man came across a pair of adders sunning themselves on a rock in Arran. He picked one up to enable his companion to take a photograph of him holding it, and even after it bit him, picked up the second, only for the same misfortune to occur. He claimed that he did not know we had poisonous snakes in Scotland, and got off lightly. However, it is probably one of the most well-documented natural history facts of all, frequently appearing as a crossword clue, or quiz question. Accidents do occasionally occur, although there is not thought to have been a death by an adder bite for over 20 years. The very young, sick or old are most at risk.

Studies suggest that 70 per cent of adder bites are in fact dry – they do not actually inject venom into their victim. Adders should be treated with the utmost respect, however. The old methods of sucking poison from a wound, or using a tourniquet in a bid to stem circulation of venom, are to be avoided at all costs. The victim should rather be kept calm and taken for immediate medical help.

Adders do not have a good reputation. Having 'a tongue like a viper,' or adder, usually implies unpleasantness, and is a most unflattering term. Many people are fearful of this beautifully patterned snake, yet they need not be. Its venom is intended for its prey and not for humans. Shepherds' and keepers' dogs sometimes get bitten, but most survive. It is more usual for an adder to rush away as it senses the approach of humans, and problems generally only occur when they are inadvertently disturbed. Adders are secretive and do not choose to live in proximity to humans. They can adapt to various moorland habitats, including those

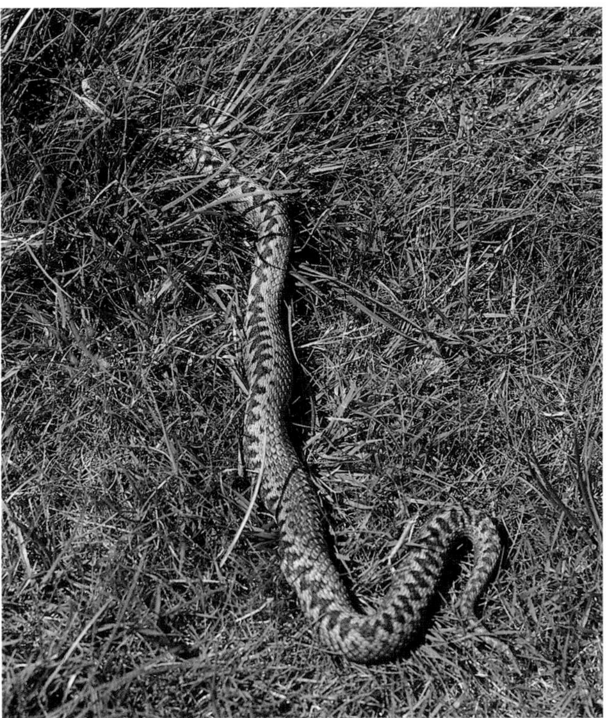

Basking female adder (Polly Pullar)

Adders and serpents

John Forbes, minister in the parish of Sleat, Skye, from 1851, was consulted once about a child who had been bitten by an adder. The traditional treatment was to cut open a live black cockerel and apply it to the wound. Forbes must have had his doubts about this, but he agreed to it, insisting only 'in the name of humanity' that the cockerel be killed first. Perhaps he thought it would help to calm the situation if the parents thought they were doing something to help. The child recovered, slowly, over the course of a year.

The Tiree minister John Gregorson Campbell (1834–1891) was told that serpents should always be destroyed, smashing their heads and throwing the tails away, otherwise they would reconstitute themselves and become monsters, capable of eating even a horse. This is the ceilidh-house equivalent of the horror movie, but even Rev. Alexander Stewart (1829–1901), known as 'Nether Lochaber', who loved wildlife and knew perfectly well that adders will always get out of the way if they can, used to stamp on them, quoting a verse from Genesis about bruising the serpent's head.

No creature is more ambiguous than the serpent. It is associated with evil but also with healing and wisdom. The thirteenth-century Franciscan Michael Scot was rumoured to have acquired his knowledge from a decoction of white serpent. The landlady of an inn in the Grampians was making it for herself, but the inquisitive scholar tasted it secretly and absorbed its powers. A similar story was told of the Sutherland physician, Fearchar the Leech.

adjacent to sand dunes, and are sometimes seen basking on rocks on a hot summer's day. Their skins are shed annually and may be left in a prominent place, thin papery remains which quickly wither and fade.

Adders vary greatly in colour. Females may grow up to two feet in length, and are usually brighter and more brown than the greyish males. Some males can appear almost black, but in both sexes it is the zig-zag diamond patterning that is distinctive. Adders were once widespread all over Scotland: the River Blackadder in Berwickshire may derive its name from the adder, although there are few in the area now. They were killed on sight by keepers and country people, and were often severed into two parts with an axe. Buzzards and hen harriers sometimes take them as prey, and on occasions drop them, leaving them stunned on a road as they fly over.

Adders hunt by scent, striking their prey with lightning speed as they inflict a bite. They then withdraw to wait quietly until the venom takes effect, returning once the victim is in its death throes. The enzymes in the venom also aid digestion. The naturalist Charles St John describes the poisonous fangs of the adder: '… they greatly resemble the talons of a cat in shape and can be raised or laid on the jaw according to the wish of their owner.' Prey is varied and may include small birds and mammals, nestlings, eggs, amphibians, and slow worms. Courtship is dramatic, with much tongue-flicking and tail-lashing. People once believed that this was a death dance. Pairs stay together for some time and their impassioned display provides a fine spectacle.

Adders are viviparous – they give birth to live young encased in an internal membrane. Even the tiny young are poisonous as soon as they are born. During the winter, adders hibernate using an old rabbit burrow, or a hole in rocks, or tree roots. Sometimes large clusters of adders will hibernate in a hibernaculum, where up to 40 have been counted together.

The island of Jura remains a stronghold for adders and there are thought to be more there than anywhere else in Scotland. George Orwell spent many years on the island. Even though he was reputed to be a great animal lover, he was described in one biography, spotting an enormous adder on the nearby island of Scarba, putting his foot on top of it, and then filleting the poor creature deliberately with his knife, much to the surprise of his companion. Adders seem to have always caused dramatic reactions, yet they are beautiful reptiles and very much a part of our native fauna.

Detail of a Pictish cross-slab at Meigle, Perth and Kinross (© RCAHMS. Licensor www.scran.ac.uk)

Serpent iconography

The serpent was also important among the Picts. At least 23 Pictish carved stones bear images of serpents, usually alongside other images. Some appear beside crosses on stones carved between the eighth and tenth centuries. They may once have had pre-Christian significance, but here they have been absorbed somehow into the Christian iconography of the North-east. In the west, the high crosses and illuminated manuscripts of the Iona school are full of serpent imagery: stone bosses in the shape of entwined snakes, and serpents in the margins of Gospel books and in the carpet pages of the Book of Kells. They could evoke the serpent of Eden, the bronze serpent raised by Moses in the wilderness, Jesus on the cross, or even the ideal disciple: 'Be as wise as serpents and as innocent as doves'. Other views survived, however, particularly in relation to St Bride's day at the beginning of February:

Moch madainn Bhrìde
Thig an nimhir as an toll;
Cha bhoin mise ris an nimhir,
Cha bhoin an nimhir rium.

(Early on the morning of St Bride's day the serpent comes from the hole; I will not molest the serpent, nor will the serpent molest me.)

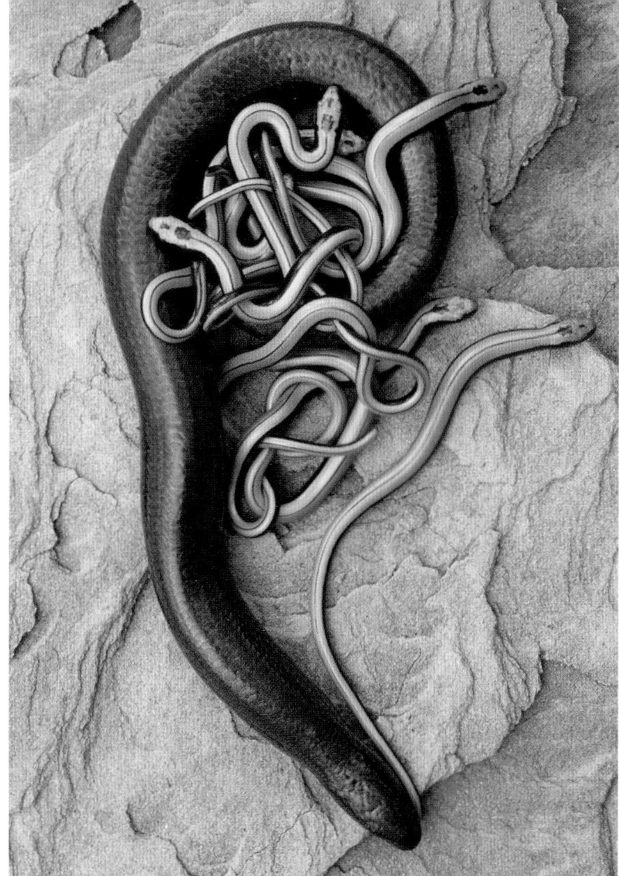

Viviparous Lizard

Lacerta vivipara
S: dirdy-locrag, dirdy-wachlag, man-keeper, lesart, heather-ask
G: *dearc-luachrach*

Like the adder, the viviparous lizard enjoys nothing better than basking in the sunshine, but will vanish in a second when disturbed, disappearing into the grasses with great speed. They are found in many moorland habitats but they tend to prefer humid conditions, and are present on many Scottish islands, although not Orkney and Shetland.

The males often have bright-orange bellies, while colours of both sexes are dependent on local populations and habitat. When pregnant, female lizards become less active, spending more of their time basking in the sun. This helps with the growth of young. After a weather-dependent gestation period of between 6 and 13 weeks, up to 11 fully formed babies are born, wrapped in a membrane from which they quickly emerge.

During the winter, groups of lounging lizards of various ages may be accidentally uncovered as they hibernate closely packed together in a woodpile or old wall, and this makes a fascinating sight.

Left. Slow worm with young (Laurie Campbell)

Below. Viviperous lizards in hibernation in rotting timber (Polly Pullar)

Slow Worm

Anguis fragilis
S: slae
G: *plàigh-shlat*, *nathair challtainn*

Often the beautiful, shiny slow worm is misidentified and thought to be a snake. It is in fact a legless lizard, totally harmless, and its smooth scales and skin can appear so gleaming that it seems as if they have been highly polished. It can be very long-lived and records show that they have reached over 50 years of age in captivity.

Slow worms, like lizards, can easily shed part of their tails if they are roughly handled. They have eyelids, unlike snakes. One of the old names for the slow worm, blind-worm, is highly inappropriate given that they are able to see. Slow worms love compost heaps and often choose these warm places for winter hibernation. Reproduction is by ovivipary; eggs developing inside the female and then hatching out as they emerge.

CHAPTER THREE

WOODS

INTRODUCTION

Trees are the largest and most important plants we have and some specimens constitute our oldest known flora. Over the centuries, many introduced non-native trees have become an integral part of the Scottish landscape and habitat.

Woodland is now at the forefront of many Scottish conservation projects. Our woods have had a chequered history. During prehistoric times, much of upland Scotland was heavily forested, providing shelter and habitat for creatures which are now extinct, as well as for numerous others that have had to adapt considerably to subsequent deforestation, such as the red deer.

At the start of the twentieth century, forest cover had dwindled as a result of years of neglect. Trees were torched during battles, or felled relentlessly for timber. The Vikings used them for building their longships and their masts, and much later during the world wars, when the country had a huge need for timber, trees were used to help the war effort. In 1919 Lloyd George said that Britain 'had nearly lost the war for want of timber than of anything else'. The same year saw the inauguration of the Forestry Commission, with the main objective to avoid such an occurrence happening again. Then came a period of intense planting: large tracts of land were covered with fast-growing commercial trees that provided little or no understorey. The dense, uniform dark green of the sitka spruce, which originates in northern Eurasia, blanketed much of Scotland with ensuing negative results for the native fauna.

Today, the situation is beginning to change. With regard to the Forestry Commission, a great deal has been achieved to reverse the effects of the destructive block planting. They work with an enlightened approach, ensuring new woods provide biodiversity and so sustain a wide range of creatures, while they also provide recreation for people, as well as meeting the need for timber.

Scottish woodlands vary enormously, but they are all of vital importance in sustaining a rich fauna. From the massive specimen trees seen in parkland or on large estates at places such as Dunkeld in Perthshire's 'Big Tree Country', to the smallest wind-sculpted rowan clinging to a rock near a wild hill summit, trees play a vital role in the ecology of the Scottish landscape. Remnants of the primeval pinewoods (the 'Great Wood of Caledon') at Abernethy, Rothiemurchus and Glen Affric, for example, are noted for their distinctive wide-ranging fauna: the Scottish crossbill, the crested tit, the now rare capercaillie, the wildcat and many seasonal migrants. Although these woods are nearing the end of their natural life, grant schemes to re-establish

Opposite. Scots pines, Glen Lyon (Polly Pullar)

pinewoods in many areas are proving successful.

The birch woods of the north grow in straggling character, reaching inaccessible places. Although they do not grow tall at higher altitudes on the poorest of soils, they add a vital ingredient to the overall picture of landscape and habitat.

The Atlantic oak woods of the western seaboard are truly astonishing – supporting a wealth of lichens, mosses, liverworts, fungi, mammals, birds, insects and plants, their lush rainforest-like growth creates an entirely unique habitat. Growing from sea level and sweeping in gnarled and twisted fashion far up the sides of steep gullies and burnsides, some stunted trees grow almost horizontally on the seashore, amid downy birch and dwarf willow. Pressure from grazing makes it almost impossible for most woods to regenerate without help, and fencing is required to allow young trees to grow.

There are now many grant schemes to help with costs of fencing and planting. Landowners and farmers are re-establishing small areas with native broad-leaved trees to provide shelter belts and amenity woodland. Even these small copses – and the wooded areas of gardens – are of great benefit, and will quickly be colonised by fauna of many types. The importance of domestic grazing animals in certain established woods is now being recognised by conservationists. Native breeds such as the Hebridean sheep and Highland cow are proving their worth in keeping invasive plant species at bay, while their grazing encourages natural regeneration.

Scrubby woods of alder, willow, hazel and other small native trees may look less impressive, but these indigenous trees are pioneer species that provide a solid base for future forest, and a valuable haven for wildlife. A few trees running alongside a hill burn often host a wide range of fauna, from the smallest shrew to the redstarts and pied flycatchers that arrive each spring from West Africa to breed.

DAWN PATROL

Badger

Meles meles
S: brock, bawsend-pate
G: *broc, tùitean, strianach*

The badger is an ancient animal, said to have been the comrade of the mammoth. It is the largest mustelid, therefore a relation to the stoat and weasel. Its name originates from the French word *bêcher* (to dig). They are indeed accomplished excavators, making themselves a complex labyrinth of underground tunnels, a sett, where a whole family exist together. Setts are well designed and take into account fluctuations in temperature so that the inmates can move between various chambers. Some setts can extend for nearly half a mile. In 2001, when a group of badgers was found to be undermining a major road near Huntly, Aberdeenshire County Council was forced into making an alternative artificial sett for them. This cost in the region of £30,000. Perhaps when viewed at current market prices, it was quite a reasonable deal for a nine-bedroom dwelling.

It is odd that an animal that is scrupulously clean should have given rise to the saying 'stinking like a badger'. They groom one another and make exterior latrine sites, bring fresh bedding to their setts every day, and meticulously remove the old material, piling it up into great spoil heaps close by sett entrances. Unfortunately they have been found to carry tuberculosis (TB) and there are serious concerns for the effect this has on cattle, especially with so many badgers living in woodland surrounding farms. Talk of huge culls to remove badgers from badly affected areas always causes conflict and debate. Work continues to find ways to eradicate a serious disease which not only affects the cattle, but also has serious emotional and financial consequences for farmers. Regular TB testing takes place, and any cattle either with the disease, or found to be carrying it, are culled compulsorily, and all livestock on the farm is unable to be sold until there have been several clear tests many months later.

A badger's digging activity can also cause problems. On some farms their exploration of rabbit holes and love of young rabbits has led to large areas being undermined; farmers complain when their cattle fall into the holes and are injured. On occasions, badgers also dig up gardens in search of earthworms or bees' nests. Finding the lawn rearranged in the morning does not endear the neat gardener.

Badgers sometimes live in close proximity to man. They are often overlooked, however, as they are nocturnal and their setts are well hidden. Tell-tale signs of coarse grey hairs caught on barbed wire, scratch marks from claws on tree trunks, or well-worn paths through the woods, and signs of new digging are often enough to confirm their presence.

A badger's black-and-white face-marking is distinctive and adds to their attraction. They have frequently been voted the most popular British mammal but despite this are still the victims of shocking cruelty. The now-illegal sport of badger baiting has gone on for centuries, using specially trained dogs against one badger in a pit area. Bets are laid with large sums at stake. With one of the most powerful jaws of all animals, the badger will fight tirelessly to defend itself, and terrible wounds may be inflicted on both the dogs and their handlers, with the poor, terrified badger fighting on to the bitter end. Culprits often boast as they show the badger's teeth marks indented on a shovel, despite having forfeited their own dogs in the process.

Badgers are playful animals, and both adults and cubs interact in boisterous play. They have a social hierarchy, with each animal recognising the other members in its group. Badgers have a catholic diet and during the autumn they feast on a varied mixture of berries, bulbs, pignuts and fruit so that they store large amounts of fat for the winter months. The harvest moon is known in Gaelic as *gealach bhuidhe nam broc* (the badgers' yellow moon) because badgers could often be seen then 'taking home their winter supplies'. Although they do not hibernate, badgers may fall into a deeper sleep during periods of hard frost and snow,

Top. Habituated badgers enjoy a free meal (Laurie Campbell)

Above. Badgers at Isle of Eriska Hotel (Dennis Hardley)

remaining underground for longer periods.

Each sett has a dominant male. Badgers have delayed implantation (see page 39), and cubs may be born at any time during the year. They remain in the sett until their eyes open, and eventually emerge at dusk to explore. There are tales of badger's funerals. Few have witnessed these extraordinary events, but on occasions badgers have been seen dragging dead family members from the sett and taking them away to bury them. They have also been heard emitting an eerie keening sound while doing so.

Valued by the Forestry Commission for keeping rabbits and wasps under control, there are special badger gates that open on both sides and swing shut as the animals pass through. Badgers are also greatly valued on the small island of Eriska, near Connel, Argyll, which has been owned by the Buchanan-Smith family since 1973. For years they have been feeding the badgers there with brown bread and peanuts. Guests staying at their hotel are enchanted by nightly visits to the bar veranda by several snuffling badgers.

The useful badger

The badger is absent from many Scottish islands, although they were introduced to Arran in the eighteenth century for sporting purposes, and are still there today. Badgers have been used for many things: they were hugely popular during Victorian times, and their skins and heads were made into sporrans, as dead road-casualty badgers and other mammals are still sometimes used now (see page 246). The men who originally trapped badgers for this purpose were called *brochans*. Badgers were also eaten; their thickset, powerful hind legs smoked and sold as 'badger hams'. Their meat and fat were seen as a cure for rheumatism and were rubbed onto the afflicted part. Badger bristles were used for shaving brushes, although now animals are specially bred for the purpose in the Far East, and brushes made from imported hair. Bizarrely, the penis bone (*baculum*) of the badger, which has a hole at either end, was once used as a tiepin. The skinned head of a badger, meanwhile, was used as a military decoration for the Argyll and Sutherland Highlanders, and their pelts frequently used for rugs.

Pine Marten

Martes martes
S: mertrick, martrik
G: *taghan* (see also polecat)

The pine marten, another member of the mustelid family, was once widespread all over Britain. In 1869 they were still common in Assynt, Sutherland, only to be nearly exterminated soon after due to the premium paid for shooting them. A high price of ten to fifteen shillings was paid for their soft lustrous pelts. Unlike the polecat, which also has lovely fur but a very strong odour, the pine marten was once nicknamed 'sweet mart' because of its less offensive perfume.

In the early 1960s, noted naturalist H.G. Hurrell wrote: 'It would delight many people if the marten repopulated certain areas, for it is an animal which has aptly been described as the most beautiful of all the fur bearers.' Today the opportunistic pine marten has indeed repopulated many of its old haunts, and is thriving. Although it is shy and largely nocturnal, it has also learned the benefits of living near man. Pine martens are omnivorous. They have an almost uncontrollable sweet tooth and are very fond of many sugary human foods. In one situation, a couple living in a remote area of the west coast have had 15 different pine martens visiting them over a five-year period. These animals come to the bird table where peanuts, raisins, grapes (preferably red), strawberry jam and digestive biscuits are left for them. They then come through the window and into the house, climbing on the furniture to gently take eggs out of their benefactors' hands. If no one is around at the allotted time, they will wander about until they find them. Life in this particular house is now totally governed by the resident martens.

Over the years, the couple have made some astonishing films of the animals in their garden, including a mother bringing her young kits to the feeding table. They have footage of the animals racing round various tunnels and obstacles specially set up for them, including climbing up

Pine martens, though shy, are incredibly curious (Neil McIntyre)

onto the greenhouse roof and sliding down the glass into a cold frame below. They help themselves to garden fruit, use runner bean netting as a hammock, and often pull out new plant tags to use as toys. Every visiting marten has been identified by its different chest markings. A dapper yellow-gold throat patch is stippled with unique marks that make individuals easy to identify.

Daily records are kept of the pine martens' visits and observed behaviour patterns. Although some experts claim that the young martens disperse in the autumn, this has been found not to be the case. Some of the youngsters return either at the same time as their mother, or with older siblings from previous years. The alpha male tolerates these youngsters.

Pine martens frequently end up in trouble. They will make dens in the roof space of houses, pulling out all the insulation in the process, and sometimes make their homes in cars. One large male discovered a way into the storeroom of the Kilchoan Village shop in Ardnamurchan. During nightly raids, he helped himself to a new box of luxury mince pies, laced with brandy, much to the annoyance of the shop's owner. The cheaper option on a shelf close by was totally ignored.

Pine martens have surprisingly large feet for their body size. Their tracks in snow appear almost as large as those of a fox. Arboreal as well as agile on the ground, their sharp, pale-coloured claws help them to grip and climb. They occasionally raid birds' nests, and ground-nesting species are not safe when a pine marten is in the area. Martens take small mammals and also eat berries and

Nuisance of the glen

Hunted and trapped with a vengeance, the pine marten was referred to as 'the scourge of the glen'. In Glengarry from Whitsun 1837 to Whitsun 1840, 246 'marten-cats' were destroyed as vermin. Four times a year, some communities called a one-day truce with martens and other predators, recognising briefly their right to exist. This happened on the old Celtic quarter days, when families in the Highlands and Islands made special bannocks and shared them with friends and neighbours. After this festive meal, the householder would go out into the fields and throw the scraps over alternate shoulders shouting:

> Here, wolf, spare my sheep
> Here, fox, spare my lambs
> Here, eagle, spare my goats
> Here, raven, spare my kids
> Here, marten, spare my fowls
> Here, harrier, spare my chickens

The wild neighbours are being bought off here, but in a sense they are also being given their due. They get their share of the feast, like other members of society, and are treated more like nuisance neighbours than vermin.

fruit. If they are able to get into a hen house, they feast on all available eggs and then, like the fox, go on a killing spree driven by the excited panic of terrified, flapping fowls. The old tales of pine martens seizing sheep by the nose and then beginning to eat them are the result of a vivid Scots imagination. They have, however, managed with great determination to drag dead adult rabbits some 70 feet upwards in order to store them in a box intended for barn owls. They are also frequently known to take over special boxes put out for nesting goldeneye ducks.

Like the badger and stoat, pine martens have delayed implantation: they mate early in the season but development of the young does not begin until the following year. Females are ready to mate at approximately 15 months old; mating takes place in July and August, and an average of three kits are born in early April of the following year. Pale-coloured at first, the young remain in the den for about two months and then start to venture further afield with their mother, who emits frequent calls and quiet noises to ensure they do not stray. As they develop confidence, however, the kits' adventurous playfulness can soon lead them into mischief, but this is part of the charm of another of Scotland's beautiful mammals.

A displaying cock capercaillie (Neil McIntyre)

Capercaillie

Tetrao urogallus
S: cobber-kelly, goat of the woods
G: *capall-coille*

The capercaillie (caper, or great grouse) has also been nicknamed the 'horse of the woods' and 'turkey of the woods' due to its size. Although closely related to both black and red grouse, its bulky presence makes it an impressive bird. There is little chance of mistaking one for any other bird in the pinewood. The bones of capercaillie have been found on many prehistoric sites in kitchen middens, and there is evidence that it was once valued for its meat. Yet the ornithologist Thomas Bewick wrote: 'It feeds on the cones of the fir trees, which at some seasons give an unpleasant flavour to the flesh – so as to render it unfit for the table.' In more modern times, its taste has been described as like that of turpentine, and only burying it for more than two weeks improves the situation. Given that the capercaillie is now one of Scotland's rarest birds, it is fortunate that they taste unpleasant.

Regarded as a game bird, there has been a voluntary shooting ban on the caper for years. The cocks are majestic, with dense beard-like feathers below their throats, beautiful fan-shaped tails and blue-black plumage. The hens are considerably smaller and have a rich russet-coloured plumage. Leks, areas where the males gather to display, may have been used by generations of capercaillie. Caper sometimes hybridise with black grouse and even pheasants, although this is not a common occurrence.

Capercaillie were extirpated during the eighteenth century due to lack of suitable habitat, and the fact that they were shot for trophies and taxidermy. In 1837 Lord Breadalbane brought 55 Swedish birds to Scotland and reintroduced them to Drummond Hill, a large forested area between Kenmore and Aberfeldy, overlooking Loch Tay. A few birds are still in the area, although they are seldom seen, occuring in very low numbers. Habitat loss is a major issue. Young chicks need a rich diet of invertebrates, many of which are found on blaeberry growing on the woodland floor. However, due to overgrazing, blaeberry has dwindled in many forests. New fences put up to keep grazing animals out of young plantations are dangerous to birds such as the black grouse and capercaillie. They have to be marked with canes or coloured net to stop birds flying into them and breaking their necks (see page 25). Foxes and crows are also a threat as they will readily eat eggs and young chicks. Consecutive years of wet summers also prove devastating to nesting efforts.

In 1988 the RSPB bought Forest Lodge at Abernethy and have since been involved in capercaillie conservation work. However, a census in 1999 brought the devastating news that capercaillie numbers could have fallen as low as 1,000 birds. A major initiative was launched to protect the birds' future in Scotland. There was a real fear that Scotland might otherwise witness the second extinction of the capercaillie. The RSPB, Forestry Commission, Game Conservancy Council and other groups rallied together with support from private landowners, and a dedicated effort is now being made to manage native pinewood sites for the birds. New woodland is being planted in many suitable areas. It would seem that this is proving successful – subsequent surveys have revealed a substantial increase in capercaillie numbers, with new leks being established by the males. With good habitat and minimal human disturbance, one of our most important birds may soon flourish once more.

Chaffinch

Fringilla coelebs
S: briskie, brichtie, chaffie, chye, shilfa, shilly, shoulfall, spink
G: *breacan-beithe*

The chaffinch is one of our commonest breeding birds, and the most common finch. It is worthy of note for the extraordinary range of varied dialects (or accents) that different populations of chaffinches use. Lars Jonsson, the celebrated Swedish bird artist and ornithologist, explained that in different areas, chaffinches all over Scotland have a slight variation in their distinctive songs, depending on the glens in which they are found. Indeed, the situation is the same throughout Europe. It takes some time to accustom the ear to these subtle changes in chaffinch song, but after a while, once tuned in, it is quite easy to hear and becomes a fascinating subject.

The chaffinch has regional accents (Malcolm Gosling)

Wren

Troglodytes troglodytes
S: wran, chitty wran, cutty wran, thoumie
G: *dreathan-donn, dreòlan*

The wren has been common in Scotland for many centuries and has always been a favourite bird. It appears almost everywhere. The wren's trilling song is loud, sweet and distinctive and its rounded shape and little erect tail make it simple to identify. It is widespread and adaptable and although it does not come to the bird table, there are few gardens without wrens. Censuses over the last 20 years

The perky little wren is present almost everywhere (Malcolm Gosling)

have shown that wrens occupy nearly every square kilometre of the country, from the loneliest crag or heather tuft, to the bleakest, most commercial of plantations.

Wrens are interesting because the male will build up to six nests, and it is the female, or 'Jenny wren', that chooses which one to use each year. Domed structures usually made of moss and lichen and lined with wool, wren's nests often appear in unlikely places. One nest built around a hook laden with horseshoes on a farrier's wall meant that the shoes could not be used that summer until the young had fledged. The patient farrier had to reorder that particular size of shoe instead.

Wrens use communal roost sites in the winter months, huddling together to keep warm. Tit boxes are sometimes used. The botanist and ornithologist Joe Eggeling once witnessed 43 wrens emerging from an old house martin's nest under the eaves. They are industrious and have large broods, as illustrated in the ditty:

The dove says coo, coo what shall I do?
I can scarce maintain two.
Pooh, pooh, says the wren, I have ten
And raise them all like gentlemen.

Wrens were once seen in rat burrows, where they found the heaps of grain taken in by the rats were heating up. This helped to keep the birds warm. Severe winters may take a heavy toll on wren numbers but they quickly recover.

Wrens were once known as 'Our Lady's hen', and it was said that harm would befall anyone who caused them ill. A short Scots rhyme referred to this: 'Malaisons, malaisons mair than ten that harry our Lady of Heaven's wren.' There are four different sub-species of wren in Scotland: the Shetland wren (*zetlandicus*), the Fair Isle wren (*fridariensis*), the Hebridean wren (*hebridensis*) and the St Kilda wren (*hirtensis*). There is an interesting size gradation, with the largest, longest-tailed and shortest-winged birds being found on St Kilda – our very own example of Darwinian evolution in an island setting.

The indomitable wren

Wrens are traditionally regarded as clever little birds, bold for their size, if a little self-important – hence the north-east proverb, 'Every little helps, as the vran said fin she pisht i' the sea'. A Gaelic tale from Sutherland tells how the wren was out one day looking for nesting materials under a pile of debris. A fox passes by and sees an opportunity:

'What will you give me if I help?' he asks.

'When I've threshed in the autumn, I may be able to give you something – *peic is ceannan* (a peck and two pecks),' answers the wren.

Fox lends a hand and comes back in the autumn to claim his fee. Wren and his twelve sons are threshing in the barn. The fox can't tell them apart so he tries flattery: 'It's easy to recognise the old hero's stroke,' he says.

Wren steps forward, bursting with pride: 'Well said, well said,' he exclaims. The fox reminds him of their bargain. Wren hops up on top of the dyke and, looking towards the house, shouts, 'It was *peic is ceannan*, wasn't it? *Peic is Ceannan, Peic is Ceannan*.' Two dogs so named come running and Fox takes to his heels.

Whoever made this story had listened to the wrens' alarm call, a staccato *chakking* noise, like miniature geiger counters, or indeed '*Peic is Ceannan, Peic is Ceannan*'. In spring, however, the wren is one of the sweetest singers in the woods, with a loud clear song remarkable for its size.

SUN-UP

Red Squirrel

Sciurus vulgaris
S: squirrel, con
G: *feòrag, toghmall*

Grey Squirrel

Sciurus carolinensis

The sight of a red squirrel in a Scots pine tree probably epitomises 'wild Scotland' just as well as that of an eagle soaring over a crag. A hugely popular animal, it is encouraged to feeders in gardens, where its daily visits are keenly awaited by those lucky enough to have them in their area. With double-jointed ankles, red squirrels have phenomenal balance, and their lightweight, long claws give them a powerful grip on branches and tree trunks. Sadly, their hold in Scotland is precarious – they were almost totally lost during the eighteenth and nineteenth centuries and were certainly not always popular. Bounties were paid for their tails, and an astonishing number of 4,727 were killed in 1903 by the Ross-shire Squirrel Club. They were also treated as vermin all over the rest of Scotland. Even worse, some keepers believed that if they caught the unfortunate animals, cut their tails off and then let them go again, they would grow another and then they might be paid again.

Today red squirrels face another survival battle. Fragmentation and loss of habitat has played a large role in their decline, but there are other factors too. It is impossible to talk of the red without mentioning the grey squirrel, a non-native North American squirrel brought to Britain in 1876. The first greys were introduced to Scotland (at Finnart on Loch Long) in 1892, and from there they successfully established themselves over a 300-mile radius within approximately 25 years.

Larger, more robust, and highly competitive, the grey easily ousted reds from much of their range, not as was initially thought through killing them, but inadvertently by devouring all their food. Grey squirrels can feed on unripe seeds and acorns, taking them long before they are ripe for consumption by the reds. They also survive better in mixed woodland and are quick to take advantage of winter stores accumulated by the reds.

Greys also carry a lethal virus which wipes out any afflicted reds within two weeks. The squirrel pox virus has now been seen in many populations of red squirrels. Their skin ulcerates from lesions all over the body, and general lethargy and weakness leads to death. Veterinary experts at the Moredun Research Institute near Edinburgh, world leaders in livestock vaccination development, have been studying the virus and are hoping that a vaccination will be available after further research and trials. This would be added to red squirrels' food.

Some feel the grey squirrel has now proved itself so successful that it is here to stay. However, there are huge efforts being made countrywide to trap all grey squirrels and exterminate them altogether. Without doubt, the grey squirrel is an example of the damage that can be done when alien species are introduced.

Young red squirrel (Polly Pullar)

Currently the only urban population of red squirrels is in Dundee's Camperdown Park within the city boundary. Grey squirrels are culled there, and much work is being done to ensure that the red squirrel population, currently thought to be in the region of 100 individuals, continues to thrive.

Roe Deer

Capreolus capreolus
S: rae, ra
G: *earb*

There are only two native species of British deer – the red, our largest land mammal, and the much smaller roe. The latter is widespread all over Scotland and has been here since prehistoric times, although it dwindled to a low number during the eighteenth and nineteenth centuries. The population has since exploded. Although they favour woodland, roe deer can live in close proximity to man in the heart of some of our cities, and will breed in parks, gardens and churchyards. Many have also adapted to life on the open hill. They have increased to such an extent in recent years that they all too often cause traffic accidents and have to be managed to keep numbers down in towns. Insurance companies in Scotland pay out millions of pounds every year for deer damage. Plans to provide continuous woodland between Edinburgh and Glasgow to help with this problem are ongoing.

Largely solitary, roe are probably one of the most beautiful deer. Bucks are territorial, although protracted periods of hard weather may make them stop defending their patch until the weather improves. Scottish roe stalking is very popular with foreigners and although stalkers take some clients out on foot, others use high seats in forestry where they wait for deer to appear.

The roe deer rut takes place in late July. Bucks then become fiercely territorial. Frustrated, immature bucks cause much damage to young trees during the rut by marking them and stripping the bark off as they rub their antlers against them. Circles of flattened grass, often in a figure-of-eight shape, are an indication of where the buck has chased a doe round during courtship.

Fawns are born after delayed implantation (see page 39) in May and June. Where food is abundant, twins are a

The Hunting Lodge, Deeside, showing roof and walls decorated with red deer antlers (© Aberdeen University, Heritage Division. Licensor www.scran.ac.uk)

Antlers

Stalkers can recognise individuals by the antlers (referred to as 'heads'). Antlers may vary greatly in length and thickness, and provide an excellent guide to those animals requiring selective culling. The conformation is awarded a points system that may lead to a head being rated as a gold-medal winner. Roe deer living in areas of rich feeding have better antlers than those on poor ground. However, injuries and illness can lead to antlers being malformed the following year. Unlike other deer in Britain, the roe's antlers are in velvet during the winter. One elderly sportsman has a huge collection of roe antlers from all over Scotland, gathered throughout a lifetime of roe shooting. Many show extraordinary malformations and deformities, and others are swept back and have few points. It is a fascinating display representing roe deer from many areas, and it also illustrates how through selective culling, gold-medal heads may be attained.

common occurrence; it is very rare for a red deer to give birth to twins. Usually the doe chooses the same area every year to give birth. The tiny spotted fawns are perfectly camouflaged and the doe leaves them hidden in deep grasses during the daytime. They are vulnerable at this early stage, and are sometimes unwittingly picked up by well-wishers who believe them to be abandoned. This is far from the case, as the doe returns at regular intervals to suckle them. Although gentle animals, a hand-reared roe buck does not make a good pet, and there have been incidents of them maliciously attacking their human carers. Does, on the other hand, are very gentle. A visiting roe deer's indiscriminate pruning often proves too much for many garden owners, while others love to see them at close proximity. However, when there are deer around, no rose is safe.

Fallow Deer

Dama dama
S: fellow deer
G: *dathas*

The fallow deer was introduced to Scotland by Normans in the eleventh century, and was a popular quarry species. Fallow deer are present on some Scottish islands including Mull, Islay and Scarba. Historians believe they were introduced to Islay by the monks at Kildalton, in the south of the island, in AD 900, and there are records of them on mainland Scotland in 1283. They are also known to have been on the small islands on Loch Lomond since very early times. In 1326 the island's owner, David Graham, signed an agreement permitting Robert the Bruce to hunt them there. Mary, Queen of Scots, reputed to have loved hunting, joined a fallow deer drive (or 'tinchel') in 1564.

In 1880 the Duke of Atholl introduced a herd of fallow deer to Perthshire. There are also records of a large herd of approximately 400 kept by Lord Ancaster at Drummond Castle near Crieff. Since the late 1950s, a thriving population centred near Dunkeld in Perthshire has become well known, and there are other small groups in many parts of Scotland, some doubtlessly initiated by escaped park animals.

Above left. Roe doe (Polly Pullar)

Above. Fallow buck, originally introduced to Britain from Europe (Malcolm Gosling)

Sika buck – considerably smaller and less impressive than our native red deer (Neil McIntyre)

Native to southern Europe, fallow are gregarious animals. They are smaller than the red deer and there are several different colour variations: a dark, melanistic form that may on occasions appear almost black; a menil or pale buff-coloured one; and a more common sandy-coated variety. A spotted pelage is evident on the summer coat of many fallow deer. Unlike all other deer found in Scotland, the buck's antlers are palmate. These hand-shaped plates may become very large, and the impressive heads of some bucks are highly sought after by trophy hunters. Being forest dwellers, they have adapted well to life in Scotland and thrive in spite of the wet climate.

The fallow deer rut takes place in autumn, which is often a good time to watch them. At this season, woodland echoes to the sound of the buck's almost pig-like grunting, which is less dramatic than the roar of the red deer stag. Fallow deer provide some of the most flavoursome venison of any deer.

Sika Deer

Cervus nippon
G: *fiadh seapanach*

The Sika originates from Eastern Asia and was first brought to Scotland (at Tulliallan, in Fife) in 1870, at a time when there was a fad for importing exotic species. Other introductions into unsuitably fenced parks made it easy for the deer to escape, and soon feral populations began to establish in various areas of Scotland, including on the Mull of Kintyre, and in Caithness and Sutherland, spreading widely through dense woodland.

Extensive coniferous forests have made it easy for Sika to thrive. Their habit of intensive bark fraying and stripping damages young trees, and most foresters try hard to cull them due to the financial consequences of their depleted plantations. Traditional stalkers are not in favour of Sika and endeavour to cull them, too often a hard task given the thick habitat that they favour. Although smaller than the

King David and the deer

'In the fourth year of his reign, this noble prince came to visit the maiden castle of Edinburgh. At this time, the whole of Scotland was full of woods, pastures and meadows, for the country was more given over to animals than to any production of corn. And round this castle was a great forest full of bears, deer, foxes and suchlike beasts. Now the Rood day was coming, known as the Exaltation of the Cross. And because this was a high solemn day, the king went to his prayers. After the masses had been said with great solemnity and reverence, many young and insolent barons of Scotland came before him eager to have some sport and pleasure by hunting with hounds in the said forest. At this time, there was with the king, a man of singular and devout life named Alkwine, a canon after the order of St Augustine, who had been confessor to King David for a long time in England, when he was earl of Huntingdon and Northumberland. This religious man used many arguments to dissuade the king from going to the hunt, saying that the day was so solemn out of reverence for the Holy Cross, and that he should spend the day in contemplation rather than in any other exercise. However, his arguments were of little avail. For the king was finally so provoked by the ill-timed solicitations of his barons, that he went to the hunt, in spite of the solemnity of this day. At last when he was coming through the valley directly to the east of the said castle, where the Canongate now lies, the swarm passed through the wood with such noise and din of guns and bugles, that all the beasts were startled from their dens. Now the king was coming to the foot of the crag, with all his nobles scattered here and there at their sport, when suddenly there appeared to his sight the fairest hart ever to be seen among living creatures. The noise and din of this hart running (as it appeared) and its awesome great antlers, frightened the king's horse so badly that no reins could hold him and he bolted away with the king, over mire and bog. Nonetheless, the hart followed so fast that he threw both the king and his horse to the ground. Then the king threw up his hands between the deer's antlers, to save himself from being gored, and immediately, the holy cross passed into his hands. The hart fled away with great violence, and vanished in the very place where now springs the Rood Well. The company returned to him in alarm from all parts of the wood to comfort him in his distress, and fell on their knees devoutly adoring the holy cross. For clearly, it could only have come by some heavenly providence. For there is no man who can explain what it is made of, whether metal or wood. Soon after, the king returned to his castle, and the following night, he was instructed by a vision in his sleep, to build an abbey of canons regular in the same place where he got the cross.'

The story of King David and the deer appears late in the history of Holyrood Abbey. This adjunct to the royal palace was founded in 1128 and already contained 'the blak croce', supposedly a relic of the 'true cross'. The earliest Latin version of the deer legend did not appear until nearly 400 years later and the Scots translation in 1536, so this is more parable than history. One of its messages is clearly that kings should listen to their spiritual advisors, but it also seems to be saying something quite specific about how a major feast day should be kept. It might even be a homily for the feast of the Exaltation of the Cross on 8 September: '… he went to the hunt, in spite of the solemnity of *this* day.' Holyrood Abbey was next to the royal deer park around Arthur's Seat. Perhaps the monks were being disturbed by the rowdyism of young nobles during their special anniversary mass or by their absenteeism. And what about the stag? Despite similarities with the conversion of St Paul (falling from his horse, seeing a vision) it seems unlikely that the stag is a symbol of the risen Christ, although it is in the similar legend of St Hubert. Here, the animal flees before the cross, so probably, to the medieval mind, he represented the wild and beautiful animal nature from which human beings sometimes have to be rescued. Is there an argument against field sports here? If so, it is very mildly stated. At most, there is a call for restraint; for not hunting on certain days. The preacher does seem sympathetic, however, towards the animals 'startled from their dens' by the guns and bugles. He also places hunting and holiness in contrasting worlds and he clearly wants us to be awed by the 'fairest hart'.

red deer, they readily crossbreed, and there is serious concern for the genetic purity of red deer. Hyrids are often hard to differentiate.

Sika deer have interesting faces that make them appear almost angry. Their antlers are less impressive than those of the red deer, with fewer points. The Sika rut takes place in the autumn as the stags emit an eerie whistling sound, thought to originate through their teeth and lips. This call is actually made using a valve in their throats. Another call is a very loud, startling yelp which is given by the females.

Polecat

Mustela putorious
S: foumart
G: *feòcallan, taghan*

Polecats are frequently confused with mink, and are often mistakenly killed when caught in legal mink traps. They may be of similar size but their markings and behaviour are totally different. Their name originates from their distinctive smell and comes from the Latin *putor*, to stink. However, the strong odour is only at its worst when the animal is frightened and ejects the scent from anal glands as a means of defence. At rest, the polecat probably smells no worse than a domestic ferret.

The polecat was thought to be extinct in Scotland by 1907, having been captured for its fur and killed because of its tendency to massacre poultry and game. Small numbers probably survived unnoticed in woodland over the last century.

Today polecat numbers are increasing steadily, and there are a few polecat hotspots around Scotland. Cross-bred with the ferret, polecat ferrets are often kept for rabbiting and hawking. Although they frequently escape and become feral, they look very different to the pure polecat with its distinctive face markings, paler buff facial mask, and dark mark running down the face to a little dark nose.

The smelly polecat

In Gaelic a *taghan* can be either a pine marten or a polecat. Only when the *taghan* is described as smelly can we be confident that the author meant 'polecat'. For example, a Hogmanay curse from Harris wished smelly polecat damage ('*cronachd thaghain tùtaidh*') on any household which did not welcome the Hogmanay guisers properly; and a protection prayer from South Uist was offered to keep domestic animals safe from predators, including the '*taghan tòcaidh na tùide*' (the swelling foumart of the stink). 'Foumart' was applied to people as a term of abuse. It turns up now and then in flytings, those contests of wit in which poets traded insults to the delight of their audience: thus Alexander Montgomerie at the court of James VI could launch his attack on Patrick Hume of Polwarth as a 'fals, feckles fowlmart'.

HIGH NOON SOARING

Goshawk

Accipter gentilis
S: goosehawk
G: *glas-sheabhag*

Once widespread in Scotland, the beautiful goshawk, like the osprey, was extinct by the end of the nineteenth century having suffered relentless persecution from gamekeepers. In the case of the goshawk deforestation added to the problem, and its ability to take prey from the smallest mammal to heavier game such as pheasants, black game and large hares quickly led to its extirpation.

With its incredible flying skills – the goshawk is able to pass through the tiniest of gaps in woodland cover with silent, almost magical manoeuvrability – this large, heavy bird of prey has long been held in the highest esteem by falconers and was once viewed as the 'yeoman's hawk'. The word 'austringer' was used for one who 'manned' the notoriously difficult goshawk. Author T.H. White, the most famous and noteworthy austringer, described his relationship with a bird, and the ensuing battle of wills and emotional rollercoaster he experienced, in his beautiful classic story of 1951, *The Goshawk*.

Very similar in colour and feather patterning to the sparrowhawk, the goshawk is one full size bigger. Females are much larger and even more fearless than their mates. There is a piercing arrogance clearly apparent in the bird's demeanour, and they have brilliant-yellow or deep-amber eyes that are renowned for a cold, almost intimidating stare.

During the 1960s and 1970s, falconers imported Continental goshawks into the country, and many hawk breeders are thought to have released birds intentionally into the wild. Coupled with others that escaped accidentally during falconry outings and successfully went on to naturalise, the population is now beginning to make a slow recovery. Shy and incredibly secretive, goshawks are often vocal during the breeding season but otherwise may go unnoticed unless they come into conflict with keepers at pheasant pens.

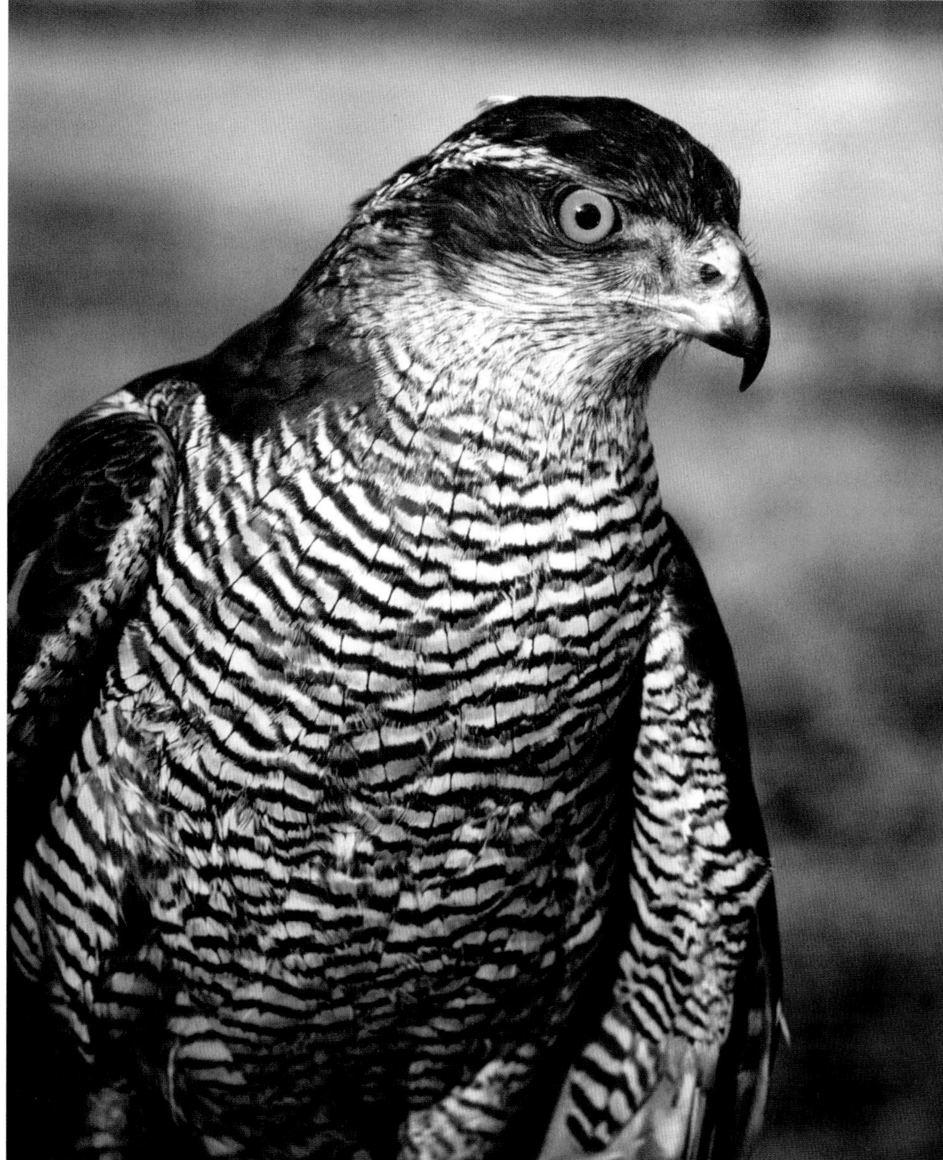

Female goshawks are bigger than their mates (Polly Pullar)

Unlike the osprey, which has had a much-celebrated comeback, the goshawk's story seems to have received less publicity but is nonetheless of equal importance. Although the population in Scotland is now rebuilding, the goshawk remains one of the gamekeeper's least-liked species, and due to this will always struggle to find its natural balance.

Red Kite

Milvus milvus
S: gled, salmon-tailed gled, puttock
G: *clamhan gòbhlach, croman luchaidh*

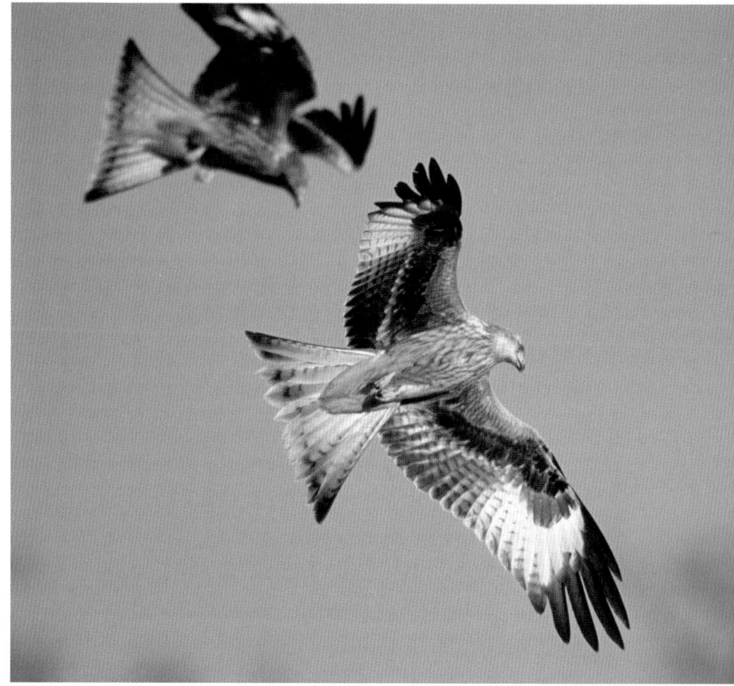

Red kites use their distictive fork-shaped tails almost like a rudder (Laurie Campbell)

Like the sea eagle, the red kite has benefited from a successful reintroduction programme. Once common all over Scotland, this regal bird of prey was revered and valued for the assistance it gave in keeping towns free of rubbish. Largely feeding on carrion, they quickly take advantage of any fallen stock.

Red kites became extinct during the nineteenth century, due entirely to human persecution. Not only were they seen as vermin and killed on sight, but taxidermists also valued them, and their feathers were used to make salmon lures. By 1870 there were only a few breeding pairs remaining in Inverness, Perthshire and Aberdeenshire. On the Glengarry Estate, there is a record of 275 kites killed between 1837 and 1840. This trend of indiscriminate killing was typical on most Highland sporting estates.

In 1989 a joint reintroduction programme between the RSPB and the Nature Conservancy Council (now SNH) saw 93 red kites imported from Sweden and released on the Black Isle in Inverness-shire. By 1992 the first pair had bred and successfully fledged one chick, and from there followed a north-west expansion of the kite population. Between 1996 and 2001, a second reintroduction phase brought 103 red kites into Scotland from Germany. They were released in suitable habitat at Argaty, near Doune in Perthshire. Today a hide allows public access to observe sizeable numbers of kites at a feeding station there. These birds have now spread to the Upper Forth Valley, and into many other areas of Perth and Kinross, and are becoming a frequent sight. A third reintroduction near Castle Douglas in Dumfries and Galloway has also proved successful.

As carrion is the main food of the red kite they remain vulnerable to illegal poisoning, although in recent years attitudes appear to have changed. There are continued problems, however, with persecution in the Black Isle area where many birds have been poisoned; this is a grave cause for concern.

Unlike other birds of prey, kites may gather in very large numbers to feed, and readily come to feeding stations. Another public hide, at Mossdale in Dumfries and Galloway, gives people a chance to see the birds in close proximity. Skilled fliers, red kites have a distinctive forked tail, brilliant-yellow eyes and, as the name suggests, a rich red-brown plumage. They are at last becoming a regular sight in many parts of Scotland, and it is hoped that with our help this magnificent bird will once again be firmly established as a common bird of prey.

The mean kite

Kites were once both disliked and admired. 'It's nae for nocht the gled whistles' (roughly equivalent to 'no smoke without fire') refers to their keen eyesight. Their proverbial greed became a metaphor for human meanness, hence the saying from Upper Strathdon: 'He's a greedy gled o' a chiel, he wid scraap hell for a bawbee gehn he wirna fleyt for burnin's fingers' (He would scrape hell for a sixpence if he weren't afraid of burning his fingers).

MIDDAY SOUNDTRACK

Great Spotted Woodpecker

Dendrocops major anglicus
G: *snagan-daraich*

There may be many birds in Scotland that are declining but the great spotted woodpecker is thriving. Numbers have increased and are bolstered because the great spotted woodpecker takes full advantage of nut feeders in gardens everywhere.

With glorious red, white and black plumage, they are flamboyant birds and are a fine sight in woodland. Their flight is distinctive, making them easy to recognise on the wing as they travel in short bounding movement, rather than in a direct manner. This makes them vulnerable to sparrowhawks, however, and many woodpeckers end up being caught in flight.

During the mid 1800s, the great spotted woodpecker became extinct in Scotland due to extensive tree felling. Enlightened planting schemes have helped this situation dramatically. For a woodpecker, however, a tree is as important dead as it is alive, providing a vital storehouse of insects, larvae and grubs, as well as a place to drill out a nest hole.

Woodpeckers are easy to sex as the male has a red patch at the back of his head, and the female has a solid black crown. Young birds also have a reddish crown, but this is quickly lost after the first moult in autumn, when their telltale red patch or all-black crowns appear.

Great spotted woodpecker males begin to drum in early spring, when woods resonate with the lovely sound. Fiercely territorial, this announces their presence to the females and rival males in the area. One particular male would use a telegraph pole, and begin on the wood area before hopping up to the top where a metal cap produced a dramatic ring.

As well as nuts, seeds, grubs and insects, woodpeckers will also take the young of small birds from their nests. This unsavoury habit seems out of keeping, but provides them with much-needed protein. They will also drill out the bottoms and entrances of nest boxes while looking for insects, and often there may be a heap of shavings on the ground below, and a disgruntled songster scolding nearby.

Forest drilling

Many old trees bear the telltale pockmarks of a woodpecker's drilling activity. Indeed, designers of protective headgear would do well to study the intricacies of a woodpecker's reinforced skull. Its brain is encased by shock absorbers to cope with the impact of drilling and drumming, and the bill is awl-shaped and more efficient than any electric drill. Once the woodpecker has listened for a hollow sound within the trunk, indicating there is a grub inside, it will begin its powerful DIY session and clock up an astonishing 40 beats per second. Their sticky tongues are elongated, more than twice the length of the skull, and can eke out food from deep holes.

Woodpeckers often wedge pinecones and large nuts in crevices and hammer them open with their bills as if using an anvil, while their long, sharp claws help them to hop up the steepest trees and allow them to hold on, even during a gale.

The great spotted woodpecker is currently thriving in many areas of Scotland (Malcolm Gosling)

Green Woodpecker

Picus viridis
S: specht
G: *lasair-choille*

It is extremely rare to see a green woodpecker in the garden. Shyer than the great spotted woodpecker, they will not come to bird feeders and the only time a visit may occur is if they appear on the lawn to look for ants. Ants form the main part of the green woodpecker's diet. Slightly larger than the great spotted, the green woodpecker is timid and secretive, only revealing its presence by giving a distinctive laughing call that has given rise to its old country nickname, the 'yaffle'. They often call prior to rain and this has given rise to another nickname, the 'rain bird'.

In Scotland the green woodpecker is widespread, although local. It favours deciduous woodland adjacent to open ground where there is short, well-cropped turf and an abundance of anthills. Its red and green plumage makes it one of the most exotic-looking British birds. There were no green woodpeckers prior to 1920 in Scotland but they have spread dramatically and have huge territories.

Jay

Garrulus glandarius
S: jay pyot
G: *sgreuchag-choille*

During Victorian times, jays were occasionally kept as pets due to their beautiful plumage and their ability to mimic. Like all members of the crow family, the jay is intelligent compared to other birds. Its brightly coloured wing bar feathers, chequered black and blue, have long been used for fishing flies, and for decoration of the rough shooter's bonnet. Due to their plumage they were once sought after by taxidermists as colourful additions to displays of songbirds.

The garrulous jay – often heard and not seen (Malcolm Gosling)

Jays may still legally be controlled. Gamekeepers account for many losses due to the jay's propensity for raiding nests – they take the eggs and chicks of a variety of songbirds. Jays thrive on acorns and during abundant years many gather together to collect them, burying large amounts in selected areas. As with squirrels, some acorn burial sites are forgotten from year to year, and new oak saplings are unwittingly propagated.

Small birds frequently mob the jay – a scolding blackbird may indicate that there is one in the vicinity. Although jays are shy and rightly wary of humans, they occasionally come to the bird table, where smaller visitors indignantly make them unwelcome.

Jays build small nests in relation to their size, and they are extremely hard to find. The birds are monogamous and pair for life. In recent years, jays have spread to most parts of Scotland and are now common further north.

The noisy jay

The well-used English word 'garrulous' comes from the Latin *garrulus* meaning noisy. The jay's Latin name is therefore highly appropriate, given that they are the noisiest birds in a wood; their calls can be heard from a great distance. The naturalist author Henry Williamson described it as sounding like the tearing of linen.

Crossbill

Loxia
G: *cam-ghob, deargan-giuthais*

Crossbills are the most specialised finches of all, and their extraordinary bills have adapted for opening pinecones. Scotland's Caledonian pine forests are home to three distinct species of crossbill: the common crossbill, parrot crossbill, and Scottish crossbill. This was not always thought to be the case, however.

One of the longest-running ornithological arguments has continued for almost 100 years. Many experts were convinced that the Scottish crossbill was simply a race of either of the other two, and not a species in its own right. It was in 1904 that a German bird taxonomist, Ernest Hartert, first described the bird as a subspecies of the common crossbill. There was not enough scientific evidence to back up his theory, however. This started a long-running argument in ornithological circles. The British Ornithologists' Union had classed the Scottish crossbill as a separate species from the common and parrot crossbills since 1980, but still its status as a separate species was not confirmed.

Following a protracted and detailed study by the RSPB, led by their senior researcher Dr Ron Summers, the findings were announced in 2006, and the argument has finally been settled. Scotland has an endemic bird – the Scottish crossbill. Dr Summers said, 'This is very significant. Now that we have shown the Scottish crossbill exists and is endemic, we must focus our conservation efforts in making sure that it not only survives, but flourishes.'

Despite this clarification there are few who could recognise the subtle differences between the various species. Differences in plumage, voice and bill structure are almost impossible to spot and unless thoroughly attuned, and equipped with software at home that can reproduce sonogram charts of recorded calls, the three are nearly impossible to differentiate. The findings of the survey also showed that flight patterns were different, and that the birds even had Scottish accents.

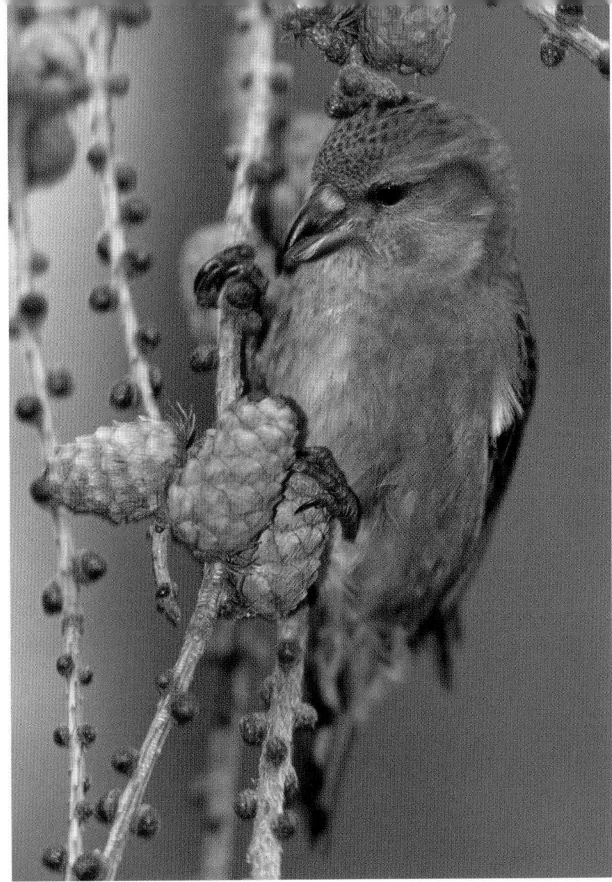

Crossbill, the subject of a long-running ornithological controversy (Neil McIntyre)

The Scottish crossbill is a species of European Conservation Concern (SPEC). Its habitat is in the conifer forests of the Highlands where the female makes her nest with conifer and birch twigs, lining the cup with moss and lichen. Young are hatched between February and June. At first, their bills do not cross over and they depend on the adult birds for food until the bill alters. In the Scottish crossbill and the parrot crossbill, the two larger species, the cross of the two mandible tips is often invisible from the side. Although there is bound to be overlap, the three species appear to show preference for different cones: the common crossbill likes feeding on larch and Sitka spruce cones with its finer bill, and Scottish and parrot crossbills, with their larger bills, prefer older Scots pine and lodgepole pine.

Crossbills occasionally invade Scotland in large flocks in summer, after a good breeding season in northern Europe. The Scottish crossbill is probably a much older species which evolved over time in our ancient pine forests, and is now restricted to the few remaining forest remnants. Future surveys may reveal that they are more numerous and widespread than previously thought.

THE GLOAMING

Woodcock

Scolopax rusticola
G: *coileach-coille, crom nan duilleag, creabhar, udacag, budagoc*

Woodcock are the only wader encountered in woodland and they have a mysterious and earthy quality. They have glorious rich-brown plumage and a prehensile bill used for constant probing in deep leaf litter. They have long been seen as a testing game bird and together with snipe and golden plover make up a trio of waders on the quarry list. Sir Alec Douglas-Home describes a shoot in 1979, when a high woodcock he hit landed in the tender of the passing train, the *Flying Scotsman*. It was left for him with the train driver's compliments at Berwick-upon-Tweed Station.

Woodcock have jinking flight and when disturbed disappear ahead and away in a flash. This adds to the challenge for sportsmen who come to prime woodcock areas to shoot them in winter. During severe winters, like those experienced recently in Scotland, shooting of waders and waterfowl is suspended for a time as the birds are weakened.

Although woodcock are present in Scotland throughout the year, others arrive in autumn from Scandinavia and the Baltic States, hence the old Lowland saying, ''Tis winter amaist when the woodcock comes'. Deciduous woodland on the islands and the western seaboard provides rich feeding grounds for them.

Woodcock have extraordinary panoramic vision: they can nearly see a full 360 degrees as their large eyes are set on the sides of their heads. While using their bills for feeding and with heads down, it helps them to keep a sharp lookout for predators. Woodcock have superb camouflage and although their nest is hidden amongst leaf litter on the woodland floor, foxes and crows may still predate them.

There are numerous tales of woodcock carrying their young between their legs in flight. They have also been seen carrying young on their backs, secreted almost under their wings. During the spring, their breeding display is noteworthy; the cocks fly back and forth at dawn and dusk emitting a gentle croaking sound, called *roding*.

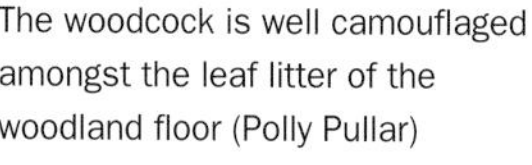
The woodcock is well camouflaged amongst the leaf litter of the woodland floor (Polly Pullar)

Barn Owl

Tyto alba alba
S: white hoolet, gillihowlet
G: *comhachag-bhàn, cailleach-oidhche*

Ghoulish shapes in the graveyard at night, and weird sounds of hissing and boiling are probably easily explained. For centuries, however, they have given rise to a great deal of controversy and speculation. The barn owl emits a range of strange sounds: wheezing, rasping and almost shrieking. Its vocalisations can be strangely eerie if you are unsure what is making them. A common call sounds like the explosive hiss of a cappuccino steamer. The barn owl often frequents ground surrounding churches, not only because the old buildings provide excellent places for them to rear their young, but also because small mammals are usually abundant in the longer grass around graves, and in the surrounding walls.

Are Ye Sleepin', Maggie?

A barn owl's plumage can be golden, like new-baked bread sprinkled with poppy seeds, and soft white underneath. Other owls, however, can look dowdy and dishevelled. All have that unnerving stare, and to see one gliding past in a dark wood on a winter's evening is still a heart-stopping experience. Owls feature in a night-visiting song by the Paisley poet Robert Tannahill (1774–1810). 'Are Ye Sleepin', Maggie?' imagines a suitor charming his way into his lover's arms by recounting all the terrors he has faced to get there:

> Fearful soughs the boortree bank,
> The rifted wood roars wild and dreary,
> Loud the iron yett does clank,
> The cry of howlets makes me eerie.
> Oh, are ye sleepin', Maggie?
> Oh, are ye sleepin', Maggie?
> Let me in, for loud the linn
> Is roaring o'er the warlock craigie.

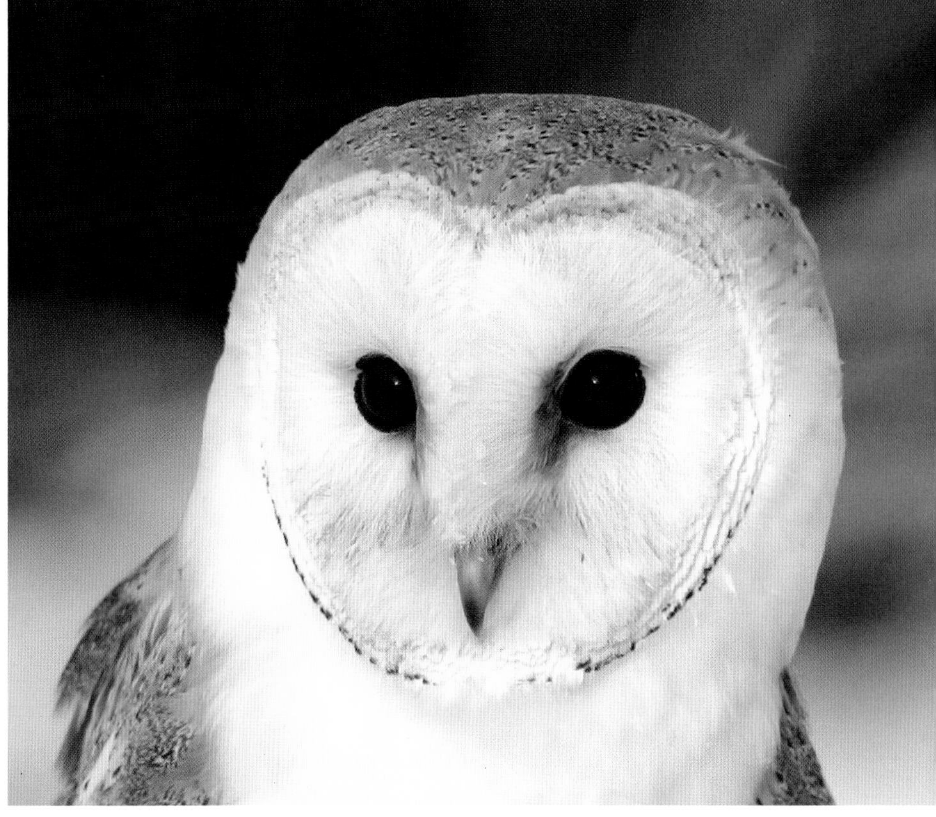

The barn owl has an almost heart-shaped facial disk (Malcolm Gosling)

In Scotland, the barn owl is at the northern limit of its range and for many years it was scarce in most parts. It is currently thriving, however, although cold winters cause intermittent dramatic drops in number due to lack of food in thick snow cover.

Schemes to re-establish barn owls in Scotland have been highly successful, with boxes put in buildings and birds fed until they begin to find enough food for themselves. The barn owl breeds well in captivity, and a productive pair may produce as many as 30 eggs a year if food is plentiful. In the past this led to problems, however, with aviary owners releasing the young birds illegally. Unable to hunt for themselves, most of these unfortunate youngsters did not make it through their first winter. Even in the wild, mortality rates among owlets are high. Many old farm steadings are now being renovated, and barn owls are losing suitable nesting habitat. With a little forethought, special holes with boxes built into the eaves of houses could provide perfect sites – an enlightened architect could find this a great selling point for a completed restoration.

Barn owls favour old-fashioned pastureland, and thrive in areas of young plantations where they hunt along forest edges. Dumfries and Galloway is a stronghold for the birds,

Hoolets old and new

In Gaelic, the barn owl is the *cailleach-oidhche* ('the old woman of the night'), and owl imagery was sometimes used to express the sadness of old age or fading glory. In a group of poems published in 1755, the 'poor old owl of Strone' (*comhachag bhochd na Sròine*) is invited to make her confession. She says she has nothing to confess: her song may be tuneless but she is neither a curser nor a liar; she has committed no theft, violated no tomb or sanctuary and been faithful in love; she is just a poor old honest woman ('*gur cailleach bhochd ionraic mise*'), she says. Poems like these have much in common with much older Irish/Gaelic laments like 'The Old Woman of Beare' and poems about the last days of the Fèinne. By the early nineteenth century, however, owlishness and modernity had made an unlikely alliance in the nickname for the night passenger service on the Forth and Clyde Canal. It carried mainly businessmen between Edinburgh and Glasgow and was known as 'the hoolet'.

and nest boxes there are regularly checked, with the young owls ringed prior to fledging. Barn owls also hunt along vole-rich motorway verges, but on occasions they are pulled into the slipstream of passing vehicles and come to grief.

Owls do not drink water unless under severe stress or in poor health, and gain enough moisture from their food. However, they frequently go to water to bathe, as keeping plumage in immaculate condition is vital. Livestock water troughs make hazardous baths as once inside, the owls find it hard to get out again and many drown. However, some farmers put a special board on the trough to prevent the problem.

With their heart-shaped facial disc and glorious feathering, barn owls are among the most popular of all birds. Due to the huge variation in plumage colouration, individual owls may be recognised in the field. A barn owl's plumage is particularly stunning. Sexual dimorphism in owls is only associated with the snowy owl. Although male owls are generally smaller than females, colour variation for sexing is not foolproof. However, there may be subtle plumage differences between male and female barn owls, with hens being generally darker, although experts maintain that this is not a reliable way in which to sex birds.

NIGHTFALL

Hedgehog

Erinaceus europaeus
S: erchin, hurcheon
G: *gràineag, uircean-gàrraidh*

The hedgehog is a primitive animal that has had little need to evolve and change. Its 5,000-plus spines and its ability to roll into a tight ball afford it perfect protection from predators; only a few badgers and foxes become adept at cracking the code of this efficiently armoured defence. Unfortunately many thousands are killed on the roads each year by increasing traffic. An approaching car triggers them to curl up on the spot, with disastrous results.

Gardeners have always loved the hedgehog because it devours copious quantities of slugs and other unwanted

Hedgehog uses

Gypsies once ate hedgehogs baked in clay and believed that cooked hedgehog cured fits. Dried hedgehog skins were fitted to the cart shafts of lazy horses and when they lent on them as they started to doze off, they were given a sharp reminder as the prickles dug into their flanks. The skins were also used for carding wool. Perhaps one of the most famous uses for a hedgehog was in Lewis Carroll's *Alice in Wonderland*, in which the Queen of Hearts used them as croquet balls.

beasts during its night-time forays. They readily take advantage of a free meal, being gluttonous by nature. People were once advised to leave out cow's milk for them, but this has been found to be detrimental, despite the fact that hedgehogs love it.

Omnivorous, hedgehogs do not hunt, but find food by wandering around eating worms, invertebrates, fallen fruit, amphibians, and eggs. Eggs of ground-nesting species are vulnerable and quickly consumed. This made them unpopular with gamekeepers: hedgehogs were culled and their corpses added to the array of bodies on the gibbet. Today hedgehogs are protected by the Wildlife and Countryside Act.

Hedgehogs frequently fall into special boxes dug beneath fences to catch rabbits. Cattle grids are another hazard, as are tennis court nets left down at night: a disgruntled snagged hedgehog will need assistance to get out again. The results of secondary poisoning from some varieties of slug pellets can also be hazardous.

To the male's relief, a female's spines are laid flat during mating. To the female's relief, the young are born with soft prickles after a five-week gestation. Sometimes grunts and snuffles can be heard and the grass is flattened where the male has chased the female round at night prior to copulation. A hedgehog's nest has an interior temperature of approximately 30°C and is insulated with a thick blanket of leaves and moss. During years of abundant food, there may be two litters. Babies born later in the season struggle to survive and if they have not stored enough brown fat in order to hibernate, they may be found wandering about in a distressed state. The SSPCA and other wildlife hospitals in Scotland over-winter these youngsters until they can be released the following spring. Captive hedgehogs often become too fat. An astonishing record-beating five-pound (two-and-a-half-kilogram) hedgehog was recently recorded – the normal weight is between one and two pounds.

Hedgehogs have a reputation for being flea-ridden and dirty. Strangely, however, we seldom hear that the red squirrel has fleas and ticks in its fur, yet like all mammals, it frequently has a selection of parasites for companions. Hedgehog fleas seldom cause problems for people, although hedgehogs do carry ringworm.

Self-anointing hedgehog (Polly Pullar)

The stone hedgehog

Hedgehogs used to be rare in the west Highlands. In some places, people were unsure as to what a hedgehog actually was. For example, Alexander Forbes from Skye was once told that a hedgehog is a small grey stone which can change shape. If such a stone was found in a cornfield, the reapers would cut carefully round about it, snipping the grain off the top but leaving the stalks standing, to avoid disturbing it.

The hedgehog's hoard

A legacy can be described in Gaelic as *cnuasachd na gràineig* (the hedgehog's hoard), after the hoard of crab apples or other fruit that hedgehogs are said to occasionally leave near the entrance to their nest. There are many tales of hedgehogs carrying fruit on their spines, and medieval illustrations also bear witness to this event. It is indeed a possibility, particularly as hedgehogs frequently roll over and could impale fruit in this way.

Hedgehogs are absent from many islands, although their introduction to some has caused problems, due to their penchant for eggs and the conflict this causes with waders nesting on the machair (see page 42). The building of causeways and bridges has made it possible for hedgehogs to find their own way to some islands without human intervention.

Hedgehogs have a wealth of country nicknames: 'prickly back hotchuss' and 'hedgepig' are still commonly used. There has always been mystery surrounding the animal. Often when hedgehogs encounter something unusual, like a cigarette end, shoe leather, or perhaps a salty human hand, they will immediately start to turn round in a contorted frenzy, covering their backs and shoulders with frothy brown saliva. The curious issue of 'self-anointing' was thus named and further explored during the 1950s by Dr Maurice Burton. Even the tiniest babies will self-anoint. Following his experiments with a tame hedgehog, Dr Burton remained unsure as to the exact reason for this behaviour, once believed to be madness on the hedgehog's part. Some even thought they had contracted rabies. Now it is generally understood that the hedgehog does this to further protect them from predators, as the saliva contains toxins which make them an unattractive snack.

Hedgehogs are full of surprises. Few realise that, underneath the brown pelmet of prickles and coarse hairs, they have quite long legs and can climb well, and run fast when the need arises. 'Aye,' said one elderly farmer, 'they are like nuns, it's seldom you get to see what lies beneath.'

Wildcat

Felix sylvestris syvestris
S: will cat, wullcat
G: cat-fiadhaich

The wild gene is strong. Attempts to tame our native wildcat have proved almost impossible. Even captive-bred wildcats will hiss and spit, stamping a front paw if approached and laying back their ears in the classic wildcat pose. Archibald Thorburn (1860–1935) depicted wildcats in this stance on many occasions in his fine paintings, and he became famous

Wildcat reflections

With so few wildcats left in Scotland, most people nowadays would be thrilled to see one. Not so in the early nineteenth century. Here is the young William MacGillivray, somewhere between Loch Maree and Poolewe in 1817:

> We betook ourselves to a cave for shelter. As we were sitting there, Mr Shand thought he observed two bright eyes in a dark hole, and was ready to swear he saw the membrana nictitans drawn several times over them. Of course, it was a cat or a marten, or an owl. So we proceeded to load the gun ....

It turned out to be the reflection of water dripping from the rock face.

for painting some of Scotland's most revered animals and birds – the golden eagle, fox, pine marten and raven. Author and film-maker Mike Tomkies said, after hand-rearing several kittens, 'They'll fight to the death for their freedom; they epitomise what it takes to be truly free'.

There are concerns that widespread inter-breeding with the domestic cat is threatening their wild credentials. Some experts claim that although it may perhaps begin to look different in appearance, certain wild traits will remain undiluted. The wildcat has ancestry dating back to the Ice Age. It has always had a fearsome reputation and was said to have mythical killing powers, yet it is probably no more likely to attack a human than any other cornered wild animal like the otter, fox, badger or seal, all of which have a powerful bite. Over-zealous keepers' dogs have probably incurred the wrath of a wildcat more than anything else, but the cats are far more likely to become victims themselves. They are run over on roads, or caught in snares intended for foxes.

The wildcat's most distinctive features are its grey-green eyes, a short and bushy striped tail with three to five rings, and a flattened ear posture. They may grow to a considerable size. Osgood McKenzie wrote in *A Hundred Years in the Highlands* that one large specimen measured 43 inches in length. Three or four kittens (in times of poor nutrition, perhaps just one) are born after a gestation period of 63 to 68 days. Male wildcats take no part in rearing offspring. The kittens accompany their mother before gaining their independence from about six months of age, when they gradually move further away from their birth site.

The wildcat was once widespread over much of Scotland but had disappeared from the Lowlands by the end of the eighteenth century. Hated by both Victorian and Edwardian keepers, wildcats were killed at every opportunity and corpses were frequently hung on gibbets alongside other mammals and birds. But it was also a popular animal for taxidermy and some of the large male specimens became a talking point in the big house during Victorian times.

Perfectly evolved, wildcats have razor-sharp claws as efficient as the talons of a large bird of prey. They are excellent climbers and masters of the art of camouflage, while their perfect stealth and precision help them to hunt. As Prof. Russell Coope, who has spent years studying them, said, 'Don't you just love the way one minute you can be watching them, and the next they have stopped moving and blend so perfectly with the landscape that they appear to have gone?' For most of the year wildcats are solitary and largely nocturnal, leaving scent markings to advertise their presence to other cats.

Wildcats have exceptional hearing and even when asleep are alert to the slightest rustle in the grass. True

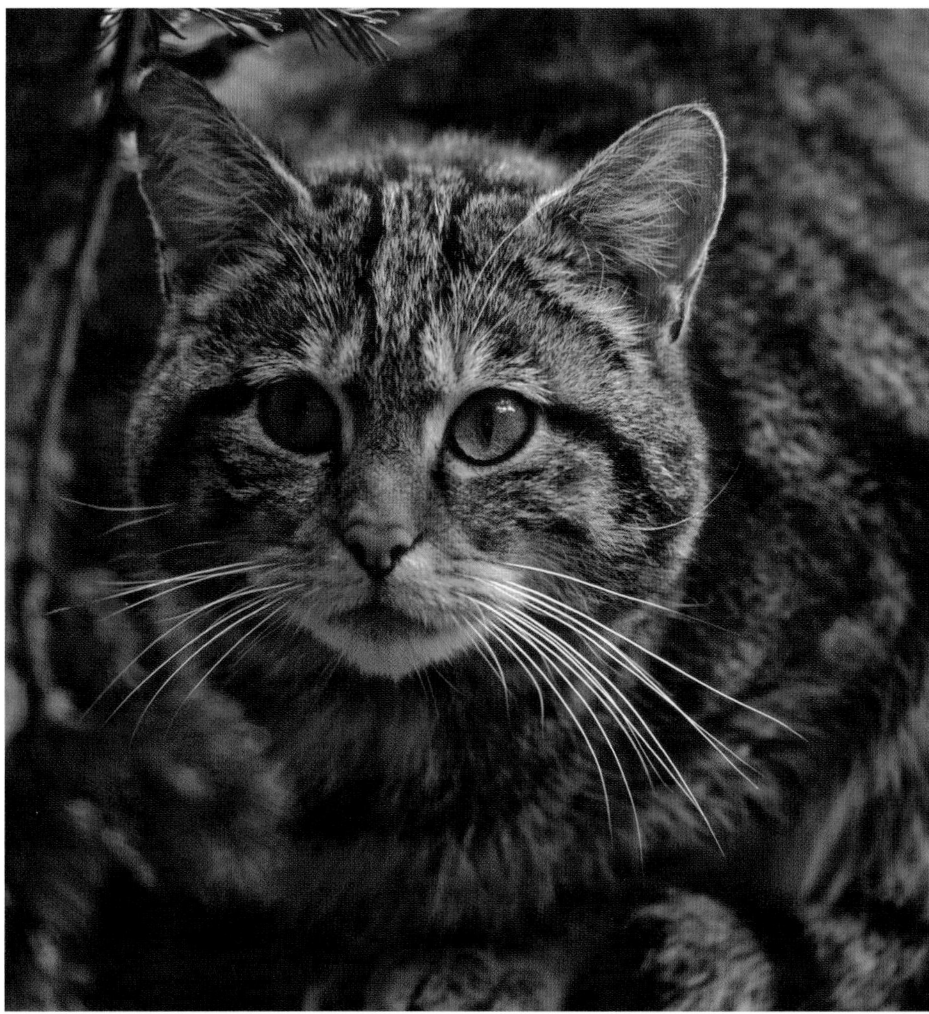

The wildcat has a distinctive stare (Neil McIntyre)

carnivores, their diet largely consists of rabbits, small mammals, birds, and on occasions, small fish and amphibians. In hard weather they will also eat carrion. Their strength means they can take prey the size of a goose. During outbreaks of myxomatosis, their favoured prey, rabbit, becomes scarce and other food has to be found. Some wildcats have been known to take lambs although this is a rare occurrence, and happily now most remaining wildcats, well-used to the perils of living too close to man, tend to avoid hill farms.

Despite concern about hybrid wildcats diluting the truly wild population, increased forestry and better habitat may mean that some wild individuals have managed to survive, and indeed thrive, in the undisturbed depths of the wildest parts of Scotland. As they are so shy and secretive, it could be that there are far more wildcats left than is currently believed. In 2010 the Royal Mail launched a range of ten Action for Species stamps featuring mammals, and the wildcat was one of the first subjects.

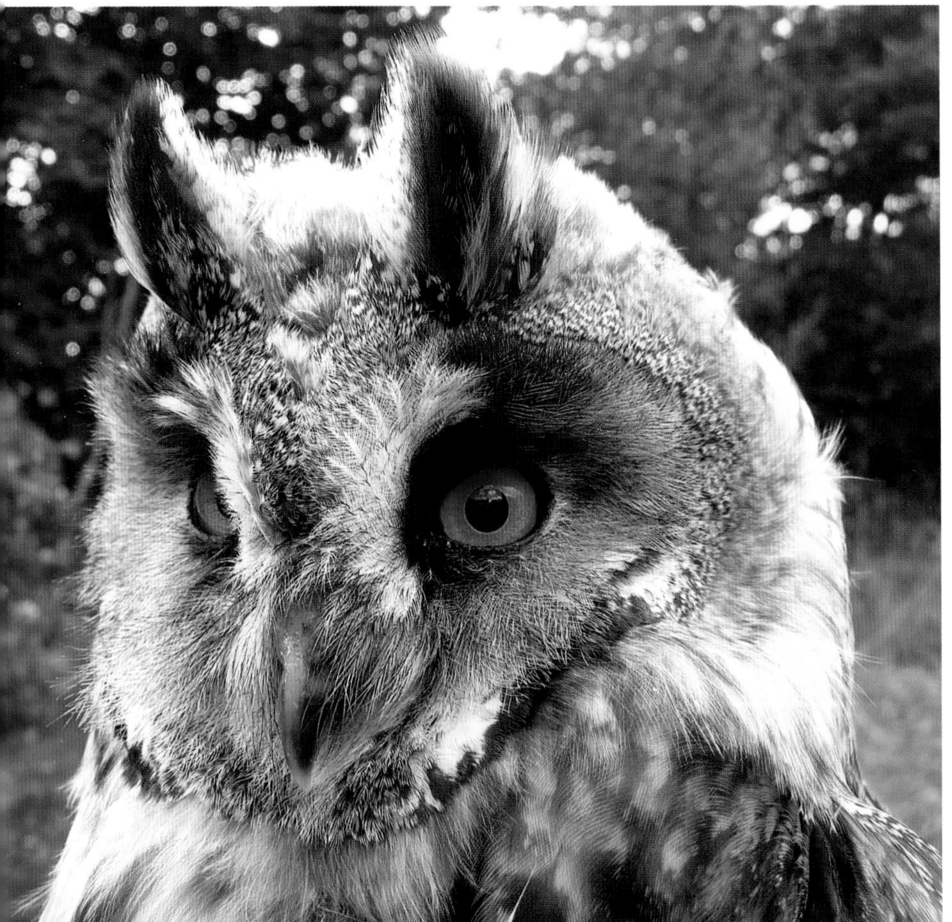

The long-eared owl is seldom seen and is the shyest of all our owls (Polly Pullar)

Long-eared Owl

Asio otus
S: horny hoolet
G: *comhachag-adharcach*

The best time of year to see the shy long-eared owl is in June when they are feeding voracious chicks. Often, on summer evenings at dusk, the young may be heard calling to their parents from a group of pine trees. Long-eared owls frequently use abandoned crow's nests, and often nest in small wooded areas on hillsides far away from human dwellings. They have also been known to nest in craggy holes adjacent to young forestry plantations, where they feed on an abundance of voles.

Unlike the tawny and barn owl that both have dark eyes, the long-eared owl has brilliant orange ones. Its long ear tufts, each made up of approximately six feathers, are there for camouflage and give the owl the appearance of being more threatening than it really is. It is often difficult to establish the fact that there are long-eared owls in a given area due to their secrecy. Often the only signs of their presence are the range of soft calls uttered in the dead of night, or the 'squeaking hinge' call of recently fledged juveniles, and regurgitated pellets found under roost sites. Unlike their close relative the short-eared owl, the long-eared owl is strictly nocturnal, except when under intense pressure to feed young. Prey is varied, although consists largely of small mammals and birds.

Tawny Owl

Strix aluco
S: brown hoolet, wood owl, ool
G: *comhachag dhonn*

There are few rural night scenes on film or television that do not feature the distinctive hooting of the tawny, or brown wood owl, the most widespread owl found in Scotland. It is also the owl with the most musical repertoire of calls, and often as birds are setting up new territories before breeding, a male and female tawny may be heard taking part in their dramatic duet. The tawny has adapted well to life alongside man. Although it favours dense woodland, it seems equally at home in parks and gardens.

Tawnies frequently become road casualties, while some become stuck down chimneys after looking for suitable nest sites. A pair may nest in an old chimney for many years and successfully rear chicks. Tawnies readily take to nest boxes but are fearsome in defence of their chicks.

Young tawny owlets are vulnerable. Thickly coated in grey down, they leave their nest holes and can quickly become soaked by summer downpours. They are then unable to get back up into the trees. Cats account for a few, but often these wayward babies are picked up by well-meaning humans, when in most cases they should be left alone. Hand-rearing is complicated. Young owls become easily imprinted on humans and once this happens, they are unfit for release.

The tawny owl has two colour phases: rufous and grey. Although birds may look entirely different they represent the same species. Males are considerably smaller. Despite the fact that owls have a reputation for being wise, they are in fact the opposite and have very small brains. Their hearing and eyesight are acute, and downy fringes to their flight feathers enable them to fly in almost total silence. They are sedentary birds: they are the most common owls on the mainland, but are not present on most of Scotland's islands.

The ubiquitous tawny owl often nests in close proximity to humans (Polly Pullar)

Bats

S: backie, bawkie, bawkie bird
G *ialtag, feasgar-luch*

Bats are highly specialised mammals. For centuries they have instilled fear in people, largely because they flit about at night, have demonic expressions and are associated with vampire myths. They are still widely reviled and misunderstood. In the Highlands, a bat inside the house was a sign of rain: 'the bat has come in, the showers will be out soon.'

There is a popular misconception that bats become entangled in people's hair, but as their navigation system is far superior to that of any satellite navigation equipment, this is pure fallacy. A minute percentage of bats carry a related virus to rabies, *Bat Lyssovirus*. In Scotland the carrier is Daubenton's bat but humans are highly unlikely to be bitten, although those under most risk are researchers trapping bats. Unlike on the Continent, very few bats in Scotland carry this disease.

Fears about bats are misplaced for they are not so different to other mammals, and although called *fledermaus* in German, meaning flying mouse, and *feasgar-luch* (evening mouse) in Gaelic, they are no relation to mice. Indeed, they have a complex social life and are a separate highly specialised group called *Chiroptera*. The word originates from the Greek and refers to the hand-like wing, a soft elastic membrane stretched over the bones of the forearm.

Although the saying 'as blind as a bat' is far from true, they do not use sight for hunting and rely more on their ears. They use a sophisticated system of echolocation, something that was only properly understood as recently as 60 years ago.

Bats found in Scotland are insectivorous, and thus are vulnerable to poisoning from chemicals and insecticides. They feed for a few hours before dawn and dusk, and can be seen emerging from or returning to their roosts, sometimes in large numbers. These sites have dwindled, particularly as more and more old buildings are lost through development and modernisation. Roost sites are legally protected and any such work has to be carried out at a time of year that will not affect them.

Hanging upside down by sharp, hooked toes helps bats to conserve energy. During the autumn they gain weight in preparation for hibernation. Their heart rate slows as they enter a torpid state, and they may also do this during periods of colder summer weather.

Although bats mate in the autumn, sperm is stored inside the female's body and she does not become pregnant until spring, providing she is in good condition. Then a single baby is born in a maternity roost site. Roosts are used seasonally and are usually made up of a particular species, and sex, males and females tending to roost separately. They must be free of disturbance and adjacent to good feeding habitat. Flying uses a great deal of energy – the common pipistrelle, our most widespread species, requires an intake of 3,000 tiny insects per night. Bats feed on midges as well as other insects, so it seems that, after all, there is good reason for us to welcome bats in our midst.

Female bats lactate for just over a month, and once the

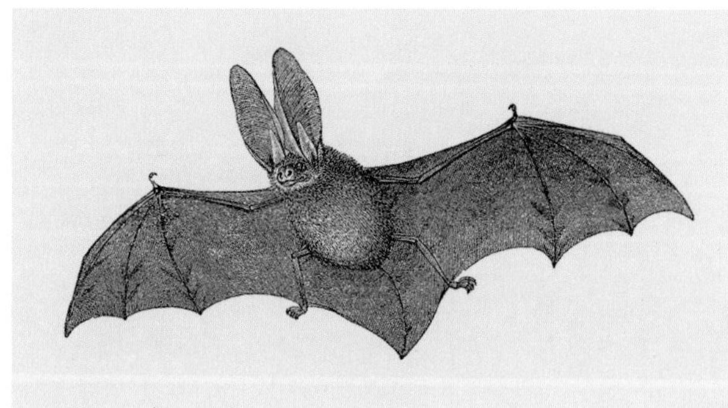

Right. Long-eared bat

Far right. Noctule bat

Scottish bats

There are 17 species of bat in Britain, 10 of which are found in Scotland although some are exceedingly rare:

Common name	Latin name	Status	Area found	Preferred habitat
Common pipistrelle bat	*Pipistrellus pipistrellus*	Common	Everywhere except Uists, Inner Hebrides	Buildings
Soprano pipistrelle bat	*Pipistrellus pygmaeus*	Common	Everywhere except the Hebrides and Caithness	Buildings
Nathusius' pipistrelle bat	*Pipistrellus nathusii*	Rare	Restricted to inner Forth and two coastal areas of Aberdeenshire	Trees Buildings
Brown Long-eared bat	*Plecotus auritus*	Common	Everywhere except the Hebrides and Caithness	Buildings
Daubenton's bat	*Myotis daubentonii*	Fairly common	Everywhere except the Hebrides	Trees Buildings Caves
Natterer's bat	*Myotis nattereri*	Uncommon	Everywhere except the Hebrides	Buildings Caves
Whiskered bat	*Myotis mystacinus*	Uncommon	North to the central belt only	Buildings Caves
Brandt's bat	*Myotis brandtii*	Rare	South-west only	Buildings Caves
Leisler's bat	*Nyctalus leisleri*	Rare	Records from Aberdeenshire and the south-west only	Buildings
Noctule bat	*Nyctalus noctula*	Rare	Records from Fife and the south-west only	Trees

young are on the wing, the colony begins to disperse. As well as old buildings and attic spaces in houses and cellars, bats also roost in caves, tree holes and old mineshafts. Despite the saying 'bats in the belfry', these are not popular roost sites, probably due to the noise and general human disturbance. Quantities of tiny droppings found on the floor are signs of an overhead bat roost. The droppings are similar in size and appearance to those of a mouse. In a large roost where the droppings become wet, the guano gives off a strong smell and the high-pitched sounds of chittering bats may also be heard. The Bat Conservation Trust works to protect vulnerable bat sites and there are also regional bat groups with specialist members on hand to give advice and information. They regularly make visits to roosts and use a special bat detector that confirms the species' presence by the pitch of its sounds. These are then replayed at a lower frequency audible to the human ear. Bat sounds are intricate and astonishingly complex.

Far left. Daubenton's bat

Left. Pipistrelle bat

THE ETERNAL NIGHT

The primeval forests of Scotland provided a rich habitat for many creatures that are now long gone. The brown bear (*Ursus arctos*), Eurasian lynx (*Lynx lynx*) and reindeer (*Rangifer tarandus*) had all been lost by the tenth century, while wild boar (*Sus scrofa*), and Eurasian beaver (*Castor fiber*) hung on for a few centuries more.

Early man, using the most primitive weapons, killed bears, hunting them for their skins and for food. The Caledonian forest was a stronghold for them, providing perfect shelter and an abundance of live prey, carrion, and other food such as berries, nuts and seeds. It seems unlikely that the bear will ever be reintroduced.

The lynx was hunted out due to its penchant for killing domestic livestock; it took sheep and even small cattle as well as roe deer and other mammals. The last evidence of lynx in Scotland dates back to AD 180 at Inchnadamph, Ross-shire.

Vast wild cattle known as auroch (*Bos primengenius*) also roamed the forests. Thought to be the true ancestors of all modern cattle, they were reputed to be enormous, with great sweeping horns. Fragments of their huge, heavy skulls have been found in peat bogs. The auroch was a dark red colour with a pale dorsal stripe down its back, and existed in the wilder reaches of Scotland until about 1000 BC. It is unclear whether they were domesticated, although their immense size would suggest that this might have proved difficult. However, they would certainly have been challenging quarry animals, and were frequently hunted.

Auroch

Wolf

The wolf (*Lupus*) was referred to as the 'volfe' or 'oof' in Scots and *madadh, madadh-allaidh, mac-tìre or faol* in Gaelic. There is ongoing controversy about the reintroduction of the wolf (*Canis lupus*), with various schools of

Friar Wolf Waitskaith D.D.

In Robert Henryson's late fifteenth-century *Morall Fabillis*, wolves often represent extortioners and corrupt officials. One of Henryson's wittiest creations appears in the story of Lowrie the fox. He is recovering from a failed raid on a hen-house and is sitting under the stars feeling sorry for himself when a shadowy figure appears:

> So saw he cummand ane littill than frome hence,
> Ane worthy Doctor of Divinity,
> Freir Wolf Waitskaith, in science wonder sle,
> To preich and pray wes new cummit fra the closter,
> With beidis in hand, sayand his Pater Noster.

Lowrie falls to his knees and begs:

> 'Ye ar mirrour, lanterne, and sicker way
> Suld gyde sic sempill folk as me to grace.
> Your bair feit, and your russet coull of gray,
> Your lene cheik, your paill pitious face,
> Shawis to me your perfite halines;
> For weill wer him, that anis in his live
> Had hap to you his sinnis for to schrive.'

The wolf hears his confession, but Lowrie is too fond of chickens to be truly contrite ('Me think that hennis ar sa hony-sweit') or to show firm purpose of amendment, so the wolf gives him a mild reproof and tells him to abstain from meat until Easter. Lowrie protests that he will die without the occasional sausage or scrap of offall: 'Neid may haif na law,' he pleads. The doctor of divinity pauses. 'God yeild you, shir, for that text weill I knaw,' he says, walking away. Lowrie has just quoted to him a text from John Gower's *Confessio Amantis* – A Lover's Confession.

The Pictish wolf

The Pictish wolf appears on the front panel of a richly decorated sarcophagus in St Andrews Cathedral museum. On the right stands the Old Testament figure of David, shepherd and future king, rescuing a lamb from the jaws of a lion. On the left is a hunting scene in which various creatures are being pursued, including a hungry-looking wolf. David is presented here as a model of good kingship. The lion and the wolf probably stand for enemies or would-be usurpers, those who would 'steal and kill and destroy'. But there is a naturalism about this sculpture too. The eighth- or ninth-century artist had clearly observed a wolf at close quarters.

The St Andrews Sarcophagus at St Andrews Cathedral, Fife (© RCAHMS. Licensor www.scran.ac.uk)

thought debating the validity of such a venture. The idea was first suggested in the late 1960s but has not progressed much further. Many feel that our modern society could not cope with a predatory animal of this kind, yet there are little or no records of wolves attacking people. Sheep and game would be an entirely different matter. Ideas about reinstating them to the Hebridean island of Rum have met with too many issues, but a different scheme to reintroduce many lost species to a large wild area north of Inverness (Alladale Wilderness Reserve) continues. The reserve is owned by Paul Lister, who intends to bring back both lynx and wolf – he has already reintroduced the wild boar.

Wolves have always provided a stumbling block. Their tendency to dig up corpses made them hated, and people resorted to burying their dead on offshore islands. The poet John Webster, a contemporary of William Shakespeare, wrote:

Send for the robin-redbreast and the wren,
Since o'er shady ground they hover,
And with leaves and flowers do cover
The friendless bodies of the unburied men,
But keep the wolf far hence that's foe to man,
For with his nails he'll dig them up again.

Wolves were blamed for all manner of evils, and dates of their final demise are vague and uncertain. Professor Derek Yaldon in the *History of British Mammals* gives the final extinction date of the wolf as around the end of the seventeenth century, but there are numerous exaggerated folk tales of the final killing of the last 'massive black wolf' well into the eighteenth century. However, wolves were never massive nor were they black. As with other extinctions, a few animals could easily have survived unnoticed for some time, especially given the wildness of much of Scotland's terrain.

The Brown Bear of the Green Glen

In the Gaelic tale '*Math-ghamhainn Donn a' Ghlinn Uaine*' (The Brown Bear of the Green Glen) a bear acts as guide, companion and protector to a boy called Iain, the youngest son of an Irish king. Iain appears to be a bit simple, but when his father loses his sight, this unlikely hero sets off to get water for him from a healing well in the Green Isle. He spends the first night in a tree:

> He wasn't up there long before he saw a bear coming with a burning coal in his mouth. 'Come down, king of Ireland's son' says he.
>
> 'Indeed I won't. I think I'm safer where I am.'
>
> 'Well, if I you won't come down, I'll come up,' says the bear.
>
> 'Do you take me for an idiot too?' says Iain. 'A shaggy, shambling creature like you, climbing a tree!'
>
> 'If you won't come down, I'll come up,' says the bear, as he starts climbing the tree.
>
> 'O God, so you will,' says Iain. 'Stand back from the foot of the tree then, and I'll come down and talk to you.' And when the king of Ireland's son got down, it was then the craic began. The bear asked him if he was hungry. 'Well, I am a bit peckish right now, if you don't mind,' says Iain. The bear went off, gallantly and cheerily, and came back with a roe-buck.
>
> 'Now, king of Ireland's son, says the bear, 'How do you like your roe-buck, boiled or raw?'
>
> 'The way I'm used to would be kind of par-boiled and roasted,' said Iain. And so that was what happened. Iain got his share roasted.
>
> 'Now, said the bear, 'lie down between my paws and forget about cold or hunger till morning.'
>
> Early next morning, the bear asks, 'Are you asleep, king of Ireland's son?
>
> 'I've slept more soundly,' says he.
>
> 'It's time for you to be on your feet then. Your journey is long, two hundred miles; but are you a good horseman, Iain?'
>
> 'There have been worse – at times,' says he.
>
> 'You'd better come on my back, then.' This he did, and with the first jump Iain lands on the ground.
>
> 'Steady,' says Iain, 'you're not bad, but you'd better come back till we try again' and he held on tight to the bear with teeth and nails for two hundred miles till they reached the house of a giant.
>
> 'Now Iain,' says the bear, 'you go and spend the night in this giant's house. You'll find him pretty grumpy, but tell him it was the brown bear of the green glen that brought you here for the night, and never fear, you'll get a decent welcome.'

Needless to say, the giant does Iain no harm when he hears that a bear is waiting outside. The creature returns next morning, carries the boy past two further giants and finally delivers him to an eagle who flies with him to the Green Isle. After many adventures, Iain arrives home, with the healing water, a courageous beautiful woman and a baby son.

Bear

Brown bears (*Ursus arctos*) were referred to as 'urse' in Scots and *mathan* in Gaelic. In Roman times, Caledonian bears were exported. This cruel trade was part of an even more barbaric entertainment industry. Visitors to the Colosseum can still see the underground passages where the bears were kept, along with other wild beasts, before being released into the stadium to fight with convicts and political prisoners before a bloodthirsty crowd.

Hercules the celebrity pet grizzly bear of wrestler Andy Robin, tree planting in 1986 (Scotsman Publications Ltd. Licensor www.scran.ac.uk)

Wild Boar

The wild boar (*Sus scrofa*) was referred to as the 'brawn' in Scots and *torc-nimhe or fiadh-chullach* in Gaelic. Once widespread, this ancient forest-dweller was hunted for centuries before it was finally lost as a truly wild Scottish mammal in the early part of the 17th century. Thereafter a few herds of wild boar were retained in parks probably mainly because of their impressive size. Others have been farmed sporadically ever since. Plans to reintroduce boar as free-living animals tend to have limited success, largely because they are included on the list of animals in the Dangerous Wild Animals Act 1976 and have the reputation for being difficult to handle. However, on some suitable Highland estates, these impressive porcines do indeed live free and are well suited for helping control bracken and unwanted scrub, especially in areas where natural regeneration of Caledonian pine is important. Wild boar, like the wolf, appear among the animal images found on Pictish carved stones.

Wild boar and young, Bamff, Perthshire (Polly Pullar)

The Dunadd boar

Most boar carvings are found in the Pictish heartlands of the north and east. The one found at Dunadd, near Kilmartin in Argyll, is unusual, however, and may be the 'calling card' of a Pictish overlord. Pigs, wild and tame, were significant in Irish mythology and Dunadd was a royal centre for the Irish/Gaelic kings of Dàl Riata from about the sixth century. It may be, then, that the Dunadd boar is a hybrid, based on Pictish design but adapted to be understood on both sides of the North Channel. It was not original to this ceremonial site but was added later, sometime in the seventh or eighth century.

Dunald, Argyll, boar-carving (© RCAHMS. Licensor www.scran.ac.uk)

The great boar of Glenshee

A 'fierce and furious' boar inflicts fatal injuries on Finn Mac Cumhaill's nephew in a late-medieval Gaelic poem known as 'The Lay of Diarmaid'. This is a tale of treachery and revenge in which Diarmaid pays the price for his affair with Finn's wife, Gráinne. The setting is Glenshee where Finn used to hunt deer and elk, but on this occasion, an enormous boar 'whom arms had never yet subdued'. The hackles on his back are poisonous and Finn hopes Diarmaid will be scratched by one of them. The hunt goes ahead. Diarmaid dispatches the 'evil beast'. Then Finn insists he measure it from nose to tail. He does so, without a scratch. 'Measure him again,' says Finn cunningly, 'against the bristles.' This time Diarmaid does scratch himself and falls to the ground. One version of the story says he could have been saved if he had been given a drink of water by a woman who had seen him naked, so Gráinne could have saved him, but Finn's jealousy is unrelenting and Diarmaid is left to die. No more is said about the boar, but even the poet admits that the big fellow was sleeping peacefully till he heard the hunters, and did his best to get out of the way.

CHAPTER FOUR

LOCHS AND RIVERS

INTRODUCTION

Much of Scotland is comprised of water: it holds more than 30,000 freshwater lochs and 6,600 major river systems, and a network of burns that run off the hills like veins in the back of a hand. Water adds to the general character of the landscape, mirroring the hills and providing a constantly changing spectrum of light and colour in all seasons. Many of Scotland's watercourses have been sculpted by great natural events, while others are being created by erosion from heavy rainfall. Man's intervention has also altered the scene: vast bodies of water are stemmed by hydro-electric dams with their maze of subterranean pipe work.

The purity of Scotland's water is world famous as the vital ingredient, together with grain, for one of our biggest exports – whisky. The word comes from the Gaelic *uisge-beatha* (water of life).

Many lochs and rivers provide superb wildlife habitat as well as opportunities for tourism and recreation. Some of Scotland's rivers are internationally famous for salmon, brown trout and sea trout. Shallow waters provide habitat for different creatures to those found in the profundity of Highland lochs such as Loch Morar, one of Europe's deepest lakes. Bog pools and vast wetland areas, meanwhile, are vital for other types of wildlife, and man-made ponds and gravel pits are soon colonised by a wide range of species. With increasing rainfall and violent storms, watercourses and lochs are constantly altering; river levels can quickly rise, although in cases of flash flooding may go down almost as fast as they came up. Animals and birds must adapt to such fluctuations.

Small hill burns are as vital as the largest rivers, providing spawning grounds for various fish including salmon, trout and lamprey. The Tay, Scotland's longest river, stretches almost from coast to coast. It begins its journey high in the undulations of Ben Lui near Crianlarich, approximately 25 miles from Oban on the west coast, ending in the Tay estuary at Dundee. On occasions, seals have been seen as far up as Stanley above Perth. The extensive Tay reed beds, some of the largest in Europe, provide breeding habitat for the rare marsh harrier and for bearded tits and many warblers.

Restoring riverside habitat is of great importance for wildlife. Water is vulnerable to pollution and intensive farming and forestry can alter its balance, with chemical leaching and run-off increasing acidity. Fish farming has also affected the ecology in many areas. Birds such as the kingfisher and dipper are only present in unpolluted waters and are therefore good indicators of a river's purity.

Some Hebridean islands are latticed with freshwater

Opposite. Loch Faskally (Polly Pullar)

lochs: parts of Lewis, Harris and the Uists are almost totally covered by them. The terrain of the islands is excellent for breeding birds, including the red-throated diver, snipe and the rare red-necked phalarope. It is also an excellent habitat for otters, water voles, amphibians and a rich community of invertebrates.

The crannog on Loch Tay (Polly Pullar)

THE BANKING COMMUNITY

European Beaver

Castor fiber
S: baver, fiber
G: *bìobhar, dobhar-chù, dòbhran-leas-leathann*

It is at least 400 years since the last beavers were hunted to extinction in Scotland. Several attempts to reintroduce them in the past failed. In the 1870s the Marquis of Bute tried without success when four animals were released in a wet area of pinewood.

During the Middle Ages, Inverness was the main centre for fur trading in Scotland and many beavers, prized for their thick pelts, were killed to supply the high demand for their fashionable fur. They were also prized for *castoreum*, a secretion found in a gland below their tails and valued for its medicinal properties, and for use as a fixative in perfumes. Beavers strip copious amounts of bark, and the salicylic acid found in willow bark is the main ingredient of aspirin and is also found in castoreum. Beaver meat was

The return of the beaver to Scotland

Plans to reintroduce beavers to Scotland have been ongoing for some time. A partnership between the Scottish Wildlife Trust, the Royal Zoological Society of Scotland and the Forestry Commission has meant that the dream has now finally become reality, and in May 2009 the first formal reintroduction of a mammal species to the United Kingdom went ahead, with beavers brought to Scotland from Scandinavia. The beavers were released in Knapdale, Argyll, in suitable wetland habitat, where they are being constantly monitored and tracked.

For years some conservationists have felt that the beaver, a keystone species (one that brings benefits to other wildlife) should be back and living in Scotland. Not everyone is of the same opinion, however, and there are those who have grave concerns for the damage the beavers may do to young trees as they spread to other habitat further outwith the trial area. Although the European beaver is reputed not to build dams as large as those of its North American relation, it sometimes builds substantial ones that alter watercourses.

Already there are many beavers thriving in locations around Scotland; possible escapees from private collections. A public outcry and subsequent huge campaign to stop SNH from trapping them began in 2010, as it is generally felt that beavers have naturalised on their own without any human interference and should now be left well alone. The best way to find beavers is to spend time listening – sounds of their eating activities may be heard long before you see a beaver. You may also see trees that have been felled, or signs of verdant greenery where the animals have been eating. The beavers are thriving and have successfully reared kits in the past few years, much to the delight of their supporters.

Reintroductions will always cause intense debate. In the right habitat, however, beavers can certainly help the landscape – they create new ponds and wet areas, and encourage the growth of young trees through their constant coppicing activity. It looks like Europe's largest native rodent is now back to stay.

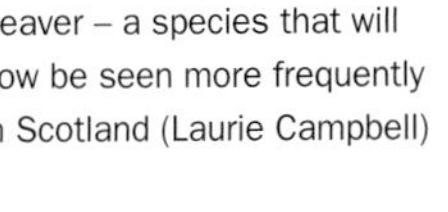

Beaver – a species that will now be seen more frequently in Scotland (Laurie Campbell)

widely eaten and Roman Catholics were permitted to eat beaver tail and paws as a substitute for fish on Fridays.

Beavers are entirely herbivorous and depend on plants, bark, twigs and vegetation. They have webbed feet and special tissue that allows the mouth to seal behind their teeth so that they may still gnaw at plant material while submerged. Ears and nasal passages are also adapted to close while the beaver is swimming. They live in family groups in a beaver lodge built out of branches and twigs.

Water Vole

Arvicola terrestris
S: water dog, water mouse, earth hound
G: *radan-uisge*

The most famous water vole of all is Kenneth Grahame's 'Ratty' in *The Wind in the Willows*. However, the water vole is not a rat but the largest member of the vole family, and it is also one of Scotland's most endangered mammals.

Highly aquatic, with thick fur and special skin flaps to keep ears watertight, the water vole is active by both day and night and consumes a surprising variety of plants. In a national survey of the species 227 different food plants were recorded.

Despite its increasing rarity, the water vole is a prolific breeder and may have up to five litters in a season. The young are frequently preyed on, however. The spread of introduced American mink has had a serious impact on numbers. Voles stir up mud as they dive for cover underwater in the hope that the murkiness will help to hide them. However, this offers little protection from such an Olympic-class swimmer and voracious killer as the mink. Otters, herons, owls, pike, stoats, weasels, rats and domestic cats also heavily predate water voles, and their life expectancy is usually little more than three years.

Voles live in multi-layered tunnels that help them cope with sudden spates. Signs of their presence are distinctive latrine sites and well-worn runs on the burn-side or riverbank. A distinctive 'plop' as they drop hastily into the water when disturbed indicates their presence although they are rarely seen. Water voles vary in colour with darker, almost black voles most common in Scotland.

A dipper returns to its nest hole with food for chicks (Laurie Campbell)

Dipper

Cinclus cinclus
S: burnbecker, esscock, water blackbird, water bobbie, water cockie, water craw, water meggie, water pyot
G: *gòbhlachan-uisge, gobha dubh an uisge, lon-uisge*

'There is a look of loneliness about this little inhabitant of the flood like the solitudes it frequents,' wrote John Colquhoun in the 1800s. Yet the dipper is a cheery little bird, like a large rotund wren that bobs and curtsies tirelessly on rocks in the heart of a raging torrent, its effervescent nature almost mirroring the boiling water.

Dippers are recognisable by their rich chocolate brown colour and smart white dicky shirtfront. They frequent many different watery places, from some of the largest Lowland rivers to the narrowest Highland burns. When feeding, they disappear under a raging torrent and re-emerge seconds later with a small aquatic insect delicacy plucked from the depths. They can dive, swim with great agility and even scuttle submerged, moving upstream against a formidable current in search of underwater larvae and tiny fish. They are as buoyant as their disposition would suggest. The chunky dipper calls as it flits low over the currents in a blurr of whizzing wings, the sharp piercing sound heard over the roar of cascading water. Males have a surprising warbling, thrush-like song (another name for them is 'water ouzel') which is heard from December to February.

The dipper has many country nicknames, including 'water peggie' and 'peggy dishwasher'. The name 'colley', and the Gaelic names *gobha dubh* and *lon-uisge* (water blackbird), refer to their dark sooty plumage.

Once blamed for taking trout and salmon ova (eggs), dippers were heavily persecuted and became rare for a while. Today, they have made a good recovery. Like the kingfisher, the dipper is an excellent indicator of the health of a river system.

Odd nesting habits

Dippers nest under low bridges or overhanging branches along the riverbank, where they make neat dome-shaped nests. They have also been known to make use of a dumped car, a fine shelter in which to raise a brood. Nests may be perilously close to waterfalls and some broods succumb when water levels rise in times of spate.

Kingfisher

Alcedo atthis
G: *biorra an iasgair, biorra-crùidein*

The usual glimpse of a kingfisher is a flash of turquoise and bright orange, accompanied by a shrill, piping call as it flits low over water and then disappears from view. The glorious blue colour is created by the play of light on a complex layering of feathers. This is called the 'Tyndall effect', named after the nineteenth-century scientist John Tyndall, who discovered the scattering of light particles and the effect it gave.

Kingfishers are superbly adapted to their watery environment and are good signs of a river's purity. Their eyes are like polarising filters and are able to adapt to the reflection and glare off the water surface. This enables them to spot small fish swimming below. With a torpedo-like dive, they disappear into the depths, returning seconds later with a wriggling reward. Their lightning-quick, accurate dives enable them to catch minnows, sticklebacks and bullheads as well as other small fish. Plumage must always be maintained and the birds spend time transferring oil from a preen gland under their tail through their feathers to keep themselves waterproof.

Kingfishers are highly territorial. The male seals the pair bond by offering a fish to his mate. At first she may play hard to get and rejects his gift, but eventually takes it from him. A nest is made in a suitable hole in the riverbank. Kingfishers are extremely vulnerable to disturbance from fishermen, dogs and excavation work carried out near the nest. Even having a picnic too close to a nest may stop the birds from returning to it and can mean that eggs chill. Pollution and summer spates are another hazard of life on the water.

Young kingfishers must learn to kill their catches by bashing them against a branch or stone before trying to swallow them. There are records of some youngsters suffocating while trying to swallow live fish.

During a hard winter many kingfishers die, unable to fish when rivers and burns are frozen. On occasion they take advantage of garden ponds, attracted to an easy meal of goldfish or other exotic ornamental fish.

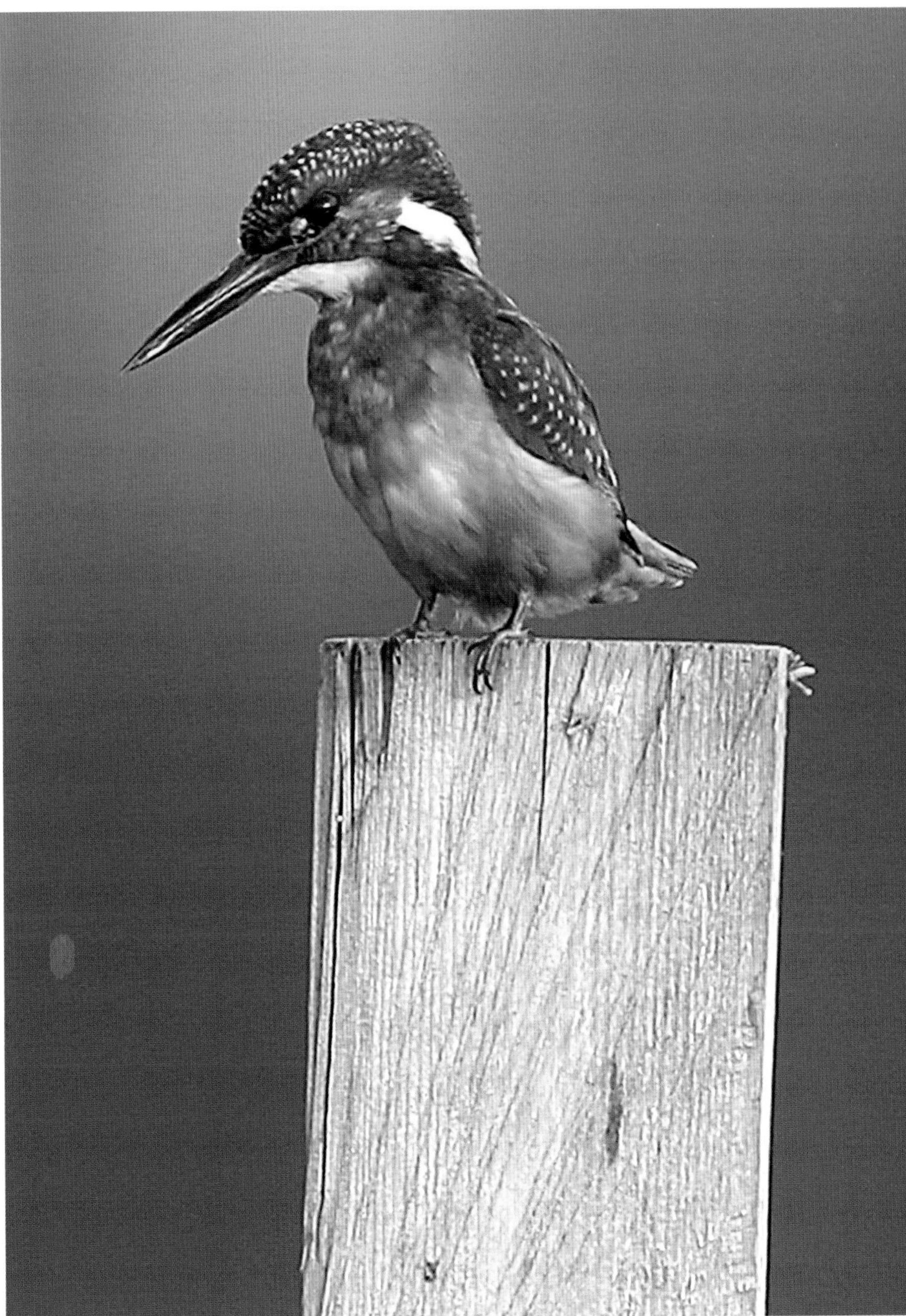

Kingfisher, superbly adapted to its watery habitat (Malcolm Gosling)

Left. The nesting moorhen is highly susceptable to flash floods (Laurie Campbell)

Right. The common sandpiper has a distinctive tail-bobbing movement (Laurie Campbell)

Moorhen

Gallinula chloropus
S: stank hen, stankie hen, water hen, cuddy
G: *cearc-uisge*

The name moorhen is in fact a corruption of the word 'mire' or 'mere', and means literally 'bird of the lakes.' Moorhens are wary birds and were once widely shot. Still on the quarry list, the shooting season for them is from 1 September to 1 January.

Moorhens have dark plumage and beautiful rich red bills with a splash of bright yellow at the tip. They also have striking red eyes. Although most of their diet consists of aquatic vegetation, they take tadpoles, small fish, worms and slugs. They have been seen killing young ducklings and small chicks. However, otters, pike, mink and herons in turn frequently prey on their chicks. In the North-east it was said that moorhens could predict the season ahead – if they were seen nesting further than usual from the water's edge, a summer of heavy rain could be expected. Their large nests are rafts made of piles of sticks and dry reed stems, and these are often washed away during flash floods.

They are referred to as 'cuddy', reference to their short pert tails, almost like that of a docked horse's tail. Another nickname, 'stankie', is probably a reference to the near-stagnant ponds they sometimes frequent.

Common Sandpiper

Actitis hypoleucos
S: fiddler, sand dorbie, sand laverock, sand lairick, tibbie thiefie
G: *luatharan, eàrr-ghainmhich, bòdhag, fidhlear bòrd an locha*

Hill burns with stony banks provide the perfect place for the delightful common sandpiper to rear its young. Largely feeding on aquatic insects and tiny fish, their constant tail-flicking movement on a prominent rock cannot be mistaken. Unlike the lapwing and oystercatcher, the sandpiper chooses a concealed nesting site and there raises chicks that inherit the frenetic tail-bobbing trait, which starts almost as soon as they leave the nest. The adults' shrill piping alarm call is audible the moment there is any sign of danger. A bird was once seen dropping into a deep pool and vanishing under the water to avoid attack from a sparrowhawk. The sandpiper's old country nicknames also include 'skittery deacon', 'steenie pouter', and 'land laverock'.

Black-headed Gull

Larus ridibundus
S: pickmaw, pickie maw, pirrmaw
G: *ceann-dubhan, stairleag, faoileag a' chinn duibh*

The black-headed gull is a landlubber and is often found inland following the plough together with the common gull. Unlike other members of the gull family, it is not pelagic and usually stays close to the shore. During spring and summer its dark, chocolate-brown hood gives it its common name, and its bright-red legs and bill make it a most attractive small gull. In recent times it has become common in parks and seaside towns, particularly in winter.

In Shetland it is nicknamed 'bakie', and in other parts of Scotland referred to as 'hooded mew'. Its association with the lapwing (or 'peewit') has given rise to another nickname, the 'peewit gull'. It often parasitises the lapwing's food as lapwings are better equipped at finding insect food on rough pastureland.

Common Gull

Larus canus
S: loch maw, louchmaa, sea maw
G: *faoileag, an t-iasgair dìomhain*

Despite its name, the common gull is not as common as many other gulls. It has recently been renamed the 'mew gull', imitative of its call. Although it may look gentle and has large, round, black eyes, like most gulls it is an opportunist omnivore. Common gulls frequently nest inland on moors and old grassland. Their eggs were frequently collected as a delicacy.

Left. Black-headed gulls are landlubbers and are frequently seen following the plough (Polly Pullar)

Right. Common gulls are also often seen inland (Polly Pullar)

Collecting gulls' eggs

Terry Duncan, in the *Ross-shire Journal* of 8 May 2009, recalls his childhood in Tain, going to the heather moor with other children armed with moss-lined buckets to collect gulls' eggs. Many of them were cracked open to make pancakes, or fried and used for baking, while others were preserved in waterglass to be used later in the year. He remembers the hazard of avoiding aerial bombardment from purple droppings as the gulls had been feeding on blaeberries from Morrich Moor. The children had strict instructions always to leave one egg in each nest.

Osprey

Pandion haliaetus
S: osprey
G: *iolair-uisge, iolair-iasgaich*

Before the Victorian era, the osprey was a common bird in the Highlands but was then shot ruthlessly. Nocturnal forays to raid nests on remote islands on lochs were commonplace in the eighteenth and nineteenth centuries. One author describes stealing eggs and then lying in wait to shoot the returning adults. It seems incredible now that he appeared surprised when the following year he found the site deserted.

By 1916 ospreys had stopped breeding altogether due to the relentless persecution. It was not until 1954 that a pair successfully managed to rear a brood at Loch Garten in Speyside. They too suffered many misfortunes, however, and were threatened by a forest fire. Their nest was robbed a few years later despite a 24-hour guard and the best efforts of conservationists. In 1959, in an inspired move that led to a total shift in people's perceptions of birds, the RSPB, under the leadership of George Waterston, built a viewing hide for members of the public. Interest was intense and during the first year there were 14,000 visitors, rising to an astonishing two million by 2001. Since then ospreys have gone from strength to strength. Writer and conservationist Roy Dennis was employed as the first warden at the Loch Garten hide. He has since worked constantly to help many species, and is closely involved in ringing and radio tracking raptors including ospreys.

There are approximately 200 breeding pairs of ospreys in Scotland today. The birds owe their success to the dedication of many individuals through their watches on nests and monitoring. Stealing osprey eggs is a practice that continues although the eggs have no financial value. In 1990 wildlife artist Keith Brockie, who has spent much time in the field ringing and studying ospreys, brought in the

The osprey – a wonderful wildlife success story (Polly Pullar)

St Cuthbert and the osprey

A late-seventh-century story about St Cuthbert describes an encounter with an 'eagle' on the banks of the Teviot. It was a fish-eater, so must have been either a white-tailed sea eagle or an osprey. Ospreys have returned to this part of the Borders in recent years, so perhaps it was indeed one of their ancestors that Cuthbert saw. He was travelling with some companions, including a little boy. They had taken no food with them, and the boy expected to go hungry since he did not know anyone who might feed them along the way. The saint assures him that God will provide and they set off:

> As they went on their way, they saw an eagle settling on the bank of the river. The boy ran towards the eagle in accordance with the command of the servant of God, and stopping, he found a large fish. The boy brought the whole of it to him, whereupon Cuthbert said: 'Why did you not give our fisherman a part of it to eat since he was fasting?' Then the boy, in accordance with the commands of the man of God, gave half of the fish to the eagle while they took the other half with them, and broiling it in the company of some men, they ate it, and gave some to the others and were satisfied, worshipping God and giving thanks.

Nowadays, we might wish they had left the whole of the fish, but ospreys were not endangered in the seventh century. What is remarkable is the author's view of providence and sharing. The saint is grateful for what God provides, and becomes a provider himself, sharing with strangers and also – significantly – with other creatures. He teaches the child to consider the needs of others, beyond his own immediate community of family and friends or indeed his own species.

Creative nesting

Ospreys nest in some unlikely places – they have been found nesting on the top of wobbling telegraph poles, and at loch-side fisheries where the birds provide a spectacle for visitors, and a free fish supper is an added bonus. In recent years they have started using pylons as nest sites, particularly in the Tummel Valley. Although living so close to electricity can prove a satisfactory deterrent to egg thieves, it has its hazards. One nest on an electricity pole was struck by lightning and the chicks frazzled to death.

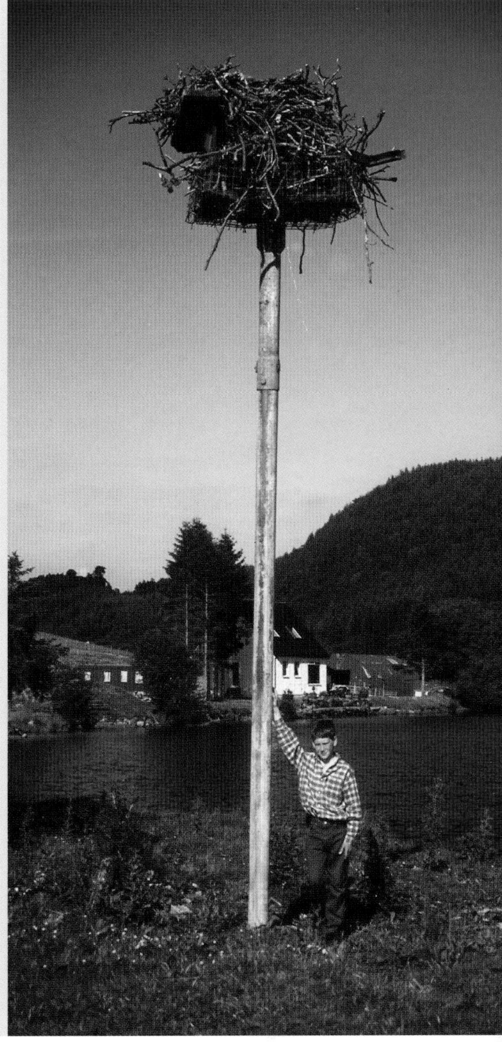

Freddy Pullar with a Perthshire osprey nest (Polly Pullar)

Marine 45 Commando from Arbroath. Some of their men dug themselves in beneath one particular nest that was robbed annually. The criminals were caught red-handed and must have been shocked to find burly marines appearing from a dugout beneath the nest. When asked afterwards about it, Keith Brockie replied, 'I was getting a bit fed-up with the current situation.'

The osprey's feet are unique, with a specially adapted hind talon to help them grip. The soles of their feet are made of rough scaly skin that also helps them to hold slippery fish. Ospreys dive spectacularly, emerging with a writhing fish that seems too large to hold. Fish can sometimes be seen wriggling wildly in an osprey's talons as it flies overhead, yet few are dropped.

Ospreys migrate to north and west Africa every year. Young birds do not return for two years. They may then pair up and make a nest but do not usually breed for at least another season.

With a wingspan of five and a half feet, ospreys are impressive. No bird has been more responsible for raising and promoting wildlife awareness in Scotland, and the osprey is one of the country's greatest conservation success stories.

The black-throated diver has benefitted from man-made nesting rafts (Laurie Campbell)

DIVERSE DIVERS

Black-throated Diver

Gavia arctica
S: loon
G: *learga, learga-dhubh, learga choilearach, broilleach-bothan*

Red-throated Diver

Gavia stellata
S: loom, leam
G: *learga chaol, learga-uisge, learga ruadh*

Divers are beautiful, streamlined birds that are frequently seen from the coast during the winter, dressed in a duller plumage compared to their summer breeding finery. Their legs are so far back on their bodies that they are seldom seen upright and find walking on land very awkward. Underwater, their long bodies come into their own as perfectly designed submarines, the short webbed feet acting as rudders and propellers. During the Victorian era, divers were frequently shot for taxidermy collections and were sometimes inaccurately represented in glass cases in a standing position, something they seldom do for any amount of time.

During the summer months, the red-throated diver comes to small, remote freshwater lochs in the north of Scotland to breed. The Shetlanders still refer to it as the 'rain goose' and often describe how it has an uncanny ability to predict rain with its long melancholy call. An old rhyme from the island illustrates the idea:

If the rain gose flees to da hill,
Ye can gang to da heof when you will;
But when sho gangs to da sea,
Ye maun draw yir boats an flie.

Parts of the Outer Hebrides and the Flow Country in Caithness provide a range of lochans where divers find undisturbed nest sites. Their calls, accompanied by that of drumming snipe and the emotive pipings of the golden plover, provide one of the finest avian orchestrations.

The black-throated diver is far less common than the red, and chooses larger freshwater lochs as breeding areas. Artificially made floating nest platforms have greatly helped the black-throated diver on some lochs.

Both red-throated and black-throated divers are vulnerable to fluctuations in the water table and to predation from mink, otters, pine martens and herons.

The black-throat is sometimes called the 'northern doucker'. On Orkney's mainland there is an area where red-throated divers breed, called 'the Loons'. The name loon originates from the Norse and is also used in North America for divers: it refers to the low moaning sounds they make.

Being rare, divers' eggs are vulnerable to egg thieves. Penalties for such crime are high – any disturbance at nesting time stops egg laying, and the chance to breed in that season is lost. Broods are small, with two or three young being the average. The chicks often ride on their parent's back, peeping out from beneath the adult's waterproof feathers.

Great-crested Grebe

Podiceps cristatus
S: arsefoot, tippet grebe
G: *lapairin, lachair*

Once pushed to the edge of extinction, the great-crested grebe has one of the most beautiful breeding displays of all birds. Dancing with agility over the surface of the water, bending its long serpent-like neck with huge crests on its head raised, the grebe's elegant water ballet is the stuff of dreams. Often a piece of weed or water flower is offered to a mate, adding to the romance of the spectacle. Its glorious silken feathers were the bird's downfall; highly sought for the millinery trade, they graced many a fashionable hat during the mid nineteenth century. The breast feathers were even sold as 'grebe fur' such was their softness, and the birds were nicknamed 'satin birds' and 'tippet grebes'. The grebe's love of small fish brought it into conflict with fishermen and added to its demise, and many were shot as pests.

On land, like members of the diver family, grebes are clumsy and ungainly due to having short legs set far back on their bodies. Several species of grebe have been given the unflattering nickname of 'arsefoot'.

Breeding great-crested grebes were first recorded at the Loch of the Lowes, near Dunkeld, in 1877 and thereafter at other important breeding lochs – Loch Leven in Fife, and Loch Ken in Dumfries and Galloway. Now numbers are stable as pairs return in late February for their annual breeding ritual. A nest is made on a floating raft of reeds and grasses and is highly vulnerable to rises in the water table. Flash floods often sweep nests away completely, and human disturbance from fast boats and jet skis can take a toll on breeding progress. Once the chicks leave the nest they ride on their parent's back. Great-crested grebes move to the coast at the end of the summer where they join a large moulting flock wintering at sea.

Little grebe – more often referred to as dabchick (Malcolm Gosling)

Left. Great-crested grebe

Little Grebe

Tachybaptus ruficollis
S: tom pudding, little douker, bonnetie
G: *spàg-ri-tòin, fàd-monadh, currghalan*

The little grebe is more commonly known as the dabchick. It is present on many lochs and small ponds all round Scotland. Like the great-crested grebe it builds a nest of floating vegetation that is at great risk from spates. The tiny young are vulnerable to predators, in particular pike and mink. Dabchicks are highly territorial. They are also quick to dive out of sight of any approaching danger and may confuse a watcher by totally vanishing and then re-emerging in thick reeds where they are unseen.

Goosander

Mergus merganser
S: saw neb, harle-duck
G: *lach fhiacailleach*

Red-breasted Merganser

Mergus serrator
S: saw neb
G: *sìolta dhearg, sìoltaich*

Goosanders and mergansers are saw-bill ducks with a cormorant-like shape. They are able to remain under water for long periods, and are unpopular with fishermen due to their penchant for salmon and trout fry. Special culling licences are issued annually on important salmon rivers where the birds present a threat to fish stocks.

The goosander favours freshwater and during the breeding season nests in hollow trees, raising a large brood usually early in the breeding season. They are common birds on large mainland rivers. Mergansers spend more time at sea, wintering in coastal waters before moving inland to breed in the spring. Although the two ducks look similar from a distance, during the breeding season the drake merganser's crest is the more spiky, and the pinkish wash to the goosander drake's white plumage makes him stand out brilliantly against dark waters.

Young ducklings are often seen riding on adults' backs or following their parents in a long, tidy line. Sometimes several females may care for many broods grouped together in a crèche.

Goosander – stunning sawbill ducks found on many rivers and lochs (Malcolm Gosling)

Above left. Goldeneye drake (Laurie Campbell)

Above right. Canada goose – an introduced species that is now very widespread (Polly Pullar)

Goldeneye

Bucephala clangula
S: gowdie duck, quink
G: *lach a' chinn uaine, lach bhreac*

Goldeneye have bright, daffodil-yellow eyes, as their name suggests. They can stay submerged for some time – an onlooker may wonder if there was a duck there after all when it suddenly re-surfaces a little further off from where it had originally been. Goldeneye nest in enlarged woodpecker holes and hollow trees, and will readily use well-situated nest boxes. Where these are in short supply, they have been known to nest communally with two females incubating in one box. The boxes are sited quite high on trees. When ducklings are ready to leave, they make a leap of faith, fearlessly jumping out like minute parachutists as they hurry to follow their grey-brown mother to water. Pine martens also take advantage of goldeneye nest boxes for rearing their own young.

GRAZERS

Canada goose

Branta canadensis
S: cravat goose
G: *gèadh dubh*

In southern Scotland, the non-native Canada goose is nicknamed the 'cravat goose' due to its white collar and black neck. It is a large, distinctive black and brown bird that was first introduced to waterfowl collections during the seventeenth century due to its attractiveness, and has since spread beyond all proportion. They may be seen in most areas, from the wilder reaches of the Inner Hebrides to parks in towns.

Its sporting potential is poor and it is therefore not a popular bird with wildfowlers. It is also highly unpopular with farmers and landowners due to the damage it does to crops. Canada geese rear large broods and a population explosion in some areas of Scotland has occurred.

The greylag goose is the ancestor of the domestic goose (Polly Pullar)

Greylag Goose

Anser anser
S: stubble goose
G: *gèadh glas*

The largest and heaviest native goose, the greylag is the ancestor of the domesticated farmyard goose and is regularly eaten, particularly at Christmas. It winters in large flocks in many areas of Scotland, favouring wetland habitat adjacent to farmland where it may feed on stubble or young crops. Its distribution is constantly changing. However, there are some core sites (referred to as 'roosts'), including the Loch of Strathbeg, Drummond Loch, some parts of the Tay valley and the Cromarty Firth. Every year, more and more greylag remain in Scotland to breed instead of heading north, and there are now large populations on some of the Hebridean islands.

With a stout orange-pink bill and pink legs, the greylag is both gregarious and noisy. Some describe its slow, ungainly walk as a nautical roll, as it waddles from side to side. When a flock lands on a field of young cereal, they damage it and compromise its growth. Greylags and other geese frequently make themselves unpopular by decimating crops, not only by consuming and damaging them but also by soiling the ground, although on poorer ground it serves as efficient manure. They soon learn to ignore alarm guns that go off intermittently with a loud bang. Some farmers leave old vehicles in their fields to try to put geese off landing there. Goose shooting is a popular pastime, and farmers with geese on their land sometimes let out shooting rights to wildfowlers. In the mid 1800s, huge flocks of greylags were apparently so destructive on arable land in East Lothian that people were employed to drive them away.

Greylag geese choose a variety of nest sites well hidden in dense vegetation or heather. Nests are lined with down feathers and although the female, the goose, does all the incubating, the gander stays close at hand and helps to rear the goslings. The family party may join with other greylags and their young, greatly increasing their chances of survival.

The fox and the goose

One day, the fox succeeded in catching a fine fat goose asleep by the side of a loch. He held her by the wing, and making a joke of her cackling, hissing and fears, he said, 'Now if you had me in your mouth, as I have you, tell me what you would do?'

'Why,' said the goose, 'that is an easy question. I would fold my hands, shut my eyes, say a grace, and then eat you.'

'Just what I mean to do,' said Rory [the fox], and folding his hands, and looking very demure, he said a pious grace with his eyes shut. But while he did this the goose spread her wings, and she was now halfway over the loch; so the fox was left to lick his lips for supper.

'I will make a rule of this,' he said in disgust, 'never in all my life to say grace again until after I feel the meat warm in my belly.'

Pink-footed Goose

Anser brachyrhynchus
G: *gèadh dearg-chasach*

This aerodynamic grey goose has a distinctive call that is similar to the yelping of a terrier. Its aerial manoeuvres as it lands on the ground or water are noteworthy, as is the way a flock flies in 'V' formation. In some years, it may be as numerous as the greylag. Birds also come into conflict with arable farmers. Wildfowlers refer to pink-footed geese as 'pinks' or 'pinkies' and await their arrival from Iceland every year for a shooting bonanza. In the past large numbers were shot and many birds were wounded, or 'winged'. Happily, this is seldom the case nowadays.

The Loch of Strathbeg in the north-east, along with Dupplin Loch, Carsebreck and Loch Leven in Perth and Kinross, are favoured staging posts during autumn. Many pink-feet then continue south-west to spend the winter in parts of Dumfries and Galloway on the Solway, also a favoured haunt of wildfowlers.

The pink-footed goose is nicknamed 'pinkie' (Malcolm Gosling)

Mute Swan

Cygnus olor
S: swan
G: *eala*

For thousands of years, people have held the swan in highest esteem and believed that after death, the human soul takes a swan's form. In the Hebrides, there are still those who believe that to kill a swan will bring nothing but bad luck and that it may harm the soul of the person that bird represents. Early records of swans in Scotland date back to the Civil War in the mid 1600s, when mute swans lived on Linlithgow Loch but departed when Cromwell's garrison occupied Linlithgow Palace. Used as food for medieval banquets, they were more popular as table birds in England than Scotland, where they have always been revered. Technically swans are owned by the monarch.

One of the largest flying birds, the swan is elegant with its pure white plumage and serene carriage as it sails effortlessly across water. They bond for life and will only take

Cù Chulainn and the bird women

There was an ancient belief that large white birds, especially swans, might be Otherworld beings, shapeshifters or people under enchantment. In one tale, the warrior Cù Chulainn gets a rare beating from two white bird-women for slaughtering thousands of their relatives. His female fans had demanded feathers to decorate their dresses and Cù Chulainn, in a rage, had gone on the killing spree which brought the vengeance of the bird-women so furiously upon him. In another tale, the children of Lir are changed into swans by their jealous stepmother and live for hundreds of years in the sea between Scotland and Ireland. Although best-known as an Irish story, a version of it was collected in South Uist in 1871. In Tiree, meanwhile, it was said that swans are 'king's children under enchantments' and can sometimes be seen in out-of-the-way places taking off their swan clothes and becoming women again.

another mate if one of the pair is lost. Contrary to their name, mute swans are not silent. Not only do they emit a range of whistling and hissing sounds, but they also make a beautiful noise in flight when the sound of powerfully beating wings can be heard from some distance. Although

The regal swan

Kings, in particular, laid claim to swans. The laws of Scotland drawn up for Charles II in 1681 list swans as crown property, along with mineral rights and treasure trove: '… although all proprietors have the privilege of fowling within their own ground, yet swans are particularly reserved to the king.'

This did not prevent the determined hunter: 'When the natives [of North Uist] kill a swan,' writes Martin Martin, 'it is common for the eaters of it to make a negative vow [i.e. they swear never to do something that is in itself impracticable] before they taste the fowl.' A token gesture perhaps, but with an underlying disquiet. Alasdair MacDonell of Glengarry (1771–1828) enjoyed swan hunting, apparently, but a 'Hunting Blessing' collected in Benbecula in the nineteenth century forbids doing any injury at all to swans, and in Barra and parts of Argyll it was still considered bad luck to kill one into the twentieth century.

The Franciscan poet William Dunbar (*c.*1460–*c.*1520) made fun of the courtiers or clergy of Edinburgh, for feasting on swan and praying smugly for their brethren in purgatory – by which he seems to mean Stirling:

That sone out of your paynis fell
Ye may in hewin heir with ws dwell,
To eit swan, cran, peirtrik and pluver
And everie fische that swowmis in rever.

(That soon out of your torment fell,
you may in heaven here with us dwell,
to eat swan, crane, partridge and plover
and every fish that swims in river)

Left. The flight of whooper swans makes a beautiful sound (Malcolm Gosling)

Opposite. Mute swan at rest (Malcolm Gosling)

they may appear serene, they can be aggressive to other birds and may cause disturbance on a loch. They have been known to catch tiny mallard ducklings and kill them by holding them under the water with their bills. They are also able to stand their ground if a human approaches too close to a nest. The exaggerated belief that they can break a human arm with one powerful beat of their large wings is surely fictitious, but they are immensely strong and can be highly aggressive. Swans will usually hiss, threatening a warning at first. The male, or cob, is larger than the female, the pen. Both birds take on parental duties and the grey cygnets stay with the adults until they have changed their drab juvenile plumage to brilliant white.

Highly susceptible to oiling and other pollution incidents, mute swans are treated in wildlife rehabilitation centres in Scotland. The SSPCA's Middlebank Wildlife Rescue Centre at Dunfermline receives swans for cleaning most years. Swans are also victims of lead poisoning due to them accidentally swallowing fishermen's weights. Discarded fishing line and hooks are another serious threat to all waterfowl. Swans may be killed by flying into electricity and telegraph wires, although in areas where there are large numbers, markers and flags on the lines has helped warn them of the obstacle.

Whooper Swan

Cygnus cygnus
S: elk, whistling swan
G: *eala fhiadhaich*

Scotland has a large wintering population of whooper swans from Iceland. Every year they arrive in small groups. They are often heard in advance, as they emit a clear, trumpeting call that gives them their common name. Whooper swans cover great distances on their annual migration and not only fly high and fast, but are also able to withstand exceedingly low temperatures *en route*. One pilot recorded whooper swans in an air temperature of below -40°C. Some wild swans spend the winter in remote glens on rivers while others choose windswept hill lochans.

During the 1960s, grain treated with pesticides killed many wintering swans and wildfowl feeding on farmland, and the whooper swan was no exception. A very small number of whooper swans breed in Scotland. A pair nested in Benbecula in 1947, and there are records of whoopers breeding in Tiree, Loch Lomond, the Shetlands and Orkney, although these incidents are sporadic. In recent years, less than ten pairs have bred successfully in Scotland.

Swans on frozen Loch Bee, South Uist (Mary Low)

Tàladh (Lullaby of the Swan)

Alexander Carmichael's introduction to '*Taladh*', one of the most beautiful songs in his collection, reads as follows:

> A woman found a wounded swan on a frozen lake near her house, and took it home, where she set the broken wing, dressed the bleeding feet, and fed the starving bird with linseed and water. The woman had an ailing child, and as the wounds of the swan healed the health of the child improved, and the woman believed that her treatment of the swan caused the recovery of her child, and she rejoiced accordingly and composed the following lullaby.

The *mànran* mentioned in line seven (*below*) is a low murmuring song, like the quiet cooing which is made by whooper swans amongst themselves.

Tàladh

Eala bhan thu,
Hu hi! Ho ho!
'S truagh do chàramh,
'S truagh mar tha thu,
'S t-fhuil a' t'fhàgail;
Eala bhàn thu,
Cian o d'chàirdiu,
Bean do mhànrain –
Fan am nàbachd;
Léigh an àigh thu,
Sian mo phàisdean,
Dìon o'n bhàs e,
Greas gu slàint' e,
Mar is àil leat;
Pian is ànradh
Dh'fhear do shàruich,
Mile fàilt' ort,
Buan is slàn thu,
Linn an àigh dhut
Anns gach àite,
Hu hi! Ho ho!
Hu hi! Hi ho!

The swan replies:

Furt is fàs dha,
Neart is nàs dha,
Buadh na làrach
Anns gach àit dha;
Moire Mhàthair
Mhìn ghil àluinn
Bhi da d'bhriodal,
Bhi dha d'mhànran,
Bhi dha d'lithiu,
Bhi dha d'àrach;
Bhi dha d'dhìon
Bho lion do nàmhu;
Bhi dha d'bheadru,
Bhi dha d'nàisdiu,
Bhi dha d'lionu
Leis na gràsu;
Gaol do mhathar thu,
Gaol a gràidh thu,
Gaol nan ainghlean thu
Ann am Pàras!

Lullaby of the Swan

You are the white swan,
Hu hi! Ho ho!
Sad your condition,
Pitiful your state,
Your life-blood ebbing.
You are the white swan,
Far from your friends.
Murmuring song-woman,
Stay close by me.
Physician of gladness,
Protect my little child.
Shield him from death,
Speed his recovery,
As you wish to.
Pain and distress
To him who hurt you.
A thousand welcomes,
Life and health to you.
Lasting joy to you
In every place,
Hu hi! Ho ho!
Hu hi! Ho ho!

Peace and growth to him,
Strength and worth to him,
Lasting success to him,
Wherever he goes.
May Mary Mother
Sweet, fair and lovely,
Be soothing you,
And humming to you,
Bathing you
And nursing you,
Protecting you
From the net of your enemy.
Cuddling you,
Guarding you,
Filling you
With graces,
Your mother's darling,
Her love of loves,
Love of the angels
In paradise.

DABBLERS

Mallard

Anas platyrhynchos
S: mallie, mire duck
G: *lach riabhach*

The ubiquitous mallard, once known as the 'wild duck,' is widespread in Scotland. It is also referred to as the 'stock duck', 'muir duck' and 'moss duck'. Due to its abundance, it is frequently overlooked. However, there can be few birds as dramatic and dapper as a drake mallard in full breeding finery, with his head of shot-green silk, brilliant-yellow bill and orange-coloured legs. The mallard, although often friendly and placid towards humans, is in fact a serial philanderer and rapist, and on occasions is known to murder its rivals.

Drakes frequently carry out gang rape and may hold unsuspecting females violently under water using their bills; this can lead to drowning. Chaucer wrote of the drake mallard, 'He is a stroyer of his own kind'. It has been said that living so closely alongside man, the mallard may have picked up some of his habits. A better explanation is that males vastly outnumber females and there is great pressure on a drake during the breeding season to find a suitable female.

Ducklings are often born both early and late into the breeding season. They are vulnerable to many predators including mink, swans, pike and otters. Many young are lost as they try to keep up with their mother in thick vegetation.

The mallard is the ancestor of the domestic duck. Highly promiscuous, it frequently crossbreeds with other species of duck. Midsummer brings the moult, or 'eclipse', when it is hard to tell the difference between drakes and ducks. During the 1950s, captive birds were released for shooting purposes. This raised mallard numbers to an all-time high. Artificially reared mallard still swell the wild population today. Duck flighting at dawn and dusk is a popular sporting pastime. Shooters wait behind butts for birds to appear, but some birds become too tame and there is a school of thought that they do not make a fair sporting challenge.

Although we are concerned about the consequences of climate change with increased flooding, the mallard is quick to take advantage. As soon as the water table rises, you can witness their almost ecstatic reaction as they paddle around any inundated area. The mallard is an opportunist, and is currently thriving (see page 243).

A dapper drake mallard in full breeding splendour (Polly Pullar)

Left. The easily recognised drake pintail (Malcolm Gosling)

Right. The shoveler has a bill like a spatula (Laurie Campbell)

Pintail

Anas acuta
S: caloo (Orkney and Shetland)
G: *lach stiùireach*

The earliest breeding records of the pintail duck are from 1869 at Loch Knockie in Inverness-shire, when a clutch of seven eggs was found and taken by Edward Hargitt. These are now in the Natural History Museum in London. Pintails are the rarest members of the group of dabbling ducks including the mallard, shoveler, teal and wigeon. Pintails are nicknamed the 'sea pheasant', 'cracker' or 'winter duck'. Two sharp-pointed tail feathers give them their name and make males easy to recognise.

The main Scottish breeding population is centred on Orkney, where birds favour low-lying, nutrient-rich lochs. Nests are usually close to water, although sometimes they are found on heather moorland. A few other island locations are chosen but it is during the winter that pintail numbers swell. They are still not an abundant duck in Scotland, however. Small numbers may be seen at estuaries and large lochs: the Solway Firth is the most important wintering area for pintail in Scotland, hosting around 3,000 individuals every winter.

Shoveler

Anas clypeata
S: spoonbeak
G: *gob leathainn, lach a' ghuib leathainn*

Thomas Bewick wrote of the shoveler: 'The bill is black, three inches long, very broad or spread out, and rounded like a spoon at the end … the insides of the mandibles are remarkably well furnished with thin pectinated rows, which fit into each other like a weaver's brake, and through which no dirt can pass.' The bill of the shoveler is spatulate and distinctive. The birds require shallow, eutrophic waters where they feed by filtering water through their broad bills to obtain nutrients such as plankton. Sometimes groups of shovelers are seen together working the water in a circle, stirring up the mud to feed. Shovelers are almost comical on land – they have notably short legs and the top-heavy bill can make them seem ungainly. However, the drakes' plumage includes a smart iridescent green head, chestnut flanks and a pure white breast. In flight, the drake's shoulders are a stunning powder-blue colour.

Teal

Anas crecca
S: jay teal
G: *crann-lach, sìolta, lach bheag, lach-shìth*

Poulterers used to refer to a teal as a 'half duck,' for it is the smallest Scottish duck, an immaculate little bird. There was great affection felt for them in parts of Gaeldom where they were known as the *lach-shìth* ('fairy duck', or perhaps 'duck of peace') and were said to be under the protection of Mary. There was less reverence for them among sportsmen: Kathleen Thomas, in her cookery book *The Sporting Wife,* writes, 'Hang for no longer than 2 days, or can be cooked freshly shot. A very tender and flavoursome bird.' Many sportsmen claim it is the most delicious of all the ducks, but as with the flavour of other game, it depends on the season and on where the birds have been feeding.

Very common in winter, most wetland areas and lochs are good habitat for teal. Their distinctive flight call and diminutive size makes them instantly recognisable in the air. Clay pigeon shooters have a setting on their traps called springing teal, reference to the birds' amazing take-off flight. If surprised while feeding on stubble fields, they will literally spring into the air. Sir Alec Douglas-Home wrote: 'All the duck tribe – and in particular the teal – lift out of the water with the speed of a well-oiled modern lift.'

Wigeon

Anas penelope
S: bald pate, pandle-whew
G: *lochlannach, glas-lach*

For sportsmen, the wigeon epitomises wild places. Backlit by winter sunlight, the drake's fine plumage – a buff-pink head and neck and chequered pattern of grey on his back – makes him a fine sight. A widespread bird during the winter, few breed in Scotland. Nest sites are chosen adjacent to remote hill lochs or isolated moorland pools. Some wigeon nest on St Serf's island on the RSPB's Loch Leven wildlife reserve. Outwith the breeding season, wigeon are common on estuaries and large lochs, and are often seen in groups feeding on mud flats or in shallow water where they find eel grass. Male wigeon emit a conspicuous melodious whistling call when a flock take to the air. Wigeon, like teal, are fast fliers.

Left. Teal have a glorious green eye patch (Laurie Campbell)

Right. The evocative whistling call of wigeon epitomises wild lochs (Laurie Campbell)

UNDER CURRENT

Atlantic Salmon

Salmo salar
S: saumon
G: *bradan*

The salmon is the most mysterious and alluring creature in Scotland. Smoked, it is still viewed as a gourmet food even though now widely available. Cooked in a variety of ways, salmon is one of the most delicious of all fish. Salmon are highly complex, however, generating an appeal that goes far beyond the culinary.

The anadromous life cycle of the salmon is intriguing. In autumn they return to Scotland from the sea and travel up the rivers of their birth, driven by a strong sense of smell and their need to spawn. They often meet huge obstacles; raging torrents and waterfalls. On their annual migration, they provide one of the finest wildlife dramas of all as they take enormous leaps out of the torrent, battling upstream to reach their final destination.

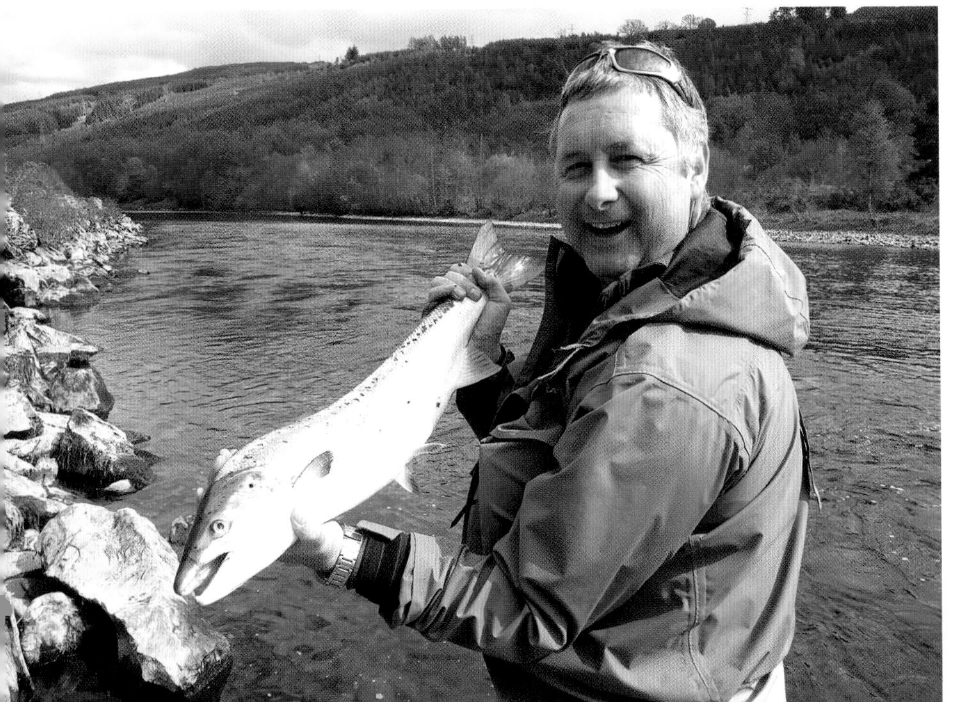
Raymond Doonan with a River Tay salmon (Polly Pullar)

Eventually the female (hen) fish lays her eggs in a 'redd' – a gravel bed in the headwaters of the river. A 20-pound female lays approximately 20,000 eggs, although most of these will not reach maturity. The eggs are fertilised by the male (cock) fish and begin to develop. From these emerge tiny translucent 'alevins'. They quickly turn into 'fry' and then develop into 'parr' at between one and three years of age. The young fish eat insect larvae and other tiny organisms, and may in turn be preyed on by large fish and brown trout, otters, mink, herons, cormorants and sawbill ducks (see page 94). The parr eventually turn into salt-tolerant 'smolts' with beautiful silver scales, which migrate out to sea in shoals. Some may remain there for a few years while others, 'grilse', return after just a year. The salmon spends more of its life at sea than in freshwater, and for centuries has been caught at netting stations around the Scottish coast as it returns to spawn.

One of the most extraordinary issues relating to salmon is that on their return to spawn they seldom, if ever, feed while in the river. Why then do they sometimes take certain flies and allow themselves to be caught by fishermen? Some believe it is purely due to the annoyance factor of having something tempting dapping the water's surface. This is one of many mysteries surrounding these beautiful fish. Some males are almost bright red on their return and are occasionally referred to as 'tartan fish', or 'kippers'. After spawning, the spent fish are known as 'kelts'. Although some return to spawn again, the majority die.

Salmon Poaching

To anglers, salmon offer the ultimate challenge. And no self-respecting poacher could ever resist the king of fish. The salmon has provoked nocturnal misdeeds, and has appeared on the tables of the rich and poor in equal measure, by fair means or foul. 'Nay! Under certain circumstances hardly would one trust even a black-coated minister

A poaching tale

Taking 'one for the pot' could be overlooked, but poaching on a larger scale or during the spawning season was a different matter. Here, a Gaelic storyteller puts the fear of God into anyone who might be tempted to try their hand:

> Alasdair Mòr, son of Iain the Strong, went poaching in the river after midnight. He met a man he did not know. He was a fine-looking man and well-spoken. 'I'll help you, Alasdair Mòr, and we'll share the fish,' said the stranger.
>
> 'All right,' said Alasdair Mòr. They worked together and they worked well too.
>
> Towards the end of the night the stranger said, 'Time to share them out, Alasdair Mòr.'
>
> 'Not yet,' said Alasdair Mòr, 'there are more fish in the pool.'
>
> They kept on working and they worked well and after a while the stranger said, 'Time to share them out, Alasdair Mòr'.
>
> 'No, no,' said Alasdair, 'there are still more fish in the pool.'
>
> They kept on working and they worked well, and soon the stranger said, 'Time to share them out, Alasdair Mòr.'
>
> 'It is just time now,' replied Alasdair, and scarcely were the words out of his mouth when the red cock crowed, and at the first crow of the cock, the stranger leapt from Alasdair's side and leapt upwards in a blaze of red sparks. Since then, no one goes poaching in the river but unbelievers without the grace of God or the fear of man. For who was this but the fiend in human shape? Since that time, no one goes poaching in the river at an unseemly time of year or an unseemly time of night.

if a salmon provoked him too sorely,' wrote Jean Lang in *Salmon and Salmon-poachers in the Border*. No other fish has such magnetism.

In 1743 the eighth Earl of Home, an angler of repute, landed a massive fish on his home beat on the River Tweed. His dog always accompanied him and the loyal animal also became adept at fishing, hauling out the salmon and placing them on the bank beside its owner. The owner of the south bank, on the English side of the river, became enraged and eventually filed an unlikely lawsuit against the dog. The case was called *Lord Tankerville versus a dog – the property of the Earl of Home*. However, the dog, representing the Scottish side, won the case. Dogs frequently acted as unwitting accomplices in poaching incidents.

One tale from the nineteenth century relates to a respected Selkirk bailiff who was blindfolded by his wife whenever salmon was on the table. The dubious acquisition of the fish served to him might have meant he had to lie in court, but as he had never actually seen it, he could not be a witness to nefarious business. Such was the salmon's flavour that he asked no questions.

Salmon poaching has lured young and old alike. Many

Spawning salmon (Laurie Campbell)

means may be employed, from straightforward stealth and patience, to more drastic measures such as dynamite, and the design of some ingenious fish traps and nets. Although most landowners turn a blind eye to the odd salmon taken by a poacher, a large explosion will be unlikely to go unnoticed.

Special gadgets have been made to perfect the technique of illicit salmon catching. The 'leister' – a sharp three-pronged tool like a trident, was manufactured by many country blacksmiths. Designed for throwing into the water, Runcimans of Yarrow made a particularly fine design with a long handle. It was ideal for 'Burning the Water', an infamous event that took place at night using bright lanterns or torches to find fish in shallow water. Shifty-looking men with large pockets and lurcher dogs were the most likely culprits and usually had a fish or pheasant hidden about their person.

A story from the Borders tells of a fisherman battling with a massive fish for a long time. Finally, in pitch darkness, the line snapped and the exhausted fish escaped and could not be located. Poachers watching from the bank witnessed the event and later acquired the fish. It was so vast that the only way they could get it home was to cut it in two and they were forced to leave one half on the bank. The huge piece that was left was reputed to have weighed 35 pounds. It was generally accepted at the time that the whole fish must have been over 70 pounds in total, which would have been a real record-breaker. However, as any fisherman will tell you, the biggest fish are always the ones to get away.

Female Fly-fishers and the Salmon

Women have caught many of the largest fish. The story of the current record-breaking salmon is well known. Georgina Ballantine caught a 64-pound salmon on a beat of the River Tay near Caputh in 1922. It has raised questions about the possibility of female pheromones attracting cock salmon. Some fishermen have even endeavoured to catch

Finn and the wisdom fish

Finn MacCumhaill is said to have acquired his gift for poetry and prophecy by eating a salmon from the well of wisdom. The story existed in writing by the ninth century, but Gaelic storytellers were still reciting oral versions of it in the nineteenth and twentieth centuries. Here is Angus McLellan's version, recorded in South Uist in 1960. The translator renders the fish in question as 'trout' but I have it on good authority that in South Uist, a *breac* is a salmon.

> 'One day, alone on the hill, the boy Finn saw a man fishing in a river and asked him for one of his trout. The man refused, but said he would put out his rod for another one for Finn. The next trout is the finest he has ever caught and he refuses to part with it. Again, he tells Finn that he can have the next one. The fisherman put out his rod again, and another trout took the bait. When he landed it, it was much finer than the first one.'Will you give it to me now?' said Finn. 'You can have it, but you must cook it without putting a mark of burning on it, and you must give me my choice portion of it.' 'You'll get that,' said Finn.
>
> 'Finn went and put the trout on a flat stone and collected wood, and made a fire before it, and the trout began to cook on the stone. Then a red-hot splinter jumped out of the fire and fell on the trout and raised a blister on it. Finn put his forefinger on it to burst it, and burnt his forefinger, and put his forefinger in his mouth. That was when Finn got the power of divination, from the trout.'

Ever afterwards, when he wanted to know the whereabouts of animals or something that was happening at a distance, he put his finger in his mouth, under this 'knowledge tooth' and the answer would come to him, so the story goes.

salmon using special flies that include female pubic hair in their design.

One of the finest salmon fly tiers in the world was a woman. Megan Boyd lived alone in Kintradwell in Sutherland, close to the River Brora, famed for its fine salmon fishing. In an obituary in the *New York Times* in 2001, Douglas Martin wrote: 'From tiny strands of hair she made magic: the classic Scottish flies like the *Jock Scott, Silver Doctor* and *Durham Ranger*; American favourites like the *Green Butt* and *Woolly Hugger*; and the fly named after her, the *Megan Boyd*, a nifty blue and black number famous for attracting salmon at the height of summer, when the water is low, hot and dead.' Megan Boyd never fished herself, yet knew more about the river and its salmon than anyone, and claimed that she would never have killed one. Through her own choice she had neither electricity nor water and worked tirelessly for up to 16 hours a day tying her legendary flies. When she was awarded the British Empire Medal, she replied to the Queen that she could not go to collect it, as she had no one to look after her dog. Prince Charles presented the award to her later in Scotland.

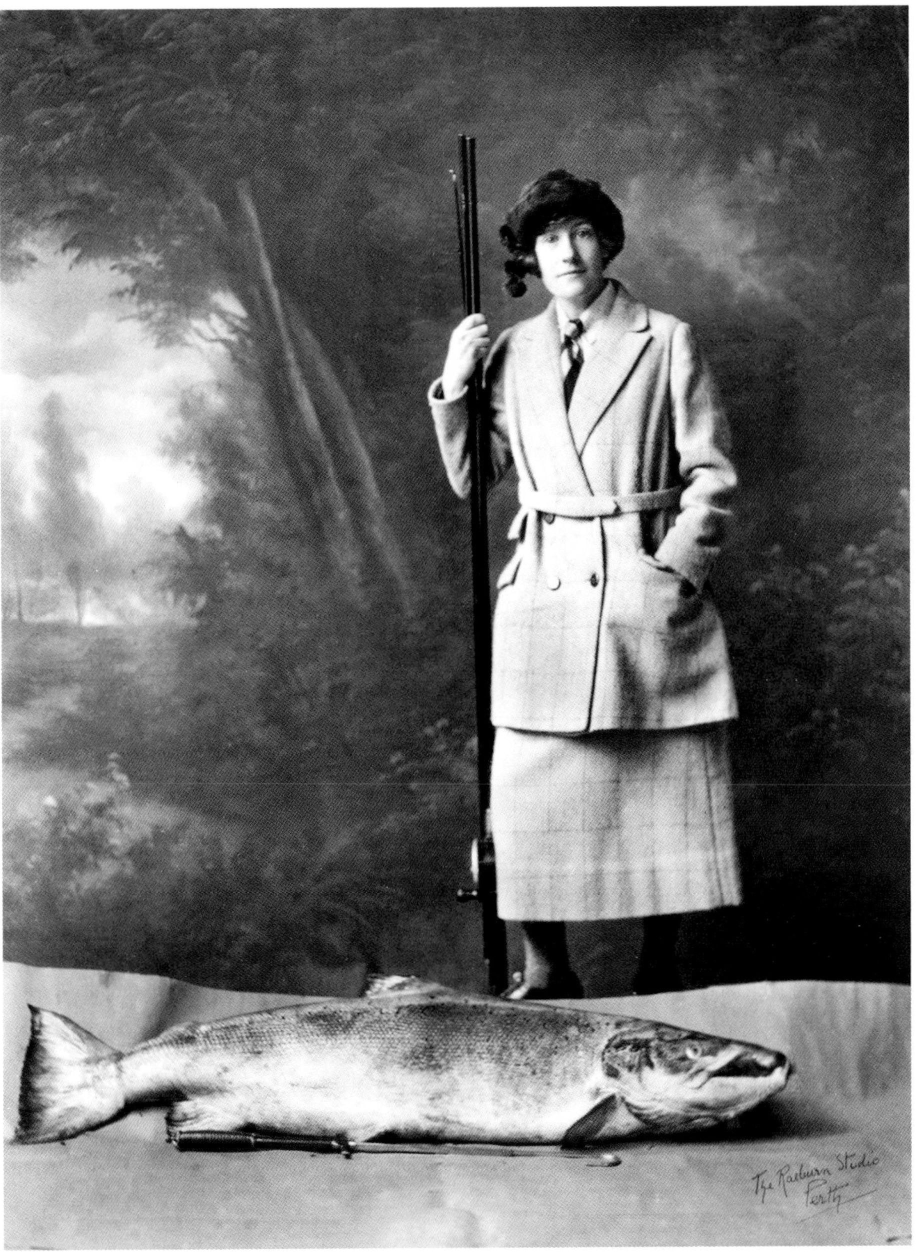

Georgina Ballantine caught a 64-pound salmon on the River Tay near Caputh in 1922 (© Licensor www.scran.ac.uk)

The Future of the Scottish Salmon

Salmon face many problems and there are concerns about their drop in number. Hydro-electric schemes on many good salmon rivers have been controversial and have doubtlessly changed the ecology of our rivers. At Pitlochry, a huge fish ladder has been made on the River Tummel. Here an average of 5,000 fish are counted every year, and are a major autumn tourist attraction with a specially constructed viewing window, walkway and underwater CCTV cameras enabling close views of salmon travelling up the ladder.

The increase of commercial fish farming all over Scotland has proved extremely detrimental to wild salmon stocks. Sea lice infest farm salmon and are a serious threat that can quickly wipe out fish stocks. Escaped farmed salmon are also changing the genetics of wild salmon as they hybridise with them, and this may be affecting their homing instincts.

Most fishermen now put back their catches after first recording the weight. Efforts are also being made to revitalise fish stocks and many rivers have hatcheries where young wild fish are nurtured before being released.

Leaping brown trout (Laurie Campbell)

Brown Trout

Salmo trutta
S: broonie
G: *breac*

Fondly nicknamed 'broonie', the brown trout favours clear oxygenated waters in areas of high rainfall. Many a Scots country child has cut their angling teeth while guddling for gleaming golden trout in a hill burn, or fishing with a long stick, using a worm attached to a bent pin on a string.

Trout in holy wells

In Ireland, holy wells were often said to contain fish, usually trout or salmon, and occasionally eels. Such fish were protected and never eaten. There are fewer reports of this in Scotland, but the well at Kilbride in south-west Skye once contained a trout which was important to local people. According to Martin Martin, 'the natives are very tender of it, and although they often chance to catch it in their wooden pails, they are very careful to preserve it from being destroyed.' He also mentions the Shiant well in the north of Skye. This was still a major centre of pilgrimage at the end of the seventeenth century, with people coming to it from abroad as well as from other parts of the island. They would take the waters, walk three times sunwise round the well and leave offerings on the capstone, all traditional activities at an old holy place. But there was more: 'There is a little freshwater lake within ten yards of the said well; it abounds with trouts, but neither the natives nor strangers will ever presume to destroy any of them, such is the esteem they have for the water.'

When held over a campfire using an improvised heather utensil, the taste of the tiniest trout will never be forgotten.

'Trout tickling' is an old technique used by the best poachers and countrymen that involves a lot of patience. Lying on the bank the tickler carefully puts a hand into the shallows and the lazing trout is gently tickled before being grabbed unawares and whipped from the water.

Brown trout spawn during September and October. The female lays her eggs in a 'redd' (a scrape cut out of the gravel in the burn or riverbed). The fertilised eggs take approximately 150 days to develop into tiny fry that remain in the nursery burn for a year before either moving to a larger tributary, loch or river, or in the case of those that become migratory sea trout, moving out to sea.

Salmon and rainbow trout farming has had a detrimental effect on brown trout populations, with infestations of sea lice from farmed fish causing high mortality rates amongst wild stock. The sea trout, also highly prized by anglers, begins its life cycle as a brown trout. Some brown trout spend all their time in lochs and rivers. Others travel out to sea where they grow larger and then return as sea trout to spawn in their natal sites some time later.

In small fishing lochs, pike heavily predate brown trout. In a *Shooting Times* article from the mid 1900s there was a report of desperate measures being employed to rid a large loch of troublesome pike on Lord Bute's island estate. It involved blowing up the water with dynamite before restocking it with brown trout. Cones of water up to one hundred feet high shot into the air and the pike must have had their comeuppance. Dynamite not only destroys live fish but their food as well.

In some lochs ferox trout are highly sought after. These predatory brown trout have aggressive-looking hooked bottom jaws known as a kype, and grow to a large size. The rapid weight increase is due to their cannibalistic habits as they feed on other brown trout, charr (a smaller species of trout-like fish, see page 109) and other fish. The rod record for one such ferox trout is a 31lb 12oz individual caught on Loch Awe. The oldest ferox trout is thought to have been 23 years old.

Charr

Salvelinus alpinus
S: red waim
G: *tarragan*

Arctic charr have inhabited Scottish lochs since the last Ice Age. They are closely related to salmon and trout and have many of the same characteristics. However, they are found in land-locked waters and in particular in some of Scotland's deeper lochs. Their colours vary greatly, and they were thought to be several different species. During the spawning season, charr's colours become impressive. Individuals may be almost blue-black, dotted with brilliant-orange spots. Charr are frequently smoked and are a delicacy, although like many fish, they should be eaten as fresh as possible, preferably straight out of the water.

In some lochs, ferox trout prey on charr (see page 108). With the increase in fish farming, charr are becoming larger because they feed on spilt fish feed. Charr are revered and fishermen regard catching one as a lucky bonus when out fishing for brown trout.

Top. Charr – lucky dip if you catch one (David Hay)

Above. Pike, or Old Lucius, is a voracious predator (David Hay)

Pike

Esox lucius
S: Old Lucius
G: *geadas*

The pike has long had a reputation for being ferocious and is nicknamed the 'freshwater shark' and 'Old Lucius'. Long-lived and with backward-facing teeth and an elongated snout, its aggression is well documented. Few creatures are safe when a pike is around – they frequently prey on both adult and young waterbirds, rats, water voles, amphibians and other fish. Their food consumption is legendary. Tales of them taking dogs and cats that approach too close to the water are probably exaggerated, although their presence in fishing ponds, trout lochs and rivers is undesirable.

Despite this, the pike is a popular fish in its own right, and for the coarse fisherman who chooses a day's solitary sport in a remote area, catching a huge pike is the high point. Keen fisherman Robert Harris once caught a large pike on a remote hill loch above Ballinluig in Perthshire, and found that it contained an undigested jack snipe. Some pike grow enormous, and females tend to be larger than males. In Loch Ken in Dumfries and Galloway, a site famed for its pike, a 73lb monster was caught in 1774. Loch Lomond, Loch Awe, and many of the lochs in the Trossachs are also famous for pike fishing.

Pike may be very difficult to catch at times and are said to be capricious in taking the bait. This merely adds to the excitement of trying to outwit Old Lucius.

Rainbow Trout

Oncorhynchus mykiss

Anglers have become accustomed to rainbow trout as part of their sport. It is hard to remember that they are not native to Britain, having been introduced from North America. The first arrived at Sir James Maitland's estate at Howietoun near Stirling in 1884. Between 1888 and 1905 many more rainbow trout eggs were brought to Lochbuie on Mull, Inverness-shire and Aberdeenshire, and the species soon became popular with anglers all over Scotland.

Rainbow trout are said to be easily acclimatised but difficult to naturalise. However, some rainbow trout now breed naturally in this country. In 1975 a self-maintaining colony of rainbow trout was discovered in a hill loch near Loch Loyne, by A.F. Walker of the Freshwater Fisheries Laboratory at Faskally. The loch had been stocked 17 years previously, with no fish introduced since.

Jim Reid and rainbow trout (Alex Murray)

The rainbow trout became important for restocking ponds and lochs. It was caught by anglers and helped to take pressure off brown trout fishing when its numbers were falling due to pollution, hydro-electric schemes and intensive fish farming. Many fish farms rear rainbows both for restocking purposes and as table trout. Hotels and restaurants take fish ideally weighing between 8oz and 1lb, and serve them grilled with almonds.

Due to their greed, rainbow trout grow fast. When farmed, their feed contains an added ingredient to help make their flesh pink. Fish that do not take up this pink colouration are not so popular for the table. People are now accustomed to eating pink-fleshed rainbow trout and perhaps associate it more with the succulent flesh of salmon. Some farmed fish can grow very large but they tend to make better eating when smoked. Many claim that smoked rainbow trout is less rich and oily than smoked salmon and actually prefer it.

Rainbow trout, as the name suggests, are beautifully marked and have an iridescent sheen. Fishermen regard the rainbow as a good fighter, and anglers with hooked fish may even be towed in a small boat up and down a pond or loch as the fish fights for its life. Very young anglers may catch their first fish at rainbow trout fisheries, and this can be the trigger for a lifetime's passion for angling.

IN AND OUT OF THE WATER

Common Frog

Rana temporaria
S: puddock, paddock
G: *losgann, smàigean, leumach*

Childhood fascination with frogspawn can forge a lifelong interest in natural history. The metamorphosis of tadpoles into perfect frogs is one of nature's many miracles.

Every year in spring small ponds and lochans become a veritable soup of fornicating frogs. Thousands of amphibians gather from the surrounding area and move to their spawning grounds, lured by the scent of glycolic acid produced from the algae in the water. The females are heavily bloated with eggs, and the smaller, eager males are ready to fertilise the seasonal glut of eggs. Each female produces approximately 3,000 eggs per season. The male frog has specially adapted pads on his forelegs that allow him to grip tightly onto the female. Following fertilisation, the eggs develop into tadpoles after three weeks. The tiny tadpoles have external gills that turn inwards after a month. By about seven weeks, hind legs begin to develop, followed by front legs when they have reached three months of age. Although ponds and ditches seem to overflow with spawn, it may be frosted and predators including beetles, herons, fish, newts, and otters, stoats and weasels devour many tadpoles. Weasels have been known to take away pairs of frogs from the pond-side, presumably to store for later. Herons too take full advantage of the buy-one-get-one-free seasonal bonanza as unsuspecting copulating frogs are hurriedly consumed.

Frogs can be found at quite high altitudes and sometimes lay their eggs in tiny freshwater pools. Otters frequently travel up hill burns in pursuit of an easy meal during the spring.

Wet weather often seems to coincide with large numbers of minute frogs leaving their birth ponds, which gave rise to the belief that it rained frogs. The date on which this happens does not vary much, with only a few days' difference in instances of particularly bad weather.

The smaller male frog grasps the egg-bloated female during the short breeding season (Polly Pullar)

A frog's colour is dependent on its habitat. Some can be a deep reddish-brown while others are almost bright green. All belong to the same species but living in acidic conditions (peaty soils and sphagnum moss) can make a frog change its guise.

Common Toad

Bufo bufo
S: taid, gangrel, yird, puddock
G: *mial-mhàgag, losgann dubh, gille-cràigein, putog*

There is a frequent confusion between frogs and toads. Toads have a distinctive warty appearance and seem less shiny when out of water. Due to their unpleasant looks, they have long been seen as venomous beasts, associated with witchcraft and bizarre medicines. The warty lumps behind their eyes secrete a toxic substance that helps

The common toad, all too often misunderstood, yet a wonderful creature in need of our utmost respect (Polly Pullar)

protect them from predators. Wheatear eggs were once thought to have hatched into young toads, and stonechats supposedly incubated them on occasions. Toads were often found in fields where piles of stones provide nesting habitat for wheatears and stonechats. The rank growth beneath provides a dank parlour for a shy toad, and this must have been the reason for such a strange belief.

Toads are less aquatic than frogs. They spend much of the year in damp, dark places but, like frogs, they have a strong homing instinct and travel great distances to traditional spawning ponds. They usually arrive between 10 and 14 days later than frogs. On occasions, local authorities have been forced to close the road leading to Arthur's Seat in Edinburgh to allow a mass of toads to cross in safety.

In the *Oban Times* of April 1985, a midsummer toad explosion was expected on the island of Luing. It was apparently not the breeding toads *en route* to their spawning ground (in a disused slate quarry at Cullipool) that caused the problem, but the fact that the emergent young toads were reported to coincide with the mass of holidaymakers taking advantage of the Glasgow Fair Holiday fortnight in July. Toads finding their way under doors and into houses, and even into beds in the area, were highly unwelcome.

The breeding time is a frenzy, and it is common to see one unfortunate female toad embraced by so many males that it is impossible to work out whose legs and bodies belong to whom. The females may be killed in this way, either strangled or suffocated by the males' mad desire to mate.

Toad's eggs are laid in long strings and attached to leaf material within the pond. Toad spawn develops in much the same way as frogspawn, which produces free-swimming tadpoles. Like frogs, toads may also vary in colour depending on the habitat where they spend most of their time.

Toads are long-lived. In captivity some have lived for over 30 years. They were once kept in cellars to keep houses free of cockroaches and other insect pests, and have long been seen as the gardener's friend due to their ability to eat copious numbers of slugs.

Due to the toad's toxins, a dog picking one up may froth at the mouth. Although this is an unpleasant experience for the dog, it is not thought to cause any damage. Human toad-eaters used to perform in circus acts and fun fair sideshows, and toads were also used for early cancer treatments. Applying one to an afflicted area was believed to draw out poisons. Farmworkers used to rub a live toad onto sprained arms or legs – there is no evidence to prove that these measures did any good, however. Toads are benign, ponderous creatures that have long been misunderstood.

The king frog of Morvern

A giant frog or toad is said to have lived in the bog at Achagavel in Morvern. A man claimed to have heard it often, yelping like a mastiff puppy, but it was never caught. At that time, in many parts of Europe, toads' heads were believed to contain a stone with powerful therapeutic properties. This made the Morvern 'king frog' an exciting proposition for hunters, and John Gregorson Campbell records an incident in which a man took his trained otter to Achagavel in the hope of making a fast buck. It was winter and the bog was frozen over, so he made a hole in the ice and sent the otter down. There he crouched, ready to smash the head of the amphibian when it appeared, but succeeded only in killing his trained otter when it came back to the surface to breathe.

Common Newt

Trituris vulgaris
S: ask, esk, man-keeper
G: *dearc, dearc-luachrach*

Palmate Newt

Trituris helveticus

Great Crested Newt

Trituris cristatus

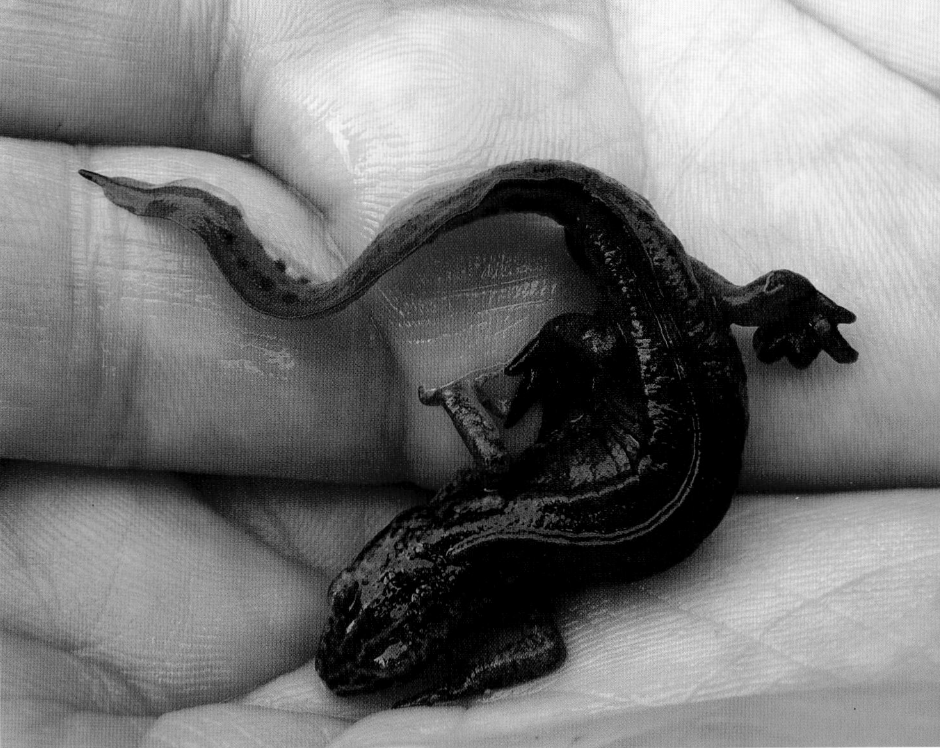

Like frogs and toads, newts have a particular attraction for children
(Polly Pullar)

Newts are frequently confused with lizards, although the former are amphibious. They hibernate in winter and often move in large numbers to their spawning grounds: ponds and small freshwater ditches. Here they attach their eggs to leaves and vegetation in the water. Like frogs and toads, the newt's homing instinct is strong and they usually return to the pools where they were initially spawned. They feed on tiny animal life: freshwater shrimps, dragonfly larvae and small molluscs.

The most common newt in Scotland is the palmate, although both the common and palmate may occur in the same places. Like other amphibians, newts start as tadpoles that metamorphose into tiny newts called 'efts'. The efts are vulnerable and are frequently eaten by fish and other predators.

The largest, most rare, and most spectacular newt is the great crested, named after the male in breeding condition which has a large crest, black spots and an orange belly. Small populations of great crested newts are only found in a few locations in Scotland and are of international importance. They may grow as large as 16 centimetres in length. Also called the 'warty newt' due to their lumpy skin, like the toad they secrete toxins from the warts. A Victorian naturalist was brave enough to put one in her mouth to see what would happen. It induced her to foam at the mouth and have minor convulsions, but she lived to tell the tale. The toxins help to protect the newt from predators. Loss of habitat is of concern for these ancient amphibians, and the introduction of fish to their breeding ponds for sporting purposes has also added to a general decline in numbers.

Great crested newts are inconspicuous, and this may be one of the reasons why they have been around for approximately 20 million years in an unaltered state.

The eel may look ordinary but its life cycle is fascinating and complex (David Hay)

Deadly eel stew

Scottish eels have usually been spared the frying pan. People have been wary about eating them, perhaps because of their snake-like ability to migrate overland and their sudden appearance, as if from nowhere, often on moonless nights. Some said they were not fish at all but horse-hairs which had grown and come to life. In the ballad tradition, eels are the main ingredient of the deadly stew which kills Lord Randall or Lord Ronald:

> 'What got ye for dinner, Lord Ronald, my son?
> What got ye for dinner, my handsome young man?'
> 'I got eels boiled in broth, mother, make my bed soon,
> For I'm weary o' huntin' and fain would lie doon.'

The source of these eels ('from my father's black ditch') sounds particularly unwholesome, and Ronald's sweetheart gets the blame for his poisoning.

PRIMAL PAST

Eel

Anguilla anguilla
S: eel
G: *easgann, sìol-mhòr*

It is said that to put a live eel in the drink of an alcoholic is a sure way to cure them of their affliction. Certainly such a bizarrely fascinating close encounter would be memorable. The expression 'as slippery as an eel' is literal, for eels are almost impossible to handle.

Eels have a complex life cycle. It begins far out in the Sargasso Sea, referred to as 'the only sea without shores', in the middle of the North Atlantic. Here adult eels lay eggs that eventually hatch into transparent larvae known as leptocephali. These develop into minute translucent worm-like creatures called elvers, which miraculously navigate the ocean currents, finding their way to particular river systems where they enter as 'glass eels'. Unlike salmon, the young eels are unable to negotiate waterfalls and instead take to land in order to reach a particular destination. Eels are long-lived. It takes a female seven years to mature, while a male needs 15 years before he is ready to breed.

Eels are caught in traps set in lochs. Special otter guards now help to protect otters from drowning when caught up in them. Eels are thickly coated in glutinous slime and experienced eel trappers sometimes use newspaper to absorb this. They are oily and high in fat, and although smoked eel has long been viewed as a delicacy in Scotland, they are an acquired taste. Eels are important prey for a large range of wildlife including otters, herons, fish, and other birds.

An old Orkney rhyme relates to the eel and is a version of the well-known nursery rhyme 'Eenny, meeny, miny mo':

> *Eenny, meeny, miny mo*
> *Cast a knot apin your tail*
> *An' then we'll let you go.*

Lamprey

S: nine-eyed eel
G: *creathall, rochuaid*

The weird-looking prehensile lamprey comes from an ancient order of vertebrates, *agnathan* (jawless fish). With no scales, gill covers nor bony skeleton, this cartilaginous creature is parasitic on other fish, feeding by latching onto them using its rasp-like tongue and sharp teeth to extract blood and tissue. There are three types of lamprey found in Scotland: the sea lamprey (*Petromyzon marinus*), brook lamprey (*Lampetra planeri*) and river lamprey (*Lampetra fluviatallis*). The Latin group name, *Petromyzonidae*, means 'stone sucker'.

Lampreys were once a delicacy, indeed such was their popularity that two English kings, Henry the First and King John, were both said to have died due to their over-indulgence as they feasted on lamprey. Lamprey is rich and fatty and both kings' greed led to severe indigestion. Smoked lamprey was also popular and is still widely eaten in parts of Europe.

Lampreys lay their eggs in scrapes among stones in running water. The young hatch into tiny blind elongated larvae called 'ammocoetes'. They live in silt for up to five years, eventually metamorphosing before migrating to sea to mature, returning to rivers to breed as adults three to four years later. Lampreys are now strictly protected and have become rare in many waters, with numbers falling dramatically due to pollution, hydro-electric schemes and general changes in the ecology of their habitat.

Lamprey showing its extraordinary mouth parts (David Hay)

Pearl mussel – discarded shells on a river bank are often the only signs of a poacher's work (Laurie Campbell)

PUSHED TO THE LIMIT

Freshwater Pearl Mussel

Margaritifera margaritifera
G: *feusgan*

Half the world's breeding population of the rare pearl mussel is found in Scottish rivers. Longer lived than the familiar sea mussel, they may be almost as large as a hand, and are almost as old as the hills.

Pearl mussels are filter feeders and are valuable for their role as natural water purifiers. Their presence in a river is beneficial to salmon and trout as well as a wide range of other fish. The female mussel develops eggs inside her shell. These are fertilised by sperm released into the water by the male. During the summer millions of tiny larvae, future mussels, appear in the river but approximately 95 per cent die. Some are carried on the gills of young fish and may drop off onto sand or gravel beds in the river, but many are consumed or washed downstream. Pearl mussel reproduction is a slow process – sexual maturity is not reached until at least ten years of age.

Pearl mussels depend on clean, clear, fast-running rivers. Although legally protected, they are seriously endangered by relentless poaching activity. Only a very few of these molluscs have a valuable pearl inside them, yet they have been exploited since the twelfth century. Alexander the First was reputed to own one of the finest collections of freshwater pearls. In 1621 the huge 'Kellie pearl' was found on a tributary of the River Ythan in Aberdeenshire. The Lord Provost of Aberdeen presented it to King James

VI, and it is now incorporated in the Scottish crown jewels, housed in the Crown Room at Edinburgh Castle.

'The Parl', a fourteenth-century medieval poem, makes reference to pearl mussels in Scottish rivers. Today, more than a third of Scottish rivers that once had healthy populations no longer have any. The battle to stop poaching continues. Many stretches of river where mussels are found are inaccessible and it is impossible to police such large areas. Often all that remains of a night's mussel poaching is a telltale heap of discarded shells on the bank.

The story of the Abernethy Pearl, or 'Little Willie', relates how in 1967, pearl fisherman William Abernethy found the largest pearl recorded in a Scottish mussel, in the River Tay. Impressively round, he sold it to Cairncross, the Perth jewellers, for an undisclosed sum. Gypsies, travellers and tinkers were usually the most adept pearl fishermen – finding a pearl was a chance to keep their large families fed for weeks or even years.

Rare black pearls and others with distinctive milky hues are highly sought, although there are stiff penalties for poachers today. Previously incorporated in brooches, rings, earrings and necklaces, Scottish freshwater pearls have a high aesthetic value and are still available as antiques.

William Abernethy displaying a pearl still embedded in a mussel, Perthshire 1973 (© National Museums Scotland. Licensor www.scran.ac.uk)

The Abernethy Pearl

Interviewing the Travellers of the North-west Highlands for his book *The Summer Walkers,* Timothy Neat reveals pearl fisher Eddie Davis's views on the Abernethy Pearl:

> After that – goldrush. Murder. They were coming up in droves. People were leaving their jobs. Eleven thousand pounds it was valued at. They were going down in wet suits. They slaughtered the rivers. They'd work the river like a factory – big gangs of them. They slaughtered the Tay, they came up the Spey, they slaughtered it. It was the new A9, it was the motorcar, you see in the old days it was all walk, camp out, walk on – just two or three of us. Like farmers, here and there we'd pause and leave a bed undisturbed for future years. But these were cowboys! By nineteen eighty, the old-time pearl fishers up here in Sutherland, we were picking at a carcase. It was the buffalo all over again! Don't get me started on that, it breaks my heart.

CHAPTER FIVE

THE SEA

INTRODUCTION

'How worthy of honour is the sea,' a saying translated from the Gaelic, '*Nach Urramach an Cuan*', bears testament to our long association with the marine environment. The sea can be said to dominate Scotland: it has provided a fine source of food and a constant challenge from the time of the first settlers to the present day. Hunter-gatherers gleaned the shore for shellfish including limpets, whelks, mussels and small crabs, while the earliest fishermen took to the water in primitive craft in search of fish. During times of famine, a small shellfish or fish may have meant the difference between life and death for the earliest settlers, and for a poor crofter during the eighteenth century.

The deeper ocean remains a mystery. However much we strive to understand its complexities, there will always be more to discover. As well as large impressive species such as cetaceans, tropical or deep-sea rarities appear on occasions in Scottish waters, driven by subtle differences in water temperature through climate change, or simply by massive oceanic storms. Sightings of sunfish (*Mola mola*), and leatherback turtles (*Dermochelys coriacea*) are being recorded more frequently in Scotland. One turtle, washed ashore in the Shetland Islands in 2000, weighed in the region of a ton and was thought to be over 100 years old. These rarities from tropical and sub-tropical waters appear here when the seas are at their warmest in late summer.

Our coastline is home to many hidden treasures. There are the long sweeping bays of the Western Isles with only the footprints of livestock and wildlife marking the flat, white sands. To the east, next to the thriving city of Dundee, the Tay estuary and nearby Tentsmuir Forest are fringed by vast seashore that provides breeding grounds for hundreds of grey seals as well as a wealth of other flora and fauna. Many little harbours along the east coast once held thriving fishing communities and they still retain their charm even though numbers of boats are severely diminished due to fishing quotas.

Some rocky shores have abundant seaweeds and teeming rock pools. Shifting shingle beaches, raised beaches, mudflats, estuaries, salt marshes and great bastion-like cliffs all provide varied environments with a specialised plant cover that is wholly dependent on the height of the tides, and on a varying degree of salt tolerance. Wind, sun, altitude, rainfall and sea spray all play a vital role in sculpting these unique habitats with their distinctive plant communities.

The shore is divided into zones: the inter-tidal or 'littoral' zone relates to the area where land and sea meets between

Opposite. Brough of Birsay, Orkney (Polly Pullar)

Unloading herring at Arbroath harbour, nineteenth century (© Arbroath Herald. Licensor www.scran.ac.uk)

the high and low tide. A nutrient-rich broth of saltwater feeds this twice daily. The inter-tidal zone may be further divided into the low tide zone, the mid-tide zone, high tide zone, and the splash zone. The largest, down to the most microscopic creatures favour particular parts of the shore. Abundant seaweed growth enables areas to maintain valuable moisture once the tide has gone out, and provides further habitat for a host of other diverse communities.

Tides are governed by the gravitational pull of the moon and sun. In a 24-hour period there are two high and two low tides, but the timing of these tides alters each day. Fishermen and those who collect shellfish use tide tables to check the optimum times for working at sea.

We love the sea despite the fact that we do not understand it completely. Busy tourist ports such as Oban in the west, with its wheeling gulls, curious seals, and stalls selling shellfish on the pier front, are proof that for many Scots, the sea and its abundant wildlife have always been a vital ingredient for our well-being.

The Fishing Industry

Fish provided an important source of food for the earliest settlers. Ancient kitchen middens at prehistoric sites in Orkney and Shetland contained fish remains, showing the value of fish as a food source at that time. The early fishermen used lines sometimes bated with limpets, as they fished to sustain their families. In medieval times, fish were an important resource and were also exported. Small fishing villages sprang up all around Scotland's coast and the fishing industry began to grow apace. The government encouraged fisheries, and boats were specially adapted to certain types of fish, with licences issued and bounties paid to owners of larger vessels.

The early nineteenth century saw the start of the 'Great Herring Boom', with an astonishing 30,000 fishing boats operating off the East Coast during the winter and spring, and off the northern coast and Shetland in summer. Herring had to be cured fast due to its fat content, and at the peak of the boom Scotland was exporting huge amounts of salted fish. Boats followed the 'silver darlings', and with them went an entourage of hardy women to process the fish. In order to catch white fish, long lines were used, bated with hundreds of hooks. Whole families helped, although on boats travelling into deeper waters, it was the fishermen themselves who had to do the work, with some lines stretching for many miles.

By the late nineteenth century steam-powered boats had been introduced. On-board winches could haul larger nets in and the catch increased in size. By the beginning of the twentieth century, a vast number of barrels of fish were being harvested annually.

The onset of the First World War took many fishermen away to fight and by the time they returned, the industry was in serious decline. By 1939 when the Second World War broke out, the decline had deepened. After the war was over, the government assisted the total rejuvenation of the East Coast fish industry, and efforts were concentrated on white fish: cod, haddock, halibut, saithe and flat fish. Mackerel were also popular. Trawling and purse netting were the main methods of catching fish. However due to over-fishing there was another serious decline in fish stocks and the industry was badly affected. Hundreds of fishermen were forced to abandon their boats, and fishing towns and villages that were once thriving hubs became ghost towns due to the resulting recession.

In recent times, the industry has been heavily regulated, with quotas on fish catches imposed on larger operators based at the bigger fishing ports of Peterhead, Aberdeen, Fraserburgh and Shetland. Huge boats with sophisticated sonar equipment, large winches and on-board fish processing plants have totally altered the camaraderie once found in the small fishing ports of the eighteenth and nineteenth centuries. The white fish industry has now become extremely complex as laws and legislation governing fishermen make it hard for them to survive. However, crashes in fish stocks necessitate quotas and only by careful monitoring will fish stocks recover. Boat owners have had to diversify and many now concentrate on shellfish, using smaller boats.

CATCH OF THE DAY

Atlantic Cod

Gadus morhua
G: *bodach-ruadh, trosg, cailleach*

The cod has been the most important fish in Scotland since the Viking era. Once abundant, it was caught in great numbers, but due to the sea's rising temperature and grossly negligent over-fishing, cod stocks continue to cause ongoing concerns and are the subject of intense political debate. Indeed, the 'Cod Wars' were sparked by arguments about territorial fishing rights between Iceland and Britain. The first scenes of confrontation began in the 1950s and continued on into the 1970s, when on occasion the Royal Navy was deployed as rival vessels actually rammed one another. Some fishermen demanded government compensation due to their loss of earnings. Finally Iceland achieved its aims and its fishing zones were expanded, much to the detriment of the beleaguered Scottish white fish industry.

Cod may grow very large: up to six feet in length (1.8 metres) and 200lbs in weight. Adapted to survive in cold, deep waters, they spawn from February to March where the water is shallower. Cod's roe is delicious and available in fish shops at this time. The parboiled roe can be fried and eaten with lemon and pepper, and is equally popular smoked. Some claim that the cod's chunky white flesh is the most delicious fish of all. Cod livers are the source of the world's best-selling food supplement – cod liver oil, rich in vitamins A, D and E, and other valuable properties. It is thought to promote good joint health.

Removing cod's roe, Gourdon, Kincardineshire (Polly Pullar)

Giant cod

A fisherman from the south end of Skye once lost his terrier to a giant cod. Believe this if you can. It leapt over the side of the boat in pursuit of the fish as it escaped being hauled aboard and was last seen disappearing into its gaping mouth. Next year, the man caught the same fish again. It was enormously fat and seemed to have something stuck in its throat. Lo and behold, there was the terrier '*agus trì chuileanan aice*' ('and with three puppies').

Atlantic Herring

Clupea harengus
S: herrin, scattan
G: *sgadan*

The 'silver darling' is a beautiful, shining oily fish which used to occur in huge shoals offshore. It was so abundant that it spawned a vast thriving industry, but sadly this fish provides a perfect example of the effects of over-fishing, for it is never seen in vast shoals today.

During the nineteenth century, you could have once walked from one end of a large fishing port to the other across hundreds of boats moored as closely together as sardines packed in a tin, such was the popularity of herring fishing. In 1907 the industry peaked and an astonishing 250,000 tons was cured and exported.

In Europe, most herring are smoked and made into kippers. Loch Fyne kippers have long been prized. They appear on the menu of many a good Scottish bed and breakfast establishment. For many years they have been caught in the waters of Loch Fyne in Argyllshire, and traditionally cured over oak fires. They are renowned to be Scotland's finest kippers. Herring are also served as rollmops, pickled in spices and vinegar and sometimes wrapped round a pickled onion. Fresh herring are often fried in oatmeal and then served with potatoes, and were once vitally important as a staple food. The fine skeleton of a herring has given rise to the popular term to describe a distinctive regular woven pattern on tweed and other material – 'herring bone'.

Fish or flesh?

A giant skate caused panic once in the fish market in Crail. Rev. James Hall records the incident in his *Travels in Scotland* (1807). Hall clearly enjoys the humour of the incident – and it does have a slapstick quality – but there were sensitivities in play:

> Some of the fishers here, had been lately much alarmed by a wonderful skate they had caught – a *lusus naturae*. This fish, having been brought on shore, lay quiet; but when they began to cut it, and prepare it for the market, it leaped from the table, bit and wounded many of them, and the pieces they had cut off leaped from place to place into the street. Amazement and terror seized every beholder, and they ran from it; but one of them, who was an elder of the Kirk, venturing to return, the rest in crowds followed him. At length they collected the pieces, which, being put together, seemed to collect new life; and having provided a decent coffin, they buried the fish, though not in the churchyard, yet as near the churchyard-wall as possible. As it was enormously large, they all supposed that it had fed upon some human body at the bottom of the sea, and had, with the flesh, imbibed some of the nature and feelings of man.

Hall had probably never been pastor of a fishing community. Burying the skate in consecrated ground was out of the question, but whoever came up with the compromise plan of laying it to rest, in a coffin, as close to the churchyard as possible, was perhaps more sensitive to local feelings. Who knows what human tragedies had occurred recently?

Haddock

Melanogrammus aeglefinus
S: haddie, haddo
G: adag, iasg Pheadail

The haddock is a member of the cod family including other important food fish: hake, saithe, pollack and whiting. Haddock is the fish of choice for the fish supper, served with copious amounts of chips, salt and vinegar.

The haddock, like the cod, is a demersal fish – it lives near the seabed. It has a distinctive black spot on each shoulder. Haddock feed on small invertebrates as well as larger fish. They are caught year round, although due to over-fishing are becoming scarce. There are many traditional Scots dishes based around haddock. 'Finnan haddie' originated from the small fishing village of Findon in Kincardineshire. These smoked haddock are poached in milk and served for breakfast, while 'cullen skink', a famed, thick fish soup, comes from the town of that name in Morayshire. 'Crappit heids' was a dish concocted in times

Haddock and herring smoking, Gourdon, Kincardineshire, 1988 (Polly Pullar)

of poverty: fish livers and oatmeal were sometimes soaked in milk and then stuffed into haddock heads and cooked.

The 'Arbroath smokie' (dry smoked haddock) is a popular delicacy, sent all over the world. Subtle flavours for the smokie are achieved using oak and birch fires. The wood used for fish-smoking can alter the flavour completely and each smokery produces its own unique taste. After the early 1990s when new health and safety regulations were introduced, many antiquated smoke houses were forced to close down. Yet it was their dense layers of tar and blackened interiors that gave the fish such superb flavour and colour. Some smoked haddock are now artificially dyed instead. Smokehouses all along the east coast hung with lines of haddock and the preparation work brought employment for countless people.

Dinno burn me beens

Roast me and boil me
but dinno burn me beens
and I'll come and lie
at thee hert-steens.

In many places, it was bad luck to throw fish bones (especially the bones of Peter's fish, the haddock) or the shells of shellfish into the fire. There are several variations of the rhyme above. This one comes from Orkney and suggests that fish will surrender themselves willingly, literally to stones around your hearth, if you respect their mortal remains. Fish bones were sometimes fed to over-wintering cattle and also made good fertiliser, so the householder who kept them might indeed have fared better than the one who threw them away.

Cullen skink

This smoked fish soup is one of the classic dishes of the world. There are fast-food versions of it, but Mary got this slow-cooked version from her mother-in-law, Biddy Low who lived in Banff, just along the coast from Cullen, for many years. Some people thicken it with potato.

Ingredients:

1 large smoked haddock, filleted
2 large onions
3 pints water
1 pint milk
1 oz butter
2 tablespoons plain flour
1–2 blades of mace
parsley
salt and pepper to taste

Method:

Chop the onions and cut the haddock into small pieces. Put the water in a medium-sized pot and add the onions, chopped fish and the mace. Simmer gently for 2–3 hours. Make a white sauce using the milk, butter and flour. When the fish broth is ready, break it up roughly with a potato masher and add it to the white sauce, little by little, stirring all the time. Remove the mace, season and serve with a sprinkling of fresh parsley.

Mackerel

Scomber scombrus
G: *rionnach*

The beautiful, gleaming mackerel is a member of the tuna family. During the summer on the west coast, we used to take a boat out in the evenings and fish for mackerel when the shoals were in the area. With darrows hung with feathers, or simply pieces of wool to decorate the lines of hooks, dozens of fish would be hauled in once we had found a shoal.

Mackerel decay quickly due to acids and a build-up of toxins in their oily flesh. Eaten almost immediately they are unbeatable, but they quickly lose their magic and many are smoked for this reason. People from Fife have always appreciated mackerel, while it was said that some traditional Highlanders would not touch them. They believed the fish would turn to maggots in their stomachs when consumed. It was once illegal to sell mackerel on Sundays, as they would not be fresh enough.

The beautiful pattern on a mackerel's side has given rise to the term 'mackerel sky'; when the sky is flecked with soft cloud in a regular pattern. Usually a good spell of settled weather follows.

Sand eels

S: sandy-giddack
G: *easgann-gainmhich, sìolag*

Sand eels may seem insignificant due to their size, but they are a vital part of the marine food chain for many species including seabirds, marine mammals and other fish. In recent years there have been serious concerns about their dramatic drop in number. Global warming has been blamed and it is thought that this is having a direct effect on the ability of sand eel to spawn. Even more worrying was the catastrophic failure of many major seabird colonies around Scotland during the 1990s, when large amounts of auk, kittiwake and tern chicks were found dead or dying of starvation, thought to have been caused directly by the over-fishing of sand eels. Industrial fishing with indiscriminate use of small mesh nets, mainly by Danish fleets, has added to the demise of the diminutive sand eel, as well as huge numbers of wild birds that rely on it for feeding. Sand

Sand eels – a vital part of the marine ecosystem (Laurie Campbell)

eel fisheries are now regulated and have been banned altogether in some areas.

There are five species of sand eel found in Scotland's seas, but the most important one is the lesser sand eel, *Ammodytes marinus*. Sand eel fishing began in the 1950s and increased rapidly thereafter. Sand eels are used in the manufacture of animal feedstuffs: fishmeal and oils for both livestock and the fish-farming industry.

SEAFOOD PLATTER

Crab

Cancer pagurus
S: cruban, partan
G: *crùbag, partan, ruadhag*

Although the edible crab is less expensive than lobster and not viewed as a gourmet food, there are many that would disagree. Dressed crab served in its shell is delicious, popular in many Scottish seaside resorts and seafood restaurants.

Edible crabs are caught off Scotland each year and most are exported to Europe. They are usually served cold and, like lobsters, are cooked in boiling water whilst still alive. Their huge pincer-like claws are where the finest white meat is found, but the brown body meat is also good. A crab's stomach is inedible and the gills, referred to as deadman's fingers, must be removed.

The words 'crabbie' and 'crabbet' are frequently used to describe someone who is bad tempered. As crabs will endeavour to give you a nip with their powerful claws when caught, they are often seen as ill-natured. Crabs are fascinating creatures, and large ones found hidden amongst seaweed are of great interest to children playing on the

Partan bree

Partan bree is a traditional Scots crab soup.

Ingredients:
1 large boiled crab
3 oz long grain rice
1pint chicken stock
1pint milk
quarter pint single cream
half-teaspoon anchovy essence
salt and pepper to taste

Method:
Remove all the meat from the crab and set aside the flesh from the claws. Boil the rice in the milk until soft, but do not overcook. Add the crab meat, retaining the claw meat until later, and rub the mixture through a sieve into a clean pan. Bring to the boil gradually, stirring in the chicken stock. Remove from the heat and add the anchovy essence, the claw meat and salt and pepper to taste. Reheat but do not boil, then stir in the cream and when hot serve immediately. Serves 4.

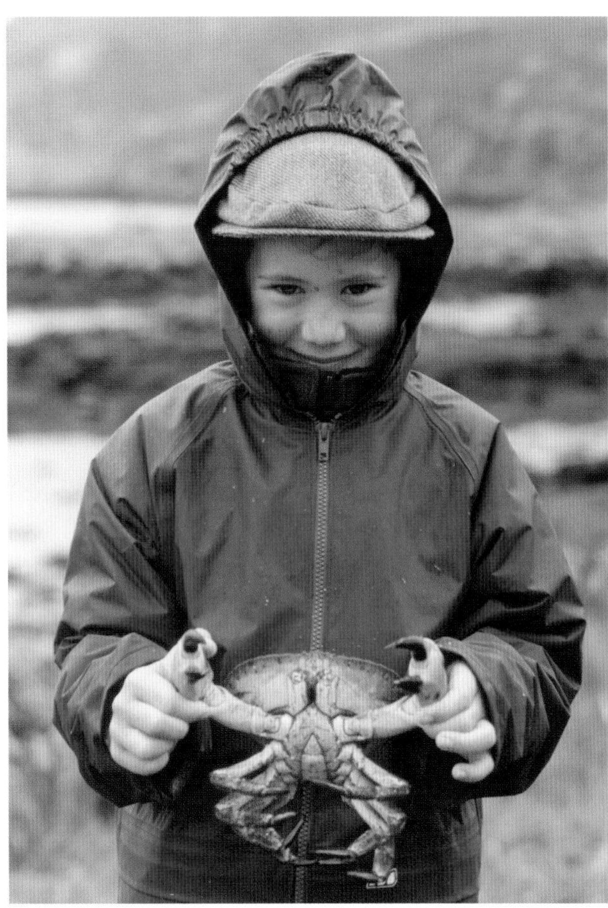

Right. Freddy Pullar with crab (Polly Pullar)

Opposite top. Lobster (Polly Pullar)

Opposite bottom. Oyster farmer Craig Archibald, Islay (Polly Pullar)

shore. The crabs often wave their large claws threateningly. They scurry off in a sideways manner due to the position of the eight legs on their bodies, the reason for this crabwise movement. Crabs eat a varied diet. They shed their hard shell each year and when the new one is still soft, they are vulnerable to predation.

Lobster

Homarus gammarus
S: lapster
G: *giomach*

Most people think of a lobster as being bright orange. While alive they are, in fact, a rich blue-black and only turn orange when boiled. Lobsters have been seen as a delicacy for many years and in the twelfth century they were caught by hand. Given that they have impressive claws of uneven sizes, a nipper and a crusher, this must have been a painful experience. The more conventional method of catching lobsters is in pots and creels baited with oily fish.

Much of the Scottish catch is sent to Europe where lobsters are extremely popular. In order to keep shellfish fresh, they are transported in special tanks called 'vivier' (from the French word *vivre*, to live). These tanks are specially designed to maintain the water conditions as naturally as possible. The lobsters have their claws banded to stop them fighting with one another on the journey. Boiling in water to kill shellfish remains a controversial subject and there are debates about whether or not lobsters, crabs, and prawns feel pain when killed in this way.

Lobsters may live for more than 50 years. They may also grow very large and heavy, although one recorded at almost 19 kilograms was exceptional. They are solitary and live in holes on the seabed, emerging at night to feed. They have four pairs of legs, and two pairs of sensitive antennae to help them locate prey. Some lobster fishermen refer to them as the 'fastest fish in the sea' – when lobsters are threatened they swim backwards at an impressive rate.

Once mature, lobsters moult annually and grow a new shell. After they are at least five years old, females will seek out males and mate when their new growing carapace (shell) is still soft. They produce thousands of orange eggs, storing them under their tails and carrying them for 11 months until they hatch as planktonic larvae. Females in this condition are referred to as 'berried' in reference to the berry-like roe. When the larvae reach a certain size, they burrow into the sand and spend approximately two years there until they eventually move to burrows of their own.

The Western Isles remain good fishing grounds for lobsters, and work is being done in other areas to make sustainable lobster fisheries: the Orkney Lobster Hatchery was started in 1985 to help create a fishery round the islands, and releases over 60,000 young lobsters each year.

Oyster

Ostrea edulis
G: *eisir*

Oysters are renowned for their aphrodisiacal properties. Opening them is a challenge, requiring deft use of a specialised, sharp knife. Oyster shells are thick and tightly fused and lead to many slip-ups and a bloodied finger. Gourmets usually eat oysters alive in their raw state, first loosened from their shells but served back in them, together with a glass of the finest champagne. Salty and slightly slippery in texture, large quantities consumed one after another are seen as an act of bravado. There is little proof, however, of their aphrodisiac powers.

Some oysters are ambisexual, starting off as males, then changing sex to reproduce before reverting to life as males again. Their nacreous (mother-of-pearl) shells often contain tiny pearls, although these rarely have any value. Oysters are raised at many suitable sites, including Loch Fyne in Argyll, and the islands of Colonsay and Islay. Craig and Tony Archibald farm oysters at Loch Gruinart on Islay, and grow the tiny spats in bags specially designed in Australia. In the warmth of the Gulf Stream, oysters thrive on rich nutrients from the sea as the water surrounding the bags is changed twice daily by the tide. They usually reach maturity at between one and three years of age. Large quantities are consumed on Islay during the island's annual Whisky Festival. At other times, they are sent abroad or marketed through Loch Fyne Oysters on the mainland.

Shellfish aplenty

'The Kyle [of Scalpay] affords oysters in such plenty, that commonly a spring-tide of ebb leaves fifteen, sometimes twenty horse-load [sic] of them on the sands. The sands on the coast of Bernstill [Bernisdale] village at the spring tides afford daily such a plenty of mussels as is sufficient to maintain sixty persons per day; and this was a great support to many poor families of the neighbourhood, in the late years of scarcity. The natives observe that all shellfish are plumper during a south-west wind, than when it blows from the north or north-east quarters. The limpet being parboiled with a very little quantity of water, the broth is drank [sic] to increase milk in nurses, and likewise when the milk proves astringent to the infants. The broth of the black periwinkle is used in the same cases. It is observed that limpets being frequently eat [sic] in June, are apt to occasion the jaundice ....'

Scallop shells encrusted with barnacles (Polly Pullar)

Scallop

G: *bainteag, creachan*

The remains of scallops and other shellfish are frequently dug up on ancient kitchen midden sites. Fossil remains of scallops date back to 400 BC. In more recent times the distinctive scallop shape has been used as the logo of a well-known oil company, Shell. Many households have empty scallop shells and use them as ashtrays, and there is an old Highland custom of drinking whisky from them.

Scallops are highly sought after, as they are one of the most delicious shellfish of all. During the 1950s, scallop dredging became popular and literally cleaned up the seabed, doing much damage to scallop numbers and the populations of countless other sea creatures. Hand-diving (literally diving under water and catching scallops by hand) is a far more sustainable method for harvesting these creatures. Scallops are bivalve molluscs that swim through the water by rapidly opening and closing their shells. They also burrow deep into the sand on the seabed. They are now regularly farmed and raised in mesh bags and, like much of Scotland's seafood, are a popular dish abroad.

Cockles, Mussels and Whelks

Barra's famous sweeping Cockle Strand beach is also an airfield, although the plane timetable must be synchronised with the tides. Cockles (*Cerastoderma edule; G: srùban*) are regularly collected there, raked up from the sand, bagged and exported. Their presence is revealed when the tide has gone out and a small jet of water from the sand confirms the presence of a cockle beneath. Cockle picking, like gathering most shellfish, is backbreaking work, but seasoned cockle pickers are adept at working out the best methods for gathering them quickly. Other important cockle beds in Scotland are found in parts of Argyll, the Firth of Clyde, and Tongue in Sutherland.

Far left. Cockles await collection on the island of Barra (Polly Pullar)

Left. Whelks (Polly Pullar)

Below. Mussels (Polly Pullar)

Whelks (*Buccinum undatum*) have been gathered from the Scottish coast for a long time. They are most abundant in the west. They are often collected in a bucket and then cooked by boiling, afterwards extracting their little curled rubbery forms with a pin and eating them with lemon juice, salt and pepper. Travelling people sometimes boost their incomes by picking whelks. On a commercial scale, large sacks are filled and kept damp until they are collected for export. Most of our shellfish ends its days in gourmet restaurants in Europe.

The common mussel (*Mytilus edulis*) is a filter feeder and is found on rocky shores. It is generally accepted that the best time to eat mussels is when there is an 'r' in the month as at other times, and during their breeding season in the summer, they are not thought to taste so good. In restaurants they are steamed with dry white wine and garlic, and served in their opened shells; the delicious wine stock is mopped up with French bread. Although still gathered wild around our coasts, they are also grown commercially, with wild mussel spats attaching themselves to specially positioned ropes. There they grow at a surprisingly fast rate. This method is totally sustainable and also provides a good habitat for birds, fish and mammals.

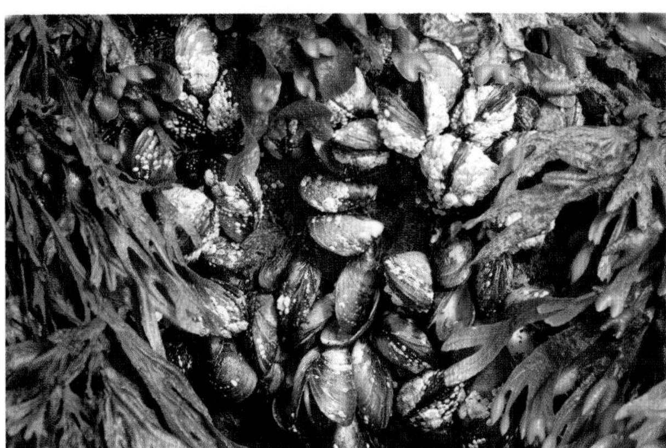

Shellfish lore

'After St Patrick's day, the limpet is better than the whelk and is said in consequence to treat it with great indignity.' So wrote John Gregorson Campbell, Church of Scotland minister of Tiree, and went on to explain, delicately, in Gaelic only: '*Mùinidh a' bhàirneach air an fhaochaig*' – 'the limpet pees on the whelk'. This was to remind people that by mid March whelks are best avoided. The whelk season, known as the 'little spring of the whelks' ran from Christmas to St Bride's day on the first of February. They were made into hearty soups or stewed in milk, the white ones (*gilleacha geala*) being preferable to the black ones (*faochagan dubha*). On Jura they might be fried with limpets, but roasting them on the fire was believed to bring seven years of famine and it was thought to be important to throw the shells away before nightfall. Shellfish, or 'ebb meat' as it was called in Orkney, was not uniquely the poor person's food, but it did help to eke out the winter supplies. Whelks, 'spoots' (razor clams), cockles, mussels, winkles and limpets were all gathered for the pot, as well as for bait or for selling on.

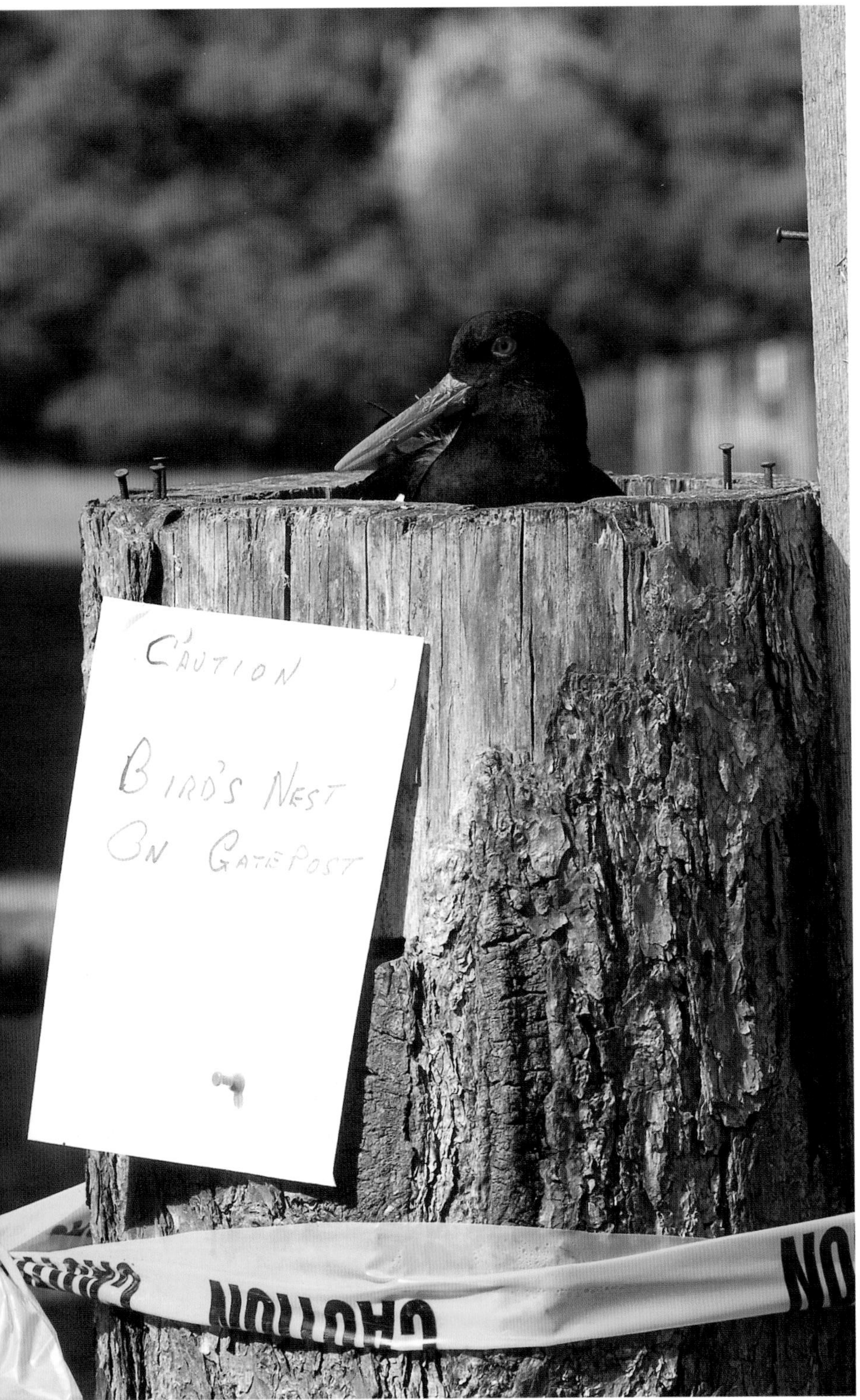

SHELLFISH GOURMANDS

Oystercatcher

Haematopus ostralegus
S: mussel-picker, pleep, reid neb, sea pyot, skirly wheeter
G: *gille-Brìghde, uiseag na tràighe*

An old Gaelic tradition states that an oystercatcher covered Jesus with seaweed when his persecutors appeared, thus hiding him and saving him from his enemies. The oystercatcher was therefore blessed – when it flies, the form of a cross can be seen on its plumage. In Uist, this cross was said to be the bird's reward. The oystercatcher's striking pied plumage, bright-orange bill and pink legs make it easily recognisable. Many oystercatchers move inland in late February to breed on farmland. Their shrill, piping calls can be heard both by day and night. They are long-lived and usually return to the same nesting areas annually. Nests are little more than an untidy scrape on the ground and are often made in unsuitable locations. Nesting on the hard shoulders of busy roads or in the middle of roundabouts in city centres can prove extremely hazardous, yet the birds seem oblivious. A pair nested on a gate post in the middle of the car park at Taymouth Golf Club for several years, and a sign on the fence read: DO NOT DISTURB – NESTING IN PROGRESS. Many a ploughman has had to carefully work round an oystercatcher's nest in the middle of a field, or move it in its entirety to a new location.

Despite their name, they do not eat oysters, consuming large amounts of mussels, cockles, and small invertebrates instead. They prize the shells open easily with their powerful bills and can cause havoc in mussel farms. In natural situations, they have no detrimental effect on wild mussel production, as birds tend to weed out the poorer mussels and leave others to thrive.

In Orkney and Shetland, their nicknames include 'skeldro' and 'shalder', and in other parts of Scotland they are often referred to fondly as the 'sea pie' in reference to their monochromatic plumage.

The Servant of Bride

In Gaelic, the oystercatcher is called the 'Servant of Bride' (*gille-Brìghde*), after the saint whose feast day falls at the beginning of February. Oystercatchers become more numerous in inland areas in early spring, and are more conspicuous everywhere as they begin looking for nest sites and defending their territories. Their insistent peeping was rendered into Gaelic as '*bi glic, bi glic, bi glic*' (be wise, be wise, be wise), although some listeners heard a more frantic note in it and told the following story:

One day, an oystercatcher got her beak caught in a limpet and called out to her mate,

> *Dè nì mi? Dè nì mi? Dè nì mi?*
> *'Ille ghuib dheirg! 'Ille ghuib dheirg!*
>
> (What'll I do? What'll I do? What'll I do? | Red-beaked boy, red-beaked boy, red-beaked boy.)

And the reply came:

> *Cùm rithe! Cùm rithe! Cùm rithe!*
> *Gon till tìde-mara na leirg.*
>
> (Hold on! Hold on! Hold on! | Till the tide turns).

She held on, most unwisely, and was drowned by the incoming tide. In another version, a different oystercatcher gives desperate advice to a rat who has got his foot caught in the same way:

> *Spìon às i! Spìon às i!*
> *Tur! Tur! Tur!*
>
> (Tear it off! Tear it off! | Completely! Completely! Completely!)

The rat escapes with his life, minus a foot. Shetlanders also knew that rats can take limpets off the rocks and eat them, and do sometimes get their paws trapped and drown when tide comes in.

Eider Duck

Somateria mollissima mollissima
S: colk, Colonsay duck, dunter, cuddy's chickens
G: *lach Lochlannach, lach mhòr, lach Aoisgeir, lach Cholbhasaigh*

There are records of breeding eider ducks on Sule Skerry from 1592, and on Sula Sgeir from 1594. They were recorded on the Isle of May in the Firth of Forth in 1710, and since then their numbers have increased dramatically; they are now widespread around Scotland's coasts. In the 1860s, eider duck eggs were sent from Islay to markets in Glasgow, but it was their down that was most sought after, to be used for bedding. Although most eiderdowns and duvets are stuffed with artificial material, or with down from domesticated geese and ducks, a few eider farms in Scandinavia

Opposite. Do not disturb – oystercatcher nesting in progress (Polly Pullar)

Below. Eider ducks, the drake with smart pied plumage (Polly Pullar)

collect the eider's soft breast feathers once the ducklings have fledged from their nests. Before his untimely death, Gavin Maxwell planned to have a commercial eider colony on Eilean Bàn, his island close to Skye.

The almost human sounds of the black and white drakes as they 'coo' and 'ah' may resound in sea bays during the breeding season. Females take to land to look for suitable nest sites, and sit tight like round plum puddings on their nests, although they are vulnerable to predation. Ducklings are sometimes raised in a large crèche, with other ducks helping to take care of them. In Orkney the eider is referred to as the 'dunter', and it was once called the 'Colonsay duck' due to the large numbers that nested on the Hebridean island of the same name.

Some 15,000 eider winter in the Tay estuary, where you can witness thousands of birds close to the shore, stretching as far as the eye can see. There they find rich pickings in the estuary's mussel beds. On occasion, special licences are issued to commercial fish farms where eider can be a nuisance as they eat the shellfish being cultivated in net bags. Oil spills are another threat, although currently it would appear that eiders are thriving.

Long-tailed Duck

Clangula hyemalis
S: coal an' can'le licht, col-cannel-week
G: *eun-buchainn, eun-binn, lach-bhinn, lach stiùireach*

The long-tailed duck was once commonly referred to as the 'old squaw', due to its upright tail feathers resembling an Indian headdress. The term is now no longer officially used in America and Canada because some feel it is offensive to Native Americans and in Canada, First Nations people. The long-tailed duck is a regular winter visitor around the Scottish coast, and a flock is often seen close to the Bell Rock Lighthouse off the east coast, near Arbroath. They are also seen on occasions at Loch Leven in Fife, and on lochs in Orkney and Shetland. Their Scots name 'coal an' can'le licht' imitates their call, which is familiar in many coastal areas. This sound has also been likened to distant bagpipe playing.

The long-tailed duck has a call like distant bagpiping (Malcolm Gosling)

Long-tailed ducks in Tiree

'In Tiree the people set small lines along the strand when the tide is out, to catch flounders and other flat fish. When the tide is in the long-tailed ducks dive for fry and sand-eels, and are caught on the hooks and drowned. During a visit to my friend and fellow-collector of folk-lore, the late Rev. Mr Campbell of Tiree, I saw at Hianaish, on the 23rd September 1887, seven of these graceful birds which had been drowned on one set of lines in one day.'

SCAVENGERS

Herring Gull

Larus argentatus
S: gray willie, pewlie, pewlie willie, willie goo
G: *glas-fhaoileag, faoileag an sgadain*

It is the herring gull's call that is most often heard in the background to film, radio and television programmes set at the seaside. This port dweller is an opportunist. It may beg for food relentlessly outside takeaway restaurants, or gather in great numbers at rubbish tips and landfill sites, where it feeds voraciously on any available scraps. Gulls often find themselves in trouble: plastic-ring holders for drinks cans caught up around their heads may lead to a painful death from starvation. Botulism and other diseases picked up in such places are another hazard of man's unwanted detritus. On one particular dump near Glasgow, so many gulls were found to have discarded condoms wrapped round their legs that the offending articles have been renamed 'gull wellies'. Young herring gulls often congregate on piers, where they soon learn to approach unsuspecting tourists carrying bags of chips or ice cream cones.

Even in its own environment, the herring gull can pose a threat to other seabirds as it frequently steals eggs and chicks. It usually nests on the edge of a seabird colony. From there, it can keep a sharp eye on an unprotected nest or a weak nestling. It also waits to steal catches from puffins as they return to their burrows.

Great Black-backed Gull

Larus marinus
S: swarbie, baagie
G: *farspach, farspag*

Author T. A. Coward wrote, 'A dead rat, dog or whale is alike acceptable to the "Corpse-eater"; where the carcase is there will the Black-backs gather, keeping the smaller fry away'. The largest gull, with its malevolent yellow-eyed stare, could be described as the yob of the bird world. Loathed by farmers and crofters, its unsavoury habit of pecking out the eyes of lambs, and the nether regions of ewes encountering lambing difficulties, has made the great black-backed gull a controversial bird.

It is a dramatic bird with superb aerial agility, however, and due to its size and presence, the great black-backed gull is the dominant species in a seabird colony. At nature reserves such as on the Isle of May in the Firth of Forth,

Left. The cries of the herring gull epitomise the seaside (Polly Pullar)

Below. Great black-backed gulls dominate a seabird colony (Polly Pullar)

signs of its activity are clear. Close to its nest site on the outer reaches of a colony, the empty sun-wizened husks of its victims, predominantly puffins and auks, may frequently be found. Black-backs can turn their prey inside out in midair to extract the fleshy interior. They then drop the skin and bones like discarded packaging.

Black-backs may be legally controlled, particularly in areas where their activities come into conflict with farming interests. Being large and imposing, this was a popular bird for taxidermy during the Victorian era, when specimens were frequently mounted in glass cases.

Lesser Black-backed Gull

Larus fuscus
S: saith fowl
G: *farspach bheag*

The lesser black-backed gull is nicknamed 'saith fowl' in Shetland and is more often seen inshore than its close relation the great black-back. It is also a scavenger and may share a breeding colony with the herring gull. Its laughing cackle is somewhat deeper than that of its relative. The strong bill has a red spot at its tip – this encourages the chicks to respond to the adult bird in 'fixed action pattern'. This is an innate behavioural response; part of the bird's genetic make-up that allows the chick to respond the first time it encounters the relevant stimulus, in this case food offered by the adult bird.

Occasionally confused with the great black-back, it is not only considerably smaller, but has yellow instead of pink legs. Although migratory, some lesser black-backs winter in Britain, while others go south as far as West Africa.

Arctic tern – glorious in flight (Malcolm Gosling)

AERIAL ELEGANCE

Arctic Tern

Sterna paradisaea
G: *steàrnan Artaigeach*

The Arctic tern is the most common tern, and is seen in Scotland during the summer months. Its annual migrations are thought to be the longest of any bird species and they are often cited as being unusual in the distances they cover. Some Arctic terns winter in South Africa, while others travel to Antarctica. Arctic terns have been recorded living for as long as 30 years, during which time they will have clocked up an astonishing mileage.

With bright-red bill and legs, black bonnets and pristine sparkling-white and grey plumage, they are a glorious sight when seen hovering above a turquoise sea in midsummer. Their forked tails are used like a rudder as they hang above the sea before softly plunging in to take sprats and sand eels.

Arctic terns nest on islands, skerries and mainland sites

all around Scotland. There was an Arctic tern colony at a gas-pipe station near Aberdeen where predation from foxes almost put paid to their breeding. However, electric netting has proved effective in protecting the site. In North Ronaldsay, the northernmost Orkney island, introduced hedgehogs take the eggs and young of nesting terns, and on Shetland there are records of ponies and sheep upsetting their breeding activities by walking through the colonies and also, surprisingly, by eating the young. Tern colonies are noisy places, and most terns will bravely dive-bomb intruders to protect their chicks.

Common Tern

Sterna hirundo
G: *steàrnan cumarta*

Despite its name, the common tern is far less numerous than the Arctic tern. They are frequently seen inland and raise young in a wide range of nest sites including fish farms, artificial mussel rafts and rooftops in various seaside resorts. There is a large breeding colony at Leith Docks, as well as in more remote locations such as the Sound of Mull. They often nest close to estuaries, choosing gravel banks and sandy shores to lay their eggs. Remote skerries and islets are also regularly used. They are frequently confused with similar-sized Arctic terns although common terns' bills are longer, less intensely red, and have a dark mark at their tip.

Common tern on island nest site (Polly Pullar)

Little Tern

Sterna albifrons
G: *steàrnan beag*

Little terns are minute, weighing just two ounces. They have yellow bills with black tips, and fly in a jerky, almost clockwork fashion above the surf as they hunt for sprats. They return to Scotland to breed in small numbers each year. Wide sand beaches like those at St Cyrus and Tentsmuir on the east coast are favoured places. They are extremely vulnerable to human disturbance because they often choose to breed on the beaches most frequented by people and dogs, which lowers their chances of successfully hatching chicks. At the Sands of Forvie in Aberdeenshire, constant predation by foxes and other predators leads to breeding failure.

A HAUNTING CRY

Great Northern Diver

Gavia immer
S: loom, leam, Allan-hawk
G: *muir-bhuachaill, bunna-bhuachaill, eun glas an sgadain*

Although there are some potentially excellent places for great northern divers to nest in Scotland, there is only one breeding record from a site at Loch Maree in 1970, and a few other unconfirmed ones. The far reaches and large lochs of the central Highlands would provide ideal nest sites, however, being largely undisturbed and inaccessible.

The largest member of the diver family, the great northern diver is impressive. Some non-breeders are seen on the sea in summer, when they sport a dark greenish-black head, red eyes and a chequerboard plumage. Their haunting cries are often heard in early summer drifting in off the sea. In winter, when great northern divers are seen in great numbers off the Scottish west coast, their plumage appears nondescript, being dark grey above and white below. During the Victorian era, they were frequently shot at sea and added to taxidermy collections.

The largest diver, the great northern, does not currently breed in Scotland (Laurie Campbell)

The salted bishop

The great northern diver may well be the bird which Martin Martin called the '*bunivochil*', also known as 'the bishop' – big as a goose, brown, white on the inside of the wings, a long broad bill and goose-like feet. It dives very quickly, he says, and is very fat. Salted, it was said to be good for sciatica.

Whales, Dolphins and Porpoises

Whales, dolphins and porpoises are intelligent marine mammals, and some are dependent on a highly sophisticated system of echolocation and a complex range of sounds for communication. They are streamlined and warm-blooded, breathe air, and give birth to live young. The group name for them is cetaceans, from the Latin word *cetus*, for 'large sea creature'. There are 83 different species worldwide, 24 of which have been recorded in Scottish waters.

Well insulated by thick blubber, cetaceans have a dorsal fin, two pectoral fins and a fluke or tail. An individual is recognisable by the scarring on its dorsal fin. Photographic records help with identification and are kept by the Hebridean Whale and Dolphin Trust, the Whale and Dolphin Conservation Society and other organisations.

Whales are divided into two groups: *odontocentes,* the toothed cetaceans, and *mysticetes*, the baleen cetaceans. Baleen plates found in the mouths of the latter group are comb-like structures that act to sieve the water for plankton and small fish. Baleen cetaceans have two nostrils or blowholes, whereas the toothed cetaceans have one. Both types breathe through their lungs, inhaling and exhaling through their blowholes. The warm air and water causes a jet to appear that can often be seen from a considerable distance. It is even possible to identify the species by the angle and height of spray each blow makes.

Whalers around the open mouth of a beached whale. (© Royal Scottish Geographical Society. Licensor www.scran.ac.uk)

Cetaceans have a gestation period of between 8 and 16 months and give birth to a single calf, born tail-first. It has to be lifted to the surface by its mother to breathe. Sometimes other female members of the group assist. The most commonly seen cetaceans in Scottish waters are minke whales, common and bottlenose dolphins, and harbour porpoises.

Whaling

There was a tradition of whaling in Scotland from as far back as the Bronze Age, when whalebone was used in the construction of dwellings. Whales washed up dead onshore were quickly dissected for meat, and it was soon discovered that their blubber contained valuable oils. Early whalers were ill-equipped with harpoons that did not attach properly to the whales. Boats kept abreast of the hunted whales while men employed lances and other sharp instruments to kill them. In 1749 the British government introduced the Bounty Act, offering 40 shillings per ton on all ships over 200 tons or more. This ushered in a huge increase in ships adapted for whaling, and by the end of the eighteenth century there were over 200 whalers.

The main whaling stations were based at Peterhead, Dundee, Aberdeen, Leith, Bo'ness, Kirkcaldy and Montrose. 'Flensing' was the method of stripping the whale of its blubber for oil for street lighting. When flensing was carried out the surrounding area was pervaded by the stench. Sperm whales also had 'spermiceti oil' stored in a large organ in their heads. At first the waxy substance was thought to be sperm, but it is actually used by the whale for echolocation and sound production. Many sperm whales were killed for this commodity for making candles,

Top. Killer whale

Above. The killer whale, or orca, is seen infrequently off the Scottish coast (Hebridean Whale and Dolphin Trust)

cosmetics and lubricants for clocks and watches. Baleen and bone were used in the fashion industry: boned corsets ensured the wearer had an hourglass figure and waspish waist measurement. Baleen was also used for umbrella ribs and bristles for brushes.

Numbers of whales killed annually were not regulated, and by 1840 they had become so scarce that many whalers were forced to give up. Larger factory ships travelled as far as the Southern Oceans, where even more whales were killed than had been in the Arctic. Men from Dundee and Peterhead went away for long periods on whaling expeditions, risking life and limb. Conditions were unpleasant and ships frequently became trapped in ice.

Scottish whaling ended in the twentieth century, although some whalers continued till the 1960s. Due to the decline in Scottish Shipping Lines, Christian Salveson of Leith diversified into whaling and for a short time dominated the industry.

IN FOR THE KILL

Killer Whale

Orcinus orca
G: *madadh-cuain*

Regularly referred to as the orca, the killer whale is seen in Hebridean waters and around Orkney and Shetland. It is the largest member of the dolphin family and may reach 30 feet (9 metres) in length. Killer whales are easy to recognise with their bold black and white markings. In some years, there are small influxes of orca in Scottish waters. Seeing a killer whale surface while you are out in a small boat is unforgettable – they are awe-inspiring creatures.

One of the sea's top predators, the killer whale adapts its diet to availability. Some pods work closely together, particularly when hunting seals. Although they have a fearsome reputation, there are no records of killer whales causing human death in the wild.

Sperm Whale

Physeter macrocephalus
G: *muc-mhara spùtach*

The largest toothed whale was once hunted ruthlessly due to the spermaceti oil found inside a special organ in its head (see page 137). Sperm whales also secrete a waxy substance called 'ambergris' from their intestines. Once used as a fixative for perfumes, ambergris is another reason why large numbers of sperm whales were killed. It was also seen as an aphrodisiac, a cure for headaches, colds and epilepsy, and much earlier as prevention from the Black Death or bubonic plague.

A few sperm whales are recorded off Scotland every year, even though they prefer deeper waters to those around the Hebrides. They can dive to great depths in search of food, and devour many different types of squid – over a ton of squid has been recorded inside a single sperm whale.

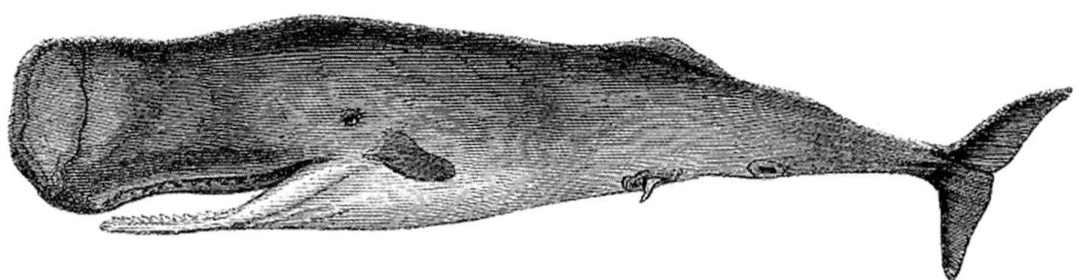

Above. Sperm whale

Bottlenose Dolphin

Tursiops truncates
S: meer-swine, pellock, dunter (all these can also be used for the porpoise)
G: *buthag*, *muc bhiorach*

The bottlenose dolphins of the Moray Firth are the most northerly resident pod in the world, numbering approximately 130 individuals. Not only is it possible to see them on special boat trips, but they are also often visible from the shore. Places such as Chanonry Point near Inverness provide fine viewing. Threats to this important pod have caused concern: too much boat traffic is increasing chances of fatal injuries by collisions with propellers, and they are also suffering from the effects of marine pollution.

Extremely playful and often seen breaching high out of the water, it is the bottlenose dolphin that was widely kept in dolphinariums. This practice has now ended, as these highly intelligent dolphins did not thrive in captive conditions.

Dolphins are thought to live for as long as 50 years. They produce a single calf biannually. They are regularly seen throughout the Hebrides and in the North Sea. Occasionally lone bottlenoses stay in one area for a long period of time and become very accustomed to humans. An inquisitive school will often bow-ride, flanking boats for some distance almost as if revelling in it.

Left. The bottlenose dolphin will play to the gallery and some appear to love an audience (Laurie Campbell)

Loupers

The 'loupers' seen by James Robertson in Loch Fyne in 1768 are bottlenose dolphins:

> This season there came into the loch a kind of fish not usually seen here, at least not in such shoals. They are named loupers by the inhabitants. They spring high out of the water; they chase, affright, and devour every other fish in the loch. This fish appears to me to be of the whale tribe. They will be from 6 to 8 feet long, nearly of the shape of salmon, black on the back and white on the belly, having two pectoral fins, and a horizontal tail.

Common Dolphin

Delphinus delphis
G: *deilf, leumadair-mara*

In the Sound of Canna, I had the good fortune of seeing a large feeding frenzy of birds in the distance where diving gannets were plunging headlong into the water. The boat was taken slowly nearer and then we drifted to watch the spectacle. A few minutes later the water erupted with splashing and over a hundred common dolphins appeared to feed on the abundance of fish. Following a group of feeding birds is often a good way of finding cetaceans. Usually common dolphins travel in smaller groups of 10 to 30 animals, but some have witnessed groups of several hundreds. They are extremely agile and acrobatic in the water and it is sometimes possible to hear their vocalisations as they communicate with one another. They have a distinctive yellowish marking on their sides, and at an average of eight and a half feet (2.59 metres) they are considerably smaller than the bottlenose dolphin.

Common dolphins can sometimes be seen in large numbers (Hebridean Whale and Dolphin Trust)

Risso's Dolphin

Grampus griseus
G: *deilf Risso*

This compact dolphin has a less streamlined shape than the common and bottlenose and has no distinctive beak. It is usually seen singly or in small groups, and does not bow ride or play close to boats like other species. It may be up to 12 feet (3.65 metres) in length and is found in deeper waters off the Hebrides where it hunts for octopus, squid and cuttlefish. Like other cetaceans, it is at high risk from contamination through the accidental consumption of plastic bags mistaken for prey. This eventually leads to death from starvation, and many beached cetaceans are found to have plastic inside their stomachs.

Harbour Porpoise

Phocoena phocoena
S: dunter, pellock (these two can also be used for the bottlenose dolphin), bucker
G: *pèileag*

The harbour porpoise is nicknamed the 'puffing pig' because of the sound it makes as it surfaces. They do not have large blowholes like other cetaceans, but there is a distinct sound as they come out of the water. They are often seen from the deck of ferries travelling to and from the islands, and are also seen from prominent viewpoints on land. They are the smallest cetacean found in Scottish waters and may be found at any time of year. They eat a variety of prey including squid, shellfish, fish and octopus, while killer whales and even bottlenose dolphins in turn prey on them. Unfortunately porpoises frequently become entangled in gill nets. As they live in waters close to human activity the noise from boats and marine activities frequently disturbs them.

IN FOR THE KRILL

Basking Shark

Cetorhinus maximus
S: hoe-mother, brigdé
G: *cearban*

The basking shark is the second-largest fish in the world. Comparatively little is known about the species, despite it occurring in some numbers in Scottish waters. This benign filter-feeding creature has huge gill rakers and a wide gaping mouth, and sieves large amounts of water to extract vital nutrients – phytoplankton, copepods and other tiny nutritious particles.

Early naturalists believed that they were sea monsters. Nineteenth-century reports from the Northern Isles describe the 'brigde' as an enormous, highly aggressive creature with sail-like fins. Their size was often exaggerated. One shark seen in Loch Broom in 1906 was reported as measuring between 50 and 60 feet (18 metres) in length. Although the basking shark may be large, the biggest are in the region of 30 feet (9 metres). Basking sharks have long been misunderstood and feared, yet they have only been accountable for the death of one human.

In 1937 a large shark breached in the Firth of Clyde near Carradale, and capsized a small boat with the loss of all three occupants. Public outcry followed and the press dined out on the story, following it with unsubstantiated evidence of a rogue shark deliberately attacking boats. Sharks breach on rare occasions, and although it is not known why, it is not thought to be through malicious intent.

It was Thomas Pennant who invented the name 'basking shark' in 1769. Prior to that they were called 'sunfish' and 'sailfish', 'pricker' and 'Muldoan'. In the Statistical Account from Loch Fyne during the 1790s, the following was written:

> The sun or sail fish occasionally visits us; this sluggish fish sometimes swims into salmon nets, and suffers itself to be drawn towards the shore, without any resistance, till it gets near the land, that for want of a sufficient body of water, it cannot exert its strength, in disentangling itself from the net, the fishers in the mean time take advantage of its situation, and attack it with sticks and stones, till they have it secure.

The riches that could be gleaned from the basking shark were discovered early, and on occasions when they were washed ashore, they were quickly cut up and exploited. In 1766 the first dedicated shark fishery was started in Canna. Shark's liver contains large quantities of valuable oil that could be used as lamp fuel, and later on for industrial chemicals. There was also a demand for fins for shark's fin soup in the Far East.

Early shark hunting was primitive and dangerous. Small boats were poorly equipped and men injured as wounded sharks battled for their lives. The first harpoon guns were ineffectual and death was usually prolonged. Shark fisheries came and went on a small scale from the Sea of the

Basking shark off Ardnamurchan Point (Freddy Pullar)

Opposite top right. Minke whale – the commonest whale in Scotland (Laurie Campbell)

Opposite below right. The humpback whale is acrobatic (Hebridean Whale and Dolphin Trust)

Opposite below left. Humpback whale

Hebrides to the Firth of Clyde. The first fishery survived until the 1830s.

In 1944 Gavin Maxwell bought the Island of Soay and began a basking shark fishery with Tex Geddes, hoping to provide enough income for them both, as well as work for some of the islanders. While Maxwell had the energy and the enthusiasm, he was woefully lacking in experience. In his thrilling book *Harpoon at a Venture,* he describes the horrors they encountered: failure of equipment and boats, and battles with vast sharks using inefficient harpoons and archaic methods for dispatching them. In a tragic irony, they discovered that all their valuable shark livers had become flyblown in storage, rendering them unfit for sale. Sharks were fished in Scotland until 1994, when nine were taken by the last shark fisherman, Howard McCrindle. He faced much opposition, and even received death threats from conservationists unhappy that sharks were still being killed, and has since been working with researchers to protect sharks. The shark-fishing industry doubtlessly had a detrimental effect on numbers. Although the basking shark is now protected, increased marine tourism has become a threat to them, with boat propellers, nets, and pollution causing damage.

Once thought to hibernate, it is now known that sharks move into deeper waters in the winter months. They are usually seen in the Hebrides in midsummer. Areas associated with an abundance of planktonic bloom are often hot spots. In the Sound of Canna in September 2004, I witnessed a huge shoal of basking sharks slowly travelling up and down the sea for as far as the eye could see, their dark fins proud of the water. I have also had very close encounters with them in Arinagour Bay in Coll, and off Ardnamurchan Point. The Sea of the Hebrides and Hyskeir, off Rum, are also favoured haunts of one of our most mysterious leviathans.

St Brendan and the Whale

There was not much to disturb a whale in the sixth century but every now and then they might have seen a leather boat scudding along, carrying men with weapons or monks on pilgrimage. Encounters like these did not go entirely unrecorded, as in this extract from the ninth-century *Voyage of St Brendan*:

> One day there appeared to them a beast of enormous size following them at a distance. He spouted foam from his nostrils and ploughed through the waves at a great speed, as if he were about to devour them. When the brothers saw this they called upon the Lord, saying: 'Deliver us, Lord, so that the beast does not devour us.'
>
> St Brendan comforted them, saying: 'Do not be afraid. You have little faith. God who always defends us will deliver us from the mouth of the beast and from other dangers.'

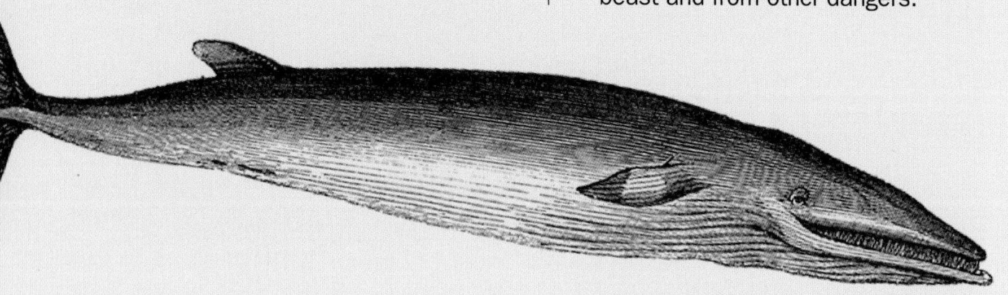

On another occasion, the monks are boiling a pot on a rocky island when it begins to pitch and roll. They drop everything and run for the boat. As the 'island' heads out to sea with their fire still burning on its back, Brendan explains: 'Where we were was not an island but a fish, the foremost of all that swim in the ocean. He is always trying to bring his tail to meet his head, but he cannot because of his length. His name is Jasconius.' Travellers like Brendan would have seen whales diving and blowing and I never pass the smooth grey islands in Loch Ailort without thinking of Jasconius. His name comes from the old Irish / Gaelic 'íasc', a fish, like the 'great fish' in the Book of Jonah. This story was a favourite in medieval Europe and probably contributed to the mistaken belief that whales eat people. Jonah's whale has also been taken as a metaphor for death, and his escape from it as a type of resurrection, so when Brendan tells his companions that God will deliver them 'from the mouth of the beast and from other dangers' he is telling them to be afraid of nothing in this life, or in the life to come.

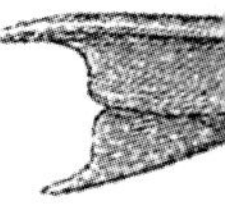

Minke Whale

Balaenoptera acutorostrata
G: *muc-mhara-mhinc*

The smallest of the baleen whales, the minke is the most common whale seen off the Scottish coast, and in particular in the seas round the Hebrides. Minke whales can grow up 30 feet (9 metres) in length and are usually seen singly. Some appear very inquisitive and have been known to 'spy hop', raising their heads above the surface to have a better view of a boat. It is also possible to smell their cabbage-like breath during these close encounters.

Humpback Whale

Megaptera novaeangliae
G: *muc-mhara chrotach*

Distinctive due to the shape of its head with its knobbly surface, this baleen whale may grow as large as 55 feet (16.7 metres) in length. Humpbacks often stun their prey by smacking the surface of the water with their tail flukes. They are acrobatic and breach clear of the water, as though playing for an audience. Their distinctive blow may rise high into the air.

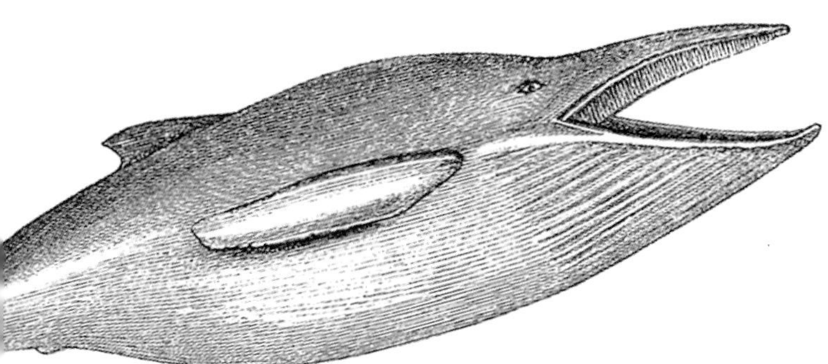

PRIZE FISHERMEN

Otter

Lutra lutra
S: otter, dratsie
G: *dòbhran, dobhar-chù, biast-dhubh*

The Small Giant

The otter is ninety percent water
Ten percent God
This is a mastery
We have not fathomed in a million years.
I saw one once, off the teeth of western Scotland,
Playing games with the Atlantic –
Three feet of gymnastics
Taking on an ocean.

Kenneth Steven, from his
poetry collection *Island*, 2009

Lithe, muscular and totally at home in the water, it is on the seashore that you are most likely to see an otter, although they are equally widespread in many lochs, burns and rivers. Otter watching demands patience: although walks on the seashore can prove rewarding, hiding behind a rock and scanning with binoculars in suitable otter habitat is the best way to see one. Shetland and the west coast are good places to see otters.

Otter in a sea of bladderwrack (Laurie Campbell)

The otter is a member of the mustelid family that includes stoats, weasels and badgers. Confusion between sea otters and river otters in Scotland leads to a belief that they are two separate species, but they are one and the same. Otters have a dense waterproof pelt, webbed feet, a long tail and a whiskered face. They are now as highly valued as golden eagles and red squirrels in the wildlife popularity stakes.

Due to their shyness, the only definitive signs that otters are present in an area may be their tracks – 'spore' left in soft mud or snow, with sometimes the scrape-mark of their tail alongside. Otter droppings, or 'spraints', are also important visual signs that are left on prominent roots, rocks and banks as territory markings. Spraints often contain traces of fur, fish bones and scales, or crabshell.

Some otters have become accustomed to life beside humans. In 2004, while I was storm-bound in a tall ship moored against the harbour wall at the Kyle of Lochalsh, two otters clambered down the pier ladders and came on board. They left a few spraints and, upon finding no fish, nipped back onto the pier. The following morning, they came on board again, crossing our boat to reach one moored alongside, where they could be heard crunching prawns. Otters frequently rear cubs at a ferry terminal in Shetland, unperturbed by human presence.

An otter's gestation period is 63 days. An average of two or three (but sometimes up to five) cubs are born in a 'holt' – a den located in a hole in a bank or amongst rocks. The young stay with their mother for up to a year and are fully aquatic after the age of three months.

The sight of a mother otter with her cubs swimming in a line has given rise to some of the speculations about the Loch Ness monster – viewed from a distance they appear as a series of humps with a tail sticking up out of the water at the end. Otters that exist predominantly in the sea frequently enter fresh water to keep their coats in good condition and to clean off salt. In spring they sometimes travel up hill burns in search of spawning frogs.

Otters are extremely popular today, but this was not always the case. In 1879 over 70 were killed during a 25-year period by a shepherd in North Uist, a pattern that continued throughout the Western Isles. Conflicts of interest between otters and salmon fishermen meant they were high on the hit list. They were also killed for their thick fur. Like badgers and foxes, the skins were often made into sporrans worn by Highland gents. As recently as the mid 1960s, otter skins were cured and sold to craft shops. Although crofters frequently benefited from otters' abandoned salmon catches, they could not tolerate their presence, claiming they also killed poultry and lambs. Otters will take hens if they are easily available, while wildfowl collections may be decimated over a period of nights if a rogue otter finds a way to get in. Their usual diet is based on fish, eels and crabs, and their powerful jaws are well able to deal with the toughest shells and skins.

The Shetlanders still call the otter 'dratsie'. In Shetland folklore, it was believed an otter descended a cliff by putting its tail in its mouth and rolling into the sea like a 'simmond clew' – a ball of straw rope.

During the 1950s and 1960s, otters came close to extinction after decades of persecution. The crash in numbers was also due to a chemical build-up of PCBs (polychlorinated biphenyls) in their bodies, along with intensive agriculture and new drainage schemes that led to habitat pollution and loss. Many otters are still being killed by heavy traffic on a vastly increased road network. Otters are sometimes caught in fish traps, lobster pots, and fyke nets – the latter set for eels. The use of otter guards over traps and nets has helped.

Rosemary and Jim Green completed many years of valuable otter research during the 1980s. By radio-tracking marked otters, they noted that certain individuals ranged for considerable distances on a nightly basis. Together with the Vincent Wildlife Trust in Galloway, they established a large otter rehabilitation centre. Through their dedicated effort, many road casualties and orphaned cubs have been rehabilitated and released back into the wild.

The one that got away

An otter from Loch Aineort in South Uist proved to be more than a match for the crofter who tried to kill him. Beaten senseless and slung over the man's shoulder, he hung there 'only pretending to be dead' while the man made his way home. On the way, however, the otter revived and sank his teeth into the man's buttocks, but the man did not let go. Instead, he called his wife to hit the creature with a stout stick. She hit it so hard that she knocked her husband off his feet, while the otter dropped to the ground and ran off. This is a true story, apparently, collected from Peter MacCormack in Benbecula, although a version of it is told in the Northern Isles as well.

In 1960 Gavin Maxwell's *Ring of Bright Water* became an international best seller, making the author one of Britain's best-known naturalist writers. The book was to have far-reaching consequences for otter conservation. His beautifully written story greatly altered people's perspective on otters even though the hero of the book, Mijbil, was an otter brought back from the Tigris Marshes in Iran. Other otters followed, and in a series of books Maxwell told their tales and those of his life living on the western seaboard, surrounded by animals.

Tragically Camusfeàrna, where Maxwell lived with his otters, burned down in 1968. Maxwell moved to tiny Eilean Bàn, an island near Skye. It was his intention to set up an otter sanctuary and private zoo there together with naturalist writer Sir John Lister Kaye, founder of the Aigas Field Centre, but he became terminally ill and died in 1969.

Maxwell's books live on. Eilean Bàn now lies under the Skye Bridge: there is a museum and otter sanctuary there dedicated to him. Gavin Maxwell's name is synonymous with otters – a bronze otter now stands in his memory near the shore at Port William, Wigtownshire, close to his family home.

The sleek but ruthless mink can wreak havoc with other wildlife (Laurie Campbell)

Mink

Mustela vison

The mink is one of Scotland's least favourite mammals. This alien was brought to Britain for fur farming from America. Records of its initial escape date back to the 1930s and since that time it has become widespread. Due to its ruthless killing and penchant for the eggs and chicks of ground-nesting birds, damage to fish and killing of the now rare water vole, mink are loathed. They are seen as a threat to game and therefore regularly come up against keepers.

Although largely nocturnal, they are often seen on the seashore hunting in rock pools for small shellfish and crabs. They also relish the eggs of gulls, waders and terns. With their thick, dark pelts, mink have a highly developed scent gland under their tail that emits a powerful odour. They are accomplished tree climbers and find suitable holes in banks or trees where up to seven young are raised. The young mink eventually disperse at approximately 14 weeks of age. Recently mink were recorded close to Edinburgh city centre, and there are fears of their possible spread into the urban environment. Gorgie City Farm, for example, was concerned about the damage that could be done to their poultry.

A special mink eradication scheme in the Hebrides has proved quite successful. Plans for a similar scheme on the Isle of Skye are also underway. On occasions, protected polecats are caught in traps as they are mistaken for mink and unwittingly killed.

Grey Heron

Ardea cinerea
S: craigie, cran, Willie-fisher, Jenny heron, lang Sandy
G: *corra-ghritheach, corra-ghlas, corra-ghrithean*

It was once believed that the prehensile-looking heron, with its long legs stretching far out behind it as it flies, had a nest with two holes in it for the legs to dangle through. The heron is widespread and takes full advantage of the increased number of fish farms where it may gather in large numbers in the hope of an easy meal.

Herons eat large quantities of fish. They wait and watch before jabbing their sharp bills underwater to spear a victim. During the spawning season when frogs and toads gather at ponds, there are always herons in attendance. They frequently devour several at once as the frenzied amphibians pile on top of one another, driven by the urge to mate. Herons also prey on goldfish in garden ponds.

Slow in flight, this large grey bird is a frequent sight, standing sentinel in almost every bay on the west coast and its isles. On take-off and in leisurely flight with its neck tucked back, it gives a characteristic, harsh *kraak* call. At the nest, herons give a large range of vocalisations including bill clicking and rattling noises.

During the breeding season, heronries are noisy, odorous places, with many pairs nesting close together. Their vast, shambling, stick nests are plastered with droppings and the young, with their wayward down, bare faces, staring eyes and flapping throat-pouches, seem almost reptilian in appearance. They are fed by regurgitation. Tread warily near a heronry, for when adults ferrying food are disturbed or frightened, a passer-by may find a load of foul-smelling fish dumped on their head.

Heronries may be found in tall stands of trees, or in the case of one heronry on the island of Jura, in a large clump of low rhododendron. An enormous heronry on high sea cliffs at Ardnamurchan Point, Britain's most westerly mainland peninsular, was abandoned during the 1930s.

The heron has suffered mixed fortunes. Seen as a royal bird during medieval times, someone found killing one would have had a hand cut off as a penalty. Conversely, later on the birds were hunted with peregrine falcons. Heron hawking became a popular sport and helped keep the birds away from fisheries. Heron numbers may drop during hard winters but these prolific breeders soon recover.

Heron proverbs

'A heron on the shore is no novelty.' This Gaelic proverb ('*Cha suaicheantas corra air cladach*'), about not reading too much into ordinary situations, reveals the down-to-earth side of Highland bird lore. Another proverb adds a touch of humour: '*"Cha doir do cheòl don chuideachd thu", mar thuirt a' chorra-ghritheach ris an fheannaig*' (Your music will not take you into company, as the heron said to the crow). In Islay, a heron on the shore was believed to be a sign of good weather, while in other places, they were a bad omen. They are named in the death-bed saying: '*An tig thu no an tèid thu, no an d'ich thu feòil churra*?' (Will you come or will you go, or have you eaten heron's flesh?). This was supposed to be asked at the moment of death, or to hasten death in someone 'too long alive'. Various interpretations have been offered for this, but it probably reflects the heron's habit of standing immobile for long periods at the water's edge, on the brink, as it were, between one world and the next. By 1976, however, Roderick MacPherson ('Goik') from Barra saw nothing at all spooky about herons. He could recall the flavour of them from his youth, when it was hunted and eaten 'like any other bird'.

Grey heron – frequently seen standing sentinel in prime fishing haunts (Malcolm Gosling)

A RARE DUNE DWELLER

Natterjack Toad

Bufo calamita

Smaller and more gregarious than the common toad, the natterjack is predominantly nocturnal. It is extremely rare, being found only in a few isolated locations in south-west Scotland, where it favours sandy heath close to the sea.

The common name 'natterjack' comes from the noisy, croaking calls emitted during breeding, between April and June. The sounds emanate from a large vocal sac under their chins. Natterjack toads favour clear, shallow, vegetation-free pools in which to lay their eggs. Long spawn strings are fertilised by the male as they are laid. By laying eggs a little later in the season than the common toad, natterjack spawn develops into tadpoles faster, due to the increased warmth of the sun. When threatened, natterjacks may puff themselves up to look larger and more intimidating. In spite of this, they frequently end up being eaten by otters, foxes, hedgehogs, herons and gulls.

The natterjack has a distinctive yellow stripe down the

Left. The rare natterjack toad is nicknamed 'the running toad' (Fergus Crystal)

Right. Hugh Miller, geologist (© Scottish National Portrait Gallery. Licensor www.scran.ac.uk)

centre of its back and is nicknamed the 'running toad' due to its active movement, whereas the common toad is ponderous by comparison.

Natterjacks burrow into the sand and can be difficult to find. Their numbers have declined drastically due to acidification from increased forestry and intensive farming activities. They have also been affected by flood prevention schemes, habitat loss and human encroachment. The salt marshes of the Solway Firth at Caerlaverock remain a stronghold.

Opposite top. Starfish (Polly Pullar)

Opposite centre. Cushion stars and sea urchins (Polly Pullar)

Opposite bottom. Goose barnacles (Polly Pullar)

Fossils and Genesis

Fossils had a major impact on theology in the nineteenth century. Already in 1517, Girolamo Fracastoro had identified them as the imprints of living creatures, but no one had been able to explain how traces of marine animals came to be buried so far inland. Noah's flood was a favourite explanation. Others thought the Creator must have made them in a playful mood and hidden them in the earth to surprise us, or that the devil placed them there to mislead us, or that they were simply shapes formed by some unknown force. In 1785, a Berwickshire man, James Hutton, published his ground-breaking *Theory of the Earth* in which he argued that the earth had been formed over immense periods of time. This brave piece of work paved the way for Rev. John Fleming, who finally found the courage to say publicly that the earth was not created, literally, in seven days. Fleming was the parish minister at Flisk in Fife when he tackled the subject in the fossils section of his *Philosophy of Zoology* (1822). He knew that he was pushing the boundaries of belief: 'the opinion here advanced is so very different from that which is received by modern authors ...' he writes, and goes on to describe fossils as the flora and fauna of previous creations, swept away by 'vast revolutions'. Fleming eventually became professor of natural science at the Free Church college in Edinburgh, New College, where he influenced several generations of future ministers.

It fell to his contemporary, Hugh Miller, to popularise this new understanding of creation. Geology could even bring him to the threshold of prayer. Strange and impressive sermons are written in the rocks, he wrote: 'the eternity that hath passed is an ocean without further shore ... nor can the eye reach to the open shoreless infinitude beyond, in which only God existed.' Before long, Darwin's *Origin of Species* (1859) would ignite a furious debate around these issues, but in the 1840s, Miller could enjoy his fossil-hunting expeditions in reflective mode, as guest of the minister of the Small Isles, on board the Free Church yacht, the *Betsey*.

Seashell games

Children in the Northern Isles used to play farms, using seashells for animals. The details vary from place to place, but in Orkney small scallop shells (*Chlamys*) were sheep and 'smerslins' or truncated gapers (*Mya truncata*) were pigs. The small, curled-up shapes of 'cattie buckies' or periwinkles (*Littorina littoralis*) come in a useful range of colours (black, white, ginger or tortoiseshell) and made good cats. The pointed end of another winkle (*Nucella lapillus*) reminded children of a dog's nose, although the bigger whelk (*Colus gracilis*), or 'big longneb', was a favourite for sheepdogs. The blue-black mussels (*Mytilus edulis*) were crows, and other shells were used for cows, horses and ponies.

Rock pools

Childhood memories of visits to rock pools last a lifetime. A rock pool is one of nature's miracles, a perfect aquarium that replicates the sea in miniature; an oasis filled with life from the tiniest plankton to the birds and mammals at the top of the food chain. Twice daily the water in a rock pool is refreshed with a rich saline soup. Marine plankton is the first link in this complex chain, together with microscopic worms, tiny jellyfish, copepods and minuscule crustaceans. Rock pools are fragile ecosystems vulnerable to human disturbance and pollution.

Creatures existing in this habitat have to adapt to salinity, light levels and temperature extremes. The best pools are those that retain salt water even during the lowest tides and are usually located on rocky shores where an abundance of seaweed grows. Water evaporates rapidly along the rocky seashore, but moisture is retained in the seaweed that clings on, providing humid pockets where crustaceans and shellfish can survive while the tide is out.

Carefully turning stones over in pools reveals a wealth of colourful plants, animals and fish: prickly sea urchins, starfish, cushion stars, brittle stars, sea anemones, shrimps and scuttling hermit crabs in their borrowed shells. All are beautifully camouflaged, and many of the rocks and small stones are covered in plants, corals and weeds of the brightest hues.

Sea anemones are a primitive member of the jellyfish family and have evolved to look flower-like, with a crown of waving, petal-like tentacles. Some of these have 'nematocysts', stinging cells that trap and immobilise prey as it passes. Prickly purple and green sea urchins graze on various weeds. They were once eaten and their soft middles scooped from their globular shells. Benign-looking starfish actually consume a wide variety of small shellfish, pulverizing them with strong jaws located on the underside of the centre of the star.

Elsewhere on the shore, old ships' timbers may reveal the curious goose barnacle. Sailors once believed these elongated, black and white filter-feeding crustaceans were emerging barnacle geese (see page 155).

Most jellyfish washed up on the shore do not sting. The large Portuguese man-of-war (*Physalia physalia*), however, has a fierce sting packed into its long, trailing tentacles which can occasionally be lethal. Nets pulled in from the sea may have these jellyfish tentacles attached and can inflict painful stings. Swimmers occasionally come into contact with them. Jellyfish are mesmerising to watch in clear water, as they swim in pulsating movement revealing their delicate colours. They are often found washed up on the shore where they are rendered immobile and prone to desiccation:

Be kind to little animals
Whatever sort they be,
And give to stranded jellyfish
A shove into the sea.

Anon.

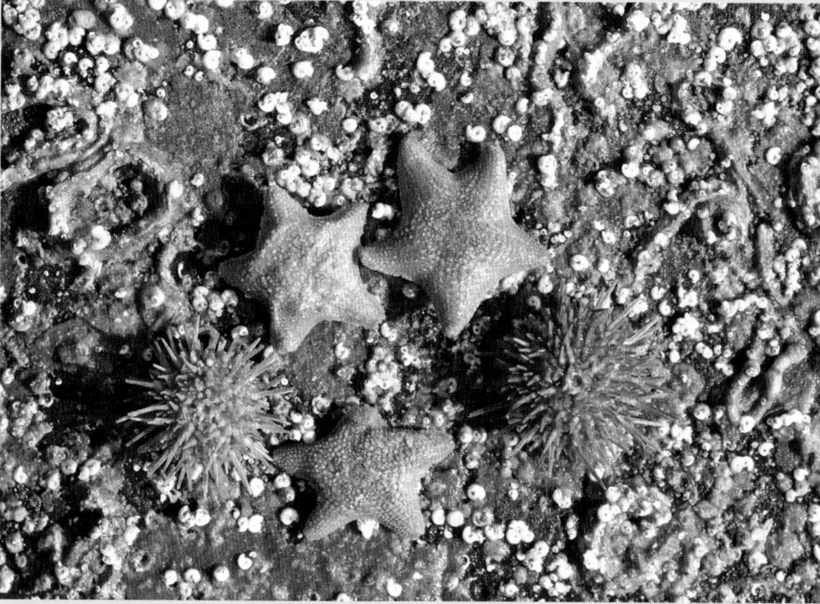

CHAPTER SIX

ISLANDS AND SKERRIES

INTODUCTION

We have an ongoing fascination for islands and visit them regularly. Some Scottish islands are approached by causeway or bridge, while others remain dependent on the reliability of ferries and the vagaries of the weather, and are often cut off for days, or even weeks at a time. Some buzz with human activity – Skye, Mull, Arran, Bute and Great Cumbrae – while others such as Mingulay, North Rona and the Flannan Isles have been totally left to wildlife.

So what is an island? Hamish Haswell-Smith in *The Scottish Islands* (1996) defines it as follows: 'An island is a piece of land or group of pieces of land which is entirely surrounded by seawater at Lowest Astronomical Tide and to which there is no permanent means of dry access.' Islands may also be in salt or fresh water, but those with the biggest attraction are surrounded by sea.

Man has left his mark and constantly intervenes in the ecology of islands, introducing species such as hedgehogs to Uist, for example, and rabbits to the Isle of May in the Firth of Forth. Rats that have been unwittingly brought to islands can devastate entire colonies of seabirds. Some species are isolated and have become unique to particular islands, such as the St Kilda wren, slightly larger than its mainland relation, and the Orkney vole. Other unique animals have their origins on islands, for example the rare seaweed-eating sheep of North Ronaldsay, the Hebridean, Soay, and Boreray sheep, and Shetland cattle. There are also Shetland and Eriskay ponies, as well as Shetland poultry, thought to have arrived with the Spanish Armada.

Scotland has over 790 offshore islands; approximately 100 are inhabitated. They are all very different in character, from the large group that make up Orkney and Shetland in the north, to the Inner and Outer Hebrides in the west; from a smattering of islands on the east in the Firth of Forth, to miniature archipelagos in the Clyde and Solway Firth. The variation in geological formations is impressive, creating distinct habitat types that play host to a wide range of flora and fauna that is not easy to observe on the mainland. The extraordinary basalt columns of Staffa with its awe-inspiring Fingal's cave, and the large basalt plug known as the Bass Rock, are worlds apart from the flat, sandy isle of Tiree, where it is said that 'should a rabbit and his mate make their home, it would sink into the sea'. Many large lochs are also punctuated with small isles that act as wildlife enclaves, such as those in Loch Lomond where capercaillie – and introduced wallabies – continue to survive.

Among the earliest settlers were monks and hermits who initially moved to the Northern Isles and later colonised the Hebrides. They came and went, leaving

Opposite. View to Rum, Eigg and Skye from Coll (Polly Pullar)

behind a fascinating history: ruins, brochs (Iron Age dry stone structures), and burial sites that are now of World Heritage importance. Remnants of our ancient past are often colonised by wildlife, as in the case of one of the finest preserved brochs which dates back to around 100 BC, on the uninhabited Shetland island of Mousa. Here, an estimated 11,800 pairs of storm petrels breed in burrows within the broch and at night emit their extraordinarily eerie calls. Many islands have been named after the first colonisers, and there is clear evidence of their settlements.

The isles of western Scotland are constantly massaged by the warmth of the Gulf Stream and have little annual snowfall. However, most islands are subject to gales of frightening velocity. They regularly drive in off the Atlantic and North Sea, and in many cases alter the landscape by shifting dunes, beaches, estuaries and shingle beds.

Islands are also dominated by strong tides: the Gulf of Corryvreckan holds the world's third-largest whirlpool, and the Pentland Firth and Sea of the Hebrides can be notably treacherous crossings for islanders travelling to and from the mainland. Swells may make landing on some islands impossible at certain times – anchors frequently drag, adding to the thrill of island-going. However, these currents also encourage large fish populations and planktonic blooms, and become important feeding grounds for cetaceans, seals, and birds.

St Kilda holds the world's largest gannetry on its sea stacks, while North Rona and the Monach Isles hold internationally important numbers of Atlantic grey seals. During storms, rare migrants find landfall on islands such as Fair Isle, North Ronaldsay, and the Isle of May where birders record arrivals as the birds are harmlessly trapped in 'Heligoland' traps, ringed and released.

Islands provide some of the finest unspoilt environments for a wealth of species and their isolation often means that there are some extraordinary surprises.

LIFE'S A BEACH

Common Seal

Phoca vitulina
G: *ròn*

The common (or harbour) seal is much smaller than the grey and has a daintier head-shape which is often likened to that of a Labrador. There is less difference in size between the sexes. Common seals live in smaller groups and despite their name and widespread distribution they number far fewer than greys. They tend to stay closer to the shore than the grey seal. Some even venture up estuaries and are seen on occasion in important salmon-fishing rivers, in particular the River Tay where licences are issued to shoot seals that become a nuisance when salmon are spawning.

Common seals are seen hauled up on small rocky islands, lying bent up in the shape of a banana as they move flippers about idly scratching themselves. Curious of humans and their boats, many come close to watch activity. When the tide is far out, some haul out onshore close to civilisation, seemingly unperturbed by its noise and hazards. Both common and grey seals drift lazily with their heads sticking up out of the water – this is known as 'bottling'.

The common seal comes ashore to breed in June. Unlike the grey seal pup, a common seal pup can swim and

Common seal and pup – North Ronaldsay (Polly Pullar)

dive within the first few hours of birth, and does not have a white natal coat as this is shed inside the womb. During their lactation period the pups double their weight, sustained on their mother's fat-rich milk (see below).

In 1988 the Phocine Distemper Virus (PDV) killed many common seals. An accumulation of toxins appeared to lower the seals' immune systems and they succumbed to the virus. The SSPCA received animals in very poor health. Some recovered and were returned to the sea. In 2002 there was a second outbreak of this deadly virus, and conservationists were concerned about the impact it would have on common seal numbers. Currently numbers appear to be stable and there have been no further signs of trouble.

Grey Seal

Halichoerus grypus
S: selch, selkie, silkie, haaf fish
G: *ròn, bèist-mhaol, moineas*

The largest proportion of the world population of grey seals is found in Scotland. By 1914, numbers had fallen to an estimated 500 due to incessant persecution, but the Grey Seal Protection Act was then passed in the same year and since then, the population has increased by an estimated 7 per cent per annum. Before the 1850s, large colonies did not exist, but as man was forced to leave many remote islands, the seals moved in. The Monach Isles, and North Rona off Lewis now have vast seal rookeries.

Grey seals come ashore to breed in October and November. A single pup is born after delayed implantation and a nine-month gestation period. Birth is fast and the new baby has a yellowish-white natal coat. Great black-backed gulls and other scavengers soon clean up the afterbirth on the shore. The pup quickly finds its mother's teat and for the first three weeks feeds on milk with a 50 per cent fat content – 12 times richer than cow's milk. With such sustenance the young seals grow at an astonishing rate, and when weaned at approximately three weeks head out to sea. Seal rookeries are noisy places fraught with jostling and fighting. Many pups are lost, squashed by the huge bulls that mate with the cows as soon as they have finished suckling their young. Twins in grey seals are a rare occurrence.

Grey seal (Polly Pullar)

It is only the largest males that mate with the females although there are continual bloody battles for supremacy. Sometimes animals may be killed in fights or die later of their injuries. Soon after seals have mated, they moult and stay on shore till this is complete. Comfortably upholstered in a dense layer of blubber, during the moult they lose a large amount of body weight.

Seals were once taken during the breeding season for meat and oil. Small boats ventured out to skerries and isles where the seals were easy prey on the shore. Armed with primitive equipment, men crept up on the unsuspecting animals and battered them to death with huge stones. Up until the end of the 1860s, an average of 50 seals was taken

Seal hunters

Seals were part of the endowment of some medieval abbeys and could be eaten during Lent, being judged more fishy than meaty. Hunters returning from Causamul off Harris in the late seventeenth century used to give the parish minister the pick of the pups. This was known as *cuilean Moire* (Mary's pup) and it had probably been part of the teinds due to the church since before the Reformation. The hunt took place in October soon after the pups were born. According to Martin Martin, the seals did not succumb easily and 'often force their passage over the necks of the stoutest assailants, who aim always at the forehead of the seals giving many blows before they be killed .... Several of the biggest seals lose their lives by endeavouring to save their young ones whom they tumble before them into the sea.' Clubbing baby seals to death in front of their mothers calls for a particularly determined hardening of the heart, and even men used to butchery could find it disturbing. For all the economic benefits of seal hunting, there are many songs and stories about seals lamenting their dead; about bad luck following the killing of a seal or the wearing of sealskin; and about selkies who lived to shame their attackers or repay an act of mercy.

annually on Hyskeir, but on other expeditions up to 1,000 seals were accounted for. Sealskin provided a source of clothing and equipment, while the rich, dark meat, likened to venison, was a valuable commodity. Some was smoked and salted over fires made of seaweed. Seal flesh was believed to be a remedy for diarrhoea and the oil extracted from the blubber was used for lamps and as a cure for many ailments. Wrapping a naked rheumatism sufferer up in sealskin for a few days was believed to ease the pain, and cattle were sometimes fed seal blubber as a cure-all.

Many sporrans are made of sealskin. Most of it was imported until recently when a ban was imposed. This caused uproar from sporran makers, who believe it is the death knell of a long tradition. Most of the skin came from baby seals in Canada, and pictures of dewy-eyed pups being clubbed to death led to conservationists petitioning to stop the brutality. Well-crafted sporrans are an art form and the market is now flooded with cheap foreign imports that use synthetic materials, much to the chagrin of skilled sporran makers. Although any hair or fur may be made into sporrans, new laws and legislation are making it increasingly difficult for sporran makers to acquire raw materials, and there are very real fears that the craft could die out (see page 252).

Grey seals have few natural predators other than man and killer whales. They are vulnerable to parasites and pollution, and are often injured by boats. They are loathed by fishermen due to the damage they inflict on salmon in nets and fish cages, and even after legal protection, many are still illegally culled. It is not only what they consume, but also the damage they do to individual fish that causes the problem. On occasions licences are issued by the Scottish Executive to cull seals in troubled areas.

Grey seals can live for up to 50 years. Males can be immense. Although the red deer stag is seen as the largest British mammal, a mature bull seal can be heavier, with some weighing over 300 kilograms. They are easily recognisable with their large Roman noses and huge broad heads. Coat colour varies considerably, from very dark to patchy shades of mottled pale grey. Some females and juveniles are blotched with yellowish markings and are often paler in colour.

Seals haul themselves out of the water daily and remain recumbent, wailing their eerie vocalisations that have given rise to myth and legend. They are also attracted to music and singing, and inquisitively come close to the shore to investigate someone playing an instrument such as a penny whistle or violin.

Every year, the SSPCA receives many orphan seal pups, some of which are picked up off beaches when they should have been left alone. At the Middlebank Wildlife Rescue Centre at Dunfermline, these pups are rehabilitated and eventually returned to the wild. Grey seals do not make good patients and despite their soft appearance have one of the most savage bites of all. Even a new white pup has a bite like a gin-trap. When cornered and threatened, they bravely defend themselves. The early seal hunters padded out their trousers with charcoal to help protect themselves. They believed that the seals would hear the crunching sounds of the charcoal and let go of their legs thinking they had crushed the bone. It is doubtful if seals are that intelligent. Certainly, however, they command the utmost respect.

The Great Selkie

'Selkie' can mean simply 'seal', but something about seals can seem almost human, and coastal communities have expressed this in stories of kinship with the seal nation, hence the other meaning of 'selkie' – a seal which comes to land and takes human form, even bearing or begetting human children.

> 'It was na weel,' quo the maiden fair,
> 'It was na weel, indeed,' quo she,
> 'That the great Silkie of Sule Skerrie
> Suld hae come and aught a bairn to me.'

The selkie in this famous ballad knows, even before their child is born, that the woman will eventually marry a gunner (harpoonist) who will destroy him, together with his seal-boy son. Other stories tell how a man once stole the seal-skin of a selkie girl while she was dancing on the shore. He takes her home and raises a family with her, but inevitably, she finds the seal-skin and returns to the sea, usually for ever. The MacCodrums of North Uist were believed to be descended from selkies, as was a Shetland woman, Baubi Urquhart, who was known to folklorists in the nineteenth century.

John Wards of Shapinsay, Orkney, told a more light-hearted seal-hunting story which he head from his grand-father: a man once set a net for a selkie, fastened the net to a rope, put the rope through the cat hole in the door of his house and sat down to wait, with the rope tied round his ankle. The selkie, when it came, was no ordinary selkie but 'a great brute of a selkie' called an 'arkma'. It pulled so hard that the man was dragged right across the room and got stuck in the cat hole. As John Wards tells it: 'there happened to be a neebor in the hoose, and she said an eerison over this owld fella. She says:

> Matthew, Mark, Luke an John
> Look this troubled sinner on.

Whether it helped or no I don't know, but they got him slacked till they got a knife-blade through the loop o the rope and they cut his leg clear. That was the owld fella.'

WINTER ISLANDERS

Barnacle Goose

Branta leucopsis
S: claik, ronthurrock
G: *cathan, giùran, leadan*

The barnacle goose comes to Scotland every winter. It was once thought to have emerged from the goose barnacle – a long-stalked crustacean found in the deep Atlantic that usually attaches to the keels of boats, ship's timbers or discarded bottles (see page 149). Nobody knew where the geese went once they disappeared in spring, and sailors even claimed that they had seen the birds emerging from the long waving tendrils of this extraordinary crustacean, the tendrils being the feathers on the chick's head.

The pied barnacle goose may be found on the mainland in great numbers at the Wildfowl and Wetlands Trust Reserve on the Solway Firth, at Caerlaverock. Its main stronghold is Islay, however. Over 30,000 barnacle geese winter on the island, particularly round the area of the RSPB's reserve at Loch Gruinart, and on Loch Indaal. Most of the birds in Islay are from the Greenland population, while those on the Solway make up most of the Svalbard population. A few also winter on Coll and Tiree, and other small, uninhabited islands where sheep-cropped turf provides good habitat.

As Islay's farmland has improved over the years with better farming practices, so too have goose numbers. The fact that they thrive on Islay's rich, short grass has inevitably brought them up against the island's farming community. Licences were once issued to shoot some of the birds, but now instead a 'goose subsidy' is paid to farmers who own the land where geese decimate pasture. There are rumours that it is easier to make money from geese in Islay than it is

Barnacle geese, Islay (Polly Pullar)

The sacred goose?

During the twentieth century, the wild goose became widely known as a Celtic symbol of the Holy Spirit. The idea sounds traditional but is hard to trace beyond the Rev. George MacLeod, founder of the Iona Community. Having said that, geese did have a special significance in earlier times, in parts of Pictland and Gaeldom. A small number of goose images appear on Pictish carved stones and although their meaning has been lost, Peter Anson knew of fishermen in the North-east who would not eat goose for whatever reason. In the early 1880s, the lady traveller Constance Gordon Cumming wrote that in the Hebrides, 'as in many other countries the goose was deemed too sacred for food.' Few, if any, of her contemporaries substantiate this, but with family connections in both Moray and Islay, Cumming could have had access to genuinely old traditions. Be that as it may, her Celtic 'sacred goose' found its way into George Henderson's *Survivals in Belief among the Celts* (1911), which is probably where George MacLeod found it. The two men were contemporaries, both based in Glasgow and both men of the cloth, although Henderson had become a lecturer in Celtic Studies. MacLeod, impatient with all forms of worn-out churchiness, preferred the wild goose to the traditional image of the dove and siezed upon it with typical audacity. With forebears in Morvern and Skye, we shall probably never know for sure whether he invented it or drew on the same lost oral traditions as Gordon Cumming.

from farming. There are those who would disagree but for the time being at least, it seems to have appeased a tricky situation and offered protection to the goose populations. Large numbers of birders flock to the islands every year to see the geese. Islay has an extensive bird list that includes many rarer waterfowl species, some travelling from North America. Of course, bird-watching visitors can also enjoy some of the island's many fine distilleries. By mid April, the geese have left and farming resumes uninterrupted until October, when the barnacle geese return, flying low over the Sound of Jura, and filling the air with their clamour, which is often likened to the yapping of terriers.

Greenland White-fronted Goose

Anser albifons flavirostris
G: *gèadh bhlàr*

Islay is not only favoured by the barnacle goose, but also by approximately 10,000 Greenland white-fronted geese. The rest of the Scottish population are found on Coll, Tiree and the Kintyre peninsula, and a few other scattered islands and remote mainland areas. Confusingly, the white front refers to a white patch around the orange bill and not to a chest mark. When mature, these large, heavy geese have dark barring on their bellies. White-fronts feed in smaller groups and are shyer and less gregarious than the barnacle goose. They were once the most common goose found in Orkney, although now only a few winter there.

The whitefront prefers feeding on boggy peat land where its large bill copes well with tough herbage and rough grasses, and due to this habit they were nicknamed 'bog goose'. The stronger bill enables the geese to uproot entire plants, an unpopular trait with farmers. They have also adapted to feed on clover and grain, and eat potatoes left in the field.

Left. Greenland white-fronted geese (Laurie Campbell)

Right. Choughs are intelligent and playful members of the crow family (Laurie Campbell)

THE COW PAT SPECIALIST

Chough

Pyrrhocorax pyrrhocorax
S: reid-legged crow
G: *cathag dhearg-chasach*

The most charismatic member of the crow family, the chough was once widespread on many rocky headlands all round the coast. The Victorians persecuted it ruthlessly, stealing its eggs and killing the adult birds to add to their taxidermy collections. By the early nineteenth century, the chough had dwindled to only a few isolated populations.

With startling red legs and bill, the chough remains extremely rare. It favours the sandy machair islands of Islay and Colonsay, and is found in very small numbers in a few other places. It requires warmer winter temperatures that ensure a year-round abundance of insect prey. For this reason, it is mostly confined to low coastal areas touched by the warming Gulf Stream.

Without cattle, the chough struggles to survive. It relies largely on dung-associated invertebrates for food, particularly those found in cowpats. Grubs are extracted by probing with its specially curved, scarlet bill. Grain and fruit are also eaten, but invertebrates are the dietary staple.

The chough has an intimate association with farming and its decline has accelerated as a result of changes to rotational cropping, increased used of wormers in farm livestock, and the loss of old-fashioned pastures.

Choughs are found all round Islay, both in the south on the wild Mull of Oa, and at Ardnave and many of the dune systems that fringe cropped turf in the north. Constant battering from salt-laden gales helps to keep vegetation short and retains the right habitat for them.

Although choughs are monogamous, they are a highly

social species that live in flocks. Non-breeding adults may help to rear young. Acrobatic in the air, they often follow people and dogs and seem to enjoy dive-bombing, filling the air with their laughing calls. There is never any malicious intent and some even think of the chough as a humorous bird. Choughs usually remain loyal to nest sites and favour cliff ledges, caves, crevices and old buildings, and are sometimes found competing for nesting space with barn owls. While jackdaws often choose old chimneys for rearing their young, the chough appears not to like being so enclosed. With farming practices becoming more intensive and more cattle kept inside to save poaching-up of the ground in winter, it seems that the chough will probably not make a comeback on the mainland. However, its future seems secure on one of Scotland's best bird islands.

Fulmers often choose old buildings and walls as nest sites (Polly Pullar)

WAYFARERS

Fulmar

Fulmarus glacialis
S: mallduck, mallimoke, mallie
G: *fulmair, eun-crom, mulcaire*

Together with the gannet and puffin, the fulmar was the mainstay of the St Kildans' existence. It provided plump nutrition, eggs in various stages of development, feathers that they could sell, and bones and skins with which to manure their frugal crops. Rent for their land was paid in feathers from gannets, fulmars and puffins and during the 1840s each family's rent cost them in the region of 168 pounds in featherweight.

The rancid fishy smell from the feathers was sought to make mattresses for the army as the terrible odour was thought to ward off bedbugs, lice and fleas. Young fulmars, like young gannets, were fat and easier to catch just before they took to the air. Ornithologist William MacGillivray wrote in 1840: 'The fulmar forms one of the principal means of support to the islanders, who daily risk their lives in its pursuit.' Unlike gannets, fulmars had another use. As any trainee bird-ringer will know, they eject vile smelling amber-coloured oil from their crops in the form of a projectile vomit. Once this is on clothing it cannot be removed despite the promise of many of today's miracle biological washing products. The benign-looking, dark-eyed fulmars eject this oil in a form of self-defence. Inexperienced ringers often take steps to avoid the first onslaught, unaware that a second and third gobbet may be forthcoming. Birds of prey may be rendered flightless due to the viscosity of this oil – peregrine falcons have had to be looked after in captivity until the affected plumage has moulted, enabling them to fly once again.

The St Kildans viewed the oil as a panacea and used it for all manner of ills. They collected it by forcing the birds to regurgitate it into a receptacle, usually a gannet's dried stomach tied onto their waists. They risked life and limb scaling the cliffs for the valuable potion that gave them oil for lamps as well as medicine.

Following a visit to St Kilda, traveller Martin Martin wrote of the fulmar oil:

> It is good against rheumatic pains and aches in the bones; the inhabitants of the adjacent isle value it as

> a catholican for diseases; some take it for a vomit, others for a purge. It has been successfully used against rheumatic pains in Edinburgh and London; in the latter it has been lately used to assuage the swelling of a sprained foot, a cheek swelled with the toothaches and for discussing a hard boil; and proved successful in all three cases.

On St Kilda many babies had mysteriously died within the first two weeks of their birth, and it was many years before the true cause of this tragedy was discovered. The islanders traditionally treated the navels of their newborn babies with fulmar oil, and initially this was blamed for their deaths. However, it was not in fact the oil that caused the problem but the dirty receptacles that housed it: they were found to contain the lethal anaerobic bacterium *Clostridium tetani*, commonly known as tetanus, or lockjaw.

Prior to the mid 1800s, the fulmar was scarce and only bred on St Kilda. Numbers increased dramatically, however, with the increase in whaling and the traditional method of 'flensing' the whales (see page 137). Fulmars take advantage of offal and were associated with the whaling industry, with its large amount of waste discarded in the sea. This led to a gradual spread of fulmars southwards from Iceland and the Faroe Islands. Once whaling stopped, the increased catches of massive trawlers suited fulmars equally well.

They have now spread to many islands. On North Ronaldsay, the northernmost Orkney Island, fulmars use the 12 miles of continuous dry stone dyke that runs round the island as an ideal place to nest, but they are also found on mainland cliff sites, and are seen rearing chicks on old buildings, castle ramparts and grassy headlands. They are long-lived and have been recorded over 40 years of age. They travel large distances, particularly prior to reaching breeding maturity, usually after ten years of age. Highly pelagic in habitat, it is their mastery of the storm as they glide effortlessly low over gargantuan foam-covered waves, rapturously in control and albatross-like, which perhaps portrays them best.

Manx Shearwater

Puffinus puffinus
S: devil bird, lyre, lyrie
G: *fachach bàn, sgrail, sgrabair*

The blood-curdling sounds of an active Manx shearwater colony at night-time have, since before the Viking era, given rise to beliefs that there were trolls or other unworldly beings existing in the hills. For much of the year, the Manx shearwater flies in great flocks low over the ocean, skimming effortlessly to within a hair's breadth of the rise and fall of the swell. However, like other members of the tubenose family, including fulmars, it is ungainly on land and gets around in a clumsy shuffling manner. As this makes it very vulnerable, it comes ashore at night and is miraculously able to locate its own earth burrow, amongst a colony of thousands, in pitch darkness. Shearwaters use burrows and underground breeding chambers as high as 750 metres above sea level. Rum holds approximately 25 per cent of the world's population and there are other small colonies on some ten other Scottish islands; Scotland is said to hold about 60 per cent of the world's shearwaters. During high summer the wild and eerie screams of the

The tale of a lovelorn albatross

The black-browed albatross (*Diomedea melanophrys*) normally frequents the southern hemisphere, although there are occasional rare sightings in Scotland. A famous lone bird was first seen on the Bass Rock in 1967. Considerably larger than our biggest seabird the gannet, the black-browed albatross has a wingspan of almost eight feet (two metres) and weighs in the region of five kilograms. From 1972 onwards, it was believed that the same bird appeared at the gannet colony at Hermaness on Shetland, to where it returned most years until it disappeared in 1995. It was christened 'Albert' by birders and seemed to be seeking a mate but although it made nests, it never laid an egg. It continually made amorous advances to neighbouring gannets, but none were in the least bit interested. On the other hand, huge flocks of twitchers were extremely interested and gathered annually to tick this unusual bird off their lists, for it was thought to be the only one in the North Atlantic at the time.

Manx shearwaters can live to a great age (Laurie Campbell)

Manx shearwater are enough to waken the dead and have earned it the nickname 'devil bird'.

On the island of Canna a vast rat population almost drove the birds to extinction, and it was not until they were culled that the shearwater colony recovered. Verdant green patches grow round the nest holes. This is due to the regurgitated sand that has been ingested by the birds as they excavate sand eels from the seabed, and also from their sand-rich guano. These lush spots are referred to as 'high altitude greens'.

Manx shearwaters share Rum with a large deer population. Researchers on the island have seen that the deer sometimes eat both chicks and adult birds, thus fulfilling their need for extra calcium, found in the bird's bones (see page 4).

On St Kilda, Manx shearwaters were taken for food and feathers. Women went out at night and took eggs which they then sold to visiting tourists. On Mingulay, many shearwaters were killed annually and salted in barrels paid to the laird for the island's rent. Their old Norse name *lyre* or *lyrie* means 'fat'. Shearwaters are one of the longest-lived seabirds in Scotland, with ringing returns revealing some birds that have reached over 50 years of age. As they spend most of the rest of the year in waters off Brazil, older individuals will have travelled many hundreds of thousands of miles during their lifetimes.

Great Auk

Pinguinus impennis
S: gairfowl
G: *gearra-bhall, colcach mhòr*

Regarded by sailors as the original penguin, the unfortunate great auk was hounded to extinction. The precise date of its tragic demise remains shrouded in sea mist like the bird's isolated habitat, but is now generally accepted as occurring in 1852. There are remains of great auks in Neolithic kitchen middens, proof that they were in Scotland for a long time prior to extinction. Their end is well documented and is one of the saddest wildlife tragedies of all. It is also a frightening reminder to us of the vulnerability of all wildlife in our care, and how easy it is to lose a species in a relatively short span of time.

Large, flightless and totally harmless, the great auk, a predominantly pelagic species, roosted far out to sea and only came to rocky outcrops and skerries to breed. During the breeding season it developed a white patch above its eyes. Its hoarse, croaking cry was said to be similar to that of a razorbill although much louder. Weighing up to 11 pounds and well covered with protective body fat, it was killed for meat, feathers and oil. It was also taken as bait.

It was never found in Scotland in large numbers but its

increasing rarity value meant it was highly sought after. In an ironic twist, the more rare it became, the more so-called ornithologists or naturalists wanted it as a specimen for their collections.

The Orcadians on Papa Westray referred to the last breeding pair as the 'The King and Queen o' the Aaks'. Jeweller and collector William Bullock instructed men to go to the island to take the last lone male, as he wanted its skin for his private museum. In fact, the price realised for such specimens meant that there was constant demand, and great auks' large eggs also fetched ridiculously high prices. In 1895 an egg made the considerable sum of £350, and a skin a few years later was sold for a similar amount. When compared to today's values the sum equates to an astronomical £20,000.

Tales vary about the fishermen who caught what was thought to be the last auk on Stac an Armin, St Kilda.

> The men caught the bird, tied a rope to its leg, and kept it for 2–3 days. The extraordinary appearance of the bird impressed the men so much that they thought it was a ghost and looked upon it as the cause of the bad weather they had been experiencing.

Donald MacQueen of St Kilda once described how he and three friends caught a great auk alive in 1821. They gave it to the factor, who passed it on to the captain of a visiting cruiser. He took it 'for the Edinburgh museum': in other words, to be killed and stuffed. But this is the story of the auk that got away. Somewhere near Arran, the captain decided it was looking dirty and needed a bath. A rope was tied to its leg and the great bird was lowered into the sea for a swim. It seized its opportunity and escaped. So there is no great auk in the National Museum of Scotland, but you can still see one in the Kelvingrove Museum, Glasgow.

Many ornithologists refused to accept the great auk was finally gone and searched for it for many years, but the last sightings were reported in 1844 in Iceland and in 1852 in Newfoundland. By then it had been lost forever. There is now a memorial cairn built by the junior members of the Orkney Field Club in 1988 at Fowl Craig, on Papa Westray. It was instigated by Ralph Faulkner, who felt the birds' loss deeply and wanted to do something to make future generations aware of the seriousness of such an irreversible catastrophe. No creature so epitomises the horror of extinction as the great auk.

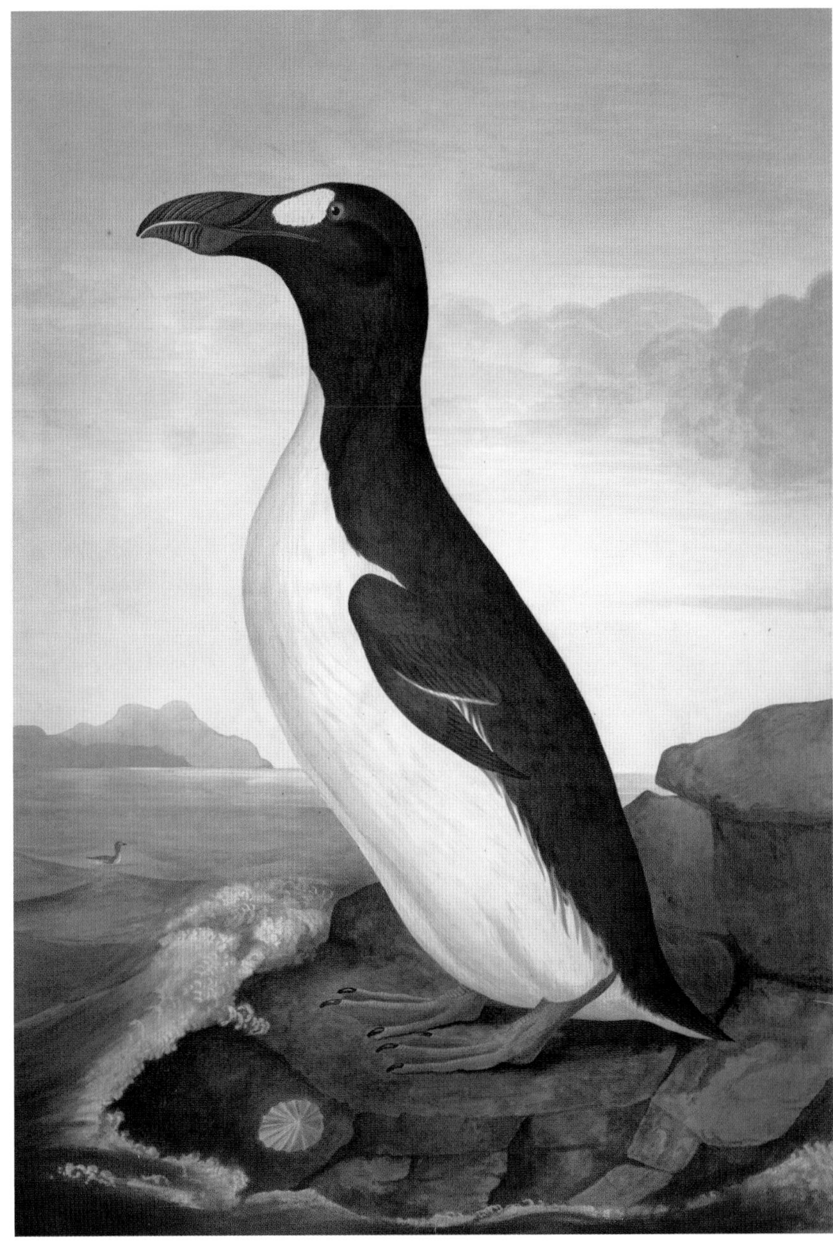

The great auk (© National History Museum. Licensor www.scran.ac.uk)

PIRATES

Great Skua

Stercorarius skua
S: bonxie
G: *fàsgadair mòr, tuilleag*

The remote Shetland island of Foula is the great skua stronghold (Polly Pullar)

Commonly known in the Highlands and Islands as the 'bonxie', the great skua is an imposing pirate, with aerial skills to match those of a fighter pilot. Once nicknamed the 'herdsman' in Orkney because it drove sea eagles away from lambs by mobbing them, it was highly popular. As more and more sheep were brought in, however, the sea eagles were persecuted and eventually the bonxie succumbed to the same fate, becoming a rare bird during the nineteenth century, when only a few bred in isolated locations.

Since law protected the bonxie during the early part of the twentieth century, it has dramatically expanded its range and has spread to some Hebridean islands around Orkney and Shetland. During the breeding season Shetland's most remote inhabited island, Foula, has more breeding bonxies than anywhere else in the world. On its breeding grounds, it is fearsome and defends its nest and young with a tenacity seen in few birds. It will attack intruders from the air and can inflict great damage with its powerful bill. Walking through the reserve at Hermaness on Unst in Shetland, even the slowest walkers running the gauntlet of overhead bombardment put on an impressive spurt. Carrying something above the head such as a stout stick can help to fend off attack although the best tactics are to steer well clear of the bird's territory.

Skuas are gull-like and agile. Although they swim well, they walk with a comical waddling gait, swaying slightly like a sailor who has been at sea for most of his life. They are mainly oceanic away from breeding areas and often follow trawlers waiting for discarded by-catch. Much of a bonxie's food is acquired by 'kleptoparasitism' – the birds steal food from others, forcing them to disgorge their hard-earned repasts. Their main victims are gulls, terns, auks and gannets. They are able to take birds too but usually only the weak, or unguarded chicks near the nest. Bonxies have been witnessed forcing adult ospreys to drop very large fish by constantly harrying them. Fishermen have seen them taking on gannets, on occasion even causing their victims to drown. Not only do they appear threatening, but they let out a deafening series of harsh, intimidating shrieks which are often enough to make a nervous bird panic, instantly drop its food and fly for cover.

THE FEATHERED FISHING INDUSTRY

Gannet

Morus bassanus
S: Solan goose, Bass goose, basser, gant
G: *sùlair, ansan, eun bàn an sgadain, tabhs, caraid-nan-Gaidheal*

There are three birds that were of vital importance to the seabird culture of the St Kildan people: the gannet, the puffin and the fulmar. The gannet, or 'Solan goose', made up part of the main food supply for the islanders by providing meat, eggs and feathers. Its huge bill was used as pegs and sometimes employed to hold down straw on buildings, its desiccated body was made into primitive footwear, and its dried stomach was used to contain fulmar oil collected directly from the birds' crops (see p. 158).

The gannet is a bird of superlatives: it is the largest British seabird, displaying a wingspan of six feet. Its plunges from great height have been recorded at 60 miles per hour, and in order to cope with this impact its skull is reinforced, while extra padding not dissimilar to a car's shock absorbers protects the neck and head. Although the gannet only stays submerged for a few minutes, its adapted nostrils and membranes over the eyes are designed to keep water out. Gannets may travel great distances in search of food.

Over two-thirds of the world's gannet population breeds in Scotland. The planet's biggest and most impressive gannetries are on the great sea stacks of St Kilda, notably Stac an Armin. This 643-foot rock is the tallest in the British Isles. Other important gannetries are found on the Bass Rock, Ailsa Craig, and Hermaness, as well as on Sùlaisgeir, some 40 miles north of the Butt of Lewis. Gannetries are visible from a considerable distance, blanched snow-white by the birds and their guano. Sailing around Stac an Armin surrounded by thousands of garrulous gannets is one of the most awe-inspiring of all wildlife spectacles. It is sometimes possible to land on the biggest single rock gannetry, Bass Rock, owned by the Hamilton-Dalrymple family for over 300 years, and now monitored and overseen by the Scottish Seabird Centre at North Berwick. Accompanied by a knowledgeable guide, this is an unforgettable experience amid the intense smell, the drifting feathers and the racket. Gannet numbers on the Bass Rock, as elsewhere, have increased dramatically in recent years. During the breeding season jet-black wings and a pollen-like dusting of soft yellow on its head, set off a mature gannet's white plumage. The bird's large eyes are rimmed with bright blue, and its webbed feet have almost

An island delicacy

Guga (young gannet) flesh was long viewed as a delicacy and helped to boost the beleaguered diets of the islanders at a time of great food shortage. Once sent to gourmet eateries in London and to the Edinburgh poultry markets, the taste of guga is notorious. It has been described in all manner of ways and appears largely to be held as a highly unpleasant dish. Daniel Defoe certainly did not appear to have much enjoyed it. During a visit to Edinburgh he described it as 'fatty, rank, coarse – and ill relish'd', while another writer said that it resembled 'a freshly killed hen that has been left in the rafters of the byre over winter and then marinated for a generation in cod liver oil'. How long can one of the last Scots' traditions survive? In the words of one young guga hunter: 'As long as a guga is in the sky, there will be a guga in the pot.'

Angus MacLeod plucking a guga on Sùlaisgeir, 1954 (© National Museums Scotland. Licensor www.scran.ac.uk)

A gannet sky-points in display beside its mate (Polly Pullar)

phosphorescent green veins.

Gannets return annually to their own particular small niche in a tightly packed colony, and there lay a single egg. The first birds to arrive often steal nest material from nests of previous years. This consists of seaweed and flotsam found at sea. A dried piece of bladderwrack may be offered to a mate during the breeding period. Courtship displays between a pair include sky-pointing their pale, dagger-like bills, and careful mutual preening. This is all part of a ritual as birds are reunited. The egg requires 40 days' incubation and the chick needs a further 90 days on land during which the adults feed it on regurgitated fish before it fledges. It then receives no further care from the adult birds. Thickly coated in white down, with its large bill peeping out, the chick resembles a child dressed in a thick fur hood.

The St Kildans sometimes caught mature birds as they arrived back in spring. However, it was usually once the chicks were fat-laden and well grown, but still unable to fly, that the hunters went on their perilous expeditions to the great sea stacks, four miles from Hirta, St Kilda's main island. Climbers were fearlessly skilled, many of them taking to the sheer, giddying bastions with bare feet and primitive horsehair ropes. Young boys became adept at climbing. Huge numbers of birds were taken, but this annual slaughter was essential to the St Kildans' survival. Thousands of birds were salted down for winter then stored in stone cleits. Totally unique to St Kilda, the cleits were built all over the island and were used to store both birds and sheep. Here meat was protected from rain, while the wind could blow through gaps in the stone to aid the drying process. Although the islanders left in 1930, the cleits remain and provide shelter for Soay sheep, native birds, the St Kilda wren and breeding migrants such as snipe.

Martin Martin, with a hint of amusement, wrote about the affect of gannets' eggs on visitors: 'The eggs are found to be of an astringent and windy quality to strangers, but it seems, are not so to the inhabitants, who are used to eat them from the nest.'

Gannets were taken in other places too. They were still collected on the Bass Rock up to 1876, when approximately 800 were taken to feed Irish labourers working on the mainland.

On Sùlaisgeir, an important, almost ritualistic Gaelic-based tradition survives from the 15th century. In August each year, the Men of Ness, on the northern most tip of Lewis, make a pilgrimage to this inhospitable outpost to harvest 2,000 young gannets, referred to as 'gugas'. The Scottish Executive sanctions the hunt, which has no impact on breeding gannet numbers, and the RSPB and SSPCA officially recognise that no cruelty is involved. Only birds of a certain size are swiftly killed and the guga hunters on the island deftly process the extraordinary harvest. Salted, and stacked in immaculate beehive shaped piles to retain the pickle, they are then covered until the much-celebrated return to The Port of Ness. On a recent visit to Ness, I was fortunate to try this notorious repast and found it not dissimilar to succulent salt mutton. The fat, however, was another matter.

Guillemot

Uria aalge
S: lavie, marrot (both also apply to razorbill), coot, queet, longie, sea hen, skout
G: *gearradh-breac*, *eun dubh an sgadain* (also applies to razorbill), *langaidh*

During periods of high gales in late summer and early autumn, it is not unusual for people to report guillemots and razorbills far inland on large bodies of water such as Loch Tay. Guillemots are normally pelagic, only coming ashore to breed. Severe gales may also cause problems for adult guillemots trying to find food for their young, and both eggs and nestlings can be washed off cliff ledges in a gale.

The guillemot's egg is not rounded like the puffin's, for if it were it would roll off the sheer cliffs where it nests. The female lays one ovate egg, a shape which makes it roll-proof. Despite this modification many eggs are still lost over the sides as birds jostle for position amid the constant coming and going from the sea far below. Usually a new egg is laid if it is not too late in the season.

A guillemot colony is extremely noisy, and the whole area is plastered with thick white guano, its strong fishy aroma hanging in the atmosphere. Although there are a few large colonies on cliffs on the mainland, most guillemots breed on islands and rocky outposts in the Hebrides, on the islands of the Forth, and in Orkney and Shetland. There are vast numbers of guillemots on the island of Westray, and at Marwick Head on the nearby Orkney mainland.

Guillemots are chocolate brown above and white below. As with other auks, divers, grebes and sea ducks this pied plumage is thought to offer camouflaged protection from predators. There is also a 'bridled' form of common guillemot where a white-eye ring is made bolder by a white strip leading back from the eye, almost resembling a pair of spectacles. This marking, along with the pied attire, adds to the general impression of a dapper gent in a smoking jacket.

The guillemot is the ultimate high-rise specialist and crams itself in with thousands of other guillemots. Sociable and sometimes viewed as comical, the Victorians once shot it purely for sport, and its eggs were collected in large numbers by the St Kildans and eaten in various states of development when they were reputed to be gamey and full of flavour. Eggs were also blown and sold as curios to visiting tourists, while the feathers and bones were used for fertilising frugal crops.

Guillemots in typical tightly packed colony (Polly Pullar)

Guillemots are all too frequently the unfortunate victims of oil spills. Although large spills are reported to the press, there are many other smaller incidents throughout the year which go largely unnoticed, yet kill birds, fish and mammals. Some years the SSPCA receives high numbers of guillemots that have to be cleaned by their specialist oiled-bird cleaning team. Another threat to members of the auk family is the loss of sand eels and sprats.

Kittiwake

Rissa tridactyla
G: *ruideag, ciodabhaig*

Kittiwake and chick on cliff-edge nest (Polly Pullar)

Generally viewed as the prettiest, most elegant member of the gull family, the oceanic kittiwake follows trawlers and feeds on discarded fish. Seldom seen inland, the kittiwake comes to island colonies to breed – the Treshnish Isles, Handa Island, Foula, and the Isle of May. The Orcadian island of Westray is home to a particularly large colony. There are also a few sites round the wilder parts of the coast, such as Fowlsheugh in Kincardineshire and St Abb's Head in Berwickshire. It is typically a bird of vertiginous cliff faces, although some kittiwakes use high buildings on which to make their nests. Ledges and crags are ideal. A pair of kittiwakes on their nest appear amorous and continuously attentive to one another. The nest site is often fringed with pink thrift and a froth of white sea campion. The noise from a kittiwake-breeding colony fills the salty air with the repetitious guttural sound that is represented in their common name.

Nesting tightly packed in high-rise cliff ledge accommodation leaves birds vulnerable. Gales and torrential rain may cause brood failure, while predators such as skuas and great black-backed gulls take chicks and steal catches from kittiwakes returning to feed young.

The kittiwake, like the puffin and various auk species, has suffered recent declines due to the over-fishing of sand eels (see page 124). Lack of this vital food led to a catastrophic drop in breeding success during the mid 2000s, and there have been major concerns about the species' future in Scotland.

Kittiwake chic

The kittiwake used to be shot in large numbers, and its attractive feathers were in demand for the millinery trade. Unfortunately, it was not only the feathers that were taken as the entire bird had to be killed, and in some cases even its wings and other body parts would be seen adorning stylish hats. During the nineteenth century, kittiwakes on Ailsa Craig suffered great losses due to the fashion for feathered headgear and many young kittiwakes were also taken, prized because their juvenile plumage was thought to be even more chic.

Puffin

Fratercula artica
S: Ailsa cock, norie, tammie norrie, tammie cheekie, patie, reid-nebbit pussy, coulter neb, sea coulter
G: *fachach, coltrachan, Seumas Ruadh, pealag, peata ruadh, buthaigre, bùigire, buthaid*

The puffin's Latin name *fratercula,* or 'little brother', shows a long-standing affection for them, and a neighbourliness worthy of the Celtic monks who used to share some of their remote island habitats.

Until the 1950s, a bakery in Stromness in Orkney used puffin's eggs with the addition of secret ingredients to make cakes and pancakes. They were said to be of outstanding flavour and were therefore in great demand. The St Kildans preferred to collect the birds themselves rather than their eggs, and caught them on Dùn, the small grassy island in Village Bay, using primitive horsehair nooses on long poles. Puffins have been eaten for centuries and it was largely the women who caught them on St Kilda, often pulling them from their burrows as well as using puffin gins. They were mainly caught for their feathers but were also an important source of food in summer when they were added to the morning porridge. The islanders collected them from the steep slopes of Soay and Boreray. The first puffin caught was plucked of all but wing and tail feathers, and then set free in order to attract the interest of others that were in turn easily caught – twenty to twenty-five thousand of them a year in the mid nineteenth century, according to one estimate.

For much of the year the pelagic puffin is seldom seen as it roosts far out to sea. During this time it becomes drab and grey and loses the brilliant coloured bill that makes it so easily recognisable. The distinctive bill is made of horny patches that re-grow annually, the male's being slightly brighter than that of his mate. The bill also gave rise to one of the puffin's popular nicknames, 'coulter neb', coulter being a Scots word for plough, and neb meaning the beak.

While they are often viewed as comical and clown-like on land, the puffin is in its element at sea. They also fly in great wheels, congregating in large numbers at daybreak and as dusk is approaching. On islands such as the Isle of May, the Shiants and Handa, this display is particularly spectacular. At a puffinry, the ground is latticed with their excavations and often subsides. Great care must be taken while walking as a heavy boot can easily cause a burrow to subside and crush a vulnerable, black-fluffed chick inside. On the Isle of May, puffins compete for burrow space with resident rabbits.

As any bird-ringer will tell you, puffins have extremely sharp claws. These are burrowing tools and are also a means of defending burrows from marauding gulls waiting nearby. The gulls are often more than a little surprised to receive a shower of earth flying out as the industrious puffin completes further DIY extensions to its burrow.

Puffin – once the breeding season is past, the puffin's colourful bill fades to duller shades (Polly Pullar)

Puffin courtship is visibly amorous. Males offer the females a piece of pink thrift or other plant material and there is much crooning and bill clacking. Strange noises also echo from the earth as birds prospecting for suitable subterranean maternity suites voice their approval. A single egg is laid and incubated by both parents and the downy puffling eventually takes to the sea under the cover of darkness. Before this, the parents are kept active and return many times with beaks crammed with sprats and sand eels, many of which will be stolen by winged bandits such as gulls and skuas.

In 1989 it was thought that 90 per cent of Shetland puffins failed to rear chicks due to over-fishing of sand eels (see page 124). This has raised grave concerns for the future of many auks and seabirds.

Such is the love for the puffin, that it frequently features on emblems, books and badges, and as soft toys. Its rounded shape has even been fashioned into pottery jugs and mugs, and it is the subject of many a postcard. The puffin is probably one of the most popular of all British birds.

Razorbill

Alca torda
S: lavie, marrot (both also apply to guillemot)
G: *coltraiche, eun dubh an sgadain* (also applies to guillemot), *duibh-eunach, sgrab, làmhaidh*

Although the razorbill is found in colonies of guillemots, it prefers to nest on the outside of the melée and does not appear to have the same head for heights as its close relation. The French call it *le petit pingouin* and it is indeed penguin-like in appearance. It is also frequently likened to a little waiter in black-and-white attire. The razorbill is the nearest relative to the great auk, looking like a pint-sized version of its extinct ancestor. The daffodil-yellow gape is a dramatic feature that is easily seen when the bird opens its bill. Razorbills lay a large, round egg and as they do not nest crammed together, it does not have to be roll-resistant. They usually choose crevices and easily accessible ledges. Eggs and chicks are vulnerable to rats and mink, and aerial predators also threaten adults returning with sand eels to feed their young.

Razorbills spend most of the year far out to sea, congregating in large rafts together with other auks. They may also be seen in estuaries and the Voes of Shetland, however. The largest razorbill colonies are found on the Shiant Islands, Berneray and Handa, but they are present on most good seabird breeding islands and on mainland cliffs, including Fowlsheugh in Kincardineshire, St Abb's Head in Berwickshire and Berriedale in Caithness.

Razorbills have seldom been killed for food although their eggs were eaten and deemed good when fresh. As with other birds caught by fowlers, the razorbill's feathers were used, and its bones and skin added to manure for spreading on fields.

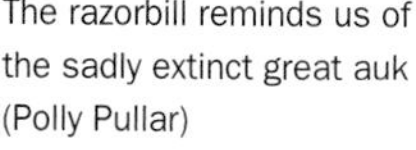

The razorbill reminds us of the sadly extinct great auk (Polly Pullar)

ON THE ROCKS

Cormorant

Phalacrocorax carbo
S: gormaw, Mochrum elder, loring, scarf, scart
(last two also apply to shag), rain goose
G: *sgarbh mòr, ballaire, cailleach dhubh, fitheach mara*

There is frequent confusion between cormorants and shags – this anonymous ode leads us to believe the two species are one and the same:

The common cormorant or shag
Lays eggs inside a paper bag.
The reason, you will see, no doubt,
It is to keep the lightning out.
But what these unobservant birds
Have never noticed is that herds
Of wandering bears will come with buns
And steal the bags to hold the crumbs.

Anon.

Although they look similar, cormorants are larger and less numerous than shags. They usually nest on islands and offshore skerries, but a few breed successfully on freshwater lochs, the largest colony being at the Mochrum and Castle lochs in Dumfries and Galloway. Outstretched wings held out to dry have given rise to a nickname, 'the Mochrum elders', for they are said to resemble the rather forbidding Presbyterian Kirk elders that once presided over the area.

Cormorants have a capacious gullet and are able to swallow extremely large fish. This has brought about inevitable conflict with anglers who see the birds as a serious threat to salmon and other fish stocks and constantly campaign to cull them, particularly on such important rivers as the Tay and Tweed. Another side effect to having cormorants roosting in trees is the copious amount of guano they produce. This can actually kill trees, leaving eerie stands of skeletal trunks in their wake. Their nick-

Cormorant

name 'Black Death' is a reference to this, as well as to the amount of fish they consume.

Although they look oddly reptilian on the rocks with their huge feet, in the water their serpentine elegance and agility is evident. As the sun hits their backs, their dull, brown plumage is transformed into a shimmering dress of many subtle hues.

MacPhee's dog

A Colonsay tradition tells how seventeen men from the island once went to shoot cormorants on Jura. Their foster-brother, Malcolm MacPhee, went with them, bringing his apparently useless dog. They cross over to Jura the evening before and settle into a cave for the night. The conversation turns to women and the brothers unwisely wish for some female company: 'Before long, seventeen women in green dresses entered the cave and went over to the beds of heather where MacPhee's foster-brothers were, and MacPhee heard the crackling sound of breaking bones.' The seventeen women then turn their attention to MacPhee but the dog puts on an unprecedented display of courage, keeping them at bay while his master runs back to the boat and escapes. But the story does not end happily. The dog returns, hurtling over the water like a blazing comet, but he in turn is now so ferocious that he goes for his master and has to be destroyed. Even so, it was observed, even the most useless dog has his day.

In the breeding season the shag has a distinctive crest (Polly Pullar)

Shag

Phalacrocorax aristotelis
S: scarf, scart (both also apply to cormorant), lorn
G: *sgarbh beag, sgarbh an sgumain*

The shag is smaller than the cormorant. During the breeding season, it is easy to distinguish due to its smart crest. Despite this, there is still frequent confusion between the two species.

Shags were once eaten, but they were reputed to be fishy and bony. So perhaps they were consumed more in desperation than for pleasure. Birds congregating on skerries were often shot at for no other purpose than so-called sport as boats passed by.

Shags are attractive birds, with brilliant, emerald-coloured eyes and glossy plumage that shines like the finest shot-silk in shades of bottle green, purple and blue when hit by the sun. It is unfortunate that their common name should immediately make us think of its modern-day sexual connotation. The NHS in Shetland decided to take advantage of this double meaning and introduced a large model shag using one of the bird's well-known nicknames 'scarf' – 'Scarfie the Safe Shag', a seven-foot model, is used to raise awareness of the growing problem of sexually transmitted diseases.

Hunting shags

Islanders still alive in the 1960s could remember hunting shags and cormorants for home use, up and down the west coast from Arran to the Northern Isles. Dawn and dusk were favourable times, when the birds came and went from their roost, but it was also possible, as on Mingulay and Westray, to hunt them at night, by muffling their boats' oars and creeping up on them while they slept. Others used guns or sticks, hitting the birds as they flew past slowly, against the wind. A Barra man told how there were two kinds of *sgarbh* – big ones and little ones. The little ones (shags) made better eating but the big ones (cormorants) kept longer, a week or more in winter. They would be plucked, singed over the peat fire and boiled with oatmeal, salt, onions and sometimes a few vegetables to make *brochan sgairbh* – a kind of porridge. The peat smoke gave them a burnt taste. The small feathers were kept for pillows.

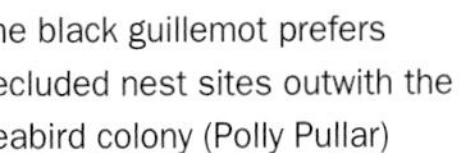

The black guillemot prefers secluded nest sites outwith the seabird colony (Polly Pullar)

Black Guillemot

Cepphus grille
S: dovekie, cutty, sea doo, teistie, sinnie-fynnie
G: *calltag, gearradh-glas*

Although the lovely, eye-catching black guillemot seems sociable at sea, during the breeding season it does not favour the densely packed colonies of its relative, the common guillemot, but prefers to lay its two eggs in a secluded rocky crevice. It is more adept at negotiating slippery rocks than the other auks.

The Shetland nickname 'tystie', from the Norwegian name for the species, is now widely used in Scotland. The black guillemot has bright-red legs and, in the breeding season, a bright-red gape is revealed as it opens its bill. In winter, however, it changes its plumage dramatically and becomes largely white. It is often visibly playful and emits a shrill and distinctive call. Frank Fraser Darling wrote: 'Play is of a varied kind and is very infectious.'

Many tysties congregate round human activity on the coast. An entire colony was almost wiped out during an oil spill at Sullom Voe in Shetland at the end of 1978. Rats can cause problems, as they frequently steal the eggs of the black guillemot.

ROCK CLIMBER

Black Rat

Rattus rattus
S: ship rat, roof rat, ratton, raut
G: *radan dubh, gall-luch*

The black rat is one of the rarest mammals in Britain. Before the early nineteenth century, the black rat was the only type of rat present in this country. It originated in Asia and was thought to have arrived during the Middle Ages. However, remains from the fifth century have proved otherwise.

Its nickname the 'ship's rat' is appropriate, for it frequently swam ashore from shipwrecks. Ironically, it was often holes gnawed by the rats in the ship's timber that led to the ships sinking in the first place. As they began to do so, the rats left in large numbers, carrying bubonic plague and other deadly diseases with them.

On the island of North Rona, black rats came ashore from a wreck in 1685 and caused havoc. They ate all the meal stored on the island and eventually both the islanders and the rats starved to death. No longer found on the mainland and exceedingly rare on islands, with the excep-

Rat satire

There were people who claimed to be able to banish rats, like the Pied Piper of Hamlin with his flute. Highlanders had other methods: they satirised them.

Aoir nan Radan (The Satire of the Rats)

Dà dhroch còmhdhail dheug is coinneamh
Air luchd nan casa caola croma,
Nam beul braoisgeach bu gheur faobhar –
Sgrios na h-aoir gun dèan bhur lomadh,
Sgrios na h-Aoine air ur n-ògaibh
'S leònadh air bhur leanaibh:
'S ann san eucoir tha sibh eòlach,
'S thèid ur fògradh air ur n-aineol

(Twelve bad encounters and a meeting be on the tribe of slender bandy legs and of grinning sharp-bladed mouths – May satire's destruction strip you bare. Friday's destruction be on your young ones and wounding be upon your children. You're no strangers to criminal behaviour, and you'll be banished to lands unknown.)

This is just a small section of a rat-satire, or curse, from Ardnamurchan. It goes on to assure the rats that if they don't leave now, things will only get worse for them. Women and girls will curse them (it was the women's work they had spoiled) and they will die a threefold death; burned, sick, and drowned in a shipwreck.

The people of Calve Island off Tobermory once paid a famous rat-curser, Iain Pholchrain, from Morvern to come over and rid the island of rats. He delivered his curse or satire extempore in the traditional way, though J.G. Campbell makes it sound more like quiet diplomacy than anything else: 'he told the rats to go away peaceably and take care not to lose themselves in the wood. He told them which houses to avoid (those of the bard's own friends), which houses held abundant stores of butter and cheese and meal.'

tion of Inchcolm in the Firth of Forth, the last remaining stronghold of the black rat is on the Shiant Islands, three islands dominating the Minch close to Lewis.

The black rat has longer ears, larger eyes and a shaggier coat than the brown rat. Its tail is longer, although overall it is slightly smaller in size. It can breed at a frightening rate, producing up to five litters a year. In situations where rats have access to plenty of food and are not persecuted, they may have as many as 15 young in each litter. Although associated with ships, like many sailors black rats are poor swimmers, but are agile climbers and can easily negotiate the steep cliffs of the Shiants, for example.

Having rats on such an important seabird colony as the Shiant Islands has been a contentious issue. The islands are very important for puffins, guillemots, razorbills, shags, kittiwakes and fulmars, but despite a rat population of approximately 3,000, there are still high densities of breeding birds. Lack of food during the harsh winter months probably helps to keep rat numbers in check. Although the rats do eat both seabirds and their eggs, they also consume vegetation, grass seeds, small mammals and invertebrates and are not viewed as a threat.

Conversely, the brown rats that arrived on Ailsa Craig on a coal puffer in 1889 caused bedlam. The island was soon overrun and the puffin colony there was almost completely wiped out. There were many half-hearted attempts to get rid of the rats until finally drastic measures were taken in 1991: the Royal Navy flew in three tons of rat poison. Care was taken to avoid non-target species, and the project proved successful.

BACK FROM THE BRINK

White-tailed Eagle

Haliaeetus albicilla
S: ern, yirn (both also used of golden eagle)
G: *iolair-mhara, iolair bhàn*

The last white-tailed (or sea) eagles bred in Skye, where an albino female was extirpated in 1918; prior to that they had been found all over Scotland, not only in wild mountainous regions, but also along coasts and estuaries, on rivers and in some surprising lowland habitats. Some inland cliffs and crags retain the Gaelic name for sea eagle. Intense persecution put an end to the Scottish population until the first reintroduction phase was initiated on the Inner Hebridean island of Rum between 1975 and 1985. Sea eagles, almost vulturine in profile, seem vast when they take to the air, as they effortlessly glide over the sea. Its nickname, 'flying barn doors', is descriptive of its massive, broad-winged silhouette, and its sheer proportions often provoke expletives.

The sea eagle is now seen as one of the most imposing and dramatic Scottish birds, although it is a bird of mixed fortunes. In *A Hundred Years in the Highlands,* written by Osgood Mackenzie in the early 1920s, there is a description of a visit to a sea eagle's eyrie to take the large, pure-white eggs, only to discover that a local shepherd had stolen them the previous day. In the end, the young Osgood MacKenzie paid the shepherd for them.

Sea eagles were previously more common than the golden eagle in many parts. They were once revered alongside golden eagles. In Pictish carvings and prehistoric remains in Orkney there are clear signs that the birds were seen as sacred and held in the greatest respect. Sea eagles were also found in ancient burial sites together with important nobles and clan members. Shetland fishermen believed the eagles had supernatural powers and they smeared sea eagle fat onto bait in the hope of improving their catches. They also believed that when a fish saw a sea eagle, it imme-

Sea eagle, now becoming a more familiar sight in some areas (Neil McIntyre)

The territorial eagle

> 'I saw a couple of eagles [on one of the Shiant Isles]: the natives told me that these eagles would never suffer any of their kind to live there but themselves, and that they drove away their young ones as soon as they were able to fly. And they told me likewise that they never yet killed any sheep or lamb in the island, although the bones of lambs, of fawns, and wild-fowls, are frequently found in their nests; so that they make their purchase in the opposite islands, the nearest of which is a league distant.'

diately turned belly up as if offering itself to the bird.

With the spread of sheep throughout the Highlands, however, attitudes quickly altered. Although skilled at plucking fish from water, the sea eagle is also an opportunist with a catholic diet, and readily takes advantage of easy prey as well as carrion. It soon came into conflict with sheep farmers and gamekeepers, and a bounty of five shillings was offered for its head. As well as plundering its eggs, the Victorians saw the birds as an impressive addition to taxidermy collections and marvelled at their eight-foot wingspan and huge impressive bills, thus sealing their fate.

The demise of the sea eagle left a void and although there were early attempts to reintroduce them, these proved unsuccessful until 1975, when the Nature Conservancy Council (NCC), now SNH, instigated a reintroduction programme centring on the National Nature Reserve, Rum. During a ten-year period 82 birds were imported from Norway under special licence and flown to RAF Kinloss. John Love of the NCC travelled to Norway and then subsequently worked with the birds on Rum as they acclimatised, fed on a natural diet before being released. With so many deer, seabirds, wild goats and fish in the vicinity, the survival rate of the released young was high.

Sea eagles take five years to reach sexual maturity. Initial breeding success was on the nearby Isle of Mull in 1985, with a pair raising the first wild chick for 70 years. Colonisation was slow but between 1993 and 1998, more birds were released in other areas and there was a gradual spread. By the 25th anniversary of the first release, 12 young had fledged from 22 pairs of eagles.

In recent years, more sea eagles have been released on the east coast, in Fife. East Scotland Sea Eagles is a joint venture between the RSPB, SNH, and Forestry Commission Scotland, and plans to release approximately 15–20 birds annually for several years. Although the birds are now well established in the west, they need help to re-colonise the eastern side of the country.

Birds of six to eight weeks old are taken annually from nests where there is more than one chick, ensuring the other chick remains with its parents. They are then flown to Scotland in August to secret locations and kept in small groups in 'hacking pens' with little human contact. Prior to release, they are fitted with wing tags and radio backpacks with a five-year battery life. Food dumps are left out but gradually the young birds wander further and further from the site and soon learn to fend for themselves.

Young sea eagles may travel great distances in search of a place to settle. They mature late and do not start breeding until they are at least four or five years old. In Mull, an area dominated by farming and tourism, the return of the sea eagle has been a great success, and it is hoped that this will be mirrored elsewhere. Farmers have been aided where sea eagles are predating on lambs, but eagle tourism has brought other benefits and many people have diversified into the holiday market. A viewing hide allows people to see birds and their young on the nest, and work is being done to promote and protect them under the auspices of the RSPB and the island's dedicated warden, Dave Sexton.

ON THE BRINK

Snowy Owl

Bubo scandiacus
G: *comhachag gheal*

The snowy owl is a bird of the High Arctic and is usually only seen as a vagrant in Scotland. Bird-watching history was made in 1967 when the then RSPB warden for Shetland, islander Bobby Tulloch, discovered the first breeding snowy owls on Fetlar.

A Mad Dash to Fair Isle

For many years now, birders have been rushing to the far north, to one of Shetland's most remote islands – Fair Isle. Lying approximately halfway between Orkney and Shetland, the island was first recognised in the early 1900s by the curator of the Royal Scottish Museum, Eagle Clarke. He had been to many Scottish islands and recognised Fair Isle as an ideal place to see rare migrants due to it being situated within a major Eurasian migration flight path. Thousands of birds, some from far afield, pass over the island each spring and autumn. When a squall begins and flying conditions become difficult, birds (in particular the young or weaker individuals) are forced to look for somewhere to land, or face imminent drowning in the sea. Fair Isle offers a crucial stop-over point for these weary migrants. It was the well-known ornithologist George Waterston who bought the island in 1947 and saw its value: Fair Isle was small and treeless enough for ornithologists to easily cover on a daily basis, recording observations and ringing data, and gaining a profound understanding of bird migration patterns in relation to the seas and the climate.

Waterston's plans to create a bird observatory there finally came to fruition in 1948. The first observatory was housed in old naval huts, but such was the popularity of the venture that by 1969 a new building was made. The island was handed over to the National Trust in 1954 but the Fair Isle Bird Observatory Trust retained the observatory and some land around it.

Over the years, an astounding list of extreme rarities has been drawn up, with birders from all over the world paying astronomical rates for flights in order to reach the island in a hurry when something of particular interest shows up. As well as a large lists of UK 'firsts' and many unique birds never recorded in Scotland before, the island has become famous for four species in particular, now known by birders as the 'Fair Isle Specials'. These four Siberian species appear annually in small numbers but are very hard to see in other parts of Europe: the lanceolated warbler, Pallas's grasshopper warbler, Pechora pipit and yellow-breasted bunting. Four other Russian rarities are also seen on a regular annual basis: the great snipe, citrine wagtail, paddyfield warbler and Blyth's reed warbler. During the autumn and spring migrations when these birds appear, the observatory bulges at the seams. Eco-friendly accommodation, at the cost of £4 million, was built on Fair Isle, opening in 2010. The UK now has the largest bird list per square mile of anywhere in the northern hemisphere. Much of this is due to the fact that vast numbers of birders spend many hours identifying rarities such as American warblers and Asian shrikes on small offshore islands such as Fair Isle and the Scilly Isles in the south-west of England.

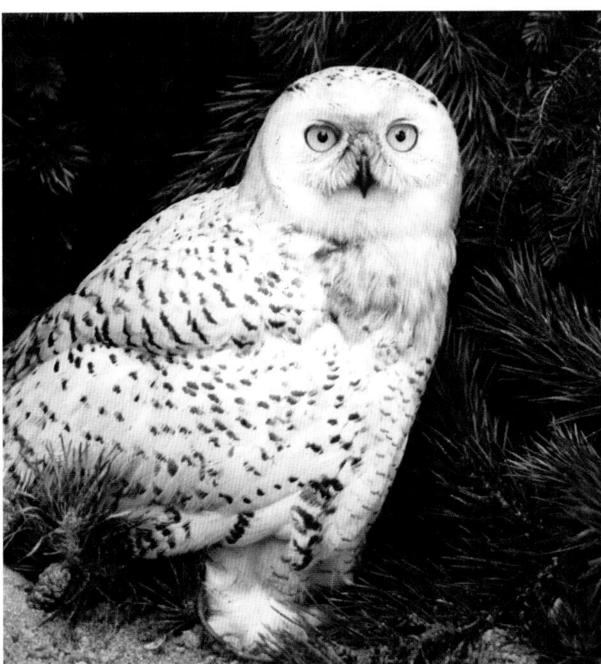

Oiled snowy owl handed to Polly Pullar for rehabilitation and release on Fetlar (Polly Pullar)

CHAPTER SEVEN

FARM AND CROFT

INTRODUCTION

Scotland's agriculture has changed beyond all recognition since the arrival of settlers from Western Europe to Britain in 4000 BC. The first colonists brought seeds with them, as well as small primitive forms of cattle, sheep, goats and pigs. These early farmers quickly spread from the south of England to the most northerly isles, fabricating rough dwellings and felling timber to make way for more stock.

The value of that early animal stock is clear today – over the millennia, various native breeds were developed, creating a legacy of farm animals individually suited to particular terrains. The hairy black cattle that dominated the Highlands from the 1600s once provided England with almost its entire supplies of beef, and they developed into today's Highland cattle.

The early settlers worked together in small groups. During the 1700s, 'ferm-touns' were established in which several families subsisted. Their beasts provided valuable food and fertilised the ground. Traditional smallholdings were often referred to as 'crofts', and in the Highlands a new focus on crofting developed. Later into the eighteenth century the entire landscape was being reconstructed to create big 'improvement' farms from the old townships, and the surplus population resettled in new planned towns such as Inveraray, or in allotted single-tenancy smallholdings on more marginal land. Crofts were recognised from Islay in the south to the Western Isles and beyond. The new crofting system provided less than a family needed to survive, meaning the crofter always had to supplement his living through other work – commonly fishing or weaving.

Crofting was originally intended to keep people in their communities. Society was rapidly changing, however, and it was to become dominated by landowners' financial ambitions, escalating rents, and the Highland Clearances for the mass invasion of sheep. These events led to the crofter's struggle for land tenure and rights, which they secured in the Crofters' Act of 1886, when their needs were finally officially recognised.

Crofting agriculture used 'lazy beds' – parallel strips separated by drainage ditches. There they grew the small disease-resistant 'bere' barley and potatoes, and took their cattle to seasonal pasturage in the summer shielings high in the glens. These sites remain green and verdant due to the animal's dung deposits from previous centuries. On many remote hillsides, when the sun highlights the ground, evidence of old 'runrig' land use and holding systems is still clearly seen.

Despite today's farms increasing in size, there are fewer farmers and employees. Most farmers have had to diversify

Opposite. Glen Ledknock, Perthshire (Polly Pullar)

in order to survive. Agribusiness is governed by complex legislation and involves endless forms that need to be filled in, while agriculture has gone from being an art form to a science. Despite this, many are slowly beginning to realise that with the downturn in numbers of such evocative farmland birds as the curlew and lapwing, our farming methods have become too intensive and the land and its natural inhabitants are suffering. Hedgerows and trees that were ripped out and felled in the 1960s and 1970s are being reinstated as wildlife corridors alongside fields, providing food and shelter for a wide range of wildlife.

From the smallest crofts in the original crofting counties of Sutherland, Caithness, Ross-shire, Argyllshire and Inverness-shire, to the large sheep and cattle-producing areas of the Borders and the North-east, the diversity of Scotland's farms is astonishing. Fewer people now live in the countryside, yet we appear to demand more access rights to it, with little thought of those whose livelihood depends on the land. Sheep, cattle, pig and deer farming plays a vital role and has been responsible for re-sculpting the landscape as we fence, plant, build and cultivate.

The important legacy of the old native breeds and their heritage value is also once again being recognised. While they may not be able to compete for speedy growth rates and increased size with modern commercial breeds, nothing beats the old breeds for character and flavour.

Aberdeen-Angus bulls at Skaill Farm, Orkney (Polly Pullar)

GOING NATIVE

Cattle

S: coo (pl. kye)
G: *bà (pl. of bò), crodh, sprèidh*

Aberdeen-Angus

> The story of the rise and progress of the Aberdeen-Angus breed of beef cattle has no parallel in the annals of cattle breeding – so local was the origin of the breed, so comparatively late was the start made towards improvement, so rapid was the progress made and so complete the conquest achieved.
>
> Barclay and Keith, *The Aberdeen-Angus Breed: A History*, 1958.

The Aberdeen-Angus is recognised as the world's finest source of prime beef. The breed was developed at the beginning of the nineteenth century from the small polled (hornless) black cattle of north-east Scotland locally known as 'doddies' and 'hummlies'. The Galloway and Aberdeen-Angus, both polled breeds, had many similarities and origins in the same early black stock.

Although private herd books were established, it was not until 1862 that the breed herd book was founded, and in 1879 the Aberdeen-Angus Society was officially launched. The Aberdeen-Angus has hit the high spots, with a world-record-breaking bull, Lindertis Evulse, that sold for 60,000 guineas in 1963 (see page 202), and another record-breaker which sold privately in 2010 for a reputed 75,000 guineas. However, having been bred too small, and then too large, and with many of the finest animals exported, breeders have had to work hard to re-establish this superb breed that now has to compete with massive beef breeds from the Continent.

In 1927 a consignment of prize bulls was shipped out to Australia, to be cared for on the journey by Aberdeenshire stockman Robert Grant. A severe storm blew up on the

The Burghead bulls

Bulls had more than ordinary significance for the people who lived on the south shore of the Moray Firth in the sixth or seventh century. No fewer than thirty bull images have been found, hefty but agile-looking, carved on stone tablets in and around the Pictish fort at Burghead, near present-day Elgin. This was one of the major power centres of Pictland, possibly a military or naval base. As with all Pictish carvings, there are different theories as to what they meant. Were they the 'signature' of a particular individual or tribe? Did they once have a religious meaning, as bulls certainly did in other parts of Europe and beyond: the Irish epic *'Táin Bó Cuailgne'* ('The Cattle Raid of Cooley') describes a war fought over possession of a mighty bull; and temples of Mithras, including one used by Roman soldiers on Hadrian's Wall, contained a depiction, carved in stone, of a bull being slain by Mithras. The Burghead bulls look more like allies than adversaries. So what did Burghead people so admire about bullishness that they wanted to be reminded of it so often as they went about their daily lives? Was it simply a fascination with power or did they also see in all that brawn and muscle – a determined life-force, a strong defender?

In the mid seventeenth century, the Presbytery of Dingwall found itself struggling with occasional bull-sacrifices, mostly in the west, although Contin and Fodderty are also mentioned. During the same period, an Auldearn woman would describe seeing elf-bulls 'roaring and skoilling' at the entrance to the fairy king and queen's palace on Dounie Hill near Nairn. Whether she knew it or not, Isobel Gowdie was in touch with an image which had been potent in her locality for a very long time.

A cast of one of the Burghead bulls (© National Museums Scotland. Licensor www.scran.ac.uk)

Indian Ocean, causing the loss of several bulls of another breed also on the ship. As the last carcass was thrown overboard for the sharks, Robert Grant was said to have chucked a heap of Aberdeen-Angus breed pamphlets over too, and shouted, 'That's a' ye'll get o' the black boys'. He was insistent that the same fate would not befall his beloved black charges.

The breed's origins were fiercely disputed, but it was eventually agreed that it was developed in both Aberdeenshire and Angus. Many breeders helped to improve and develop the Aberdeen-Angus, but there were three in particular whose input and knowledge proved invaluable: Hugh Watson of Keillour in Angus, and William McCombie of Tillyfour and Sir George MacPherson-Grant of Ballindalloch, both in Aberdeenshire. Each man concentrated on different aspects of a breed which has experienced mixed fortunes. The Aberdeen-Angus is currently found in more than 60 countries, however, and is still without doubt the producer of the finest beef of all.

Ayrshire

The early Ayrshire-type cows were referred to as 'Dunlops' and 'Cunninghams' and had long sweeping horns that have since been bred out for ease of handling. Many farms kept an Ayrshire cow for the provision of milk for the house. This beautiful breed was first recognised in its own right

The Ayrshire cow has a gentle temperament and longevity (Polly Pullar)

in 1814, and the first Herd Book Society was established in 1877. Colours and hide patterns may vary – from red and white, to almost pure red, and pure white. The Ayrshire is small and hardy but in recent years has lost popularity to imported dairy cows, Holstein and Friesians, both of which have capacious udders and produce an astonishing amount of milk per year. However, biggest does not always mean best and the Ayrshire's small, neat udder is less prone to mastitis, and she can produce milk for longer periods than her supposedly superior competitors. She is also thrifty and will lactate even while on a low plane of nutrition.

The Ayrshire has a reputation for her mild temperament, ease of handling and calving, and lack of health problems. Her milk is high in butterfat, contributing to a fine flavour. Ayrshire cattle are often favoured for small organic systems.

Beef Shorthorn

Nicknamed the 'great improver' for its ability to enhance almost any breed when crossed with it, the Beef Shorthorn is now finding popularity once again as the ideal animal to use on hill cows, due to its ability to thrive on poor ground. Red and white, and roan are the common forms. A docile nature and kindly eye are breed characteristics.

The Beef Shorthorn, also known as the Scotch Shorthorn, was altered during the 1830s. Aberdeenshire cattle breeder Amos Cruickshank enhanced many of the breed's finest traits through selective breeding until an improved type was fixed.

Beef Shorthorns have been exported worldwide as they manifest the essential qualities of a good suckler cow: strong milking ability, ease of calving and excellent fertility. According to one of Scotland's most famous cattle breeders, James

Cattle raids

Martin Martin describes cattle raiding as a normal, even honourable, part of Highland life. Edward Burt, an accountant visiting in the 1720s, voiced the southern perspective which was then gaining ground: 'The principal time for this wicked practice is the Michaelmas moon,' he writes, 'when the cattle are in condition fit for markets.' He calls the perpetrators 'banditti' and complains about the low rate of prosecutions, but there was a time when cattle raiding was almost regarded as a kind of championship between clans. The pipe tune '*Thogail nam bò*' ('To lift the cattle') celebrates the audacity of the MacFarlanes on moonlit nights, and the toast '*Geumnaich bhà*' (the lowing of cows) is probably not as peace-loving as it sounds. Cattle raiding was by no means confined to the Highlands, although it continued for longer there. The Border rievers were also cattle raiders and the Devil's Beef Tub above Annandale was once a holding area for livestock 'lifted' from their neighbours.

A reiver comes to a sticky end in a fourteenth-century poem about St Ninian: it tells how he used to visit his cattle in the hills and bless them, making a circle round them with his staff. The herdsmen were supposed to keep them within that circle all night, but on one occasion they fall asleep and a party of reivers swoop down, eager for booty. Suddenly however, a 'bule fers and fel' charges at one of them and 'in the wame racht hym sic a rout, til al his guttis schot oute'. He is dead by morning. The romance of cattle raiding means nothing to this ethically-minded poet. He calls the victim a 'maister thef', not a dashing young hero, but he also presents Ninian as the kind of saint who would give a man a second chance. He resuscitates him and blesses his contrite, shaken accomplices.

Left. Beef shorthorn bull (Polly Pullar)

Above. Galloway bull perfectly at home on Islay (Polly Pullar)

Biggar of Kirkcudbrightshire, 'No single breed can do every job, but the Shorthorn is as good as you will get, and is the base of most other cattle. It has laid a good foundation for improving other native breeds all over the globe.'

Galloway

This ancient breed was once the only one found in the south-west of Scotland. Some would say that the Galloway is now Scotland's purest remaining breed of cattle as they have had little other influences added to their bloodlines and remain highly suited to the extreme wet conditions in western Scotland. Like the Aberdeen-Angus, the Galloway was developed from small, polled (hornless) cattle and initially both breeds were registered in a Black Poll Register.

Although the two breeds may have had similar beginnings, the Aberdeen-Angus was bred to mature rapidly and with the ability to thrive in intensive situations. The Galloway cow, on the other hand, is perfectly suited to being a hardy hill cow, rearing her calf successfully on the roughest terrain. Due to her thick, mossy, double-layered coat, she can also survive the worst abuse that the climate can hurl at her.

Galloway cattle are of three main types: the predominantly black Galloway (which may also be red or dun); the Belted Galloway, which has a distinctive white belt round its middle; and the White Galloway, with smart black points.

The Belted Galloway is more usually known as the 'Beltie'. The unusual white belt was introduced from an infusion of blood from Dutch sheeted Lakenvelder cattle during the seventeenth century. The Stuart family of the Old Place of Mochrum, Wigtownshire, were famed for their Belties and it was these animals that were the founder members of the Belted Galloway Herd Book. The Beltie came perilously close to extinction but Flora Stuart, famously known as 'Miss Flora', worked continuously to promote the breed both at home and abroad, producing many supreme animals. Born on the Isle of Bute, she dedicated her life to her cattle, and was revered in many countries in her role as president of the society. Her death in 2005 left a void and there is no doubt that, without her work, the Belted Galloway would not be the popular animal it is today.

Charm for rutting

Rarely has Christian spirituality been as earthy as in this 'Eòlas na Daire' (Charm for Rutting) with its rather surprising attribution –

> Eòlas na dàire 'rinn Moire 's a Mac,
> 'S thubhairt Crìosda fhèin gum bu ro-cheart,
> Air a' Chiad Luan,
> 'Chur a' chruidh gu luath a dhàir,
> Gun fharlaogh 'n a dheigh
> Ach laoigh bhreaca bhoirionn uile gu leir.

(The charm for the rutting made by Mary and her Son, and Christ himself said it was right, on the first Monday, to send the cattle quickly to the bull, so that no ectopic pregnancy should follow but only speckled female calves.) Taking the cow to the bull counted as a 'work of necessity and mercy' and could be done even on the Sabbath. The necessity was an economic one, but a determined cow could insist that it would be a mercy too. Conception and calving were also believed to be affected by the moon and tides. 'She'll calve in the full tide, next week' is still heard occasionally on Skye.

Highland cow and calf, North Uist (Polly Pullar)

Highland

The Highland is one of the oldest British breeds of cattle. The first Herd Book was published in 1885, and while other breeds may have gone out of fashion, the Highland has held its own and is now found worldwide. Early ancestors of the Highland cow were discovered in archaeological evidence dating back to the sixth century, and there are written records of small, hairy black cattle from the twelfth century. Often referred to as 'kyloes', they were stunted due to the poor habitat and bad weather of the remotest parts of the Highlands. Slightly larger animals of the same type were raised on the mainland on better keep and referred to as 'Highlanders'. The dominant colour in the early days was black, although the Highland cow today is predominantly red, with brindle, yellow, dun, white, black and silver also in existence: all are accepted breed colours.

Although modern Highland cattle have altered in stature, they are long-lived, extremely hardy and well suited to poor grazing, just like their ancestors. There are records of cows producing calves into their teens, which is unusual among faster-growing, intensively bred cows. The distinctive long, flowing coat and sweeping horns are part of the breed's undoubted attraction – no bovine is more photographed or more representational of wild Scotland than the Highland cow. A group of Highland cattle is referred to as a 'fold' and not a herd as in other breeds. The word originated from when the animals were kept enclosed in stone-built pens.

Ena McDonald and her family from North Uist have a large pedigree fold of Highland cattle that has worked the machair (see page 223) for many generations. They are well aware of the sensitive nature of the habitat and still farm the land using traditional methods. They believe that there is no better grazing beast for this fragile ecosystem than the Highland cow. During the winter months, the cattle are put onto a tidal island that has remained uncultivated for decades, and graze the machair close to their farm. Heavier breeds of cattle would be more inclined to do damage. Although predominantly a beef breed, crofters often milked their Highland cows. Ena McDonald milks one of her cows daily for the family's use.

Luing

The tiny island of Luing, lying in the Firth of Lorne south of Oban, is home to a unique breed of cattle. History was made in 1965 when an Act of Parliament officially recognised the Luing as a breed in its own right. The accompanying press report read as follows:

> Following a prolonged study of the breeding performance of the cattle developed over the last 17 years by Messrs. Cadzow Bros. on the Island of Luing, Argyll, the Secretary of State has accepted the recommendation of the Licensing of Bulls Advisory Committee that the Cattle should be recognised as a distinct beef breed. The Breed will also be recognised in England and Wales.

The Luing was the brainchild of the highly respected Cadzow brothers – Shane, Denis and Ralph, who made their name as unsurpassed agriculturalists and stockmen. Although they farmed on the productive arable ground of the east of Scotland, they had bought the island of Luing and wanted to breed cattle there and take them to the rich ground of the east for fattening. They needed to produce hardy animals that could also be kept as breeding cows, and could withstand health problems associated with inhabiting an area of incessant rainfall.

They acquired top quality Highland x Shorthorn heifers to form the basis of a new herd. On these they used Cruggleton Alastair, a Beef Shorthorn bull of the old-fashioned type, bred by renowned cattle breeder Bertie Marshall, from Wigtownshire. The bull left a distinctive mark on his offspring and eventually two sons from this mating were used on their half-sisters. Through the Cadzows' knowledge of line breeding and in-breeding, a type was fixed with all the qualities they were seeking and the hardy, commercial

Beltane and winter traditions

Beltane, at the beginning of May, was once an important time for protecting cattle and other animals. On Beltane Eve, according to John Gregorson Campbell, cattle would be sprinkled with urine and daubed with tar to protect them from witchcraft. The minister of Logieriat, between Dunkeld and Pitlochry, saw Beltane as mainly a cowherds' festival, although it was ancient and used to be celebrated by everyone. In the North-east, rowan twigs were hung around the entrances to byres and stables to keep the witches away; and in many places, cattle would be driven through or around the Beltane bonfire to 'sain' them against disease and evil influences.

The long winter was marked by occasional treats and celebrations. In the Northern Isles, cattle received a special sheaf of corn (their 'hallow') at Hallowmas (All Saints' Day). In the North-east, a sheaf was given to all the cattle and horses on Christmas morning, and juniper burned to keep them from harm.

In the Highlands, juniper was also burned at the beginning of Shrovetide (Lent) to 'sain' or protect the cattle during the long hungry weeks before the grass began to grow again. Inevitably, not all of them made it through to spring and a Gaelic proverb shows just how far their owners could be from a purely commercial relationship with them. It was a lean time for crofters as well, but they could still feel sorry for their beasts and wish that in the next world, they would be amazed by the abundance of food: 'Said March to February, "Where left you the poor stirk?" "I left him with Him who made the elements, staring at a stack of fodder."' (*Thuirt an Gearran ris an Fhaoilleach,"Càit an d' fhàg thu 'n gamhainn bochd?" "Dh'fhàg mi e aig an Fhear rinn na dùilean, 's a dhà shuil an an t-sop."*)

Luing cows and calves, Isle of Luing (Polly Pullar)

Fairies, witches and traditional healers

If a bull fell over a crag, he was sometimes said to have been shot by fairy arrows. If a cow's milk failed completely, the fairies might be blamed. To keep them sweet, Highland women would give them a share of the milk each day, pouring it into a hollow in the ground or a cup-shaped stone. Some of these are called 'gruagach' stones, after the gruagach or curly-haired one who was more goddess than fairy originally. If a cow gave only watery milk which would not turn to butter, witchcraft was sometimes suspected. Fairy-lore was often assimilated to witch-lore so the distinction is hard to maintain. Indeed, measures which were taken in Scotland against witchcraft were still used against fairies in Ireland; but it was widely believed by the end of the seventeenth century that 'women by a charm, or some other secret way, are able to convey the increase of their neighbour's cow's milk to their own use.' There are countless stories, and indeed court records, about these alleged offences. Probably the cow was undernourished, but as witch hysteria swept the Lowlands (and occasionally the Highlands) in the late sixteenth and seventeenth centuries, traditional healers were as much a target as those engaged in real or imaginary mischief.

There was a market for their skills none the less. When William Reidford of Lilliesleaf had a sick cow during the harvest of 1627, his mother sent for Isobel Howetson. She 'charmed' the animal in the field and it recovered, though she herself lay on the ground afterwards, gasping and groaning. This is very similar to the description of Agnes Sampson at work in the 1590s. At other times, she used prayers, stroking the animals' backs and bellies while saying a Hail Mary. She was executed as a witch in 1591. Isobel Howetson was also called to a farm in Midlem to treat a sick child. The child recovered, but within 24 hours one of his father's calves was dead. She confessed that it was her fault. The last we hear of her is in Selkirk jail.

hill breed that would become known as the Luing was born.

The Luing is an animal deep-red in colour, although there are variations – roans, brindle and white are a throwback to their Highland and Shorthorn ancestry and are also acceptable. They have a high fertility rate, are easily calved and have now gained popularity for production of the Sim-Luing, resulting from a cross with the larger continental Simmental bull.

In 1972 the Cadzow brothers won the Massey Ferguson National Award for Services to United Kingdom Agriculture, but modestly stated it had been a team effort, with much co-operation from the stockmen on Luing and members of the Breed Society.

Shetland

The diminutive dual-purpose Shetland cow is one of the rarest native breeds and has long been viewed as the ideal 'crofter's cow'. They were also used as draft animals

Shetland cow and calf, Burland, Trondra, Shetland (Polly Pullar)

harnessed to the plough. Their ancient lineage dates back to the first domesticated animals that came to the Shetland Isles with the Vikings. Appropriately the cattle, more usually referred to as 'kye', have slightly upward-curving Viking-style horns.

The Shetland cow was a vital part of life in the islands. Families depended on them to provide both milk and calves – premature loss had devastating consequences and was seen as a bad omen. The animals had to survive on the poorest fodder and frequently, like the Shetland families, had to withstand famine during long winters, emerging from the byre so weak with malnutrition that they required lifting. The Shetlanders were so devoted to their cattle and they in turn to their owners that sometimes when they were forced to sell them on, they went with a piece of their owner's sack cloth tied to their backs. For this reason, they became known as 'clootie cows'.

Many different forms were once common, but eventually the dominant form became black and white, although red and white is not unusual. The cow's tremendous ability to produce a large thrifty calf when crossbred was almost her downfall, and numbers of purebred animals fell until they were almost lost altogether. Due to the dedication of a few breeders and assistance from the Rare Breeds Survival Trust, they were saved and numbers have risen again. Although the modern Shetland cow is well nourished and therefore larger than her forebears, it is said that she still retains many of their tough traits and characteristics, including the superb Shetland temperament.

Sheep

Blackface

The Scottish Blackface, or 'Blackie', is a horned breed that thrives on the highest hills. There are three distinctive types: the Lanark, the Perth and the Newton Stewart. Each is suited to the particular habitat of the area. The most numerous and popular type is the Lanark Blackface. All have an influx of blood from each type, and some are now having Swaledale blood added to them.

Early paintings show the old Scottish Dunface and the Short-wool, ancestors of the latter-day Blackie. Their faces were more pointed and they had a lighter bone structure and longer fleeces. The gnarled and curly horns of the Blackface tup are highly sought-after by crook makers who carve them into many different shapes, although the traditional shepherd's 'cromak' is the most popular and is used

Blackface ewe, the most widespread sheep in Scotland (Polly Pullar)

as a work tool by stockmen everywhere.

Prices of prize Blackface tups are steeped in mystery, and astronomical figures have been reached. Sales of rams are always auspicious events and command much interest, with breeders able to recognise sheep sired by a particular tup. Unlike other breeds, the Blackface Sheep Society does not have a Herd Book.

Once called the 'Short Sheep of the Forest', the modern-day Blackface still holds her own against other breeds and is the most numerous sheep in Scotland. She is wily, hardy and produces excellent lambs, and when crossed with terminal sires, she can compete with many other larger breeds.

Boreray

On the St Kildan island of Boreray, amid summer breeding colonies of over 50,000 gannets, the small Boreray sheep lives a feral life. Descended from the Dunface, or Old Scottish Shortwool, and then crossed with the Scottish Blackface, the sheep have been left untouched since the St Kildan people were evacuated in 1930. A few were taken off the island to establish mainland flocks during the 1970s. There are approximately 400 Boreray sheep on the island. They have adapted well to the most savage Scottish environment of all, maintaining their numbers through natural fluctuations, without human intervention. The Boreray is listed as 'critically endangered' by the Rare Breeds Survival Trust and its grazing has become a vital part of maintaining the sward for the island's flora.

Castlemilk Moorit

The rare Castlemilk Moorit owes its survival to Joe Henson who bought six ewes and a ram in 1970 for his Cotswold Farm Park. The sheep came from the Castlemilk Estate near Lockerbie. They had been advertised as 'Moorit Shetland sheep' but Joe Henson realised they were quite different and was impressed by their great beauty. The animals had many characteristics of the wild mouflon and also of Manx Loghtan sheep from the Isle of Man. Records from Sir Jock Buchanan-Jardine's estate proved that he had bred the sheep by crossing moorit (a brown colour found in primitive sheep breeds) Shetland sheep with both the mouflon and Manx Loghtan, and a type had been set.

Tragically most of the remainder of Sir Jock's flock had been lost. However, Joe Henson was determined that the breed should not only be saved but also officially recognised. In 1984 the Rare Breeds Survival Trust finally classified the breed.

A sheep of many names

There is surprisingly little folklore about sheep in Scotland, far less than about cattle, but sheep-farming was important and has its own rich vocabulary. Indeed, this would be true of all farm animals. A sheep is not just a sheep or a cow a cow. They are named differently according to age, sex and breeding status: *yow* (ewe), *tup* (ram), *hog* (a lamb before shearing), *wedder hog* (a castrated male lamb before shearing), *wedder* (a castrated male lamb after shearing), *custom wedder* (a wedder paid as rent in kind), *rin wedder* (a wedder given in part-payment for rent), *gimmer* (a two-year-old female), and a *yeld sheep* (a sheep with no lamb), not to mention a *Dunbar wedder*, which was not a sheep at all but a salt herring. There are many variations and names to do with colour and temperament. Gaelic has at least as many names, if not more, for cattle and sheep.

Castlemilk Moorit tups: this breed fell into single numbers in the 1960s (Polly Pullar)

The Castlemilk Moorit is renowned for its delicious lean meat with a slightly gamey flavour, and its soft moorit-coloured wool is highly sought-after by hand spinners. Despite the breed's tiny gene pool, the sheep have been found to have few health problems compared to larger breeds with a massive gene pool. The tups have huge, gnarled horns and a fighting spirit said to have come from their Corsican mouflon ancestors.

Hebridean

Before the nineteenth century, the Hebridean sheep was widespread in many of the outer islands but numbers fell dramatically when it was replaced by the larger and more popular Blackface. It became a fashionable addition to parkland in England due to its attractiveness and unusual horns. The Hebridean's origins are much debated: it was once referred to as 'St Kilda sheep' as there are records of dark-woolled sheep on St Kilda from before 1880, but records from elsewhere gave rise to an accepted name change during the 1970s when the Rare Breeds Survival Trust agreed it should be called the Hebridean.

A member of the northern short-tailed group of sheep, the Hebridean has many primitive characteristics. Sheep with four horns are still bred although there is currently a trend towards breeding animals with only two. Some of the tups have vast horns like those of wild billy goats, and it was doubtlessly this dramatic feature that helped to save the breed in its early days. During the 1980s and 1990s, the Hebridean was reintroduced to many of its island haunts through the breeding and promotional work of the late Donald Ferguson of North Uist. The Hebridean is excellent in conservation grazing schemes and is also ideally suited to the organic system of farming. When crossed with a large terminal sire, excellent fat lambs are produced.

North Country Cheviot

The North Country Cheviot has been in Sutherland for over 200 years. The great agricultural improver Sir John Sinclair of Ulbster, Caithness, had set up the Wool Society in 1791 due to increasing concerns about the loss of quality wool in British sheep. At this time wool was being imported. He was thoroughly impressed with the 'long sheep of the hills' – the Cheviot, found in the border country in the Cheviot hills – and took some north to his Caithness estate. They did exceedingly well and soon many thousands were taken to hill areas. Through selective breeding over time, the sheep increased in size and hardiness and became known as North Country Cheviots, or 'Northies'.

Left. The Hebridean is now a familiar sight in the islands once more (Polly Pullar)

Right. The North Country Cheviot is the dominant breed in Sutherland and Caithness (Polly Pullar)

North Ronaldsay sheep are governed by tide timetables (Polly Pullar)

Perfectly suiting the inhospitable ground of Sutherland and Caithness, the Northie is widely used in many other hill areas and is often crossbred to produce a fine, fat lamb. It has since evolved into three distinctive types: the Hill (or Lairg), the Caithness, and the Border.

Year of the sheep

The arrival of the Cheviots signalled the death-knell of many small communities in the Highlands. The year 1792 is still remembered in Sutherland as 'Bliadhna nan Caorach' (the year of the sheep). Under normal circumstances, crofters had nothing against sheep and often kept a few themselves. But now, vast areas were given over to them and people who had lived there for generations were driven out, regardless of age or circumstances. Within a generation, fifteen thousand people had been forcibly removed from the Duke of Sutherland's estates alone. Ewan Robertson (b.1842) from Tongue composed a song about it. Here is the opening verse:

Mo mhallachd aig na caoraich mhòr –	My curse upon the great sheep –
Càit a bheil clann nan daoine còir	Where now are the children of the kindly folk
Dhealaich rium nuair bha mi òg	Who parted from me when I was young
Mus robh Dùthaich 'IcAoidh na fàsach?	Before Sutherland became a desert?

The Lairg Sales were initiated in 1895, as Sutherland Estates needed somewhere close by to sell their large numbers of stock. The venue proved to be ideal, being adjacent to the railway. The annual North Country Cheviot event has since become one of the most important in northern Scotland, bringing buyers from far and wide. Sellers may have just one or two sheep, or a vast number, and the livestock pens outside the market-building bustle with activity as the small town of Lairg is transformed.

North Country sheep men are not only known for their skills in stockmanship, but also for their revelries. It is said that often the only way lairds can find their shepherds in their inebriated state after sales, is by recognising the various tweed breeks of different estates in the crowd. Such events are vital to the survival of rural communities, and are the lifeblood of the area.

North Ronaldsay

Over the centuries, North Ronaldsay sheep have adapted to survive on seaweed. The small island's lush grass is reserved for larger farm animals, so this athletic sheep is kept on the seashore by 12 miles of continuous dry stone dyke encircling the entire island. This Grade A-listed structure is as important as many of Scotland's better-known architectural edifices.

Prior to lambing, North Ronaldsay ewes are brought to the in-bye ground to give birth to their lambs. In a unique management system, in the instances of twins, only one lamb is kept as the rigours of life on the seashore mean a ewe would be unable to rear two. A few weeks after lambing the ewes are returned to the shore and remain there till the following spring. The whethers (castrated males) are kept until they are between four and five years old and are then killed for meat. The succulent mutton is low in cholesterol and lacking in fat, and has an unsurpassed flavour that fits a niche market in the south.

The North Ronaldsays are similar to Shetland sheep, and probably share Norse ancestry. The high iodine content of the seaweed they consume ensures they never suffer from foot rot like other breeds and they have little or no health problems. As seaweed is low in copper, and the sheep have adapted to survive without it, they need to be given a copper substitute when they are taken to the mainland.

The life of the North Ronaldsay sheep is governed by tide times. As soon as the sea retreats, troops of sheep skip down to the water and venture far out to the uncovered skerries. Here they feast on their two favourite seaweeds, dulse and laminaria, often amid groups of slumbering seals. The island maintains approximately 3,000 sheep, managed by an ancient Sheep Court, which was originally based on the island's six crofting townships with 12 wise men that controlled decisions. The local laird chaired meetings. Today all North Ronaldsay sheep owners are members of the Sheep Court.

Milking sheep

Sheep were kept for milk as well as for wool. One of Robert Burns' most enduring love songs begins with a hidden reference to this:

> When o'er the hill the eastern star
> Tells buchtin' time is near, my jo …

'Buchtin' time' was when the ewes were brought to the buchts (also 'boughts') or enclosures for milking. Ewes can be milked single-handed, but it is quicker and easier with help and a twentieth-century account from Berwickshire gives some idea of the close physical co-operation that was required: the sheep were put into a narrow alleyway three abreast; the man would stand astride the middle sheep, pinning the other two against the wall with his knees; the woman would then come in behind and milk them quickly into a tankard or a jug. Edwin Davidson only saw this once, in about 1914, and no doubt there were other ways of doing it, but it is easy to imagine the banter and repartee that went on during the short season that the ewes were in milk.

On the edge – a Shetland ewe in Scotland's most northerly outpost, Hermaness, Shetland (Polly Pullar)

Shetland

Norse settlers arrived in the Northern Isles with small sheep similar to today's diminutive Scandinavian and Icelandic breeds today. Like all Shetland's native livestock, the Shetland sheep is small and finely boned, and has been improved as changing fashions have altered market demands. Shetland sheep are hardy and long-lived: they have been known to go on breeding for up to 15 years. Like other primitive breeds of sheep, the Shetland has a short tail and is known for its agility. There is great variety within the breed, not only with type, but also with the range of colours and markings, from greys to rich browns, blacks, silvers, creams and greys, each with descriptive names including 'katmoget', 'bleset', 'krunet', 'shaela', 'moorit', and 'yuglit'. However, flock book Shetlands tend to be pure white. It was these extraordinary colour variations and the soft quality of the wool that spawned an entire industry as Shetland knitters produced garments from un-dyed wool that became highly sought-after. The work was carried out by the womenfolk and involved laborious tasks such as carding and spinning, skills acquired over generations. Wool was plucked from the sheep by 'rooing'. White wool was dyed with lichens. The 'Fair Isle' pattern found on woollen garments is still available today and there are a few islanders who continue to produce this traditionally patterned knitwear.

Although tups have impressive horns, the Shetland ewe is polled (although some of the early primitive types had up to four horns and a few are still kept by enthusiasts, ensuring their survival). On the remotest Shetland island of Foula, the sheep retain many of these characteristics, including some of the most dramatic markings and colours of all sheep breeds.

Soay

Frequently described as a 'living fossil', the Soay sheep is more caprine than ovine in many of its habits. As the St Kildans witnessed, the Soay was extremely hard to catch and could seldom be rounded up like other breeds, having the speed and agility of a mountain goat. With a divide-and-confuse mentality like other primitive breeds, the Soay shares many characteristics with its ancestor, the wild mouflon. Soay colours are moorit, fawn, dark brown and black, and animals still retain the distinctive mouflon colouration on the underbelly. Originally kept on the St Kildan island of Soay, meaning 'Island of Sheep', most Soays are now found on the main island of Hirta.

The Soay's wool was never clipped but was plucked by the islanders in a method known as 'rooing'. It was then hand-spun and woven into distinctive St Kilda tweed, which was paid to the laird in lieu of rent, or to tourists visiting the islands. The St Kildans frequently filed their dogs' teeth or removed some of them altogether to avoid damage to the sheep as they tried to catch hold of them.

Despite the departure of the islanders in 1930, the Soays remained and have continued to live a wild existence ever since. They are the most primitive of all Scottish breeds, with next to no infusion of other bloodlines. Even Soays kept on the mainland retain their wild character and are notoriously hard to work with a dog.

Left. Soay tup on Hirta, St Kilda, showing mouflon colouration (Polly Pullar)

Right. South Country Cheviot ewes and lambs (Polly Pullar)

South Country Cheviot

Small and extremely hardy, the 'Southie' is reputed to be the oldest recognised sheep breed in the country. It is famed for its wild nature and prime carcass quality.

Modern influences have altered the breed considerably from the wiry animals that first roamed the Cheviot Hills. The Southie has had an infusion of other blood added, including that of the fine wool-bearing Merino, and its fleece was once in demand to supply the Borders Woollen Mill industry. It was the Cheviot that was taken to the far north of Scotland to Caithness, Sutherland, and Ross-shire during the time of the Highland Clearances at the end of the eighteenth century, and it was this introduction that drove local people away, forced to abandon their croft lands to make way for the lucrative four-footed arrivals.

Nothing wasted

As with cattle, there was the usual round of seasonal work: lambing, milking, marking, castrating, shearing, smearing and dipping. Some sheep were paid over as rent and others were killed and salted for use throughout the winter, but nothing was wasted. The lungs, heart and liver were mixed with oatmeal and spices and sewn into the stomach bag to make haggis. In some places, the oesophagus was filled with melted tallow to make 'ruffies' – a sort of candle. The skins were made into bouys or floats for the fishing nets. Only rarely were they cured to make rugs. Unless you were very wealthy, fresh mutton was for feast days and special occasions only: Christmas and Michaelmas, Hallowmas in the Northern Isles, weddings. The sheep would be shorn each summer and the fleeces washed, carded and spun, and knitted into jumpers and stockings or woven into tweed.

Scraps of stray wool, gathered off the hill, were used as dressings under the toes and helped to sooth the injuries got from walking barefoot. Far less sensible was the Northern Isles' cure for smallpox: sheep-droppings boiled in milk. A similar concoction ('pushlocks') was given in the North-east for whooping cough and also for jaundice. Sleeping among sheep was said to be a cure for 'the lingering disease', whatever that was.

Horses and Ponies

Clydesdale

Nostalgia surrounds these gentle workhorses that have their origins in the Clyde valley. It was during the 1600s that the Duke of Hamilton imported six black Flemish coaching horses to cross with traditional farm horses, generally referred to as 'Scotch mares'. Impressive results were achieved with the infusion of new blood and soon the animals gained a reputation for being the most superior draught horses in Europe. They were in great demand, as farmers and carters saw their potential and tried to acquire them. Eventually, through the work of a few famous breeders, including the Patersons of Lochyloch, the new breed spread to other parts of Scotland, and in 1877 the Clydes-

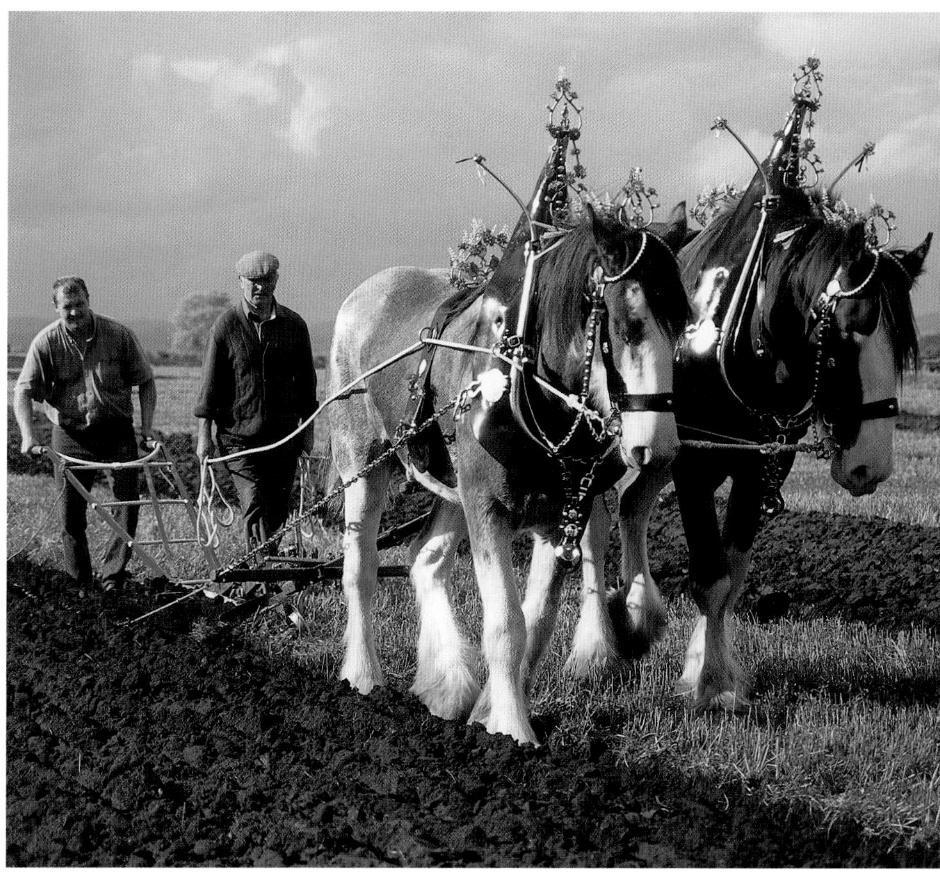

Clydesdales in traditional show harness at a ploughing match (Polly Pullar)

'Weel mounted on his grey mare Meg'

There are countless stories in Gaelic oral tradition about horses having the second sight. If a tragedy occurred, it would be remembered that a horse had been shying for weeks at a certain boat on the shore or at a bridge where the news was heard, or had broken loose and bolted unexpectedly as if sensing something untoward. In Argyll, it was said that a stallion would protect his rider in the presence of evil, but that a mare would turn and attack him. No one seems to have told this to Tam O'Shanter's Meg, the mare who saves him from the 'hellish legion' in the ruins of Alloway kirk. Perhaps things were different in Ayrshire. Burns was brought up on tales of the supernatural, so they were just as current there, but in Ireland, it was the mare, especially the 'true mare' (the seventh filly) who was powerful against evil, so perhaps there was some influence from across the water. Burns was more than happy to send up the idea of the witches sabbath, but he keeps the image of the horse as protector against evil, so that Meg becomes the only real heroine of his story.

dale Horse Society was formed.

A few outstanding Clydesdale stallions were travelled around central Scotland to serve mares. Stallions were licensed by the Department of Agriculture for particular areas, but then there were the inevitable poaching horses that could be used on the cheap, and often caused much controversy in a pedigree. One famous pedigree animal, The Baron of Buchlyvie, became unwittingly involved in a lawsuit between its owners William Dunlop and James Kirkpatrick. After a long and heated battle, the court decided that the animal should be put up for sale and the proceeds split. In a packed market in Ayr in 1911, Dunlop pushed the bidding to a world-record price of £9,500 and Kirkpatrick was forced to pay back his share.

The early horses ranged in height and colour – bays and dark bays with white blazes and large white socks were favoured and were encouraged in the breed as seen today. Long silky hair on the lower part of the legs (called 'feather') was important, and in the show ring much attention is paid to this attribute. Clydesdale owners have always protected their animals' feathers and often use leather guards or 'spats' to stop the mud from causing damage.

A Clydesdale's strength and gentle temperament was also vital and ploughmen became totally attached to the animals in their charge. Clydesdales are still decorated with coloured raffia and handmade ornaments called 'segs'. Diamond rolling is the specialised plaiting of coloured cloth, ribbon or wool. These creations are added to the mane and tail, with coveted prizes for the best-decorated animals.

In the early 1900s, the Clydesdale was in great demand. During its heyday there were approximately 140,000 working on farms throughout Scotland and the islands. In towns they pulled dreys and did other draught work, and many were exported to Canada and America where they are still popular today.

The dreaded horse disease 'grass sickness', together with the arrival of the tractor, ousted Clydesdales from most farms, particularly in the North-east. By the 1950s, although some dedicated farmers hung onto their animals, the Clydesdale had all but died out.

Recently, the Clydesdale has had a welcome revival and is now seen at every agricultural show countrywide. Due to the efforts of a loyal band of breeders, Clydesdales have now returned to a healthy number.

Eriskay Pony

Smaller than the Highland Pony, the Eriskay was the original 'crofter's pony' and was used in the Western Isles for carrying peat, fish and seaweed. Akin to the Pictish ponies found on carvings, the Eriskay pony had Norse and Celtic connections. It survived due to the inaccessibility of Eriskay and other nearby islands, and does not appear to have had an infusion of blood from larger breeds. With fewer feathers at its heels, a slightly larger head, and a smaller build than the Highland, its similarity to that breed has caused controversy. Due to the dedication of a loyal group, including a vet, a priest, a doctor, a scientist and Eriskay crofters, the Eriskay was finally officially recognised as a breed in its own right in 1997. It has now been placed on the Rare Breeds Survival Trust's endangered list.

The Eriskay is increasingly popular and its long, close association with man is reflected in its loyal temperament, like that of the Shetland or 'crofter's' cow. Usually black, grey or brown, the ponies do not grow larger than 13.2 hands high and are ideally suited for children or light adults. They seem happy to join in all activities. They were often used by children on the islands for getting to school and would wait all day, grazing the meagre landscape until it was time to take their charges home again.

Horseman's Word

Ploughmen, like a guild or trade union, guarded their skills carefully:

> As will be readily understood, it was the great ambition of most young ploughmen to graduate into their brotherhood as soon as possible; such were athirst to learn those mysterious secrets which would give them skill with and domination over horses – particularly over 'wicked' horses – and for the prestige and deference which such skill would bring them from their fellows. Several ploughmen with whom I was on friendly terms were held in high respect – not unmixed with awe! – on account of the undoubtedly remarkable 'way' they had with horses, and the process of being 'brothered' to the horses was usually quite seriously regarded, and very secret.

Remedies from mare's milk

Mare's milk was widely believed to be a cure for whooping cough. Some said it should be given on aspen spoon, but there is no mention of that in Essie Stewart's account of being forced to take it as a four or five year-old. The Stewarts were Travelling People and her uncle milked the mare for her at the roadside in Sutherland in 1946: 'It was thin, very thin, like skimmed milk, sweet tasting. You had to drink it warm, straight from the pail, that's what he said. My mother dipped a tin cup and made me drink. It was frothy, almost golden yellow.'

An Eriskay pony. Photograph taken in 1934 by Werner Kissling

Shetland

Pound for pound, no breed is stronger than the diminutive Shetland pony. There are records of the presence of these small animals in the Northern Isles for over 2,500 years. They formed an integral link in the islanders' existence, carrying all manner of loads. They were used for 'flittin' the peats' on all of Shetland's islands. They were also used as draught animals and there are old photographs of them carrying fully grown men as well as children.

Famine was a feature of Shetland life and often in the harshest winters, their animals succumbed to the vagaries of the climate, and starvation. The ponies had to survive as best they could and this led to them becoming one of the

Night riders

Witches were said to be able to change men into horses. A minister in Assynt had heard of two lads working at the same big house, eating the same food. One grew thin and tired. The other remained strong and healthy. The thin one always slept on the outside of the bed, so one night they changed places and the strong one stayed awake. Before long, who should appear at the bedside but the lady of the house. She shook a bridle at him, changed him into a horse and off she rode with him to a witches' gathering. To cut a long story short, he eventually manages to get the bridle off, shakes it back at her and turns her into a mare. He then takes her to the blacksmith and gets her shod. In the morning, the lady of the house is found whimpering under the blankets with horseshoes nailed to her hands.

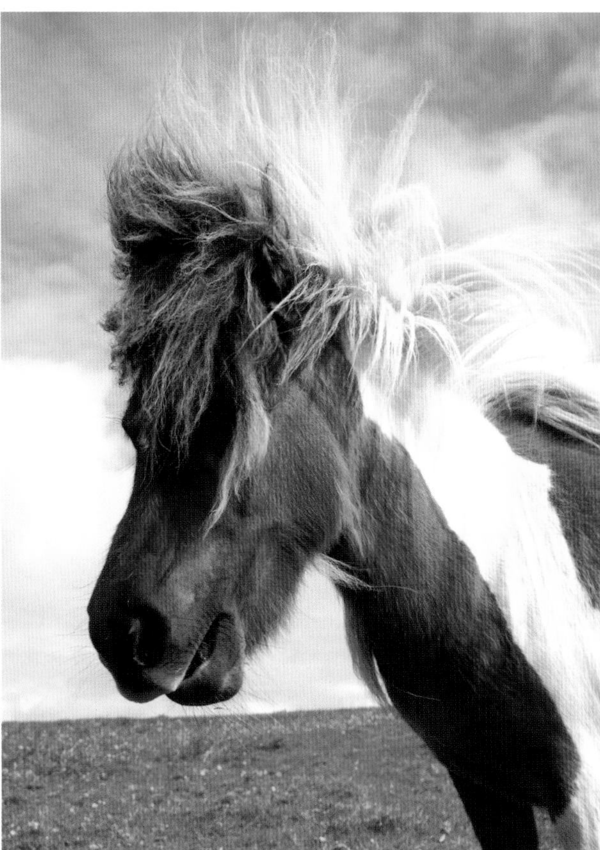

Right. Shetland pony (Polly Pullar)

Opposite top. Commercial pigs (Polly Pullar)

Opposite bottom. Free-range crossbred piglets (Polly Pullar)

toughest native breeds of all. Due to the Shetland's isolated location, the breed has remained remarkably pure.

Their small size was to have a detrimental effect on the breed when they were highly sought as pit ponies following the Mines Act of 1842, which banned women and children from working down the mines. Thousands of ponies left the islands, in particular the smallest males. The Marquis of Londonderry, a mine owner, soon realised that taking so many good animals from the islands was causing not only a deficit, but also a lack of quality. He began an intensive breeding programme on the islands of Bressay and Noss using some of the best stallions available. Many of today's Shetland pony bloodlines descend directly from the excellent ponies he was responsible for breeding.

Highly popular as children's ponies, the Shetland is now found worldwide. It retains many of its island characteristics, not least of all a cheeky disposition and great strength and stamina. It needs firm handling. Due to its size, it is often over-pampered. However, as one knowledgeable Shetland stud owner commented, 'Treat these wonderful hardy ponies like big horses and they are always trouble free.' Shetland ponies may be any colour except spotted. Piebald and skewbald are common, and it is important that they have dense manes and tails to help protect them against the worst of the Shetland weather.

Goats

S: gait, gayt
G: *gobhar*

Scotland does not have a native goat, although crofters and smallholders once kept many goats. Their milk was thought to have health-giving properties and was highly valued for keeping consumption at bay. In areas where goats were kept, they did much damage due to over-grazing and their ability to either get into, or get out of, places where they were not meant to be. Some lairds did not allow crofters to keep them due to their destructive nature.

Morality and blessings

Goats could represent either end of the moral spectrum. A selfish goat appears in one of Duncan Williamson's stories from the Traveller tradition. Designed to teach children how to share, it tells of a man who adopted a kid goat which turned out to be a malicious liar and the four-footed equivalent of a cuckoo in the nest. Even the foxes suffer from its machinations and it is only driven off eventually by bees. Outside of allegory, however, goats were regarded in much the same way as other animals, and might be included in prayers and home-made rituals. A blessing for harvest time includes goats among the animals whom God is asked to protect: '*Cuimrich gach mins, ciob, is uain, gach ni, agus mearc, is maon*' (encompass each goat, sheep and lamb, each cow and horse and store).

Pigs

S: grump, grumphie
G: *muc*

While a few crofters kept a pig for fattening, there has never been a native Scottish pig. It is hard to see why this might be, but as pigs are not grazers and tend to decimate the land, they would not have easily fitted into the impoverished husbandry system which dominated most of the Highlands and Islands. They are also incredibly strong animals and could force their way out of all but the best-made enclosures, or indeed excavate an escape route. These reasons would be more than enough to deter early Scottish farmers from keeping them, especially in the far north. Most pigs were reared for the pot, fed on meagre household scraps.

In 1814, however, Robert Henderson wrote in *On the Breeding of Swine in the Hebrides*:

> I would recommend it to the inhabitants of these islands that they should immediately introduce this

stock into their respective abodes. Nowhere do I know a country so well adapted for rearing swine as the Western Isles, where there are large tracts of pasturelands, in which swine will feed all the summer months among their cattle and sheep, and will resort to the shores and pick up seaweed and shell fish, which are excellent food for them.

Pig-keeping in the city

Pig-keeping was not confined to the countryside. Complaints about 'filthie swyne' turn up regularly in the record books of Scottish burghs, as they howked up the streets, destroyed vegetable gardens and ate people's produce. Their destructiveness was proverbial. 'The swine hiz gane throw't' meant a project was in tatters. In 1542, the burgesses of Edinburgh had to be reminded that it was unlawful to keep pigs unless they also employed a swineherd, and that the stairs and passageways of the High Street were to be cleared of makeshift pens: 'That all ... persouns haifand ony cruvis for swyne at thair stairis and sydewallis fornent the hie streitt or in commoun venellis ... remoue the samyn.'

Most people were happy enough to eat ham, bacon and pork, when available, but pigs themselves were widely regarded as unclean animals. In the North-east, a pig-bite was believed to cause cancer; and pigs, like witches, were said to bear the 'devil's mark', a crescent-shaped pattern of spots on one of their forelegs.There are health risks associated with pigs and these are probably at the root of religious objections to pig-meat, but the seal of St Anthony's Hospital in Leith depicts a pig, close by the feet of the patron saint of swineherds and people with skin diseases. St Anthony's pig was famous enough to appear to devastating effect in Sir David Lindsay's sixteenth-century *Satyre of the Thrie Estaitis.* A trader in bogus relics offers for sale 'the gruntill of St Antony's sow, quhilk bare his haly bell.' The bell gave protection from hellfire, he explains, as if some of this immunity might have rubbed off on the pig, but there are no takers for the magic snout.

Poultry

There are few native breeds of Scottish poultry, yet fowl of all descriptions have always played a vital role in crofting and farming, with smallholders keeping a few birds for eggs and meat, and perches made within some croft houses for their birds to roost on. One of two traditional Scottish breeds, the Scots Grey was once known as the 'Shepherd's Plaid' or 'Chick Marley'. Now extremely rare, in recent times it has been bred almost exclusively for the show market and has lost many of the traits that once made it popular. The Scots Grey's origins stem from game fowl bloodlines. 'Cuckoo feathered', it has dapper chequered black and white plumage.

The Scots Dumpy is smaller and squatter as its name suggests. It has a rounded appearance and a slightly waddling gait. It may be black or cuckoo-patterned. Its little legs restricted its foraging activities to near the homestead and meant that its meat was succulent and tender compared to that of more active fowls. The Scots Dumpy was almost lost altogether. However, a pure strain was brought back to Scotland from Kenya during the 1960s, having been taken

Right. Shetland ducks at Burland croft, Shetland (Polly Pullar)

Far right. Shetland hen showing characteristic 'tapp' of feathers on her head (Polly Pullar)

there by Lady Violet Carnegie in 1902. Since then numbers have been steadily increasing although the dumpy remains exceedingly rare. There are records of many types of shorter-legged birds referred to as 'crawlers', 'creepers', 'stumpies', 'hoodies' and 'bakies'. Poultry similar to the dumpy was taken onto encampments near battlefields, as it was said that their acute hearing would warn of approaching dangers and then they would crow a warning. They were also said to have been trained to crow to order.

Distinct poultry breeds in the Shetland Islands are believed to have arrived with Norse settlers. Geese are the oldest domesticated birds. Unusually, the Shetland goose is sex-linked: unlike other geese, it can be sexed upon hatching. Shetland geese forage on seaweed and thrive on the poorest keep. Mary and Tommy Isbister of Trondra have fine examples of Shetland geese, hens and ducks, and have not only researched their history, but also worked hard to find birds to add to the limited gene pool to keep them as close to the original stock as possible. The Isbisters discovered the last of a line of Shetland ducks on the island of Foula and have since succeeded in breeding ducks true to type. There are two types of Shetland hen, the larger having a characteristic 'tapp' of feathers on her head.

Hens

Cocks and hens were forever under the eye – and overhead – in the simpler houses. The tie beam of the roof was sometimes known as the 'henbauk' because that was where the chickens roosted. The hens would seem to be constantly 'talking' to each other and to themselves while the cock strutted about with an agenda of his own. In international folk tales, the language of the birds is usually accessible only to specially gifted individuals, but people all over Scotland have composed brilliant imitative sayings based on what they 'hear' in bird-calls. Here is one from somewhere near Turriff in Aberdeenshire, about four rather indecisive hens making plans for the day:

> The first hennie comes oot an' she says:
> 'We'el awa,' we'el awa;' we'el awa.'
> The neist hennie comes oot an' she says:
> 'Far till? far till? far till? far till?'
> The neist hennie comes oot an she says:
> 'Tae Turra, tae Turra, tae Turra, tae Turra.'
> The neist hennie comes oot an she says:
> 'Fat tae dae there? fat tae dae there? fat tae dae there?
> The cock he comes oot and he says:
> 'Tae buy tobaccaoooo.'

Cockerels

Inevitably, cockerels were taken more seriously than hens. Their crowing was believed to banish ghosts, demons, bogles and fairies. If a cock crowed before midnight, however, it was a portent of death, especially if his feet and wattles were cold as well, and he would be looking towards the fatal spot. Sometimes a cock would be buried alive under the bed of a person with epilepsy, or on the spot where their first fit had happened. Reports of this came from many parts of the country. Colin MacDonald remembered his parents going to such an event on the eve of the twentieth century, somewhere near Strathpeffer. A little girl had been having fits for two or three years, and the doctors could do nothing for her. It was decided, as a last resort, to try using a cockerel sacrifice. An elder of the church was involved, together with 'an old woman of the glen' who knew about such things. After prayers for the girl's recovery, the floor was lifted and the cock buried alive. Whether substitutionary sacrifice or animal-helper dispatched to the Otherworld, it made no difference to the cock, but the prayers that were said were to the Christian God, and the people were uneasy about what they were doing: 'I don't know if I believe it or not,' said Colin's mother, 'but we were asked to go and we couldn't refuse. Besides, you never know.'

A typical mixed group of farmyard fowls (Polly Pullar)

THE MAINSTAY

Border Collie

S: dug, doag, tike
G: *cù, leth-chù*

In 1824 the Ettrick shepherd James Hogg wrote in *The Shepherd's Calendar*: 'Without the shepherd's dog, the whole of the open mountainous land in Scotland would not be worth a sixpence. It would require more hands to manage a stock of sheep, gather them from the hills, force them into houses and folds, and drive them to markets, than the profits of the whole stock were capable of maintaining.' James Hogg knew much about herding dogs and their affinity with man, their adaptability and intelligence. He told tales of dogs performing death-defying feats while locating sheep stuck in deep snowdrifts.

The early ancestors of the Border collie were highly valued from the outset. Although many were seen as fulfilling a role as workers, others became so much a part of a man's life that when they died, there was incredible sadness as unique partnerships were terminated.

There is much dispute about the origins of the word 'collie'. Some say that it comes from the word coal – meaning black, or from the Middle English, while others claim

that it stems from an old Gaelic word meaning 'useful'. Certainly the latter is highly appropriate for the working farm dog that has its origins in the border country between England and Scotland. Collies arrived with the influx of Lowland breeds of sheep to the hills and glens of Scotland. The early herding dogs were frequently nervous around people but this trait was soon bred out and their natural ability to gather sheep and other livestock was enhanced. Although they may have lacked in style, they were hardy, intelligent and highly valued.

There are records of dogs working sheep as far back as 1557 when in Dr Caisus's *Tretise of Englishe Dogges*, farm dogs were 'not huge, vaste and bigge but indifferent stature and growth'. This is a fairly accurate depiction of the collies of today.

As better sheepdogs were developed, there were unofficial displays of their prowess, with farmers keen to show off their dogs' abilities in a series of trials held in remote areas. However, it was not until the end of the 1800s that the first official sheep dog trial was held in Wales. The dog that is still recognised as being the forefather of the breed, Old Hemp, bred by Adam Telfer, won it. Many went on to use Hemp on their bitches and he sired dozens of litters of excellent puppies. Hemp was one of the first dogs to have looks, style, eye and temperament of the ultimate herding dog.

The word 'style' refers to the way in which a collie carries itself when around stock, and it should always have an inbuilt gathering instinct and an 'eye' always on the sheep. Good collies have many of the same traits as the wolf and although they are not killers, they use similar circling movement to the hunting technique of their predator ancestors. This, together with a constant eyeing, intimidates the flock into moving just where the handler requires it to be.

Although the earliest collies were referred to as working dogs, sheep dogs, farm collies, and a selection of other names, it was not until 1915 that the Border collie was officially recognised by James Reid, secretary of the International Sheepdog Association. It has remained one of the most popular breeds and is not only highly valued for farm work but is also generally viewed as being the most intelligent and easy to train of all breeds. The Search and Rescue Dogs Association, who use them for locating people on the hills following avalanches and accidents, and also to locate bodies in criminal investigations, find Border collies excellent for the purpose.

Opposite. Robert Harrison of Glen Artney and his collie (Polly Pullar)

Left. Border collies, highly intelligent and rewarding when trained (Polly Pullar)

The Border collie comes in many different guises, with a short coat, referred to as 'bare-skinned', or with long, silky hair. It may have smart prick ears, or ears in almost any position, and although black and white is the dominant colouring, there are also collies of sable, red, brown, blue merle and tricolour forms. The modern Border collie, like many farmers, may have filled out a little round the girth, as it tends to spend more time checking sheep from the back of a quad bike rather than covering the huge mileage each day of its forebears.

The Border collie is highly strung and was never a dog for an inactive person. Many have found an excellent role in obedience and agility classes and can be taught a vast array of skills in a short time.

Collie nomenclature has been stuck in a rut for generations. Names given to working dogs tend to be of one syllable as it is impossible to shout instructions across a high wind-blown hill to a dog with a long, fancy title. Moss, Jed, Glen, Fly, Gyp, Di, Ben, Bess, Lass, Nell, Clyde and Cap are just a few of the typical names used for Scots farm collies. On occasions while working such hardy sheep as the Blackface, which may turn round and send a dog packing, tempers may be sorely tried and the poor dog may answer to nothing whatsoever and instead head for home.

The introduction of the electric fence has added another hazard to sheep work. No collie will stand a kick off a high-voltage fence without retreating in terror. Although sheep are reputed to be stupid, I have witnessed many a fly hill ewe pushing a dog in the direction of a live fence. Some trial-winning trainers claim that there are no bad dogs, just bad owners.

Collies in the divine service

Border collies were once part of the religious life of the Yarrow valley. During the eighteenth and nineteenth centuries, there were outdoor communion services in summer, in the hills between St Mary's Loch and the Loch o' the Lowes. Famous preachers would be invited to prepare the people for the sacrament, and on one memorable occasion, a collie quietly upstaged the minister. There was no irreverent intent; quite the opposite. The shepherd was as devout as the rest of the congregation, but the day was wearing on and the ewes had to be gathered, so he slipped out, had a few words with his dog and returned silently to his place. The dog took to the hill. Before long, sheep started appearing on the ridge.

> 'See yonder, Robin, saw ye ere the like of yon?' said one old shepherd to another. 'John Hoy's "Nimble" gathering the Chapelhope ewes her lane, while he's sitting yonder. I'm no wondering, on a night like this, that the dumb brute should be led to do the deeds of the carnal day. We have heard muckle anent thae hills, but now we may say, we have seen mair than ever we heard of. See till her, Robin, man; she has brought the Lang Bank ewes forrit to the Ox-cleugh, and she's taking the brae again to gather the Brown Law.'

Gradually, the eyes of the congregation were drawn more and more towards the wonder on the hill and away from the preacher, till at last she had all the sheep down at the buchts, ready to be milked. It is fascinating to see how this was understood, not as a distraction, but as the workings of providence: God was leading Nimble to take care of earthly matters so that John could attend more fully to the things of heaven. But the theologising is secondary to the amazement ('See till her, Robin, man!') and Nimble was still remembered in 1818, nearly fifty years after the event. Was it necessity or theology that allowed collies to attend the morning service, just a little further down the valley at Yarrow Church? There, dogs would lie under the pews while shepherds worshipped God. The arrangement was far from trouble-free. There were occasional scraps and howls during the Psalm-singing. The dogs learned to recognise the end of the service, so that the congregation had to remain seated during the benediction, to forestall the joyous uproar.

THE AGRICULTURAL HEYDAY

Droving

From the thirteenth to the sixteenth centuries, cattle were the mainstay for those living in the Highlands. The small, hardy black animals, the forerunners of today's Highland cow, often constituted the only source of income for many poor families. They provided meat, milk, and if their owners were lucky, a small income. Rents could be paid in butter and cheese. Horns were used to make buttons, spoons, and other items. There was huge over-production of animals. Like the cattle, the people were hardy but often they could not sustain their animals through the harsher winter months and many died of starvation. They were therefore forced to sell some of their animals to those who came bargaining from other areas. Men travelled the Highlands mustering large numbers of cattle that were walked south to be sold in more prosperous areas. They eventually became known as 'drovers', and by the mid seventeenth century there was such an enormous trade in cattle that Scotland became widely known as 'the grazing field of England'.

In 1663 some 18,000 cattle passed through the border town of Carlisle on their way south. Droving was a high-risk, low-gain occupation. Rieving (the stealing of cattle) was commonplace and usually took place under the cover of darkness. Many of the rievers were armed and highly dangerous and would quickly hijack a passing herd. Crossing the wild and rugged terrain was fraught with difficulties as cattle were lost in bogs or were drowned, pulled under by vicious racing currents in places such as the Kylerhea narrows between the Isle of Skye and Glenelg on the mainland.

Some cattle were tied nose to tail and driven across the water by the drovers in small craft. In other cases cattle were crammed in boats lined with scrub to absorb their dung as the stress of the journey proved to have a laxative effect and they slipped and injured themselves, the dogs or the drovers.

Topsmen often accompanied the drovers, travelling ahead to pick out softer routes that would be easier on the

Droving cattle on the Isle of Skye (© Scottish Life Archive. Licensor www.scran.ac.uk)

cattle's hooves. They arranged for night grazing for the beasts and lodgings for the drovers, although they often slept outside beside their animals. Food was scarce for the men. They made rough black pudding by bleeding the cattle and adding the blood to oatmeal and onions. Small inns and houses on the way bolstered their spirits when lodgings were found, but someone always had to remain with the cattle to ensure their safety.

Gravel on some of the new Wade roads was not good for the animal's feet. Many were shod during the journey. Farriers, such as one at Crossgates in Fife and another at Trinafour in Perthshire, specialised in producing metal shoes for cattle. The outer edge of the hoof was covered, or sometimes leather shoes were fitted instead.

The two great cattle markets – or trysts – were held at Crieff and Falkirk. Here the immense cash crop of up to 30,000 black cattle was brought for sale, and then driven on south. Often animals might have already travelled many hundreds of miles through some of the most perilous territory in Scotland.

The trysts were colourful events and bustled with activity, as Gaelic and Scots mingled with many different strong English dialects to create a bazaar-like scene.

Gisborne's *Essay on Agriculture* of 1854 described it as follows:

> The scene, seen from horseback, from a cart, or some erection, is particularly imposing. All is animation, bustle, business and activity; servants running about shouting to the cattle, keeping them together in their particular lots and ever and anon cudgels are at work upon the horns and rumps of the restless animals that attempt to wander in search of grass or water.

Droving had all but died out by the time roads into the Highlands were appearing and railways had become part of modern life. By the 1830s, more and more cattle were kept in enclosures, and the wild, hirsute cattle drovers were lost to the new agricultural scene.

Perth Bull Sales

The Perth Bull Sales were one of the high points of the livestock calendar and put the small county town of Perth

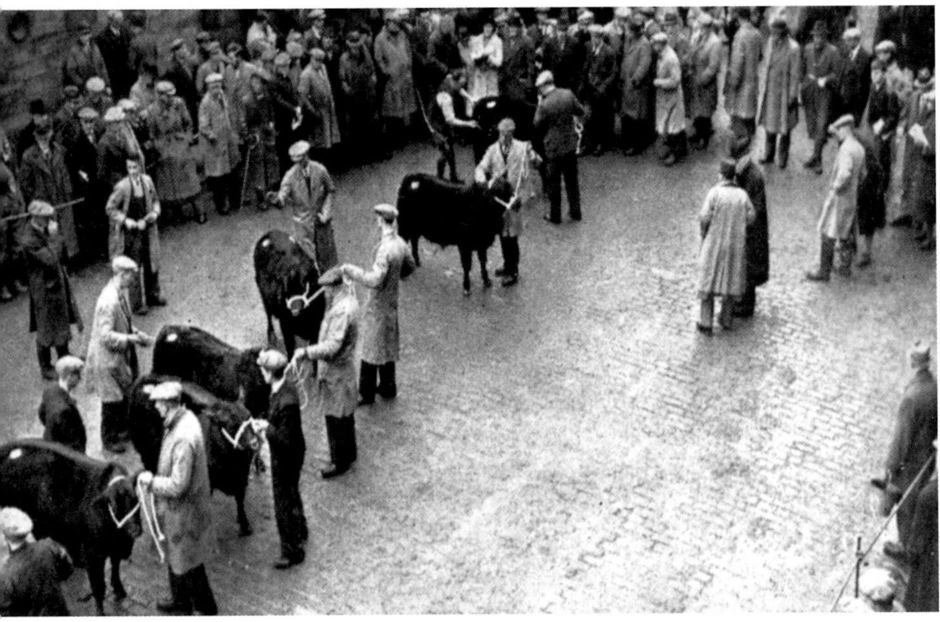

Aberdeen-Angus at the 1941 Perth Bull Sales (Farming News)

firmly on the world map. It was in 1865 that the first sale of Beef Shorthorn cattle was held in the town. It was officiated by John McLaren Fraser who had learned his trade in a local firm of agricultural valuers and estate agents, MacDonald and McCallum. The sale proved a great success and livestock premises were opened in Mill Street in 1863. In 1872, a similar sale of Aberdeen-Angus cattle was held. When one of the founding partners died, John McLaren Fraser was made a partner and the new firm was titled MacDonald Fraser and Company.

Fraser was keen to expand and although many sales were carried out on farms, the growth of the railway system brought new opportunities. Livestock could travel by train, and for purebred cattle such as the Aberdeen-Angus and Beef Shorthorn this proved ideal. Eventually a purpose-built livestock mart was established in Caledonian Road, close to the town's railway station. Not only did the stock arrive on special extra trains, but also buyers from all over Britain travelled north for two annual sales of pedigree stock. The business expanded, with new cattle sheds and auction halls providing venues for prospective buyers to view livestock. Many studied the animals as they were walked to the mart from the station. Unusually, judging was held outside in the street. Extra staff was taken on by the railways to deal with the huge influx of animals and passengers. MacDonald Fraser opened marts in other towns round Scotland, although it was the Perth Bull Sales that remained the mainstay of their business.

After World War II, the Bull Sales experienced a boom as buyers from all over the world descended in great numbers, keen to take some of the fine Scottish bred Aberdeen-Angus and Beef Shorthorn back to countries such as Canada, USA and Argentina, where many fine blood lines remain to this day.

The rich and famous (company directors, actors including John Wayne, and cattlemen with equally great amounts of cash) were regularly to be seen amongst the tweed-clad locals, eyeing up the bovine talent. 'The Fair City', as Perth is nicknamed, also boomed due to the extra business the Bull Sales brought. With such growing interest in the cattle, it was inevitable that records would be regularly broken as bidders pushed prices sky-high and beyond. Eventually, such was the popularity of the two breeds of cattle that a week was set aside for each. The exorbitant prices raised eyebrows as previous records were smashed.

In 1963 an astonishing record price was reached for Lindertis Evulse, from Kirriemuir, an Aberdeen-Angus bull that had just won his showing class. The electric atmosphere in the market that day has been described by many who witnessed the incredible events that followed, as the gavel finally fell at 60,000 guineas – a new world record. Owners Sir Torquil and Lady Munro must have found it hard to believe, but Black Watch Farms in New York then exported their animal. Incredibly, headlines were made a second time some six months later when Evulse was found to be infertile. However, insurance brokers Lloyds of London paid up and the buyers remained undaunted and continued to pay astronomical prices for Aberdeen-Angus at Perth thereafter.

In 1962 MacDonald Fraser became United Auctions and by the mid 1960s prices were falling. By the early 1970s, interest in native breeds was in stiff competition with the newly arriving, fast-growing large Continental breeds:

Simmental, Charolais, Limousin, and Romagnola. With advances in road transportation, the need for extra livestock trains and stockmen had disappeared, and animals were no longer to be seen parading the streets of Perth. In the Perth Sales heyday, one bull had even escaped, found his way to the High Street and had accidentally gone through a shop window. It truly was a case of a bull in a china shop, although there is no record of how much damage was done. In 1989 the market moved again to new premises at Huntingtower on the outskirts of Perth. Despite a new venue and it remaining a hugely important event, it was not to last. In 2009, the Perth Bull Sales was once more uprooted, this time to a purpose-built agricultural centre at Stirling – the end of an era that had seen the Fair City of Perth become one of the most important livestock centres in the world.

Cattle parade at the Royal Highland Show, Hazlehead Park, Aberdeen 1959 (Royal Highland and Agricultural Society of Scotland)

Royal Highland Agricultural Show

The Royal Highland and Agricultural Society of Scotland was established in 1784, but it was not until 1822 that the first show was held in Edinburgh's Canongate. There were reputed to be only a small number of exhibits at this event: approximately 75 cattle, eight Leicester sheep, and a couple of pigs.

To begin with, the show moved from town to town, and in 1948 when held at Inverness, King George VI, father of the present Queen, bestowed the event with its royal title. In 1960 the show became permanently based at Ingliston on the outskirts of Edinburgh. It has become a prestigious annual event, with over 5,000 animals exhibited from Thursday to Sunday in the second last week in June. In 2010 the Royal Highland Show celebrated its 50th Anniversary at Ingliston. One of the event's most coveted prizes is the Queen's Cup, which rotates between all breeds.

The heavy horse turnouts and bustling action of the main ring lure the crowds, and in recent years, the show has been not only recognised as Scotland's finest for agricultural matters, but also as a celebration of Scotland as a whole. The grand parades of stock round the main ring are a wonderful spectacle. I remember watching as a donkey foal went into orbit on hearing the skirl of the bagpipes, causing chaos among the ordered ranks of horses, ponies, and cattle, and providing much entertainment for the massive crowds. All livestock being shown remains on site for the duration of the four-day event, and this in itself is worth witnessing as the animals, deeply bedded in fresh straw, doze after the rigours of the show ring. The livestock owners provide another fine spectacle while fastidiously preparing their charges, primping and preening, shampooing, combing and trimming them and often finally blow-drying them with massive hairdriers. For the farming world, it is not only an important showcase of the country's ability to breed superb stock, but also a vital appointment in the social calendar, as the drover's bars and various other watering holes do roaring trade. Many livestock secrets are given away as Scotland's whisky industry is given an annual boost during show week.

The show has been cancelled once since it has been at Ingliston, during the Foot and Mouth outbreak in 2001. This halted all animal movements throughout Britain and did much damage to the livestock industry as a whole.

FORAGE HARVESTERS

Brown Hare

Lepus europaeus
S: baudrons, bawd, bawtie, cutty, donie, fuddie, lang lugs, maukin, pussy
G: *geàrr, maigheach, mial-bhuidhe, sgiarnag*

It was inevitable that a creature so supremely fleet of foot should have become a valuable quarry animal. Hare coursing was introduced by the Romans and became highly popular until animal rights groups finally won the battle to ban it at the beginning of 2005. It still continues illegally, however, when poachers venture onto farmland with their lurcher dogs and take up the chase. In central Scotland greyhound racing on tracks, using a fake hare running in front, is big betting business and attracts much support.

I will never forget the first time I heard the almost human cry of a wounded hare. The hare continued the soul-searing noise for some time. Indeed this pathetic sound inspired Robert Burns to write a poem titled 'On Seeing A Wounded Hare Limp By Me, Which A Fellow Had Just Shot'. Burns was on his farm at Ellisland in Ayrshire when he witnessed the shooting and wounding of the animal, and on hearing its distressed cry threatened to throw the perpetrator into the River Nith. Some say that due to this sound they will never shoot a hare for fear they do not kill it outright.

A brown hare crouches to aid the camouflage effect (Polly Pullar)

Although the beautiful brown hare may look similar to a rabbit, it is very different. It is unusual to see it in large groups, and it tends to join up with others to feed and breed rather than existing in a colony. Unlike rabbits, hares do not make burrows but use a 'form' – a simple scrape in the grass for both shelter and giving birth. Hares have never been domesticated in the same way as the rabbit, although small numbers were once kept in enclosures. They are highly nervous and their meat was not as popular, being more sinewy than that of the rabbit. Hare fur was sometimes used to make felt.

The exciting courtship displays of 'mad March hares' can be seen from early spring through the summer, although it is usually during March that they are witnessed at their best. Hares are promiscuous and often the crazed boxing and acrobatic high kicking is because the doe may not be ready to mate and tries to fend off persistent bucks. Often many males will pursue her, jostling to drive one another off the chase.

Although the hare cannot compete with the fecundity of the rabbit, in exceptional conditions, up to four litters a year may be produced. Leverets are born fully furred and with their eyes open, unlike the bald, blind, baby rabbit. On occasions a doe may become pregnant again before she has given birth to the litter she is carrying, something highly unusual among mammals, but foetuses at various stages have been found inside dead hares.

A doe is remarkably brave in defence of her young. I remember watching one with her two leverets in a field of cattle. A cow came close and blew inquisitively on the youngsters. The hare quickly reared up on her hind legs and boxed the cow several times squarely on the nose and sent her packing.

Loss of hedgerows and changes in farming methods has led to a downtrend in hare numbers – more crops are sown in the autumn than previously and there are fewer hay meadows. Many leverets are lost in grass-cutting machines

In a hare's likeness

Virtually any animal could be suspected of being a witch in disguise, but there are a great many witch stories about hares. This could be partly due to the publicity given to the confession of Isobel Gowdie at her trial in 1662. Isobel confessed that she often changed into a hare and roamed the countryside with other women similarly disguised, causing malicious damage and consorting with the devil. On one occasion, she said, she was pursued by a neighbour's greyhounds, but managed, just in time, to get home and repeat the disenchanting spell:

> Hare, hare, God send thee care!
> I am in a hare's likeness just now,
> But I shall be a woman even now –
> Hare, hare, God send thee care!

She believed herself to be guilty of terrible crimes, for which there was no forgiveness, and urged the court to punish her severely. Probably, as Sir Walter Scott said, the poor creature was suffering from 'some peculiar species of lunacy', but behind and beneath Isobel's nightmare world lies a local version of what Carlo Ginzburg has called 'a deep stratum of peasant myths lived with extraordinary intensity'.

They had not always been peasant myths. Kings and their families, professional poets, and even the occasional saint and angel, change into animals and back in early Irish and and Welsh literature. Shape-shifting is a very old, international motif which derives from a world-view in which the soul can take up residence in different bodies, temporarily or through several lifetimes. Christianity had no problem with the journey of the soul, but animal transformations were another matter. Indeed, the spiritual life has sometimes been seen as leading away from animal nature. So as the learned classes turned their attention elsewhere, the old myths became more and more the preserve of the people who kept them alive in stories, songs and in a kind of home-grown spirituality which was more or less Christian, but still in touch, to some extent, with older strata of belief.

and are killed by traffic. Permanent grass pasture and young forestry plantations are often favoured, but damage done to trees is unappreciated by foresters, while grazing hares in a field of young barley may mean a farmer reaches for his gun. Hares can be shot at any time of year and are often culled where they are causing damage. The rough shooter may also take a hare to add to the game bag and after it has been hung for about a week, it may be prepared and made into an old-fashioned dish called 'Jugged Hare', in which the animal's blood is a vital ingredient and is finally mixed with port or other alcohol.

Hares frequently eat their own droppings – this is called 'refection'. They consume large amounts of cellulose that is hard to digest and by eating droppings they are in effect giving themselves a second chance to metabolise this valuable food source. When feeding in open fields, they will sometimes sit tight with ears flat against their heads, barely moving a muscle until a human or dog is almost on top of them. Then they will jink away, seldom running in a straight line, always altering their route, part of their superbly adapted capture avoidance tactics. The saying 'first catch your hare' bears testimony to their speed and ingenuity, as it takes a swift dog with much skill to keep up with one.

Rabbit

Oryctolagus cuniculus
S: bawtie, cuning, kinnen, mappie, map-map
G: *coinean*, *coineanach*, *rabaid*

The ubiquitous rabbit was introduced by the Normans, brought to Britain as a valuable source of meat and fur. At that time it was managed like farm stock and kept in huge walled warrens where it bred in profusion. Between 1214 and 1249, Alexander II of Scotland had his royal warrens protected from poachers by statute. Records from the king's warrens at Crail in Fife show that an annual salary of 16s 8d was paid for the services of a rabbit keeper. During the

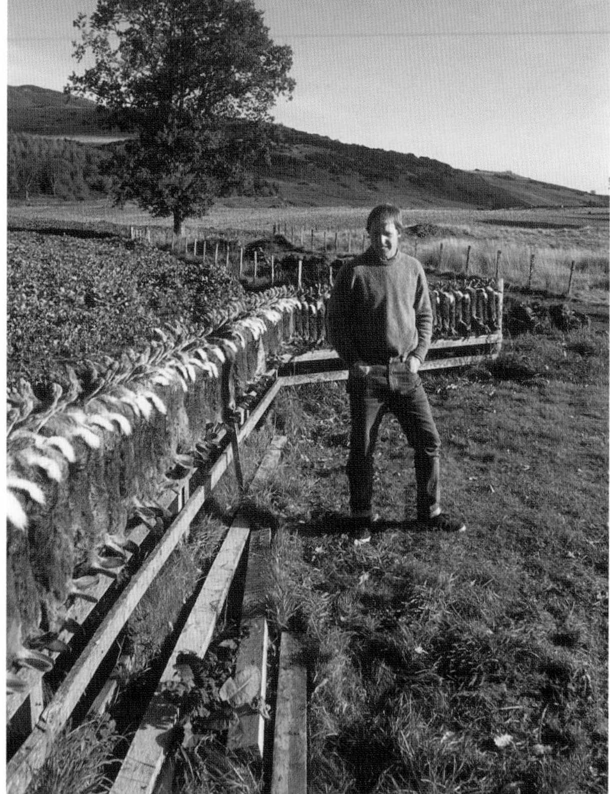

Jock MacDonald, keeper on Drummond Estate, with his handiwork (Polly Pullar)

1490s, the Earl of Orkney was paid part of his annual rents in rabbits. There are records of rabbits on Little Cumbrae Island in the Clyde in 1453, and bizarrely records of 'conyngis' (rabbits) on the Bass Rock in 1584 – a place that hardly seems suitable for such creatures. In 1750 at Lossiemouth in Morayshire, rabbits were thought to have escaped from a ship moored close by. They quickly spread and soon took over the dune systems.

By the end of the eighteenth century, rabbits had colonised almost every corner of Scotland. Views had rapidly altered and although the delicious white meat and soft pelt had once been valued, they were seen as a serious agricultural pest, and have remained so ever since.

The rabbit has always been the staple fare of the poacher and few landlords had much argument with the poor countryman who took fat rabbits home to feed his starving family. In 1954, however, even poachers became less enthusiastic about rabbits, or 'coneys' as they were frequently called. The highly contagious rabbit disease myxomatosis, spread by fleas, had finally reached Scotland. The first outbreak was reported at Durris in Aberdeenshire. The disease then became rife as it was deliberately spread around the country in a bid to rid farmland of the rabbit plague: Rabbit Clearance Societies were set-up, and myxomatosis was the most effective way of keeping populations in check. 'Myxie' causes afflicted rabbits to be covered in weeping sores with suppurating eyes that swell to the point where the animals become blind. Rabbits are rendered almost immobile and soon succumb to high fever.

Although there are currently outbreaks of myxomatosis every few years, some rabbits have become immune. Rabbits are the staple fare of many birds including eagles, buzzards and ravens, and also many mammals. Badgers frequently dig out nests of young rabbits. On the Isle of May and other important seabird breeding sites, rabbits constantly compete for burrow space with breeding puffins.

Ferreting is a popular sport and can be carried out with a bird of prey to catch the rabbit as it bolts from a hole, or simply with nets pegged round the burrow exits. Once the ferret is put into an occupied warren, then a patient wait follows, and there may be loud thumps from within before a rabbit darts out in a panic. A fully grown rabbit can be surprisingly hard to grab and may pull the net free, so most ferreters also have terriers or gundogs to help. Other efficient methods of rabbit culling are snares or special box traps, which are set in well-used rabbit runs through a fence. Once the rabbits are used to going back and forth over the box, a trap door is left open and many rabbits can be caught in a single night in this way.

Mice

S: mous
G: *luch*

Mice have a very short lifespan and are vulnerable to extremes of weather and lack of food. The ubiquitious house mouse (*Mus musculus*) was originally a Neolithic stowaway and has been in Scotland ever since. As soon as the days begin to shorten, most old houses harbour these unwelcome guests. We hear them in the attic space, running frenetically back and forth – even a tiny mouse can sound as if it is wearing clogs and appears much bigger than it is so that people frequently think they have rats. These adorable-looking grey-brown creatures with their beady black eyes cause untold destruction. They eat wiring and chew their way through many household objects. The use of plastic water pipes in houses can lead to major floods when mice nibble holes and water eventually seeps through ceilings. Archie Fletcher of Persabus Farm, Islay, told his family that as a boy in the 1930s, he slept on a mattress stuffed with chaff and would frequently be woken in the night by mice eating its contents, and had to kick out with his feet to get rid of them.

Mice, although tiny, cause unnecessary fear. Some find they are unable to handle them and therefore will not remove them from traps, while others merely scream hysterically on sight. A friend living alone in a remote cottage in Angus had a plague of mice but was too revolted to remove them from traps. Instead she lifted them using a shovel and then flagged down passing motorists asking them to remove the bodies.

Many different mousetraps have been fabricated, some of them ingenious, with several holes able to trap up to six mice at a time. Others involve luring mice up a pipe with food where they eventually fall into a bucket of water and drown. Poison is frequently used but in some cases mice become immune to it.

The wood mouse (*Apodemus sylvaticus*) is sometimes called the long-tailed field mouse. Although very similar to the house mouse, it has larger eyes and ears and is often slightly browner in colour with more patches of yellowish fur. Their tails are almost as long as their bodies. Presence of house mice in a building is often noticeable by their pungent aroma, something that is not as prominent in the wood mouse.

Mice are sexually mature at just over a month old and they breed prolifically. They have a short gestation period of 20 days. They can breed from early February through to October, so a house may soon be overrun. House mice thrive in the presence of humans. Empty houses are not as popular as homes where crumbs and food remains are left lying about.

On the island of St Kilda, two endemic subspecies of mouse were officially recognised, the St Kilda house mouse (*Mus musculus muralis*), and the St Kilda field mouse (*Apodemus sylvaticus hirtensis*). Both forms are larger than their mainland cousins. When the islanders left in 1930, the house mouse only survived for a short time and has since disappeared altogether. However, Frank Fraser Darling found house mice on Lunga, one of the Treshnish Isles in 1937, despite the departure of its human occupants some 80 years previously. He found that, unlike the house mice on St Kilda, the Lunga mice had adapted to al fresco living. They were quick to take advantage of the visitors' temporary camp, however, and swiftly moved in with them. House mice are renowned for their playful, spirited nature and these mice showed signs of cheeky behaviour.

Some think the St Kilda house mouse could have evolved as a unique species, but became extinct within just 1,000 years. Research is currently being done on why the remaining St Kilda field mice are so much larger than those on the mainland. It is thought that as they have no real predators, and have to cope with the island's savage weather, they increased in size.

Cheddar cheese is frequently referred to as 'mousetrap'

Young woodmouse, sometimes called the long-tailed field mouse (Polly Pullar)

Mouse lore

There is more about rats than mice in Scottish tradition, although sometimes the two are treated together. In the Hebrides, children left their milk teeth for the tooth mouse rather than the tooth fairy, but most mousy creatures were unwelcome.

The *luch-sith* (fairy mouse) could harm a beast if it ran over it. If a field mouse ran over your foot, it was said to cause paralysis. But roasted mouse was said to be a cure for whooping cough and jaundice, and was most effective if you took three.

due to the mouse's love of cheese. During the 1960s, my parents went to the Summer Isles Hotel with a view to buying it. The owner showed us round and took us into the larder where a vast cheese bell stood on a shelf. He told us that they prided themselves on providing their guests with excellent mature Stilton, and with much aplomb lifted the lid. Underneath was a tiny mouse cleaning its whiskers having had its fill of cheese. It was doubtful if the guests were ever any the wiser.

Rat

S: ratton, raut
G: *radan, gall-luch*

There was a certain fatalism about rats. It was even said that rats leaving the house were as sinister as rats leaving a sinking ship, although the opposite makes more sense; that an invasion of rats meant you would soon be either dead or homeless and the rats had come to 'summonce' you out. Harder to shift from his home was the old Shetlander whose son found him fishing for rats through a hole in the floor using a limpet and line – he had a 'kishie' (creel) beside him full of dead rats, so the story goes.

Rats for evermore

It is difficult to imagine a rat infestation worse than the one endured by young Ned Robertson when he was a stable lad in a farm near Biggar. He makes light of it in the following interview, given many years later in 1972. The older men went into town in the evenings, but young Ned didn't lack for company:

> We slept abin the horses. And rats for ever more. Oo got what they ca'd a ticky bed. That was a kind o a strippit big sack or something filled wi' caff … [chaff] oot the barn. It was fine the first nicht, but the next nicht the rats had it torn to atoms. Oh, they were into the bed aside us. Oh, an' I'll tell you what, they'd gae through ablow your back, and a good big yin, it didnae feel as thick as that finger. They could streetch theirsel like an eel, and they never, well, I was young an sleepy, never heeded them.
>
> Oo wasna alood tae hiv a licht, the fermer wouldna let us hiv a licht, but oo'd stole the … well we didna steal it, but oo got the doups oot o his gig, well, the lichts o his gig, y'see. It burnt doon tae aboot an inch, and then there was what oo ca'd the can'le doups, when he changed his can'les, oo'd grab the doups. Now, we got a wee clog, an oo drapped a bit oil on it, and he didna see the licht up in … it was so small y'ken, but when you lichted that licht there was a great scram'le o rats wantin into the beam ends o the rebbie [?] and they squealed for to get in, and I know they werena three minutes in, jince you'd see the three noses come oot like that, and by God they were oot in legions efter.
>
> And the fermer kept a stallion and they were in the courts doon below us a' summer and they were aye getting' feedin' and they were knockin' the feedin' ow'er o the side o their dish and … the rats lived on't you see. And then they bored into the beddin'. Well, it was like peat moss, and they made burrows in that where the stallion bade.
>
> Well there were yae day the farmer says, 'You're a nice chap, a young fellae', says he, 'I think we'll clean oot the stallion hoose'. So oo got the great big stable barrae, that was a big barrae at oo hid tae lift the manure o the horses, an they scoored wi' spades and grapes, an I had the barrae, to hurl the rats away, an there were over four hundred in it, and when I gaed to lift the barrae they slid like fish, they slippit off and slid off, there was that many on the barrae … An' oh, a lot o them got away, but they could get a nest wi' … wi' takin' a square moo'd shovel and comin' doon on a nest wi't … Dugs was no use. No. Traps was no use. No use whatever. So that was the thing up there, but oo got accustomed wi' them, and I think, I think it were only yince yin that I flung off, well it'd be comin' … they were always … but they liked gettin up into your oxter.

THE EARTH MOVER

Mole

Talpa europaea
S: mowdiewort, modewarp, moudie
G: *famh, ùir-threabhaiche, dubh-threabhaiche, dallag*

Fields punctuated with a rash of molehills are a familiar sight. The little gentleman in black velvet is oddly absent from many Scottish islands, however, including Islay and some of the Outer Hebrides. An x-ray photograph of the ground beneath a mole's heaps would reveal a complex labyrinth of tunnels that would put motorway planners to shame. Despite their small size, moles are some of the best earthmovers of all. With their strong shovel-like front feet, they can dig at a rate of 18 feet per hour. Some enormous mole heaps, or 'fortresses', can be found on damper ground that is prone to flooding. The collective noun for moles is a 'labour' – an appropriate monicker for these industrious mammals.

People do indeed make mountains out of molehills – the mole has been heavily persecuted for centuries, but it continues to be widespread and numerous. Moles incur wrath when their evidence appears all over immaculate lawns, graveyards, golf courses and newly sown fields. Methods that have been employed to try to eradicate them include a huge selection of traps, worms dipped in strychnine, pesticides, smoke bombs, explosions, vibrating devices, floods and gas. Mole catching has long been steeped in mystery, with catchers reticent about their methods and reluctant to give away trade secrets. In some areas, lines of dead moles attached to fences are proof of the catcher's skill.

The problem of moles was recognised as far back as 1566 when an Act of Parliament was passed offering a bounty for eliminating them. Not only were mole catchers remunerated for the number they killed, but they could also sell their beautifully soft skins. These were an added bonus and were made into waistcoats, britches, muffs and hats during the early part of the twentieth century. Moleskins were widely used by plumbers to temporarily patch burst joints in pipes.

Traps and the poison strychnine were the two most widely used methods of mole despatch until 2007 when strychnine was banned. Since then, professional mole catchers have been even more highly sought as frustrated farmers and gardeners are unable to get rid of moles, and despair at the ruination they cause. However, some professional gardeners have come to value the beautifully tilled, well-aerated soil left by moles. The head gardener of Drummond Castle gardens at Crieff made sure it was collected for use in potting young plants.

Moles are active all year round. They consume large amounts of earthworms, immobilising them by biting off their heads. Often their worm larders contain many hundreds. A mole needs a constant supply of high protein food; being so frenetic, it must consume between 50 and 100 per cent of its bodyweight every day.

Moles have tiny eyes, but the belief that they are blind is unfounded. They have superb sensory powers and a strong pig-like snout. Their short tails have spiky hairs that help them detect the movements of worms and invertebrate prey. Moles are usually only seen above ground when they are searching for bedding material, or have been dug out of their tunnels by larger animals. It would appear that they are unpalatable, since owls and other raptors shun

With large, strong front feet, moles can move an astonishing amount of earth (Polly Pullar)

them. Even when I have had injured birds of prey in captivity and offered them dead moles, they have been left untouched. Moles decay rapidly, giving off a strong smell, and this may be part of the reason why they are not a popular food source.

Moles breed once a year, with three to six babies born after a four- to six-week gestation. The babies are blind, bald and helpless and do not start moving about until they are about three weeks old. Both parents care for them, although if the female mole is killed, the father abandons their litter. By two months of age, the youngsters are able to start digging, and are sexually mature at about a year old.

AVIAN AGRICULTURALISTS

Common Buzzard

Buteo buteo
S: bizzard, puttock
G: *clamhan*

Almost 150 years ago Sir William Jardine wrote, 'The buzzard is a fine accompaniment to the landscape whether sylvan or wild or rocky'. In 1776 Pennant wrote that it was the commonest of the hawks. Due to law enforcement, the buzzard has been spared almost two centuries of persecution and although it is still the victim of illegal killing, its numbers are currently healthy; along with the sparrowhawk, it is Britain's most numerous raptor. Many gamekeepers claim that there are far too many buzzards and that they should be culled. This is something that always generates intense debate. The buzzard's presence next to pheasant-rearing pens is never popular and poults may be taken as easy prey, thus incuring the gamekeeper's wrath.

The buzzard is all too frequently the unfortunate victim of poisoning as it is a lazy feeder and will always take advantage of carrion. Its diet is extremely catholic: although rabbits tend to be the main prey in areas where they are abundant, any carrion is acceptable including road kill. During large outbreaks of the deadly rabbit disease myxomatosis, buzzard numbers plummet accordingly. Small mammals and amphibians are also taken, and I have seen buzzards carrying adders and slow worms. Buzzards in our fields frequently spend much time looking for earthworms on molehills. Their pellets reveal that they also eat large amounts of beetles and other invertebrates. One pair of buzzards on a large farm near Auchterarder learned to take hens and killed several in a short space of time, although this is unusual. However, if the living can be made easy then a buzzard may take advantage.

It is possible to see buzzards in almost every habitat in Scotland, although they tend to favour farmland areas adjacent to woodland, and are also often seen near motorways where vole-rich verges and road kill provide a varied menu.

Although the buzzard is approximately half the size of the majestic golden eagle, it is frequently mistaken for it by the uninitiated on a first trip into the Highlands. This has earned it the nickname 'the tourist's eagle'. I am frequently told by holidaymakers of a huge eagle perching by the road on a telegraph post. It is a fair assumption that if it is seen on a post near the roadside it is not a golden eagle, as perching on telephone poles or posts is something that eagles would seldom do. In the Highlands, it is sometimes possible to see buzzards mobbing eagles and then the size difference becomes clear. Like the eagle, the buzzard has a dramatic flight display during the breeding season, and will lock talons with its mate in midair, tumbling in freefall before separating just above the ground and soaring far into the sky again.

Nests are made in trees or on crags and if neither is available, birds will nest on the ground. The young are coated in thick, white down and are fed by both adults. The nest is a bulky structure and is often used in subsequent years. The mewing of the buzzard can be heard almost everywhere and in the late summer, as the juvenile birds are learning to hunt, it almost takes the form of incessant whining when they nag their parents for food. Round bales in newly harvested fields make ideal perches between hunting forays around vole-rich end rigs.

I have had many injured and orphaned buzzards over the years and find that not only are they easy to handle, but they are also less prone to stress than other raptors. Three tiny eyases brought to me when their nest tree was accidentally felled were hand-reared successfully. I continued to put food out for them once they were free. They remained around the farm for many years and helped to keep the rats at bay.

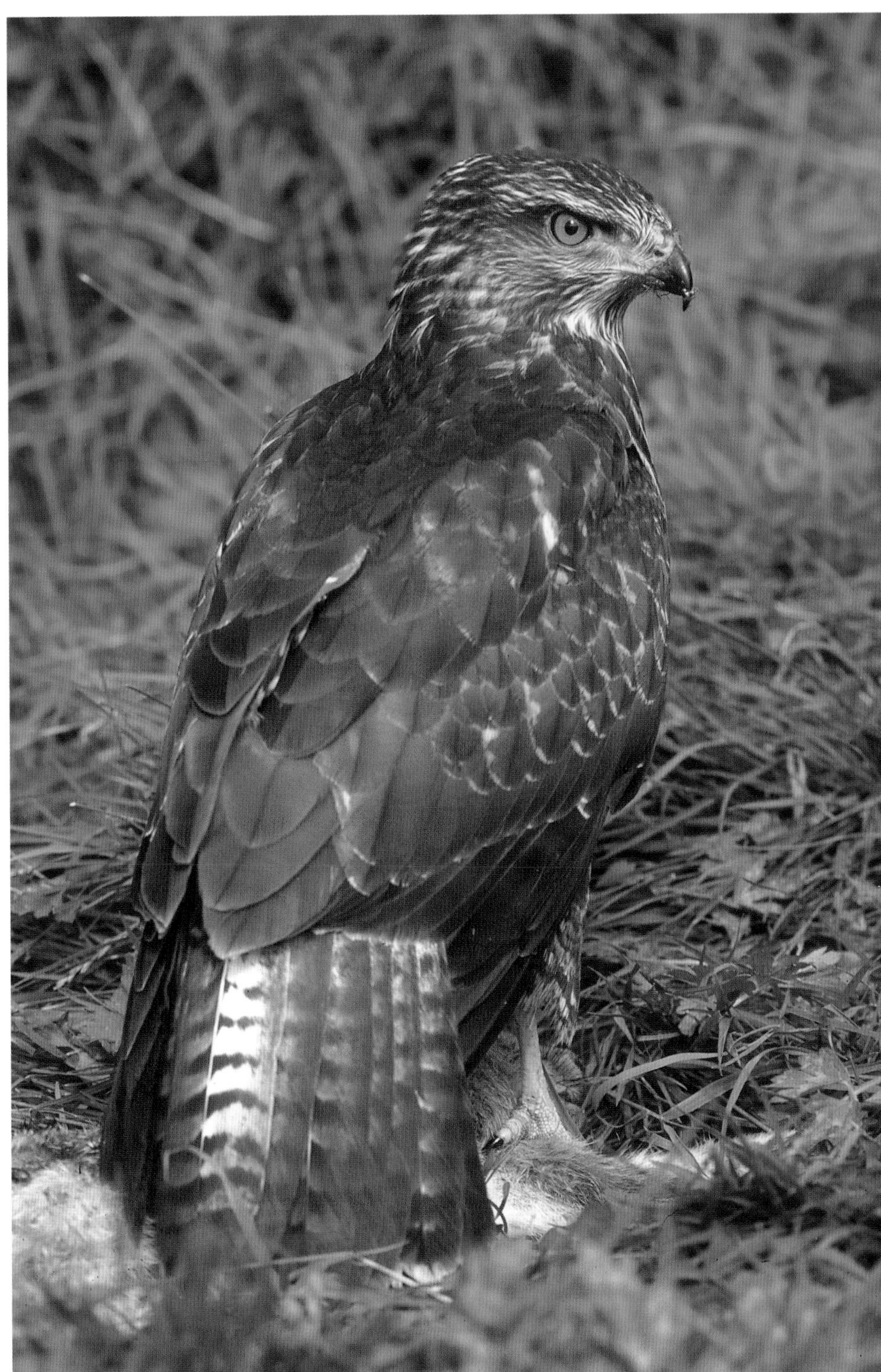

Common buzzard feeding on a rabbit (Polly Pullar)

The grey partridge in fact has plumage of many beautiful varied hues (Malcolm Gosling)

Decline of the partridge

During the late nineteenth century, partridges were plentiful on Lowland farms. Unfortunately, this delightful bird has suffered more than any other game bird as a result of changes in agriculture, and by the 1950s a worrying decline had begun. Introductions of grey partridges to many locations including some of the islands have not proved successful, although the non-native French red-legged partridge appears to be thriving. Farms that were once rife with weeds, providing plenty of seeds and insect life for partridges to feed on, are now kept tidy with the increased use of weed killers, and grey partridge numbers continue to plummet. Schemes to help farmers implement changes to agricultural policies can be highly successful, however. One example is 'beetle banks', which have been introduced to provide food for birds that otherwise could go hungry.

Grey Partridge

Perdix perdix
S: aiten, pairtrick, perdrix
G: *peurtag, cearc-thomain*

> If ever there was an advertisement for plump domesticity it is the partridge. It is well deserved for they are monogamous, and a pair, given reasonable conditions in the mating season, will produce large families well into the teens, and they will look after their young with fussy and businesslike efficiency.
>
> Lord Home, 1979

Unlike the pheasant and other introduced game birds, the grey partridge is a fine parent and will defend its tiny bumblebee-like young against predators, endeavouring to lure them away with broken wing action. A covey of partridges often roosts in a circle with the sleeping birds facing out so that they are aware of advancing dangers. Despite this, they are still extremely vulnerable to predation.

The grey partridge is depicted in the Game Conservancy's logo. The onomatopoeic Latin name, *Perdix perdix*, refers to their noisy, rasping calls, which have been likened to the continual swinging of a gate with rusty hinges. They are often heard as a disturbed covey explodes from undergrowth.

Most partridges are found in the drier parts of eastern Scotland where large fields of grain provide suitable habitat. During extreme weather, grey partridges have been recorded in some surprising places, however. They appeared in the streets of Edinburgh city centre during the severe winter of 1882, and although grey partridges are normally sedentary, they have been seen flying out to sea during bad weather.

Swallow

Hirundo rustica
S: swalla
G: *gòbhlan-gaoithe, ainleag*

House Martin

Delichon urbicum
S: mairtin, wunda-swalla
G: *gòbhlan-taighe*

The well-known saying 'one swallow does not make a summer' may be true, but the sight of the first one as it arrives back after winter is enough to make us think of warmer days ahead. Often swallows, house martins and sand martins return to Scotland when snow is still on the ground. Early sightings are often near water, where birds, exhausted after a long flight from Africa, gather to feed on emergent insects.

Farmyards all over Scotland once had several pairs of swallows, but with major agricultural changes, outbuildings being converted into houses, and increased use of pesticides, numbers have fallen dramatically. Many hirundines (birds of the swallow and martin family) are lost over the Sahara on their long migrations.

It is the female swallow that chooses a mate. Males with the longest tail streamers are preferred. Their glossy metallic blue-black plumage and chestnut heads are stunning as they perch in lines on telegraph wires, chattering to one another cheerfully. Large groups of swallows and martins are often seen during sultry weather, swooping low over fields of long grass while hawking for insects. The unpopular midge is a valuable food source. Nests are often made in unusual places and although swallows once favoured rocks and cliffs, they now tend to nest in close proximity to man. They may choose a site over the top of an open doorway, which poses a few problems for the human residents.

House martin feeding young in typical eaves nest site (Lawrie Campbell)

Swallow lore

Swallows were once thought to hibernate, hiding away under water in deep, murky pools where they lay wing-to-wing, foot-to-foot, beside one another. Swallow broth was thought to cure epilepsy and stammering; the birds have always been seen as a good omen. Nest desertion was viewed as a bad sign, however. Swallows may lay in each other's nests, and it is not unusual for there to be cuckoldry, leading to egg dumping. Swallows have long been viewed as a symbol of grace and speed.

Swallows do not tend to nest in colonies, whereas the house martin does exactly that. We have eight house martin nests in the eaves of our house, including one sited right over the top of the burglar alarm. The sitters do not appear to be perturbed by the alarm's intermittent flashing. We eagerly await the birds' return in spring, and we are concerned when numbers appear to drop. Garden plants grown beneath may suffer as a result of the excess ammonia in the bird's guano, but the joy of having the constant activity and chatter from both swallows and house martins is more than compensation for a few lost flowers. It is illegal to remove nests, although this unfortunately happens too frequently.

Swallow

House Sparrow

Passer domesticus
S: sparra, sparry, spurg, speug, spurdie
G: *glaisean, gealbhonn*

Seeing a house sparrow in the garden these days is a rare occurrence. They were once extremely common on farmland and frequented byres and farm buildings almost everywhere, making full use of any available space in which to build a profusion of messy nests. Their familiar chirruping sounds were synonymous with arable farming. Sparrows are still regularly referred to as 'spuggy' or 'speug' in parts of Scotland, while in others areas the nickname 'Philip' is imitative of their call.

Sparrows were regularly caught in nets when they became a nuisance on crops or in gardens. They were also shot, and falconers often trapped them for feeding to their captive birds of prey.

Some towns and cities still have large numbers of sparrows while in others there has been a huge, inexplicable, widespread decline. On some Scottish islands, not only have the human occupants moved to the urban environment, but so too have the sparrows.

The tree sparrow (*Passer montanus*) looks very similar to the house sparrow but has brighter plumage and is slightly more elegant. It is also becoming increasingly rare, but in some areas populations have been maintained by nest box schemes, particularly around Blairgowrie and Coupar Angus in Perthshire. It was the naturalist Sir Robert Sibbald who officially listed the tree sparrow as a different bird in 1720.

Sparrows are renowned for their noisy public copulations. There are fewer nesting spaces for them as more old buildings are being renovated, although these small birds are renowned for their unusual choice of sites. One pair successfully reared several broods in the rigging of a coal boat, and they were regularly fed by the crew. Nests may also be made from strange materials, as in the case of one made almost entirely from discarded cigarette butts.

The cheeky house sparrow is now in serious decline (Polly Pullar)

Jackdaw

Corvus monedula
S: jackie, kae
G: *cathag, cnàimh-fhitheach*

The opportunistic jackdaw is a small, cheery-looking member of the crow family with a smart grey mantle and grey-blue eyes that miss nothing. Ubiquitous, gregarious and omnivorous, jackdaws are found wherever there is a chance of food and shelter, from mountains to estuaries, where they have been seen taking wader chicks and the young of other birds.

Old chimneys, buildings, rock crevices, hollow trees and even rabbit holes make popular nest sites, and frequently jackdaws post large amounts of sticks into chimneys that fall into the fireplace or become jammed in the flue instead. Many chimney fires have been caused as a result.

Jackdaws are often seen on the backs of sheep and cattle, picking off parasites, and I have seen them pulling wool out too, to comfortably line their nests. Sheep do not appear to mind and probably find the jackdaw's probing bill relieves the itch from parasites. Jackdaws are easily tamed and learn to imitate the human voice when kept as pets. A young jackdaw brought to me became a perfect nuisance and stole a large bunch of keys from a windowsill and then flew off into a nearby wood where it deposited them, leading to inevitable mayhem. Jackdaws also compete for chimney space with a pair of tawny owls in an old bothy adjacent to our house. They continue to push sticks down on top of the sitting owl.

Like rooks, jackdaws are colonial. During the 1970s, a large colony on St Serf's Island on Loch Leven had to be eradicated because the jackdaws consumed the wild duck eggs, leading to total brood failure. Farmers frequently view jackdaws as pests and many are caught legally in Larsen trap. Vast flocks of jackdaws from Scandinavia arrive in Scotland in late autumn and gather at roost sites in central and eastern Scotland. Washing lines often have to be taken down due to the mess from large numbers of birds, as in

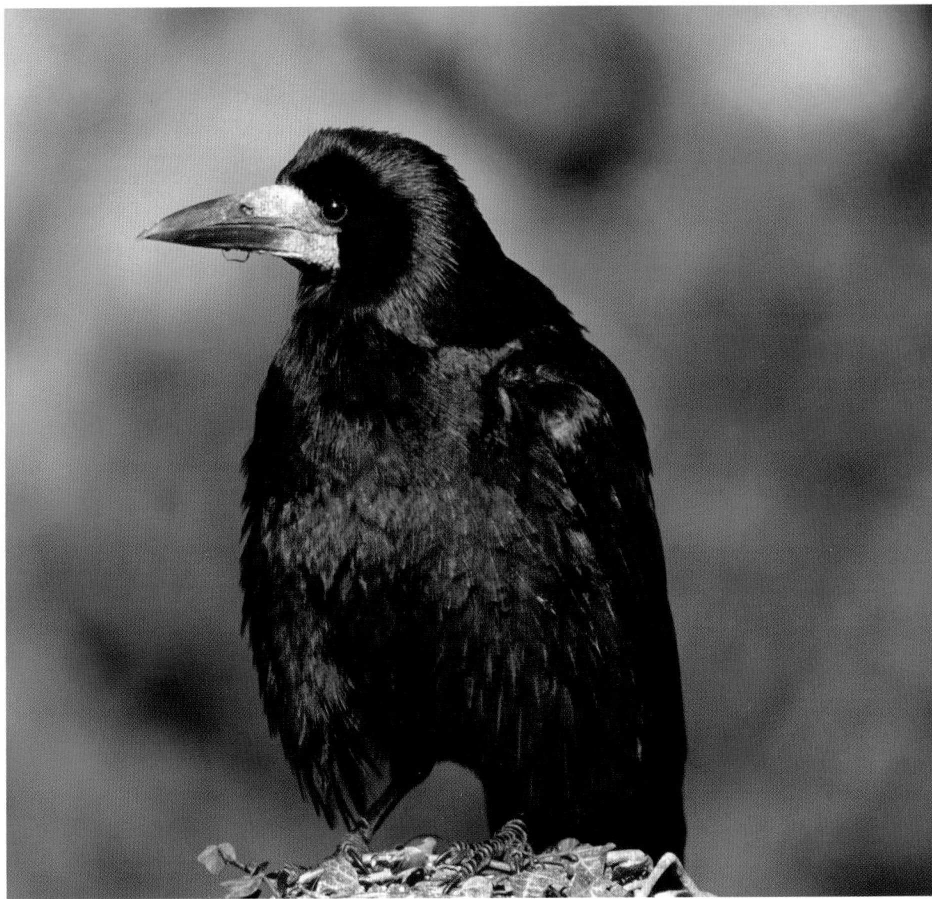

Left. Jackdaws frequently nest in the chimneys of both abandoned and occupied dwellings (Polly Pullar)

Right. Like all members of the crow family, the rook is surprisingly intelligent (Laurie Campbell)

the case of a record roost of rooks and jackdaws at Moness, Aberfeldy. Like starlings, jackdaws may congregate at roost sites in incredible balling flights, sweeping through the air in impressive formation.

Rook

Corvus frugilegus
S: corbie (also used for raven and hooded crow)
G: *ròcas*

Scottish rookeries are much larger than their English counterparts, with an average of 6,000 nests being recorded annually at Hatton Castle, Aberdeenshire from the 1940s to the 1970s. This site remains the stronghold for the rook in Britain, but today's population count hovers at around 2,000 pairs there.

Rooks flourish adjacent to farmland and can frequently be seen following the plough or in stubble fields where they consume numerous cereal pests including cockchafers and leatherjackets. They also feed on spilt livestock feed and are sometimes seen at rubbish tips. They frequent upland pastures where they find copious craneflies. The desertion of a rookery was seen as a bad omen, and in Orkney it was believed famine would follow.

Rooks are present in most areas, including some Hebridean islands. They were previously widely eaten and were often made into rook pie. Young rooks are still occasionally shot, particularly when they are almost ready to fledge and are at the 'brancher' stage when they have plenty of stored body fat. One Glaswegian restaurant has been serving a popular seasonal rook pie to its customers.

Like all corvids, rooks are intelligent. They are sociable and have been seen in circles with a bird in the centre, giving rise to the idea that they hold rook 'parliaments', referred to as 'craa courts' in some parts of Scotland. A 'parliament' is the collective noun for the species. Like jackdaws, they are frequently confused with carrion crows but their more ragged appearance and distinctive bare grey faces are immediately recognisable.

Scarecrows in fields of grain were originally made to ward off rooks rather than crows, but all corvids soon become accustomed to them and are sometimes seen using them as perches. Hand-reared rooks make good pets as they become very attached to people, but their cleverness frequently leads them into mischief. Perhaps this is the origin of the term to 'rook' someone, meaning to dupe or short-change them.

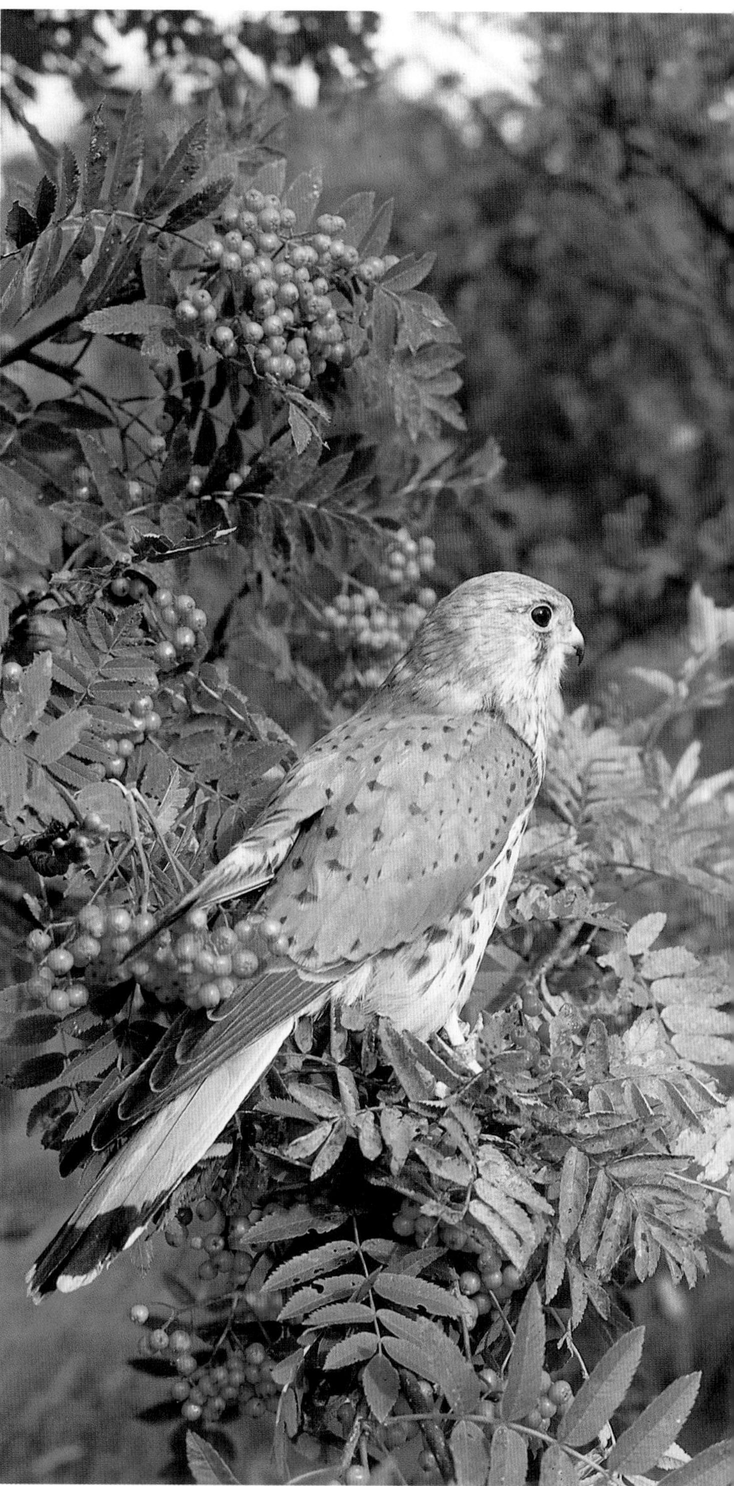

Adult male kestrels have a blue tinge to their heads and a slate-grey tail (Polly Pullar)

Kestrel

Falco tinnunculus
S: keelie hawk, reid hawk, stanchel, willie-whip-the-wind, wind cuffer
G: *deargan-allt, clamhan ruadh, speireag ruadh*

One of my first close encounters with a bird of prey was with the diminutive kestrel. While at school during the 1970s, I had the good fortune to be involved with hand-rearing a two-week-old kestrel eyas (chick). It became extremely tame and eventually two of us endeavoured to train it to catch mice and small birds. The kestrel was never highly valued as a falconer's bird and was lowest in the hierarchy of suitable birds of prey for the budding falconer. It was given to the knave, or servant, and although it did not have great hunting prowess and was viewed as a mouser, it would indeed serve a valuable purpose in teaching the handler about bird of prey husbandry, as I learned with that kestrel. The Rev. C.A. Johns wrote in *British Birds and their Haunts*, 'The Kestrel was formerly trained to hunt small birds and in the court of Louis XlII, was taught to hawk for bats'.

The kestrel is easy to recognise and is frequently seen hovering alongside motorway verges. Together with many other vernacular names, including 'wind cuffer' in Orkney, 'keelie' and 'moosie hawk', it is sometimes called the 'motorway hawk'. The kestrel's commonly used nickname, 'windhover', refers to the way it remains almost motionless in the air while scanning for a tiny movement in the tussock grasses below.

Kestrels are birds of open country and may be seen in most areas hunting along the end rigs of fields, both on arable and upland ground. Deforestation must have suited this bird well, although young forestry plantations provide good hunting grounds for voles and other small mammals. Mature forestry is far from suitable for the kestrel. During the vole plagues of 1890 in Roxburgh, Dumfries, Lanark and Kirkcudbright, farmers became almost desperate about the terrible damage inflicted by the rodents. That year birds of prey, previously slaughtered on sight, were left well alone and proved their worth when large numbers of short-eared owls and kestrels appeared and killed many voles. Peter Adair, in a survey published in 1892, collated information from farmers in troubled areas, and there were reported to be 18 kestrel and short-eared owl nests in the Devil's Beef Tub alone.

Despite the fact that the kestrel poses little or no threat to game, it was not exempt from the killing fields of the Victorian era. Charles St John made a derogatory comment about the gamekeepers at the time: '... therefore the poor kestrel generally occupied a prominent place amongst the rows of bipeds and quadrupeds nailed on the kennel, or wherever else those trophies of his skill are exhibited.'

Foxy red-brown, male kestrels have a blue-grey tinge to the top of their heads and a grey tail, whereas the females and juveniles have barred plumage. Kestrels do not make elaborate nests and usually only have a single brood, although they will sometimes lay again if a clutch is lost early in the season. I have seen them on crags very close to nesting peregrine falcons, and I have also found nests out on the open moor. One pair of kestrels chose the wing of a vintage aeroplane that was being restored. All work had to stop until the young had successfully fledged.

I am often handed young kestrels in autumn when the first cold spells leave them weak with hunger. They respond well to time in captivity and can soon be released again. One particular young male appeared in the field outside my house. It was so weak that it let me approach to pick it up and became unusually tame. I had it for many years and it accompanied me all round the country and came for walks perched on my shoulder, and due to this I have always had a particular soft spot for this small, common raptor.

Lapwing

Vanellus vanellus
S: peewit, peesie, teuchit, wallopie, wallopieweet, tieve's nacket
G: *curracag, adharcan luachrach*

Mention the words lapwing, 'peewit' or 'green plover' to any true countryman and they will perhaps reminisce about the days when these beautiful members of the plover family graced farmland all over Scotland. Like the curlew, the lapwing is a harbinger of spring and comes to farmland and open moor to breed towards the end of February. Currently in decline, the lapwing fills people with nostalgia and although it was not always seen as so, it is a valuable addition to the bird life of the farm and croft. Changes in farming policies, however, led to the intensive cropping of upland pasture which has altered the situation for the lapwing.

The lapwing's call is easily recognisable and gave rise to many variations of the most commonly used name – 'peewit'. There is probably no Scottish bird with more vernacular names than the lapwing – 'peeweep', 'peesie', 'wallopieweet', and 'tieve's nacket' are but a few examples.

From a distance, lapwings may appear a dull, darkish brown and white, but viewed up close when the sun hits their plumage, a beautiful palette of colours is revealed; a silky sheen of pinks, mauves, bottle greens and gold. The male has a longer crest than his mate and is easy to recognise. During the breeding season, the aerial dance of the lapwing and its joyous call has cheered many a hill shepherd and farmer as he goes about his work. Often while ploughing and sowing, he will stop to lift the eggs, moving them to a safer place rather than risking them being damaged by machinery, such is the esteem in which the lapwing is held. Many people are highly concerned about the drastic fall in numbers. Even as far back as 1842 there were records of similar concerns, when advances in agricultural cultivation led to fewer lapwings successfully breeding. Large numbers of lapwings were killed for food and their eggs were regularly collected and sent to English markets where they were deemed a delicacy. Myths also circulated that the birds were associated with evil.

Nesting on open ground, both male and female take turns to brood their eggs and both care for the tiny, grey down-covered chicks. Despite this, they are extremely vulnerable to predation and human disturbance. Wheeling high in the air above perceived threats, the adult birds noisily dive-bomb intruders near their nest.

The Hebrides and the Northern Isles remain a stronghold and numbers are considerably higher there than on the mainland. In particular, the lime-rich machair (see page 223) suits the birds well, and large numbers return each spring to raise chicks on the flower-studded pastures adjacent to the shore on islands such as Tiree, the Uists, Islay and North Ronaldsay. By the end of September, most birds have returned to tidal flats and stubble fields near the coast, with large flocks wintering at Caerlaverock, in Dumfriesshire.

The collective noun for lapwings is a 'deceit', a name earned in the days of the Covenanters when men were hiding on the hills to avoid ambush and capture. Lapwings defending their nearby nests made such a racket that the men's hideaway was revealed. Due to this, lapwings were once called 'de'il's plover'.

Viewed in sunshine close-up, the lapwing's stunning colours are revealed (Malcolm Gosling)

The 'Teuchit Storm'

Some time around the middle of March, the lapwings arrive on a cold blast of wintry weather known in the North-east as the 'teuchit storm'. They like short tussocky grass. An old peat moss is ideal, but a farm favoured by lapwings was not necessarily a good farm to work. Thomas Carlyle complained that when he first saw his new home in Craigenputtoch, it was so broken down and neglected that he would 'almost rather build a ring-fence round it and leave it gratis to the tee-wheets.' Nowadays, he could have done just that, and applied for a Country Stewardship grant to keep them there, but in 1827, lapwings had little economic value. Egg collectors might come looking for them. The eggs were supposed to enhance fertility, but small boys were more interested in adding to their collections and were not greatly deterred by the prospect of getting wet:

> Wallopie, wallopie, weet,
> Harry the nest, an' rin awa' weet.

Pheasant

Phasianus colchicus
S: feesant, fasiane, ephesian
G: *easag*

The pheasant probably has the most stunning plumage of all British birds, yet it is also reputed to be one of the most stupid. Vast annual introductions add to the wild population and all too frequently young newly released poults end up dead on the side of our busy roads. Some roads provide such levels of pheasant carnage that they have become popular places for people to stop and pick up a free meal. A French man living in Scotland was astonished to see all this good food going to waste and frequently served up what we called *faisan ecrasé en route* (pheasant crushed on the road).

The pheasant has its origins in the bogs and swamps of Asia Minor and the Far East where it has a very different lifestyle and is far from stupid. It was initially thought that it arrived with the Romans, but research has revealed that it was here prior to the Norman Conquests. Despite this it is still viewed as a non-native species.

Pheasants are widespread and numerous all over Scotland and there are few islands without them. Large numbers are bred for game shooting every year, reared intensively in pens, and then released into the wild. Many of these birds naturalise and swell the already large wild populations. There are new breeds of pheasant with more fabulous plumage variations: Chinese, Japanese and Mongolian. Other colourful species such as Reeves, Golden and Lady Amherst's are occasionally released, and resulting hybrids with exotic colour schemes are sometimes seen.

Hen pheasants do not make attentive mothers. Heavy summer downpours account for many poults; they are often separated and cannot keep up with her in long undergrowth and quickly chill and die. Foxes, mink and other predators, not to mention poachers, are extremely partial to pheasant and many are taken in addition to the estimated 4.5 million birds shot in Scotland each year.

The ring-necked pheasant may have Eastern origins but is now perfectly at home in Britain (Polly Pullar)

Skylark

Alauda arvenis
S: laverock, larick
G: *uiseag, fosgag Moire, topag*

The skylark may have few bright colours and could be placed in the 'LBJ' (little brown job) category, but its trilling song has long been the subject of poem and prose as the epitome of freedom. The collective term for larks, an 'exultation', beautifully depicts all that is special about this little bird. The skylark's unsurpassed melodic song was once heard over every field and hedgerow in Britain, as it soared higher and higher into the sky, filling it with its glorious voice.

In 1890 a vast pie to celebrate the opening of the Forth Railway Bridge was reputedly made with over 300 larks. Thousands of skylarks were taken each year, some killed

Skylark song

'Up and awa' and awa' wi' the laverock, up and awa' and awa' in the morning ...'. Andy Hunter's song about setting off for a day in the Kilpatrick hills continues a long tradition of celebrating larks in Scotland. They were protected, not so much by law as by the delight people took in hearing them. Hence the saying from the North-east:

> Malisons, malisons mair nor ten
> Fa herries the nest of heaven's hen,
> But blessins, blessins, mair nor three
> Fah leuks at ma eggies an lats them be.

for food, while others supplied the demand for cage birds. Some suffered terribly and were even blinded as it was thought they would sing better. Numbers fell further when changes in agriculture, the widespread use of pesticide and weed killer, and an increase of spring-sown cereals altered their habitat beyond recognition.

When heard, the song of the skylark seldom fails to cheer, reminding the listener of open, wild places. People still refer to 'getting up with the lark', for an early start in the morning. An old Scots rhyme also makes reference to the bird's early activity:

> *Larike, larike lee,*
> *Who'll gang up to heaven wi' me?*
> *No the lout that lies in his bed,*
> *No the doolfu' that dreeps his head.*

Starling

Sturnus vulgaris
S: stirlin, stuckie, stushie
G: *druid*

During the mid 1700s, starlings were extremely common, but they had all but vanished by 1800. A combination of cold weather and changes in farming policy is thought to have contributed to their demise. The warmer air of the Gulf Stream has helped them increase in number once more, which is why the Hebrides have become a stronghold for this fabulous bird. From a distance, the starling appears rather dull, but in sunlight its feathers are not only punctuated with pale spots, but also shot through with a wealth of iridescent colours. Huge banks of rotting seaweed on the islands also provide a rich source of small flies and invertebrates and many starlings are seen gleaning the tide line.

In the Outer Hebrides, letterboxes have to be fitted with special covers to stop starlings from taking them over as maternity suites. When doors are blown off telephone boxes in the ferocious gales that sweep in off the Atlantic, starlings quickly make use of the shelter as a nest site.

The starling can imitate other birds and humans. A starling adding a totally unrecognisable voice into the equation often catches out those who are keen to memorise bird song. Due to their vocal skills, starlings were once caught and sold as cage birds. The largest flocks were originally seen in towns, and this is true today, with vast numbers congregating in some urban areas. Here they are quick to emulate the cheeky whistles of builders and even learn to time it as females pass by.

The collective noun for starlings is a 'murmuration'. The sight of a massive flock displaying in the air before they roost is now recognised as one of the most impressive of all wildlife events. Starlings fly in incredible formations, rising and falling with ultimate skill, sometimes dotting the air like thousands of dark snowflakes. This vision has reduced even the hardest souls to tears and is testimony to the power of nature.

Left. Wonderful mimics, starlings also have surprisingly exotic plumage (Polly Pullar)

Right. Some of our most common birds such as the wood pigeon are stunningly beautiful (Laurie Campbell)

Woodpigeon

Columba palumbus
S: cushat, cushie, cushie-doo
G: *calman-coille, guragag*

Despite its name, the woodpigeon is largely associated with farmland, where it takes advantage of any cereals, game crops or brassicas and feasts on them until it has caused total decimation. A shot pigeon frequently reveals a crop bursting with undigested grain, peas, clover, and other food matter.

Pigeons are viewed as a serious agricultural pest. During the 1950s, the government funded culls and the Ministry of Agriculture paid a cartridge subsidy to farmers, who in turn were happy for people to come and shoot them on their land. Pigeons have excellent eyesight and are also extremely wary – shooters may have a long wait for the birds to return to their roost sites. Pigeons also fly fast and high, adding to the challenge.

Frequently overlooked as dull, the woodpigeon is a beautiful bird, with patches of bright metallic green highlighting the sides of its pink-blue feathers, and dramatic white flashes on its flanks and neck. Its mournful cooing in a wood is often the only sound to break the silence of a sultry day. Pigeons thrive best in areas of woodland adjacent to arable farmland but can equally exist adjacent to hill farms where there may be turnips, grazing rape and kale for sheep. Highly adaptable, they will eat almost anything, including beech masts, acorns, ivy berries, and any garden produce, much to people's annoyance. Newly sprouted shoots can be wrecked in seconds, as any gardener will testify. Pigeons will consume their own bodyweight approximately every four days.

It is little wonder that the woodpigeon is so numerous, for pigeons' nests have been found in every month of the year and in some extraordinary places where there are no trees, including scrapes in the ground on open heather moor. Orcadian woodpigeons quickly learned to use ground nests. The squabs (young pigeons) are fed on protein-rich milk made in the adult's crops. A pigeon's amorous courtship and soft cooing have given rise to the term 'lovey dovey', often applied to young lovers. 'Pigeon holes' for storing letters and other items are a reference to the entrance holes in 'doocots', the beautiful shelters for domestic pigeons that are distinctive in different regions of Scotland.

My mother sometimes shot a few pigeons on the farm for dinner. She always removed the rich, dark-red breast meat, leaving the rest, and used this to make delicious meals. Sparrowhawks appear to do the same thing: we find the rest of the carcass left lying with a heap of feathers after a sparrowhawk has been at work. Live pigeons were once cut up and the parts added directly onto adder bites, as this was thought to be a cure.

Sometimes pigeons are seen in vast numbers. In 2003 approximately 25,000 pigeons were seen after dawn over Barry Buddon near Arbroath, and there are many other records of equally large flocks. They are present on most of the islands although rarer in some of the Outer Hebrides where woodland is scarce.

Yellowhammer

Emberiza citrinella
S: skite, yoldrin, yorlin, yarlin, yaldie, yeldrick
G: *buidheag*, *buidhean na coille*, *buidheag-bhealaidh*

The yellowhammer is also known as the 'Scotch canary'. Intensive use of chemicals on farmland has done nothing to improve conditions for this charming bird, and it is declining all over Scotland. Scrub and areas of gorse close

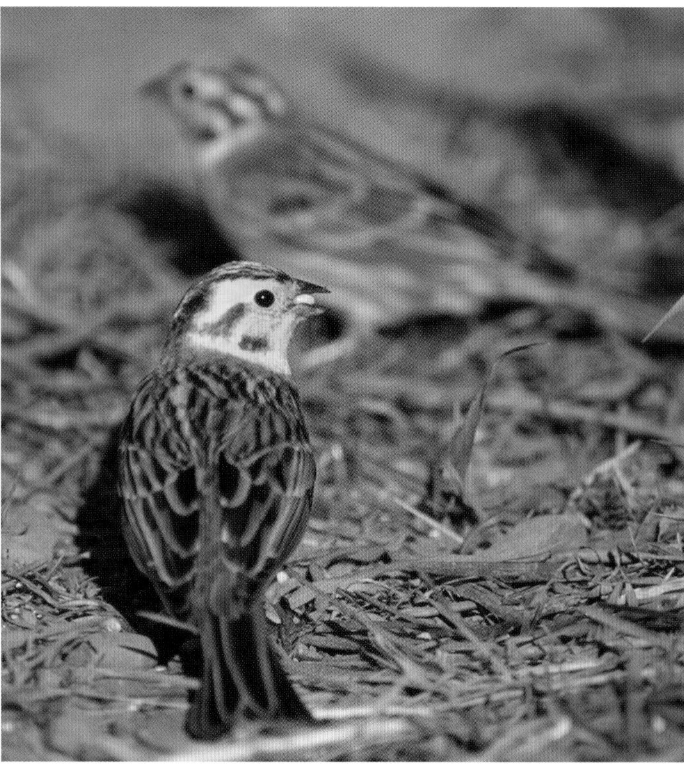

One of the most charming farmland birds, the yellowhammer is now sadly in decline (Laurie Campbell)

Persecution

'The bonnie wee yellow yite' has only recently shaken off a sinister reputation. Perhaps it was its sulphur-yellow head which made people uneasy. It is said to have a drop of the devil's blood in its veins and its nest would be destroyed wherever it was found. The unfairness of this was keenly felt by the Paisley poet Robert Tannahill in his song 'The Midges Dance aboon the Burn'. While other birds sing happily in the summer gloaming, the yeldrins (yellow hammers) pour out their distress.

> Beneath the golden gloamin' sky,
> The mavis mends her lay,
> The redbreast pours his sweetest strains,
> To charm the ling'ring day;
> While weary yeldrins seem to wail
> Their little nestlings torn,
> The merry wren, frae den to den,
> Gaes jinking through the thorn.

Machair, Isle of Coll – beautiful as it blooms in summer, the machair is dependent on a carefully managed grazing system (Polly Pullar)

to unimproved pasture where there is an abundance of farm weeds is ideal habitat for them. Large amounts of grain spilt in fields provided excellent feeding for many birds including finches and buntings. Today's efficient machinery, however, seldom leaves any gleanings.

The yellowhammer has also been nicknamed the 'scribbling lark' due to the irregular lines on its eggs. Poet John Clare wrote:

> *Five eggs, pen scribbled o'er with ink their shells*
> *Resembling writing-scrolls, which Fancy reads*
> *As Nature's poesy and pastoral spells –*
> *They are the yellow hammer's and she dwells*
> *Most poet-like, 'mid brooks and flowery weeds.*

MACHAIR

The word 'machair' comes from the Gaelic for a low-lying fertile plain. Machair is one of the rarest habitats in Europe. It is only found on the north-western seaboard of Scotland and Ireland, and consists of a lime-rich, shell-strewn dune pasture, dependent on a carefully managed grazing system.

The best examples of machair are found in the Hebrides: the Uists, Barra, Coll, Tiree and Islay. Crops of bere barley, oats and rich grass are grown in the lee of protective dunes that are constantly reshaped by Atlantic storms. In heavy rain and gales, artificial fertilisers quickly leach out of the ground and for many years, crofters and farmers have used kelp as fertiliser instead. This helps to maintain valuable moisture in thin calcareous soil.

In late spring, the machair bursts forth in a series of impressive colour phases as a profusion of wild flowers emerge, including many orchids unique to the Hebrides. Cattle are vital to the machair: their dung not only helps improve the pasture, but hosts many invertebrates for feeding waders, shore birds, and the rare corncrake.

In 1764 the Rev. John Walker wrote of the machair, 'About the first of June when the cattle are put upon it, it is all over as white as a cloth, with daisies and white clover. In that season, there may be seen pasturing upon it at once, about 1,000 black cattle, 2,000 sheep and 300 horses intermixed with immense flocks of lapwings and green plovers.' This is proof that the machair has been valued for some time, both for farm livestock and for the precious habitat it provides for birds.

Where does the corncrake go in winter?

Where do corncrakes come from? From under the ice, according to an old belief recorded in North Uist. Puzzled by their absence for most of the year, and perhaps noticing that they cannot fly during the breeding season, it was supposed that they spent most of their lives underwater, in the lochs, even under the ice. They would emerge in spring, but never stray far from the water. Their call was a sign that the danger of frost had passed.

The harvest corncrake

In Gaelic, the corncrake prays for a good harvest:

> *A Dhia nam feart,*
> *A Dhia nam feart,*
> *Cuir biadh sa ghart,*
> *Cuir biadh sa ghart.*
>
> (O God of the powers, O God of the powers,
> Put food in the field, Put food in the field.)

This sounds just like a corncrake calling: the rhythm, the internal rhymes and especially '*feart*' and '*ghart*'.

MACHAIR DENIZEN

Corncrake

Crex crex
S: craik, weet-my-fit
G: *trèan-ri-trèan*, *tràc an arbhair*, *traona*, *garra-gart*

If you visit corncrake habitat such as the RSPB's Balranald Reserve in North Uist during early summer, you will witness a flurry of activity. Every year, keen birders descend on such places, known hot spots for one of our rarest birds, the corncrake. The bird-watchers get out of their cars slung about with cameras, telescopes and binoculars, as a repetitive noise starts coming from the grass – a telltale rasping sound, often likened to that of a football rattle. They rush to try to spot where it is coming from. All too often the maker of the sound, the extremely shy corncrake, does not reveal itself, infuriating the birders by remaining hidden. Frequently heard but seldom seen, the corncrake is a skulking member of the rail family and was once a widespread summer visitor to many parts of Britain.

During the first half of the nineteenth century, Advocate Lord Cockburn wrote in *Memorials of his Time*, 'I have stood in Queen's Street, or the opening at the north-west corner of Charlotte Square, and listened to the ceaseless rural corn-craiks, nesting happily in the dewy grass'. Corncrakes were clearly spending their summers close to the centre of Scotland's capital city. Like the grey partridge, the corncrake has an onomatopoeic Latin name. Sadly, the introduction of mechanical hay mowing saw numbers plummet as many birds were killed at their nests by the rotating blades of the new machines. The retreat was swift: by 1940 the only large populations of corncrakes were found in the Hebrides and Northern Isles.

The corncrake arrives from North Africa in mid to late April and starts to call almost immediately. People living in close proximity often complain bitterly about the incessant din, but having spent much time in the Hebrides, I find the sound oddly soothing, although it does begin well

Corncrake – skulkingly shy, it is more often heard than seen (Laurie Campbell)

before the crack of dawn and continues on till far into the night.

Once a male has found a female and they have mated, she lays half the clutch of eggs. He then disappears, and immediately starts to call again to attract a second wife before his first has even begun to brood the 8–12 eggs. The black, down-covered young take approximately 18 days to hatch. After the first brood is almost two weeks old, the female abandons them and finds herself another mate too – not necessarily the first one. With corncrakes it would appear that a change is as good as a rest. She lays again and usually a second brood is reared. Once chicks are independent, adult corncrakes moult. During this flightless period, they gain extra weight to sustain them on their long migration to Africa. They are seldom seen in flight as they are nocturnal migrants, and little is known of their winter behaviour as they are even more skulking in winter in Africa, where they prefer the dry, dense grasslands near water on higher ground.

Special schemes to encourage farmers to harvest their crops in a corncrake-friendly manner have proved highly successful. By mowing from the centre outwards instead of the other way round many deaths are avoided and young birds are able to escape being cut by the mower blades. Corncrakes require long vegetation both early and late in the season, and the ditches and bogs of the Hebrides provide dense wild flowers including flag iris and cow parsley, wild carrot and other leafy vegetation. Not only does this provide locations for secrecy but also plenty of invertebrates, worms and slugs.

Corncrakes have short lives. Each spring the young return to their natal area and once again, the air is filled with the sounds that have proved cryptic to birders for years. Some cheeky Hebridean starlings have become adept at imitating the clandestine corncrake, and much amusement is had when a birdwatcher realises that he has been misled and has not been scanning the undergrowth for a corncrake at all.

ROYAL BRITISH

CHAPTER EIGHT

ABOUT TOWN

INTRODUCTION

The urbanisation of many rural areas is an unstoppable process. Only 5 per cent of the British population now live in the countryside. Towns and cities sprawl further and further into green spaces and although much is lost from a wildlife point of view, there are many overlooked oases in the midst of towns where a wealth of creatures are thriving. Some animals and birds have adapted far better than others and are able to cope well with man and his constant development.

In thousands of town gardens everywhere, birds are encouraged and fed throughout the year, and mammals (such as foxes, hedgehogs and bats), amphibians and reptiles also take full advantage of these excellent refuges. During the recent hard winters in Scotland, the amount we spent on wild bird food was testimony to how much we value wildlife. Many companies selling bird nutrition ran out due to the high demand.

Abandoned buildings and warehouses provide secure breeding places for animals and birds, while motorway verges and roundabouts are resplendent with wild flowers, small trees and shrubs, with abundant food sources for a large variety of wildlife. Old railway embankments, rich with uncut herbage, are excellent haunts for breeding butterflies and small mammals. Increased numbers of insects in turn help bats and birds. Herons, otters, and even kingfishers have now been recorded on many canals and rivers flowing through towns, particularly where efforts are being made to clean up watercourses.

Rubbish tips and landfill sites may seem undesirable as residences but they can be highly valuable to gulls, corvids, foxes, and many other creatures. Old churchyards, cemeteries and densely planted crematorium gardens in the midst of cities are frequently viewed as being some of the best urban wildlife havens of all. One pair of roe deer set up home in a churchyard in the centre of Glasgow and managed to exist there despite having to dodge the traffic. Owls frequent graveyards where the old turf and longer grass provide good habitat for voles and mice.

Even birds such as the majestic peregrine falcon, usually associated with the steepest mountain crags and sea cliffs, can exist in a city. Peregrines frequently breed on high buildings including church spires. Here they benefit from the abundant food supply of multiplying feral pigeons.

Town councils and other organisations often have wildlife gardens where children can learn to dip for insects in suitable ponds, and witness at first hand the breeding progress of amphibians. They may learn about food plants for particular species of butterflies, and the value of even

Opposite. Edinburgh from the Castle (Freddy Pullar)

the smallest patch of land left to nature. City Farms also provide important places for educating young people. The well-established Gorgie City Farm in Edinburgh's heart attracts many young visitors every year. They are able to learn about a range of farm animals and small pets there, as well as garden birds and bugs. Increasingly urban children are losing touch with the natural world. In a recent survey, many thought that milk originated from a supermarket and not from the mammary ducts of a cow.

Large waste tips from the mining industry are referred to as 'bings'. This Scots word means 'heap' or 'pile up' and is also used to describe a slagheap. Coal bings are the most frequently seen and can be a large intrusion on the landscape in their raw state. While many have been reclaimed and cleaned up, others have been left on purpose. These bings provide a unique environment of a particular type depending on the properties of the associated mineral, and are quickly colonised by distinct plant and insect communities. This may eventually serve as part of an important wildlife corridor in a built-up area. Research carried out in the 1980s on bing sites near Glasgow revealed plants of high conservation value including rare grasses, mosses, and orchids, as well as more obvious fauna including foxes and badgers. Although man is constantly altering the ecology, it is important to realise that in turn there can also be benefits for a large range of species.

URBAN GARDENERS

Blackbird

Turdus merula
S: blackie, merl
G: *lon-dubh*

One of most common garden birds is also blessed with one of the finest of all bird songs. There are few sounds in the dawn chorus to equal that of an amorous male blackbird with his dapper dark plumage and brilliant orange bill. One of the easiest ways to locate a roosting owl hidden in the leafy canopy is to follow the persistent, tinny alarm calls of a scolding blackbird. Cats, jays and mustelids can also trigger an angry response.

Easily tamed, blackbirds are familiar to almost everyone and despite their ubiquity, are hugely popular. They have been recorded in 90 per cent of all Scottish gardens. Large flocks of blackbirds coming in from Scandinavia swell numbers each autumn. Some gardens may have numerous birds and they may remain there throughout the coldest months, feeding on a surprisingly eclectic menu. Blackbirds

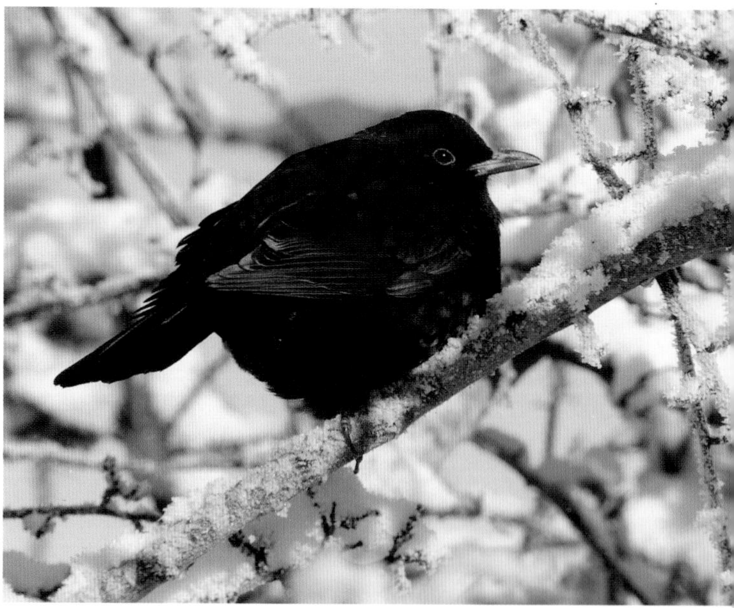

A male blackbird has one of the finest voices of the dawn chorus (Polly Pullar)

are often one of the earliest birds to nest. Before there is sufficient cover, they may be highly vulnerable to predation by cats. Their distinctive straw and grass nests have a hard-baked mud cup inside. The dark-brown female huddles in to incubate and is just visible, with her bill and tail feathers sticking out at either end. Once the young fledge, they hang about the garden waiting for food, chirruping loudly until the adults fly in with the next earthworm or grub.

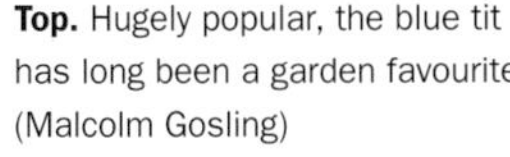

Top. Hugely popular, the blue tit has long been a garden favourite (Malcolm Gosling)

Bottom. Great tit (Malcolm Gosling)

Blue Tit

Cyanistes caeruleus
G: *cailleachag cheann-ghorm, snoil-eun*

Great Tit

Parus major
S: oxee, saw sharpener, blue bunnet
G: *currac baintighearna*

The titmouse family are some of the most endearing of all garden visitors. Small, colourful, cheeky, adaptable and entertaining, the blue tit and great tit are widespread and numerous. Attracted to peanut, seed and fat feeders in gardens almost everywhere, their plucky acrobatics have attracted generations of armchair birders.

Both species freely make use of nest boxes, providing hours of entertainment with their bustling breeding activities, and even more delight as large numbers of tiny young take their first precarious flights. Many of the fledglings appear on the bird table where adults feed them.

The blue tit has gathered several affectionate nicknames such as 'tom tit', 'blue bonnet' and 'bottle tit'; the latter due to its ability to peck open the foil tops of milk bottles in the days when every household countrywide had their milk delivered.

Pecking putty around windows is another favourite tit occupation – in woodland, however, they peck at bark and

The dunnock may seem dull compared to other garden birds but it has extraordinary sexual habits (Malcolm Gosling)

moss in search of insects. Broods of tits may be large: it is usual to have 11 or 12 chicks, although up to 15 have been recorded. Despite this, mortality rates are high and up to 70 per cent of young do not survive their first winter. Populations fluctuate according to weather conditions and food availability. During a three-week period approximately 8,000 caterpillars are required to satiate a large brood. Weasels sometimes find their way into nest holes and boxes, and great-spotted woodpeckers too may predate young.

The great tit, with its distinctive eye patches, is sometimes nicknamed the 'ox eye', 'yaup' and 'saw sharpener', the latter due to one of its calls. Great tits have an astonishing repertoire of approximately 40 different calls. Often an unrecognisable birdcall can be explained as coming from a male great tit showing off.

Dunnock

Prunella modularis
S: whin-sparrae
G: *gealbhonn nam preas, gealbhonn-gàrraidh, donnag*

The dunnock's jaunty song is similar to a shorter version of a wren's song. Its high, slightly sharp call has been likened to the sound of a squeaking wheel.

This small, dull-brownish bird skulks like a mouse under shrubbery. It has recently become known for certain extraordinary aspects of its mating behaviour: the female takes two partners, which eventually leads to a sperm war. While she may mate with both males, each one in turn frantically pecks at her cloaca prior to mating in a bid to get her to eject the sperm of the rival male. Tests have proved that the resulting chicks may be the progeny of either father. This unique behaviour is called *polyandry* and is only employed by approximately 2 per cent of bird species. The dunnock builds its nest in a low bush and once the young are hatched, both males and the female bird attend to them.

Robin

Erithacus rubecula
S: reid rab, red rab, mason's ghost
G: *brù-dhearg, ruadhag, robaidh-raoighde*

Chaucer called the robin 'tame ruddock'. This perky, beady-eyed bird has long followed gardeners, often perching close by on a spade or wheelbarrow handle, cocking its head before hopping down and pulling out a freshly exposed earthworm. In medieval Scottish woodland, robins followed wild boar around the forest in a similar manner, gleaning wriggling pickings from the grubbed-up earth.

Harming a robin has long been viewed as bringing bad luck. Few were caged in Scotland or eaten as in other parts of Europe, and the robin has largely been seen as a benefactor rather than a bird of ill omen. The bird was given its common name as far back as the fifteenth century. Centuries later, Victorian postmen who wore red waistcoats were nicknamed 'robins'. Images on nineteenth-century Christmas cards showed a robin bringing letters; this began the bird's ongoing association with the festive season.

Although we often refer to the robin as the 'cock robin', both males and females have red breasts. Contrary to popular belief, the robin is not the sweet individual that we think

we know. Pugnacious males defend their territories, often killing an impostor that dares to intrude. A robin's thin, melancholy song fills the autumnal air and reminds us that winter is fast approaching. Robins also sing at night. Their tetchy alarm call is frequently heard, particularly in the presence of cats or birds of prey.

St Mungo and the robin

The sixth-century St Serf of Culross is said to have had a tame robin which he fed by hand. One day it was accidentally killed by a boisterous crowd of St Mungo's fellow students. Mungo prays over it and it revives. At this point, the author feels the need to justify St Serf for taking such pleasure in the little bird: 'Perhaps it will seem a wonder to some that a man so holy and righteous would take delight in respect to the play or gestures of a little bird. But let it be known to those of such thoughts that righteous men at times need to be softened from their own sternness ...' The robin is also the bird on the Glasgow coat of arms, through its association with Mungo. It was widely seen as a sin to kill a robin or rob its nest, because it had a drop of God's blood in its veins. By contrast, any kindness done to a robin was sure to be rewarded.

Song Thrush

Turdus philomelos
S: mavis, mavie, throstle
G: *smeòrach*

The poet Robert Browning wrote:

> *That's the wise thrush;*
> *He sings each song twice over,*
> *Lest you should think he never could recapture*
> *The first time careless rapture.*
>
> 'Home Thoughts from Abroad',
> from *A Victorian Anthology* (1895)

A song thrush's beautiful song often becomes more complex with age and some individuals master a repertoire as varied as that of a nightingale. The rich fluting notes are often varied in tone and given in a series of threes. The song from many males is heard in woodland at dawn and late into spring evenings, providing an evocative concerto.

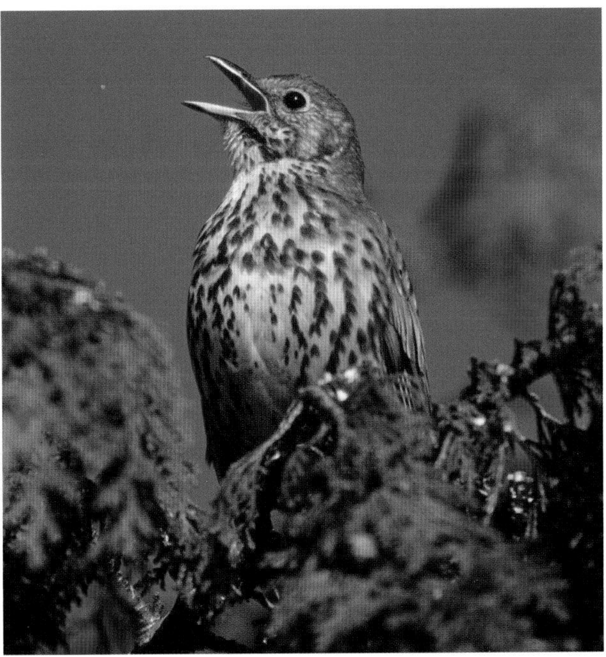

Above left. The benign-looking robin is known to fight to the death while defending territory (Malcolm Gosling)

Left. The song thrush has a varied repertoire of melodic song (Laurie Campbell)

A song in May

A thrush singing on a May morning is a favourite image in Gaelic song. After the Disruption, in May 1843, when the Free Church split from the Church of Scotland, thrushes in the Highlands were said to be singing –

An Eaglais Shaor, 's i as fheàrr,
An Eaglais Shaor, 's i as fheàrr;
Na Moderates, na Moderates,
Chan fhiach iad, chan fhiach iad.

(The Free Church is best, the Free Church is best. The Moderates, the Moderates, are worthless, worthless.)

Song thrushes have suffered a recent decline due to agricultural intensification, pesticides and the removal of hedgerows. Loss of permanent pasture for livestock has further added to the drop in number. It is fortunate that more song thrushes are now over-wintering in Scotland as they are heavily persecuted in Europe: tinned thrushes are occasionally available in some Continental food shops.

At daybreak, the beautiful spangled thrush may be seen with its head cocked to one side listening for movement from the ground, or patting its feet on the dewy lawn in a bid to bring earthworms to the surface. Thrushes use a flat stone as an anvil for smashing snail shells so they can extract the succulent contents. These improvised anvils, found with remnants of snail shells, are a welcome sight for gardeners who are growing greens nearby.

The thrush's anvil with tell-tale broken snail shells (Polly Pullar)

NEIGHBOURHOOD WATCH

Magpie

Pica pica
S: pyot, deil, devil's bird, maggie
G: *pioghaid, athaid, breac-mhac*

The noisy, chattering call of the magpie is a familiar sound. This cheeky, pied member of the crow family is taking full advantage of increased urbanisation, as well as thriving in woodlands in most areas. Like all corvids, the magpie is intelligent and inquisitive. They were first recorded in Scotland in the seventeenth century, but by the late 1900s they had been exterminated from many parts. Persecuted on sight, they were culled in large numbers by keepers and farmers. However, the population has recently exploded. Although it is legal to kill them or catch them in Larsen traps, it is hard to keep on top of numbers, particularly as many places have fewer keepers.

Magpies make themselves unpopular in gardens and there is constant controversy about their unsavoury habits: they pull bird's nests to pieces, eating both the eggs and fledglings of many species, and regularly steal food from other birds. They have been known to learn how to open rabbit and guinea pig hutches, and have pilfered food and tiny helpless young. Their cockiness knows no bounds and they may pull mischievously at the brush of a town fox, or the tail of a cat, to encourage it to drop whatever delicacy it is eating. Ironically, their dramatic spread has been greatly helped by the increased number of wildlife casualties on our busy roads. As soon as a creature is hit, then a magpie seems to appear, ably dodging the traffic almost as if playing Russian roulette in order to feed on the hapless victim. Amazingly, cars hit very few.

Magpies pair for life, build large domed nests, and have an average of four to six young. They are omnivorous. When food is plentiful it is cached for poorer times ahead. They also have a liking for shiny objects and sometimes go in through open windows to steal jewellery and trinkets

Magpie lore

It is often said that a single magpie is unlucky, hence the rhyme 'One for sorrow, two for joy' but in fact, magpie omens used to vary throughout Scotland. In the south, a magpie flying round a house meant a stranger was coming. If someone in the house were sick, the stranger in question might be the Grim Reaper. In the Highlands, a single magpie was only unlucky if you saw it before breakfast. If it was hopping around in front of the house at any other time of day, it was a harbinger of good news, likewise if it landed on the road in front of you when you were travelling. In the North-east, the saying was –

> Ane's joy
> Twa's grief
> Three's marriage
> Four's death.

In Rhynie magpies were seen as tell-tales (children used to chant 'Clypie clypie clash-pyot') and in Strathdon, they were much disliked by smugglers since a magpie chattering around a stash of illicit whisky was a sign that the gauger or exciseman was on his way.

from dressing tables and windowsills. People who find it hard to throw things away and collect many belongings are often referred to as 'magpies' for this reason. And the term 'thieving magpie' is widely used to describe a dishonest person. Being intelligent, a magpie can recognise its own reflection in a mirror – something that is unusual amongst birds.

Sparrowhawk

Accipiter nisus
S: blue hawk, gleg hawk
G: *speireag, speir-sheabhag*

The sparrowhawk is a highly efficient killing machine. It has a cold, yellow-eyed stare and a highly nervous disposition. It favours feathered prey. Falconers find these diminutive birds hard to train, but claim that if successful, the birds turn into supreme hunters. Many people despise this beautiful little raptor. Often all they see of it is a cloud of feathers and a flurry of brown and grey as it plucks another unfortunate victim from the bird table. Sometimes the body of its prey is ruthlessly plucked in view of the shocked observer – something that does little to help the plucker's reputation. Sparrowhawks and other raptors are constant scapegoats and are blamed for the decline in songsters. Domestic cats, however, pose a much more serious threat to our garden birdlife, accounting for millions every year.

There are many reasons for the general decline in songbirds, including habitat loss and climate change. Sparrowhawks are unpopular with gamekeepers because they take small pheasant poults. Sometimes even the sparrowhawk's presence near a release pen is enough to send the incumbents into a mad panic which may on occasions lead to mass mortality through stress.

Male and female sparrowhawks have the largest size difference of any birds of prey – while the tiny male weighs just 5 ounces (150 grams), his mate is double the size and therefore can take impressive prey such as woodpigeons, jays and even adult game birds on occasion.

Sparrowhawks are superb in flight, true avian speedsters. They have unsurpassed manoeuvrability and they fly low, jinking in and out of obstacles with the skill of a honed

The sparrowhawk is often misunderstood but is in fact a beautiful, integral part of Scotland's fauna (Polly Pullar)

stunt pilot. Pairs also spiral high above their territories on clear days as part of the breeding display. However, their mad dashes along hedgerows, through closely packed trees, and even down streets or housing schemes, sometimes end in grief. I have had many injured sparrowhawks handed to me over the years. Often birds have been stunned after flying into large glass windows or patio doors in pursuit of a songster. One particular casualty was disentangled from a line of supermarket trolleys it had crashed into as it chased a blackbird.

All raptors are nervous, but one of the most neurotic members of the clan is the sparrowhawk. When injured or in captivity, some succumb to the stress of being handled. At a wildlife rehabilitation conference, a London Zoo vet advised me to give them a minute dose of a well-known nerve-calming drug. This does two things: it makes them calm and very hungry, both advantageous in a captive situation. I have had far fewer losses since.

Although largely associated with gardens, the sparrowhawk is equally at home on moors and in woodland. It builds a deep-cupped nest of twigs high in a tree fork and lays an average of four to six eggs. Several pairs may nest quite close to one another in a wood, in a kind of 'loose colony'. While the female incubates the eggs and broods the unfledged chicks, the male brings a constant supply of food. The young birds are frequently heard in high summer, emitting their tetchy calls, as they demand more food from their over-stretched parents.

The Hawk Watch Project

Since 2009 Mike Thornton of the Edinburgh Hawk Watch Project has been monitoring sparrowhawks within the city by-pass boundary. There are many misconceptions about the sparrowhawk and the aim of the venture is to develop public awareness and dispel the myths surrounding raptors in general. The public are encouraged to record their sightings and to participate in the programme.

Nests are monitored with cameras, and in 2010 it became possible to view the birds at the Environmental Gateway Centre at the Royal Botanic Garden in Edinburgh, and also on the Hawk Watch website. Much is being learned about the birds and their breeding behaviour in urban areas, and it is hoped that in future it will be possible to view other urban raptors such as tawny owls, buzzards and kestrels.

HIGH RISE SPECIALISTS

Swift

Apus apus
S: cran, crane swallow, jack-a-dells
G: *gòbhlan dubh*, *ainleag dhubh*, *gòbhlan mòr*

The swift is the stunt pilot of the avian world. Poet Edward Thomas (1878–1917) wrote:

> The swift with wings and tail as sharp and narrow
> As if the bow had flown off with the arrow.

Although they are often mistaken for swallows or martins, swifts are classified in a category by themselves. Both mating and feeding is carried out on the wing. The only time swifts are not airborne is during the breeding season when incubating their eggs. They once chose caves and cliffs as nest sites, but have adapted well to nesting in the eaves of tall buildings in town and centres.

Swifts' visits to Scotland last little more than three months. They arrive late in the season and leave early. Even newly fledged young migrate south almost as soon as they leave the nest.

Due to their exceedingly short legs it was once thought that swifts were footless, and their distinctive shrieking calls and sooty colouration gave rise to associations with the devil. They are extraordinary avian visitors, however. With scythe-like wings, swifts perform a Red Arrow-style display as they wheel in death-defying formations around church spires and tower blocks, a spectacle which is wonderful to watch.

SPRING CADENCE

Willow Warbler

Phylloscopus trochilus
S: wheelie-oe, willie muff, willie muftie
G: *crionag ghiuthais*, *ceileiriche a' ghiuthais*

The willow warbler is Scotland's most numerous summer visitor. By early May its distinctive cadence of sweet notes is heard almost everywhere as entire scrub-covered hillsides erupt in song. It totally transforms the dawn chorus and is a sure sign that spring is on the way. Small and greenish-yellow in colour, the willow warbler has the most easily recognisable song of all the warblers.

A willow warbler feeds its chicks (Laurie Campbell)

LIVING WITH MAN

Brown Rat

Rattus norvegicus
S: ratton, rotton
G: *radan*

Feared, hated, and persecuted, the paradoxical brown rat is the most successful mammal of all. It has been blamed for all manner of horrors and indeed may spread and carry many diseases that include several zoonoses (infectious diseases that can be transmitted from animals to humans), such as Weil's disease (*leptospirosis*) and salmonella.

It is strange that a creature which is viewed as being filthy and disease-ridden is actually an extremely clean animal that has a complex family life, and only exists in such gigantic numbers because of the filthy manner in which we as humans conduct our lives. It seems we make it blissfully easy for rats to exist, leaving half-eaten take-away packaging and many other delectable delicacies most attractive to the gourmet rat about town. It is said that you are very seldom more than a few feet away from a rat, be it in your attic, garden, drain or sewer. A most unsettling thought!

It is estimated that there are as many rats as humans in the British Isles – approximately 62 million – and given the ideal habitat we provide for them, in a good year this frightening statistic may rise even higher. This rodent, with impressive fecundity, starts breeding at the age of ten weeks, and can produce up to five litters a year with as many as 12 or more babies a litter. Even if less than half the offspring produced are female, it still means that a pair of rats can produce a whole plague, amounting in real terms to many thousands per annum. Luckily, a rat's life is short and young rats have a low survival rate due to poisoning and predators.

In Scotland, rats tend to be more noticeable in winter when they move into farm buildings and houses, creating mayhem wherever they go. They wreck a vast amount of the world's food crop each year, not only as a result of their own feeding needs but worse still due to contamination from their urine and droppings. Most country dwellers are well aware of the telltale signs of shiny, liquorice torpedoes left round feed sacks in outbuildings, but in towns rats are seldom seen. Poison is expensive and indiscriminate. Domestic and wild animals can be killed by secondary poisoning through consumption of rat carcasses. Recently rats have become resistant to many poisons, thus exacerbating the problem.

Rats find their way into buildings through the smallest gaps – a half-inch hole is quite big enough for forced entry – and with their greatest asset, their sharp teeth, they will gnaw their way through not only electric wiring but also most of the other things we value in our day-to-day lives.

Greatly misunderstood, rats are biologically little different to mice. They do bite when cornered although would rarely, if ever, fly for the throat as has been documented. They are territorial and become familiar with their patch using incredibly sensitive, tactile hairs to feel their way along well-worn runs. They are also superb swimmers and climbers. They immediately notice when there is something new in the way such as a trap. This is why it usually takes some time before you will catch one. Being omnivorous, they are able to exist in a sewer or a hedgerow, town garden or remote Scottish island. However, they suffer population crashes and explosions according to food availability but, although many die during times of famine, enough survive to rebuild numbers with alacrity.

The brown rat is not a native of Scotland. It arrived here

in the mid-1700s on ships coming to Britain from Russia. Its sheer size and strength meant that it easily ousted the smaller, daintier black rat which arrived much earlier (see page 171).

Rats have been immortalised through well-known children's heroes such as Roland Rat and Beatrix Potter's Samuel Whiskers – they are usually portrayed as the bad guys. Even though owls, birds of prey and domestic cats account for some reduction in rat numbers, with such vast amounts, natural predation is never going to make a true impact on the total. Like it or not, rats are here to stay.

Pigeon

S: dou, croupie
G: *calman, smùdan, dùradan*

Feral pigeons (*Columba livia var. domestica*) have been present in towns for generations and frequently strut down the High Street, clustering in groups around famous buildings, where they are unpopular due to the mess they make. They are blamed for spreading diseases and are seen as pests. Every year, councils spend thousands of pounds endeavouring to exterminate them – often in vain. Spikes are put up below windows to deter them from perching on the sills, and the birds are frequently driven away and stopped from building their untidy dropping-spattered nests.

Many people love pigeons, however, and enjoy feeding them in city parks and gardens. The town pigeon originated from the wild rock dove (*Columba livia*). Although the rock dove is now scarce and only found in remote craggy parts of western Scotland, it frequently interbreeds with its townie relation.

Adapting to a life in close proximity to man has had its advantages, and not all feral pigeons are persecuted. They often have access to a ready food supply and may rear up to six broods annually, feeding their plain, downy squabs on rich 'pigeon milk' regurgitated from their crops. Abandoned buildings and old warehouses provide a wealth of nesting opportunities.

Town dwellers appear to either love or loathe the widespread feral pigeon (Polly Pullar)

Conflict with birds of prey such as sparrowhawks and peregrine falcons is something that causes consternation among pigeon racers and fanciers. In Crieff, one particular pigeon fancier lost nearly all his birds to a pair of peregrines, yet he could do nothing to protect them, as law protects falcons. His distress illustrated the frustration of pigeon breeders all over Scotland. Many pigeon rings are found at peregrine eyries and are often secreted away by bird ringers to avoid trouble. Pigeon breeders maintain a great rapport with their pigeons.

Carrier pigeons were once trained to take secret messages during wartime. These could be hidden on the pigeon's body. Pigeons fly silently, so they usually went undetected. Some were even awarded medals for their bravery. Although they are often seen as 'stupid', this is far from the case as pigeons are versatile birds and as the wartime heroes prove they were even useful to society.

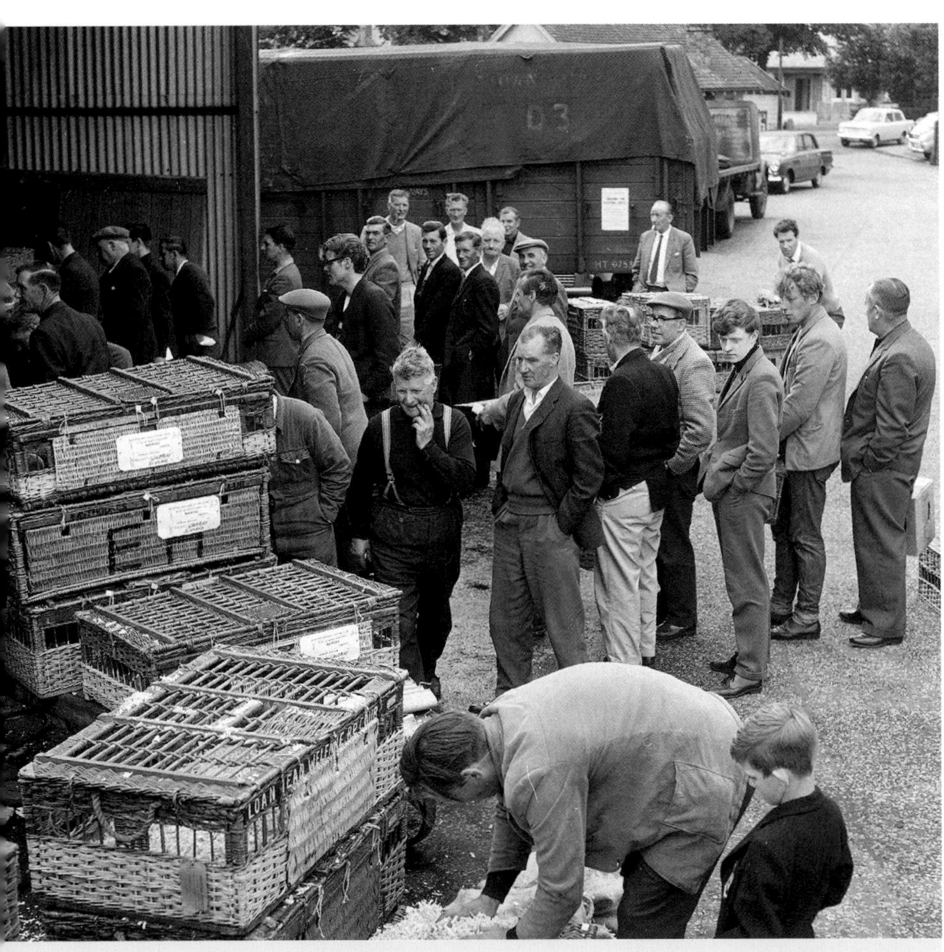

Above. Pigeon fanciers at Corstorphine Railway preparing for the Vauxusher International Pigeon Race (© The Scotsman Publications Ltd. Licensor www.scran.ac.uk)

Right. Is the grey squirrel now firmly here to stay? (Malcolm Gosling)

Pigeon racing

Pigeons have been domesticated since around 400 BC. They have also been bred as homing and racing pigeons. Pigeon breeding is sometimes as involved as the breeding of great racehorses – much attention goes into producing champion racing birds.

The Royal Pigeon Racing Association was formed in 1897, and today over one and a half million young racing pigeons are ringed annually. People from all walks of life take part in this growing sport. Birds are ringed with rubber leg rings and may race distances between 60 and 500 miles. Once the pigeons return, the ring is immediately removed and placed in a special clock that records the time taken. Over £100,000 has allegedly been paid for an outstanding racer, and the sport is highly speculative.

A Grey Area

Grey squirrels (*Sciurus carolinensis*) are seen in most city parks. The grey was introduced from North America and it is larger and more robust than our native red squirrel (see page 57), causing serious concerns about their spread – a battle is now being waged as hundreds of grey squirrels are caught in live traps in an attempt to remove them altogether. It is an uphill struggle to get rid of them since they breed prolifically. Not all trapped squirrels go to waste, however. One enterprising Glasgow restaurant has become known for serving grey squirrel rillette, paté and tortellini, and claim that it is a delicious wild food not dissimilar to rabbit. Apparently their customers love it.

There are some people who believe that the grey should now be allowed to stay as it has colonised Britain so successfully, but evidence proves that their presence is damaging to natural red squirrel populations. Greys

Left. The vital importance of habitat protection for frogs should not be underestimated (Polly Pullar)

Right. The tawny owl adapts well to life alongside man, though casualties are inevitable (Polly Pullar)

become bold and like all rodents have incredibly efficient teeth, and have been known to bite when handled. In town gardens where food is put out for birds, special 'baffles' may have to be added to nut feeders to stop grey squirrels from stealing food. Ingenious methods and hilarious acrobatics have been employed by greys as they endeavour to get through the added armoury. Success is nearly always guaranteed for these determined creatures.

A Frog Hotel

People go to extraordinary lengths to protect the wildlife in their gardens. In March 2009 the first Frog Hotel was opened, in Redhall Walled Garden in Edinburgh. This feature was designed specially to protect breeding amphibians from predators including herons and gulls. As well as offering various secure chambers attractive to amphibians there is also a compost café. Organised by the Action Earth Campaign, the idea is to encourage other groups to make specialist secure retreats for amphibians.

An Owl Window and a Canned Owl

Both barn and tawny owls have learnt to exist in towns. Old buildings provide good nest sites and the growing rodent population in all cities is an added advantage as owls are highly efficient rat killers. Many owls are killed on the roads each year, in particular when hunting along vole-rich motorway verges at night, when birds can be dazzled and dragged into the slipstream of vehicles.

Former Labour politician Tam Dalyell has what he describes as an 'owl window' at his family home, the House of The Binns, near Linlithgow. This has been home to the Dalyell family for nearly 400 years and is now owned by the National Trust for Scotland. It was the view of the Chief Inspector of Ancient Monuments that this special slot had been left in the house to enable owls to come in at night to kill off the inevitable rodents accumulating around the spilt grain in the old bake house.

Due to living in close proximity to man, owls frequently end up in difficulty. One tawny owl travelled almost 300 miles as a figurehead embedded in a lorry grill, after having been hit shortly after Norwich. When the lorry arrived at the depot in Edinburgh, the comatose bird was found. It had a miraculous escape, however, and was released once it had recovered from its terrifying ordeal.

Urban Undertakers

Many members of the crow family have adjusted to town life. Rubbish tips swarm with corvids as the opportunist birds rally to the challenge of sifting through millions of tons of our discarded food waste in search of another repast. Huge rookeries may appear in parks and town gardens and are often overlooked, even though people complain of the noise and the terrible mess. Visit one at sundown on a summer evening and the spectacle of the air filled with hundreds of birds flying in formations as they finally turn in for the night is unforgettable.

Jackdaws and carrion crows also frequently breed in the heart of cities. In spring they can be watched in parks as they collect dog and cat hair to line their nests. They also collect copious amounts of twigs that they post into deep chimneys, often unaware that the material falls right through, providing perfect kindling for the building's occupants. Like the magpie, jackdaws have a liking for shiny objects and will steal when the opportunity arises.

Members of the crow clan generally occupy car parks at motorway service stations; the black scavengers hang about round bins and thrive on a diet of discarded chips, burgers and other unwanted food. It is appropriate that the crow family are dressed in black, as they are the undertakers of the avian world. As they patrol motorway verges any unfortunate creature that meets a premature death under the wheels of vehicles is swiftly given its last rites in an efficient clean-up operation.

Fox about Town

Although there are huge numbers of foxes in the countryside, it is far more likely that you will see one in a town or city. It is at least 60 years since they moved into the centre

Left. Rooks frequently take advantage of motorway service stations (Polly Pullar)

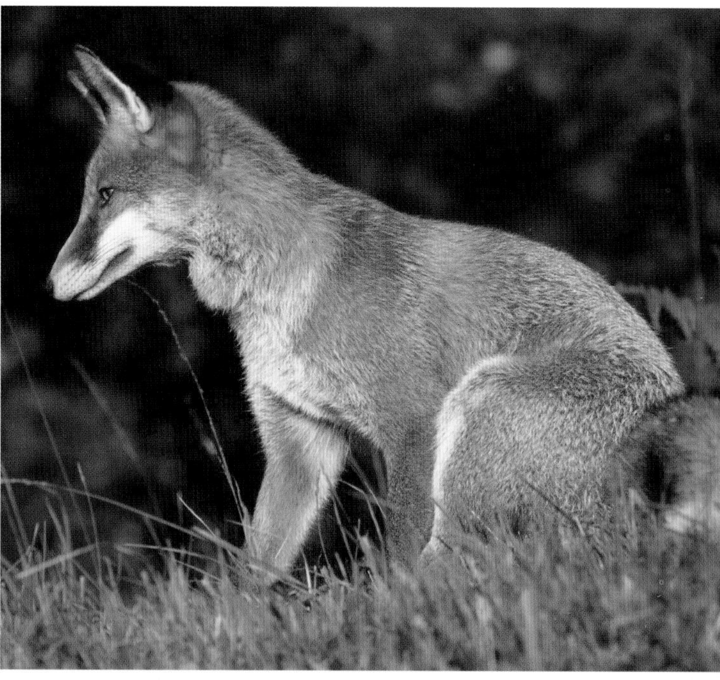

Right. It is now far easier to watch foxes in towns than in the countryside (Laurie Campbell)

of Glasgow, and they are widespread in most urban areas. Foxes make dens in any available locations including landfill sites, rubbish tips, building sites, gardens and parks. They have taken full advantage of man in different ways.

While the country fox is adept at raiding the hen run, the streetwise vulpine prefers fast food and visits the local convenience food outlet instead, returning to the den to feed cubs Indian or fried chicken takeaways, or fish suppers. Some foxes become very tame and there are seldom reports of any trouble or vicious behaviour. Other fox behaviour is less appreciated, however. During the mating season, the noise of a shrieking vixen is enough to waken the dead, and since foxes often frequent graveyards, the sound can be hair-raising. At least the fox's breeding call is only heard for a few short weeks in January or February.

Foxes make themselves unpopular by littering gardens with the remains of their stolen dinners. They undermine garden sheds and other suitable denning areas. Stories of them spreading disease are exaggerated. *Toxocara canis,* a parasitic roundworm, can be passed to humans but this is extremely rare and is more likely to come from the family dog than from the neighbourhood fox. Some urban fox populations are afflicted with sarcoptic mange. Caused by a tiny mite, 'fox mange' will gradually debilitate an infected animal through hair loss and terrible itching. The entire body becomes riddled with sores, and death follows within a few months if left untreated. As foxes with the condition appear to be in a dreadful state, the misconception that they are unhealthy is fuelled, but most people are of the opinion that city life without foxes would be more dull.

Badgers in the Botanics

Badgers frequently exist on the outskirts of urban areas and have caused chaos with their excavations in such places as Edinburgh's Royal Botanic Garden. Badger watches in springtime allow members of the public to see the animals at close proximity and can be an exciting part of a town visit, but the gardeners at the Botanics were understandably

Reynard in Paradise

In a famous incident some years ago, a fox halted play at Parkhead football ground in Glasgow's east end. The song-writer Michael Marra was listening to the Celtic–Aberdeen game on the radio when he heard the incredulous commentator gasp. A fox had run onto the pitch. 'In 'Reynard in Paradise' Marra imagines the moment from the fox's point of view.

Men can be graceful
This much I know
They say I'm aware of one big thing
But I'm not so slow
I used to live in a place where the people wore red
And they howled and screamed and blew their horns
And they wished my family had never been born
I left the day that my brother went down
I headed in through the East side of town
I never heard a harsh word as I made my way
The people gave each other the time of day
I found this place in the middle of the night
When all was quiet and it felt just right
I made my way underground
I felt safe and I felt sound
Then one day the whole world came
They stood round the field and they spoke about the game
One at a time they made their way
Then the lights came on it was bright as day
There on the field to my surprise
Right in front of my very eyes
The people in red had come to town
But they had no Horses and there were no Hounds
They began to dance and I heard an old man sing
And there on the field what appeared to be
A working model of the one big thing
They could dance and sing,
A working model of the one big thing
Men can be graceful
This much I know

less impressed when several families of badgers moved in during the summer of 2010. Indeed one gardener was quoted as saying: 'They have very strong snouts and they make snuffle holes in the grounds to get the worms and other grubs and these holes are all over the beautiful lawns'.

Badgers near Edinburgh Airport, and close to the location of Edinburgh's new controversial tramline, have had to be relocated due to the threat posed by development work close to their setts. Arrangements for such a house move has to first be approved by SNH. A new sett is then built to particularly high specifications before the old one is removed. Usually this proves successful.

Gulls

There are few seaside resorts and towns without gulls. If there is a bird with entrepreneurial skills then it is surely the herring gull. Due to their pushy nature and determination to maximise all opportunities, they have become a real pest in many places. In Arbroath and other small towns around the east coast, control officers are used to deter birds from nesting on buildings. In recent years, falconers have been employed to help, and brings in Harris hawks and falcons to drive the gulls away. It is ironic that we treat gulls as pests when it is our litter and mess that attract them. Some gulls have become so used to humans that they take little or no notice and have regularly been known to attack and injure. They may swoop down to try and extract food from a passer-by and have on occasions inflicted peck wounds and scratches.

In 2009 a herring gull made its mark in a shop in the middle of Aberdeen where it was found to have a passion for a well-known brand of chilli-flavoured crisps. Much to the amusement of the shop's customers, the gull stole crisps every day from a stand close to the open door, before ripping open the bag with its powerful bill.

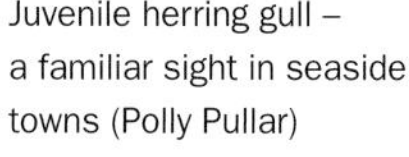

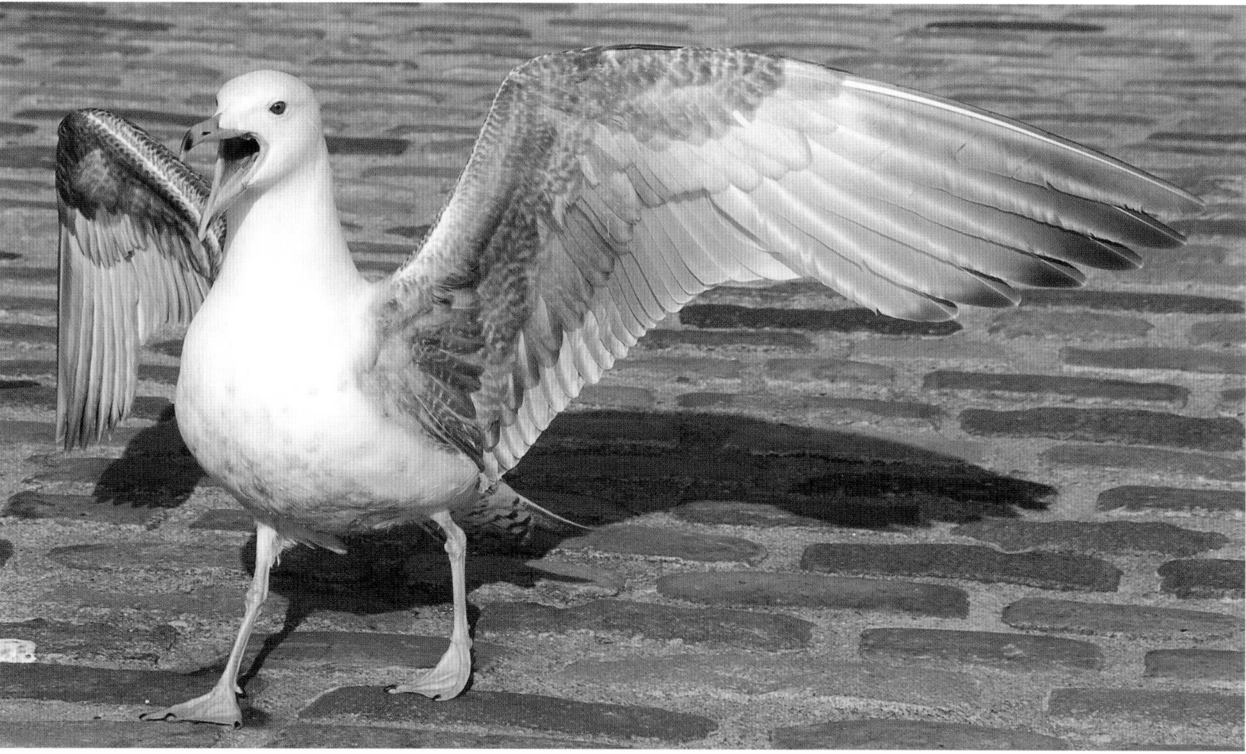

Juvenile herring gull – a familiar sight in seaside towns (Polly Pullar)

Waterfowl

Four birds in particular have quickly established in the urban environment: the mute swan, mallard, coot and tufted duck. They are now a regular sight in many parks and gardens and often wander into town to acquire a meal using their utmost charm. The mallard is the most appealing and waddles close to humans in search of food. Swans cause more problems because they are large and intimidating and although they become tame and love to be fed by members of the public, they tend to stick closer to the water's edge. The mallard, however, will not hesitate to wander right down the High Street, and for this reason it often ends up in trouble, with ducklings becoming separated from their parents. Mallard ducklings have been found in shopping centres, cattle grids, storm drains and even public conveniences. Eggs are also laid in unsuitable places – one mallard duck laid a large clutch in a tub of flowers in the Winner's Enclosure at Perth Racecourse. Former prime minister Sir Alec Douglas-Home says in *Border Reflections*, 'In my year at No. 10 Downing Street a mallard duck nested in some low *Hypericum* just outside the Cabinet Room. Eventually she left by the back door, and so a little later did I.'

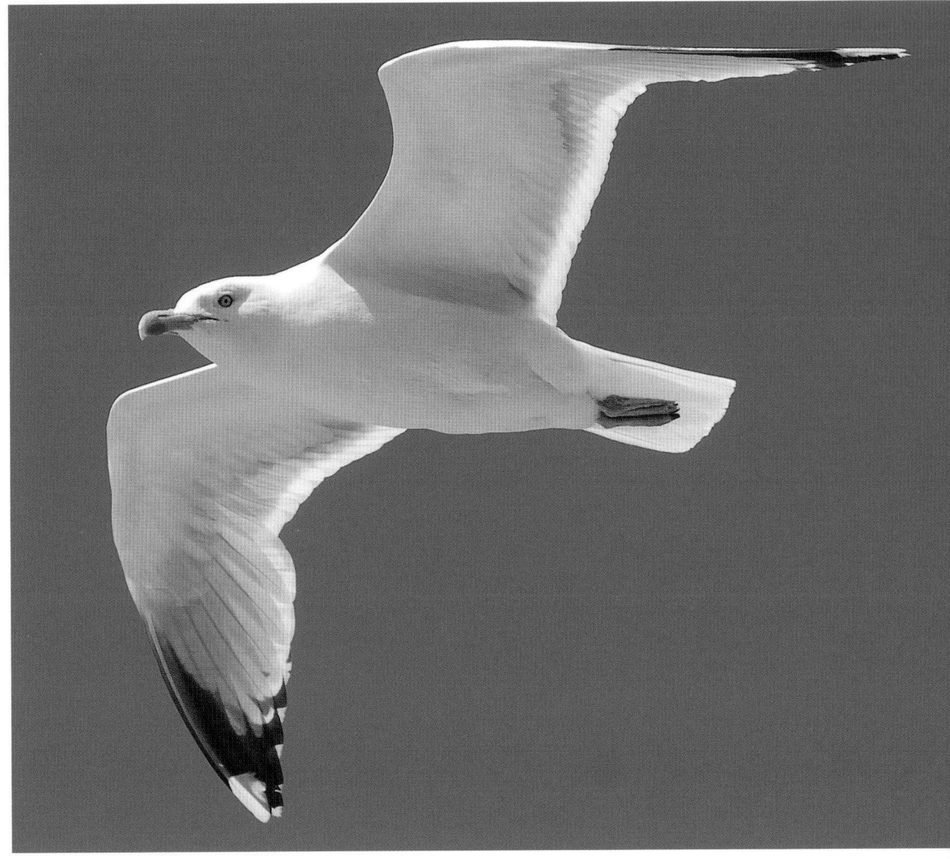

The herring gull has a distinctive call and great aerial agility (Polly Pullar)

Swans on the Nor' Loch

There used to be swans on the Nor' Loch in the centre of Edinburgh, where Princes Street Gardens are now. The Burgh Council saw it as their duty to protect them, and other wildfowl, from people like Quentin Bowston who shot a swan 'with ane hackbut' in December 1589, without even leaving his house. It seems that several men were involved. Did they lean out of the window? Over the garden wall? Bowston later named his fellow miscreants and promised that there would be no more shooting. He was fined and ordered to provide a new swan to replace the one he had killed. Clearly, the citizens of Edinburgh enjoyed their ornamental birds.

A record from the spring of 1677 makes this clearer still. A man gifted four swans to the town, in the hope that they would breed and stay. Vandalism continued to be a problem however, and the town crier had to be sent round warning people of the hefty fine laid down for anyone who disturbed them.

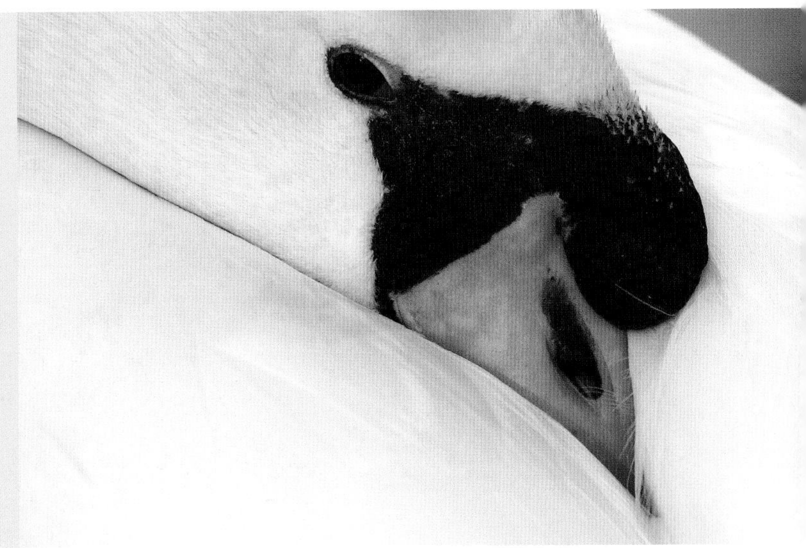

Above. Mallard – our most widespread duck is common in the urban-environment (Polly Pullar)

Right. Tufted duck (Malcolm Gosling)

Tufted Duck

Aythya fuligula
S: tuftie
G: *lach sgumanach*

The tufted duck is widespread. It is equally as likely to be seen on a town pond or canal as on a wild and windswept loch on a Hebridean island. In recent years, it has become almost as familiar as the mallard, and like the mallard, it is able to survive in close proximity to humans. The first records of tufted duck breeding in Scotland came from Perthshire in 1849. It then expanded rapidly and thrived. At that time, large amounts of gravel were extracted to make a network of new roads. Excavated gravel pits remained and filled with water to become vegetated artificial ponds – perfect tufted duck habitat.

The tufted duck, a member of the group of 'diving ducks', not only dives deep, but also stays submerged for some time as it searches for molluscs, crustaceans, insects and spawn. It also feeds on tadpoles, frogs and small fish. The drake's crest is longer than that of the duck and his smart pied plumage has given rise to the nickname of 'magpie diver'. In Islay, the tufted duck is referred to as a 'douker'.

Faithful cohorts: milk horses

The last milk horses in Edinburgh were owned by Scotmid dairies, formerly St Cuthberts. Shortly before the horses were retired in 1985, one of the drivers, William Skedd, was inteviewed by Gail Christey from the School of Scottish Studies. He describes the horses like workmates, each with their own personality:

> . . . I was up a stair, an' it was bucket morning [the day refuse bins are collected]. Another nice day, sunny day. Ah hud a horse called Molly. While I'm

up the stair, she's into the buckets [waste bins]. Well, the lid o' the bucket got caught in her bridle. This wumman called up the stair, 'Willie, your horse is away.' I was doon the stair like a shot! An' I had to go to catch it, I'll tell you that. An' the mair it's gaun, the harder the lid o' the bucket – a metal one – is clattering. However, afore she got to the main drive it fell off. That was a funny incident, but it could have been a serious accident. But these things happen when you're drivin' horses. You see, when you're driving the horse the only thing ye can dae is pit the brake on. But, you've got the milk to deliver; you take it, ye ken, your horse he'll stand fur ye, but there's a thousand and one things that'll frighten the horse. Ye can even get a bird, a sparrow, tae land on the horse's bridle, that'll frighten it. But, as long as your brake's on, you're all right if you've got a good brake. It'll pull the van away, but it' ll no' be able to run. No, if you've got a good load, he'll still pull it. An' if he pulls it, the harness could go; he could burst the traces.

Tracer horses

Mary Low's father, Jim Farquhar, had vivid memories of the 'tracer boys' who used to ride Clydesdales, sometimes at the gallop, from Edinburgh's Princes Street down the long steep hill towards Leith, sparks flying up between the horse-shoes and the granite setts. Tracer horses were the result of animal welfare legislation and the foundation of the SSPCA in 1839 and were still in use a hundred years later. They were needed to help pull heavy trams and wagons loaded with grain, coal, timber and other goods, from Leith docks up into the city. There was a stance at Shrubhill where boys and horses waited together for a hire. Then the tracer would be harnessed alongside the haulier's own horse and a boy would accompany the load up the hill, but from the top, of course, they had to be brought back down and the quickest way was the ride them: no hardship at all to a city lad and the envy of many a schoolboy.

A Scotmid milk horse on its last round, 1985
(© The Scotsman Publications Ltd. Licensor www.scran.ac.uk)

Ken, wi' a dead weight, he could still burst the traces or the heid straps … .

'You always put the brake on, aye. You take bucket morning, see the bucket motor? [refuse lorry] An the noise o' the bucket motor? Some horses cannae take it. Mick would go balmy! He doesnae like drills, he doesnae like bucket motors, he doesnae like anything like that. Wee Billy's all right, he'd stand all right. Eh, Trigger, he wid stand a' day – it doesnae bother him. Ranger, it doesnae bother Ranger either. Ye see, horses are temperamental, they've a' got thir ain outlook.'

Beyond the grave: Greyfriars Bobby

The most famous stray dog in Scotland has to be the one who lived in and around Greyfriars churchyard, Edinburgh, in the 1860s. Generations of schoolchildren were brought up on the story of Bobby, the Skye terrier who came to the city with his master, a shepherd, one market day in 1858. The old man took ill and died and was buried in a pauper's grave in Greyfriars churchyard. Bobby guarded the spot for years, leaving it only to be fed by the landlord of a local hostelry. Such is the story as told by American children's writer Eleanor Atkinson in 1912, and again in a Disney film in 1961. A new film was made in 2005, with a West Highland terrier in the leading role. This time he was a guard dog belonging to a Constable John Grey whose job it was to guard cattle in the Grassmarket at the night. The rest of the story is substantially the same: his master died and was buried and Bobby stayed by the grave 'under the shelter of an old pillared tomb-stone' until local people, touched by his faithfulness, started feeding him and letting him into their homes. Times change, and recently other writers have attempted more factual accounts of the Bobby story. It seems that the real Bobby was a mongrel who lived in the grounds of George Heriot's School till the

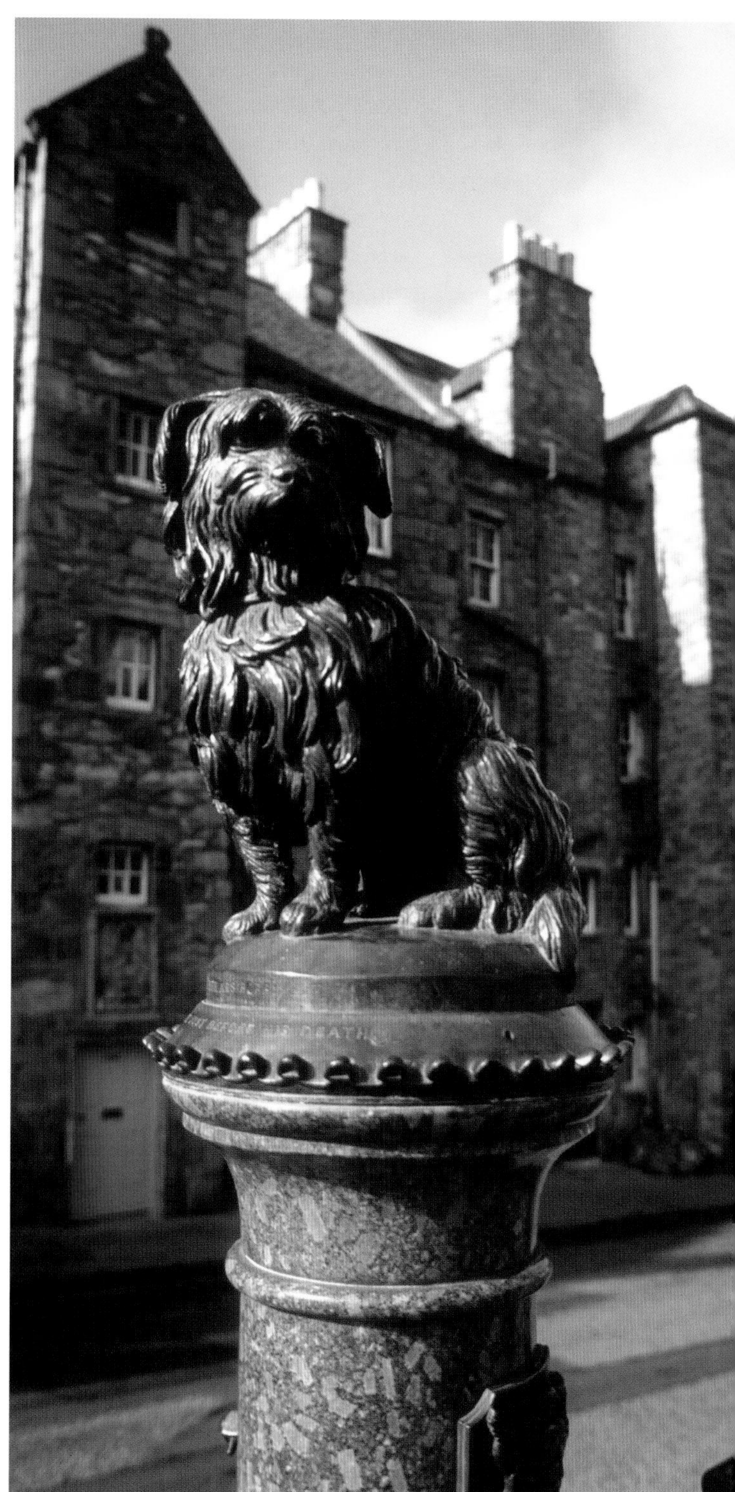

Greyfriars Bobby (© Neil Sinclair. Licensorwww.scran.ac.uk)

gardener threw him out. He relocated to the churchyard next door where he was befriended by the sexton, James Brown, and the owners of a hostelry round the corner. No one seems to know how the story grew up that he was lying on his master's grave but he quickly became an icon of doggy nobility. There must have been something appealing about Bobby and something kindly about James Brown or their relationship would never have got off the ground in the first place. There was however, a business aspect to it, especially after May 1864, when Bobby became a national celebrity thanks to an article in the *Inverness Advertiser*. From then on, money changed hands as Brown regaled people with the story and tourists flocked to see the tenacious mongrel emerge from Greyfriars every day at one o'clock sharp and trot along to the hostelry, by then a coffee house run by the Traill family. The Traills had themselves photographed with him, but Bobby never really belonged to anyone and it was a different set of neighbours who came to his rescue three years later when a law was passed requiring all dogs to be licensed by their owners or be destroyed. In the end, the Lord Provost was persuaded to pay Bobby's dog licence for life. His statue can still be seen at the top of Candlemaker Row and his photograph in the Museum of Edinburgh, along with his inscribed collar 'from the Lord Provost' and his dog dish.

CHAPTER NINE

WILD WORK

For as long as there have been human beings in Scotland, they have made use of the creatures they have lived beside, forging a relationship with them in many different ways. Whilst the earliest settlers were wholly dependent on wild animals and birds to provide them with primitive tools, food and clothing, gradually they also learnt to domesticate small sheep and cattle. As agriculture progressed, oxen and horses were used as draught animals. Animals and birds were also used for medicinal and religious purposes. Feathers were used for decorations and in early times worn by clan chiefs and other noblemen, while during the Victorian era, the fashion for feather decorated hats caused a drastic drop in numbers of some birds, in particular the kittiwake (see page 166).

Today we continue to make use of animals but in a vastly different way. While many of those uses are immediately obvious from the provision of fish, meat, milk, eggs and other foodstuffs, to wool, feathers, and by-products for dozens of things we use daily, other uses may be less so.

There are probably few people who do not own at least one pair of leather shoes, a belt, handbag or a wallet. All these are sourced from animals – usually with leather made from cow or pig hide. Many high-end perfumes contain animal by-products – some still contain 'ambergris' a substance extracted from the intestines of the sperm whale and used as a perfume fixative. Rennet – a natural enzyme produced in the fourth stomach – the *abomasum*, of a young calf, is used as a coagulant for milk to make puddings and other human food, though there is now a synthetic alternative. The hooves of cattle are boiled up to produce 'keratin' used as a flame retardant by fire fighters, and bones and skins may be processed for bone meal, glues and to add to chemical preparations. Sand eels and other fish are made into meal for livestock feedstuffs, and the guts of cows are still occasionally employed to make strings for tennis rackets. Down feathers from ducks and geese fill expensive pillows, duvets and clothing. Perhaps surprisingly there are traces of animal placenta – in particular that from a sheep, in many beauty products. Animals have long been used for testing purposes for new medicines and cosmetics, supposedly for the good of the human race, but often to the detriment of the unfortunate beasts, as in the case of such controversial processes as the 'Draize' eye test, known to cause intense pain and discomfort. Happily, animal testing is under constant review, and in many cases it has been banned altogether.

Animals are also widely used for recreational purposes, for sport and entertainment. From the close bonds we form with dogs, cats and horses, to exotic collections of fur and feather, man's relationship with animals has always been varied.

We use guide dogs for both the deaf, blind and handi-

Opposite. Polly Pullar feeds an injured red deer calf (Iomhair Fletcher)

capped, and train many different specially bred animals to help us in our day-to-day lives; farm collies, gundogs, hounds and terriers are used in agriculture and hunting. Dogs are also used for Search and Rescue and have become extremely important working as sniffers to find drugs and other illegal substances.

Men and women have ever shaped the landscape, and in a twist of irony, though responsible for creating some of the most beautifully wildlife rich habitats, they are also responsible for wreaking havoc making it often impossible for creatures to survive symbiotically beside us. Though attitudes are changing constantly, many wild animals struggle to keep up with man's domination. While they can adapt to change over a long time period, the speed in which we alter their habitat often makes this impossible and leads to casualties. There will always be the need for wildlife hospitals and havens where animals can hopefully be repaired and recuperate following many of the horrible incidents that befall them due to our activities. Traffic accounts for thousands of casualties each year. We both use and abuse animals and our relationships with them can be beautiful and ghastly in turn. Luckily there are now those on hand who work to rectify just some of the many problems urbanisation and our encroachment causes.

Hand-rearing an orphan red squirrel (Polly Pullar)

Our constant need for more income and food means that the small native farm animals that were once highly valued are being replaced by faster growing breeds from the Continent. Due to their largesse they in turn may alter the balance as they need more food and larger fields, and in this way inadvertently change the landscape too. Mounting pressures on farmers and landowners mean that some may be less tolerant of sharing the land with creatures considered as pests and they may be removed as a result.

Strict new laws that come into effect nearly every day also alter the balance. Many old crafts have died out altogether simply because legislation makes it hard to continue. It is rumoured that perhaps even horns and antlers will one day be deemed as a health hazard governed by new laws, despite the fact they have been used for generations with no ill effects. This will make it impossible for horn carvers to continue. Like fashions, our outlook towards creatures is constantly changing. The wearing of fur has become less acceptable yet despite this concern we still abuse them in other ways.

With an increasingly urban population many young people may never have the chance to witness wild creatures in their natural settings, or to forge a beneficial relationship with a domestic pet, or learn some of the old rural skills. Far too many children are unaware of where their food originates.

The people who are included in this chapter represent some fine examples of those that have made a way of life working with animals. Wildlife crime and animal cruelty has been on going since time immemorial and sadly is almost impossible to wipe out with or without strict laws, but there are those who strive to conquer this problem.

In the case of craftsmen and women who still work with animal parts to make beautiful creations, they provide an integral part of our natural heritage. Enlightenment and education will play a key role and it is only if we can work with animals in a humane manner, while using them respectfully, that man's relationship with them will continue and go from strength to strength.

Uses

The Taxidermist

The word taxidermy comes from two Greek words: *taxis* (arrangement) and *dermis* (skin). It is the process of mounting dead creatures for display purposes, with the aim of replicating their living presence as accurately as possible.

Taxidermy became highly popular in the nineteenth century, with many 'bird stuffers' producing work in Scotland. Peter D. Malloch of Perth was not only a taxidermist of repute, but also a specialist in producing barrel-shaped cases for his plaster-cast fish. He was an expert on trout and salmon and his vast knowledge of insect life led to him becoming a superb fly-tier. Other Scottish taxidermists included William McCleay of Inverness, Small of Edinburgh, F.C. Waters of Aberdeen, and Cecil Bisshopp [sic] of Oban. Some of their work is still available, although it may be faded, collapsed and moth-eaten: some specimens are scarcely recognisable.

The penchant for producing animals in anthropomorphic displays, wearing clothes and engaged in duels or human pastimes, is no longer popular. During the Victorian era, there was also a trend for producing macabre hybrids ('rogue taxidermy'), in which bizarre creatures were constructed from the parts of several animals and birds.

Some of this early work, where a case was frequently tightly packed with a huge array of raptors shot purely for the purpose, conveys the attitudes of the period. When something rare and interesting was seen, unenlightened Victorian naturalists reached for their guns. Some of the early pieces also show a lack of field knowledge. Taxidermy began to attract criticism, and poorly mounted specimens were rejected in favour of more naturalistic settings.

George Jamieson, one of Scotland's most respected taxidermists (Polly Pullar)

George Jamieson, one of the longest-serving taxidermists working in Scotland today, is largely self-taught and as a teenager took guidance on the subject from an old book dating back to 1873. He modestly says: 'The real thing is perfection, and however hard you try you will never get it right,' but his work – that of a true artist – must be as near perfection as it is possible to achieve. It is vital to know the animal or bird in the field and to be able to recognise and reproduce its character and movements. Jamieson views everything through naturalist's eyes – he has a passionate interest in wildlife, forged in his formative years. As a small boy, he spent many hours in the field. This shows in his work, and it is no surprise that he has worked with nearly all Scottish species, as well as some from further afield. His subjects are legally taken game and road casualties, or animals that have died naturally. He is equally at home with a tiny goldcrest as with a huge red deer stag, although the methods for dealing with each differ widely.

He lives and works at the eleventh-century Cramond Tower on the Firth of Forth. In this inspirational setting he tirelessly produces commissions. They come from many sources all over the world: museums, advertising agencies, government organisations, individuals, estate owners, film directors and private buyers. He was one of the earliest members of the Guild of Taxidermists – and through their accreditation scheme, work is monitored to ensure it is of a museum-standard of excellence. Many species now require a special licence.

Today, the term 'stuffed' is dimly viewed, and the word most frequently used is 'mounted'. Animals and birds have to be either sent to the taxidermist immediately, or stored in a freezer – the fresher the corpse, the better. A rough sketch or template of the bird or animal prior to skinning is vital to ensure that wings and legs are in the correct position when the skin is put back over the model. The subject will then be skinned – for a bird, George likens this to removing a glove. Next all the muscle is painstakingly picked out with a scalpel. A wood, wool or polystyrene body-shape is made and eventually after many hours of work this is put back into the skin. Wires are inserted to keep wings, legs and limbs in the right place, and various muscles and eye sockets are filled with special clay. Casts of mammal body shapes have to be made and the skins tanned, a complex process that takes at least ten days to complete. The correct eyes are very important and although George has a stock of some of the most common species, others have to be specially ordered from Germany. He often adapts his own methods to deal with a particular animal or bird, and says that he is always learning, and perfecting his techniques.

George runs taxidermy courses and explains that corvids are good for beginners as they have little or no fat, whereas ducks and geese are so fatty and their skins so papery that they take far too long to prepare. His main work comes from mounting red deer stags' heads, and he has also done several entire stags for large displays. Hedgehogs are fiddly due to the spines. Some mammals may be prepared for making into sporrans. Fish are cast in fibreglass and the final model, with an average of 5,000 scales on just one side, has to have each scale individually painted no less than three times. The original fish often ends its days as a smoked delicacy.

Taxidermy is an art form. A good taxidermist must not only be a skilled craftsman and artist, but must also understand anatomy. Taxidermy plays an important role in education: a well-produced specimen may be the only chance that a young person has of getting close to some of our native species.

Poor Bruin

During a trip home to Harris in 1817–8, the young William MacGillivray found himself involved in the shooting and taxidermy of a bear. He describes the episode in his diary: 'Today I got up about six and left Rodill, after having promised to go down tomorrow before ten to stuff the bear, which is about to be killed.' He does not explain whose bear this was or how it came to be in Harris, but it was clearly a live bear. The diary entry for the next day records, 'Poor Bruin was shot through the head. After breakfast I skinned him, and after dinner made up a body of sticks and hay for him – and that was all.' It is not often that MacGillivray personalizes an animal like this ('him', not 'it') and things go from bad to worse when he realizes he has made a mistake: 'I found that I had taken a wrong method in stuffing the bear.' It all sounds rather futile. Was it the tired old bear of some travelling showman, a trophy-pet grown large and worrisome, or had the poor creature been brought to Harris especially to be sacrificed on the altar of interior design?

The Sporran Maker

Old photographs from the early 1900s often show men in Highland dress wearing animal sporrans. At Perth Racecourse during the 1930s, photographs of race-goers reveal the popularity of otters, badgers, wildcats and foxes as fash-

Kate Macpherson sporrans (Kate Macpherson)

ionable sporrans. This traditional craft has largely died out. Many people are concerned about using animals in this way. However, as more and more animals are unwittingly killed on increasingly busy roads, Kate Macpherson has been putting them to good use while keeping a traditional craft alive. She points out that these beautiful specimens would otherwise be totally lost and left to rot beside the road. She also points out that most of us wear leather shoes and have leather bags and belts sourced from animals. Fake fur is environmentally unfriendly, being an oil-based product that is totally un-renewable.

Based in a workshop on a remote farm close to Beauly, Kate Macpherson is one of the few sporran makers left in the country to complete the craft from start to finish. She trained as a taxidermist with Mike Windham-Wright in Argyll and later completed a saddler's course, enabling her to make the entire animal sporran from scratch.

Suitable casualties are immediately put in a deep freeze

Fox sporran – Kate Macpherson makes the entire sporran including the leather work (Polly Pullar)

It's complicated

Fashion items made of fur or feathers are provocative, no doubt about it. You have to put aside certain feelings about the original owners, as women used to do when wearing fur coats. Animal mortality is a fact of life but enjoying it requires a certain bravado which the five-year-old Colin MacDonald (1882–1957) cultivated only with difficulty and never completely mastered. Here he describes an incident that happened on his first walk to school, aged five:

> There were three of the gamekeeper's family from far up the hill-side, two cousins from just above us, and three of our nearest neighbour's bairns. Lower down we collected the MacKays, and when we came to the railway crossing we were joined by a bigger contingent from the Bottacks. Of course, I was the show-piece, and very shy and embarrassed, I felt the crowd's attentions. Instead of crying – as I very nearly did – I picked up a stone from the railway and threw it as far as I could along the line. It was a sort of gesture of independent manliness which I was far from feeling. Speak of 'shots at random sent'! That stone happened to come bang down on the steel rail, about ten yards away, a fraction of a second after a young linnet had alighted at the identical spot. It was instant death to the linnet. The bigger boys were impressed by such marksmanship: what an eye! What an aim! I felt momentarily proud of a feat which – quite undeservedly – jumped my stock in the market of that somewhat callous lot of hooligans' esteem; but indeed my triumph held a cankerous seed, for, as I looked at that pathetic fluffy little heap, still warm and trembling, which but moments before had been the incarnation of joy and gladness, a tear rolled down my nose and I had to laugh in raucous bravado to avoid disgrace. That little linnet remains the only song-bird I have injured in my life; and when at the last bar of judgment I shall be asked, as I still dread – 'Why did you do it?' – the only plea I can tender is that I didn't mean it and that it has been a lifelong regret.'

and then the part that is to be used, normally the head for a full-mask sporran, is tanned and painstakingly dealt with in the same manner employed by a taxidermist. The process is long and fiddly. All Kate's sporrans are laboriously hand-stitched. While the issues of a ban on sealskin have altered the situation for some sporran makers, Kate has turned to deer hair and often uses the spotted pelts of fallow deer, or the rich russet-red ones of a roe deer in its summer coat.

Unusually, Kate makes sporrans from pheasants, mallard and other birds, and she once made a sporran from a beautiful salmon skin. The pheasants are particularly popular with teenage boys. She uses antler to make buttons and toggles for closing the sporrans. Foxes, pine martens and badgers prove the most popular. Many sporrans are commissioned, tailored to suit the wearer's needs exactly, including those for children. From sporrans made for members of the Tartan Army to wear at football matches, to military sporrans using wild goat hair, and the dressiest sporrans with silver tops (or *cantles*) for use with formal attire, anything is possible.

Strict laws dominate her business and she must be able to prove that the animal was found legitimately. Wildcats, otters and beavers cannot be made into sporrans even under special licence. Mink are increasingly used as their pelts are luxuriant and attractive, and with the spread of pine martens to many areas, more are succumbing to road accidents. Many women had fur stoles, or sable and mink coats, most of which end their days in charity shops, and these too are cleverly recycled to make quirky sporrans. Some sporrans incorporate Kate's humorous side. If an animal has ticks on it, she may leave one on and see if the wearer eventually discovers it.

The Horn Carver

In his heyday working full-time as the horn carver of Lawers, overlooking Loch Tay in Perthshire, Cameron Thomson used over a ton of antlers every year. He bought them from local estates, the finest antlers coming from

Rannoch: 'Aye the deer at Craiganour produce a right tarry kind of dark horn, with nice white points, just perfect for my needs.' Cameron is originally from Aberdeenshire and now in his eighties, he is still making glorious creations. It all began as a hobby, which led to almost 50 years of horn carving that also included using the horns of sheep and cattle. Driven by the need to create, he uses the antlers for cutlery handles, dog whistles, candlesticks, walking stick tops, pendants and lamps. He also sculpts animals, fish and birds, egg spoons, eggcups, beakers, and mugs from cow horn. He shows me a bracelet on a deerskin strap with little squares of horn depicting a salmon, a stag, a thistle and an eagle – fauna that epitomises Scotland. Not content with horn carving, he also bought treated deerskins, and made these into popular handbags using a specially designed sewing machine.

Cameron was in great demand to make traditional shepherds' crooks from the horns of blackface tups, and commissions have come from all over the world – one crook was made for the prime minister of Australia, while

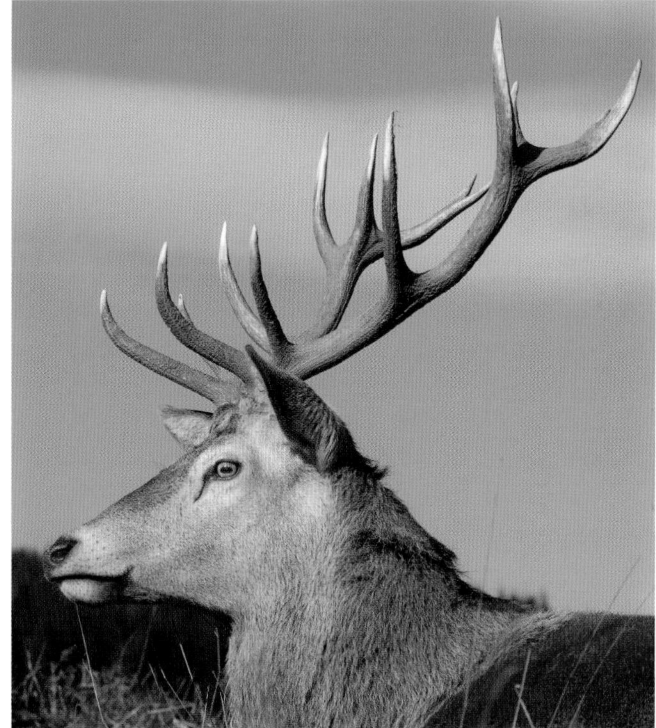

Above left. Cameron Thomson, the horn carver – a master of his craft (Polly Pullar)

Above. 'Wildwork' by Cameron Thomson (Polly Pullar)

Left. Once shed, antlers like these are highly sought by the horn carvers (Polly Pullar)

Whizzers and dirlos

In Shetland, toys were sometimes made from bones or feathers. A 'snorro-bone' (pig's foot bone) was threaded onto a loop of wool and twisted tightly. If you looped this round your thumbs and pulled it in and out, it made a snoring noise. We had cardboard versions of these in the Lowlands and called them whizzers. We got them out of cereal packets, pigs' feet being in short supply. Another toy was the 'hen-pen-durlo' – a potato stuck with hens' feathers and set down in a windy place to run around like a crazed bird. Footballs were also made of pigs' bladders, washed, dried and covered with canvas.

a crook with a religious symbol was made for the Bishop of Sudan.

Even though he is now retired, Cameron will continue his carving and creating purely for his own pleasure, a true craftsman using traditional skills with some of Scotland's most natural materials.

Abuses

The Wildlife Detective

There has always been conflict between game shooting interests and birds of prey. During the Victorian era, the mass slaughter of raptors and corvids in favour of grouse and pheasants was simply an everyday occurrence. This carnage led to a devastating dearth of many species, and some were extirpated.

Although attitudes have since changed, it would appear that we still have a long way to go. Raptor persecution continues and there are horrendous wildlife crimes still taking place in Scotland. Poisoning occurs for various reasons: the shepherd protecting his lambs from foxes, the keeper protecting game, or even the pigeon fancier keeping birds of prey away from his pigeon lofts. It is indiscriminate and highly dangerous. Poisoning on shooting estates is once again rife.

From his early days as a police constable working in Tayside, Alan Stewart has become Britain's foremost nature detective. His rural background and interest in agriculture and the countryside was the perfect foundation for a life dedicated to wildlife. Knowledgeable about the ways of poachers and how the shooting fraternity operates, he has an innate understanding of the fragile line dividing the interests of conservation and shooting, and its emotive issues.

Wildlife criminals come from all walks of life, from the unemployed to wealthy company directors. Some poachers offend for the excitement; others in the case of badger baiters and hare coursers may be exceedingly violent.

In 1993 Alan was promoted to Inspector for Perth and Kinross, and later Crieff as well. He has probably had more dealings with salmon and deer poaching than anyone and retains a great sense of humour while relating priceless tales: that of the wily salmon poacher with a huge vanload of fine fish who even had the brass neck to offer police officers a few fish to take away with them, is particularly memorable.

Despite great changes to the Wildlife and Countryside Act, it is still exceedingly difficult to get a conviction. 'There were many changes made in 2004 and up to that point the act was hopeless. Now if crimes against wildlife are committed they are punishable by imprisonment, and we have the power of search without warrant and can bring a case to court up to three years after the event – this is excellent but there is still a long way to go.' Yet in 2008, when over 30 poisoned baits were found on fence posts on an estate in Angus, there was not enough evidence for the police to submit a case for prosecution; a disappointing outcome.

Alan Stewart was first made a wildlife liaison officer (WLO) in 1993. Police forces all round the country are now employing specialist wildlife crime officers (the title changed across the UK around 2002) and that has without doubt helped.

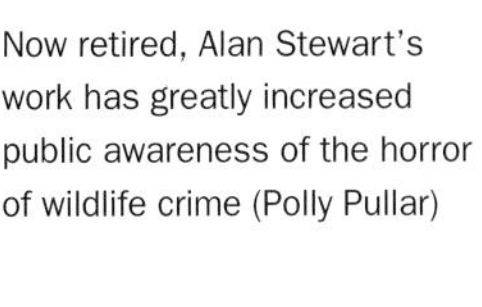

Now retired, Alan Stewart's work has greatly increased public awareness of the horror of wildlife crime (Polly Pullar)

Despite problems securing convictions, there have been many success stories. 'Operation Easter', launched in 1997, involves every police force in the UK. It has almost put a stop to egg thieving and cut the number of incidents right down. Together with the RSPB, Alan took on this project and through intelligence gathered, many thousands of eggs were recovered from illegal collections and the egg thieves jailed or heavily fined. In 2008 an astonishing 7,130 eggs were confiscated – the most, up to that date, from a single collector. Rare species such as the black-throated diver, golden eagle, sea eagle, greenshank, dotterel and red-necked phalarope are vulnerable, and although there is no monetary value in stolen eggs, thieves greatly fuelled by bravado become obsessed with collecting.

Even clearing active house martin and swallow nests off buildings, or evicting bats from a roost under the eaves when a house is renovated, is breaking the law. Currently, with people struggling to make ends meet, incidences of deer poaching have risen. Grallochs (the guts of a deer) are sometimes found by roadsides, while in other cases wounded animals die later revealing that they have been shot with weapons of unsuitable calibre, leading to immeasurable cruelty.

Thefts of the valuable pearl mussel from Scotland's rivers are ongoing (see page 117). It is impossible to police remote areas. Although intelligence comes from SEPA, water bailiffs, fishermen, walkers and canoeists, it is often too late. The penalty per mussel is a £10,000 fine or a year in prison: few cases are brought to court, however.

Badgers are frequent victims and baiting is one of the most harrowing crimes. Some farmers do not want badgers on their land due to the threat of TB (tuberculosis) and have resorted to filling setts up with slurry (see page 51).

Legal Larsen traps used for catching corvids are sometimes misused and raptors caught in them are killed instead of released. These traps must have both licence and police contact numbers so that anyone suspicious of their misuse can ring for advice. With increased marine tourism, there

Sly thief, sorry saint

St Columba had two tenants. One had a family and the other had not. The rent was the same in each case. The one who had no family complained to the saint of the unfairness of his having to pay as much rent as the other considering his cicrumstances. The saint told him to steal a shilling's worth from any person, and to restore it at the end of a year. The man took the advice and stole a small book belonging to St Columba himself, and thereafter he proceeded to the Outer Hebrides, where he permitted people to read the book for a certain sum of money. The book was read with great avidity, as it contained all the 'Eòlais' [healing prayers, charms] composed by the saint for the curing of men and cattle. Thus it was that these 'Eòlais' came to be so well known in the Western Islands. The farmer went back to St Columba at the end of the year, having amassed a considerable fortune, and restored the book. The saint immediately burned the book, so that he might not on its account earn a reputation which he thought he did not deserve.

are sometimes reports about disturbance to cetaceans, and illegal killing of seals.

Much of Alan Stewart's work involves education. Wildlife crime officers and other organisations work hard to raise public awareness, often by visiting schools. Enlightening children to the importance of protecting wildlife is of vital importance.

The Wildlife Hospital

Urbanisation causes problems. There is far more injured wildlife found as a result of human activity than there is in the wilder parts of Scotland. Roads account for many thousands of casualties each year. Pollution and litter cause much distress, injury and death, and activities such as grass and hedge cutting, strimming and bonfire making, can all lead to severe injury and loss of life. Dogs and cats cause much damage to wildlife – uprooting nests, killing adult mammals and birds while they are out foraging for their young, and massacring whole nests of offspring. Young animals are also all too frequently picked up when thought of as abandoned. Most of these should have been left well alone, as in most cases the mother will return.

Dedicated husband and wife team Gay and Andy Christie with roe buck (G. & A. Christie)

There are small wildlife hospitals based around Scotland. Some are run by individuals who work tirelessly for the good of the creatures they are brought, and others are also set-up as charities. They fundraise and post information of their work on websites and through newsletters, and all require great dedication. The best wildlife hospitals are those that endeavour to return their casualties to the wild – often this can be very difficult.

It is vital to ensure that there is a constant available food source until the bird or animal has acclimatised. On occasions this may be for an indefinite period. A large percentage of mammals and birds reared by their own parents do not make it through their first winter – a hand-reared creature or one with even the smallest disability has an even lower chance.

Husband and wife team Gay and Andy Christie, from Beith in Ayrshire, run the largest independent wildlife hospital in Scotland, Hessilhead Wildlife Rescue Trust. It was set up in 1986 although they had been rescuing animals and birds for a good deal longer – indeed, their entire house and garden had been taken over by them. Up to 2011, they were treating an average of 3,000 casualties each year. Garden birds are their most common patients, followed by hedgehogs, swans, ducks, foxes, owls, and a dozen or so otters each year. They also receive a few seals, unusual raptors, pine martens and other creatures. Nothing is ever turned away. Now with a staff of four, and a regular team of 15 to 20 volunteers, they also have vet and conservation students, many from abroad, who can stay for up to six months. Their help is invaluable and there is often a constant exchange of ideas and information. The Christies

Poisoned buzzard (Alan Stewart)

Ace with Animals

Kelso vet Brian Wain was respectful of people like 'Tubby Anne' from 'up Hindhope' in the Cheviots. She had no scientific training but was 'ace with animals', he said: she had a tripod hound, a horse with no hoof, and she gave them all names. I asked him if he thought this was a female trait, remembering when no self-respecting zoologist would give an animal more than a number and a brief physical descriptor. Not at all, he said. He also knew a man near Kelso, very good at mending broken bones in birds and animals, and he gave them all names too. People would take sick animals to him, said the vet, without a trace of antipathy.

have a list of 200 volunteers who they call upon to drive casualties to the hospital.

Hessilhead is centred on 20 acres and includes a swan and seal pool, hedgehog unit, a surgery and x-ray facility, and over 60 outdoor aviaries and pens. Their logo has the words 'Rescue, Repair, Rehabilitate', and due to their incredible dedication and hard work, they both received the MBE for services to Scotland's wildlife in 2003.

The Scottish Society for the Prevention of Cruelty to Animals (SSPCA) opened a new state-of-the-art wildlife rehabilitation centre at Fishcross, Alloa, in 2012. They are the only specialised unit in Scotland for oiled-bird cleaning. They receive an average of 3,500 injured animals a year, including about 80 grey and 20 common seals. They

Young hedgehogs (Polly Pullar)

Iomhair Fletcher with recovering red deer calf (Polly Pullar)

constantly advise people to leave young pups found on beaches and instead to ring for advice before picking them up. Storms and human disturbance can separate pups from their mothers. The centre's manager, Colin Seddon, tries to educate both the public and members of his team so that they are aware of the moment when it is necessary to intervene. Seals in the Firth of Forth are monitored by the SSPCA, and those that are rehabilitated will be released back into the sea as soon as possible. The SSPCA will euthanise any casualties that are too badly damaged to be returned to the wild, and always endeavours to return animals and birds to their natural habitat where possible.

The beginnings of the animal welfare movement: from David Hume to the SSPCA

The urban wilds of nineteenth-century Scotland could be desperate places for human beings and also for other animals. Horses were worked hard and long, pulling carts, cabs and even buses. Abbatoirs were more or less unregulated. Cock-fighting and other blood sports were seen as quite acceptable, and were even glorified. An early voice of dissent came from the philosopher David Hume. Already, in the mid eighteenth century, he had suggested that 'the laws of humanity' bind us to treat animals with kindness and compassion – this at a time when other thinkers were either oblivious or frankly hostile. Hume read, and may have honed his ideas against those of the Cartesian philosopher Nicolas Malebranche, who argued that we have no duties at all towards animals; they were like wonderful machines – incapable of pleasure or pain, desire or fear. Had Malebranche ever met an animal, one wonders? In every croft and farmtoun, there were people who attended naturally to their animals' needs. On the big Lowland farms, the society known as 'The Horseman's Word' required new members to swear that they would never ill-treat any horse, or see ill done without reporting it.'

The Victorian city was another matter. In 1822 an Irish MP, Richard Martin ('Humanity Dick') steered the first animal welfare legislation through parliament in England. At first judges were reluctant to convict, seeing the matter as too trivial for the courts. Also, there was a widespread belief that animals exist to serve human needs, and for that reason alone. This Aristotelian idea had become firmly lodged in Christian theology in spite of the complex and nuanced picture in other parts of the tradition. A change of attitude was needed as much as the proper enforcement of Martin's law. To this end, the Society for the Prevention of Cruelty to Animals (later the RSPCA) was launched in a London coffee house in 1824. Fifteen years later, the Scottish Society (SSPCA) was convened.

The great and good were out in force for the inaugural meeting: the Lord Provost of Edinburgh, Sir James Forrest of Comiston, three members of parliament, several baronets, four senior military men, and a cohort of doctors, lawyers, ministers and other gentlemen. Several eminent churchmen also took an interest. Thomas Chalmers of the recently formed Free Church was one of the first patrons of the society. As early as 1826 he had been preaching from the text: 'The righteous man regardeth the life of his beast,' urging people to open their eyes and, in a remarkable turn of phrase, to extend their 'compassionate regard over the whole of sentient suffering nature'. Other patrons included Professor George Baird, a former Moderator and principal of the university, and two Episcopalian bishops. The only woman on the list of office-bearers was 'Mrs Gibson, patroness'. It would be good to know more about her, but this quiet activist had been paying preachers to win hearts and minds on the subject since 1825, and the Martha Gibson sermons could still be heard in Scottish towns well into the twentieth century. So the churches played their part, but the echoes from David Hume's dinner table in Edinburgh's New Town can also be felt in the society's opening statement, that 'cruelty to the brute creation is contrary to Scripture and humanity'.

There were many setbacks, but in 1850 a specifically Scottish Act of Parliament prohibited 'the ill-treatment and over-driving of animals' as well as 'fighting or baiting any bull, bear, badger, dog, cock or any other kind of animal'. Inspectors were appointed and paid, and branches began to be opened all over the country. The Highland and Agricultural Society joined up. In Dunfermline, 510 linen workers, all women, joined at a cost of a penny each. New challenges arose all the time. In the early 1870s horse-drawn trams began to be used. These were larger and heavier than buses, and the strain showed almost at once. A report commissioned in 1873 found that up to a third of Edinburgh's draught horses were lame, many too lame for any kind of work. There was particular concern about Leith Street, where the gradient could be lethal. Tracer horses (see page 245) were eventually introduced on this section. Over the years, the society pressed for other improvements: vehicles with brakes, water troughs, and nose bags. Cabbies who looked after their horses well could earn a sovereign and a silver badge. A licensing scheme was introduced for drovers, to prevent worn-out animals being walked over long distances. The inspection of slaughter houses became routine. A vigorous education programme was launched and schools were encouraged to include kindness to animals on the curriculum. Gradually, Britain became known as a nation of animal lovers, although animals continued to suffer, on the battlefield, in the laboratory and in food production, as well as from plain old-fashioned cruelty and neglect. New challenges arise all the time and we still need to 'open our eyes to the whole of sentient suffering nature', if only because all life is interconnected in a way which our ancestors glimpsed, but did not have to act on as urgently as we do now.

CHAPTER TEN

CREATURES OF THE MIND

Scotland has a long tradition of imaginary animals. The Loch Ness monster looms large in our tourist literature. The water horse was once believed to lurk in lochs and rivers across the land. The very term 'cryptozoology' – the study of lost or imaginary species – seems to have been coined by the Edinburgh-born naturalist Ivan T. Sanderson, who took a special interest in water monsters and yetis. In 1997, a whole new generation of dragons, centaurs, salamanders, basilisks, phoenixes, and hippogriffs emerged into a quiet corner of the same city, from the pen of J.K. Rowling. But creatures of the mind are not just for children. Glasgow novelist Alasdair Gray gave us 'dragonhide' and 'going salamander' as symptoms of psycho-social meltdown in his 1981 dystopia *Lanark,* and imaginary beasts feature in some of our earliest Scottish writing for adults, from the River Ness monster described by Adomnán of Iona in the seventh century, to the 'serpentis, leopardis, beris, unicornis and griffonis' which appear in the late medieval Buik of Alexander. Both Sir Gilbert Haye and John Barbour regaled their aristocratic readers with tales of lands infested by such beasts, and high-born heroes like Alexander the Great who rode undaunted through them.

Of course, what is imaginary today was less so, or not at all, to people living in a relatively unexplored world. In a sense, even today, all non-human animals are creatures of the mind since we can never know what it feels like to be one of them. It is hard enough to know what it feels like to be another human being, let alone a badger or a basking shark. All we have to go on is imagination – and it can take us far – but in pre-scientific times, imagination ruled to such an extent that the present author confesses to getting a bit impatient at times. Those of us who like our animals real can grow weary of fictions about creatures which exist only in the human mind. So, fantasy animals, who needs them? Do we need them at all? The evidence, from all over the world, suggests that we do, and that even if we could purge our thinking of them somehow, they would return in the form of daydreams, dreams and nightmares. They 'exist' because they give shape to certain kinds of experience. Monstrous, funny, awesome, disconcerting and mystical, many creatures of the mind were once believed to exist in exactly the same way as badgers and basking sharks. Others probably came about through garbled descriptions of animals which today are captured on camera. Is there still something out there? I know people who believe that there is. In other parts of the world this is mainstream, but few Scots would admit to it today, except perhaps in places like the Findhorn Foundation or the Tibetan centre at Eskdalemuir.

Opposite. The fourth tapestry in theStirling Tapestry project, entitled *The Unicorn Is Found* (© Historic Scotland)

Out of the Depths

A native tradition of water monsters first appears in writing at the end of the seventh century in Adomnán's Life of St Columba. While travelling in Pictland, the saint happens upon the grieving relatives of a man who had been savaged by a 'water beast' in the River Ness. Rashly, some might say, Columba sends another man into the water: 'the beast was lying low on the riverbed, its appetite not so much sated as whetted for prey. It could sense that the water above was stirred by the swimmer, and suddenly swam up to the surface, rushing open-mouthed with a great roar towards the man …' Columba makes the sign of the cross and commands the beast in the name of God to stop where it is. 'Do not touch the man,' he shouts. 'Go back at once.' He does not exterminate the creature – unlike many another Celtic hero – just sends it back where it belongs. Fear of drowning and fear of the abyss are both addressed here. Terror need not have the last word, suggests the storyteller: there is a power more ultimate than the beast.

Adomnán would have been familiar with biblical water monsters like Rahab and Leviathan and with comparable creatures from his native Ireland, but there were other sources to draw on as well. Visitors to Rome might have seen similar monsters represented there, the great sea dragon for example, which appears on the imperial Ara Pacis or 'altar of peace'. The Vikings would bring their own sea monster traditions. What these were we can only guess, but one Icelandic saga collection, the Prose Edda, describes a giant serpent, Jörmungand, who lives in the sea, encircles the whole world and is so powerful that even Thor will die fighting him in the end. The Viking-descended peoples of Orkney and Shetland believed in the Stoor Worm, a sea monster that could devour ships and sweep away whole villages with his tongue. In Ireland and Gaelic-speaking Scotland, a late-medieval story of Finn Mac Cumhaill tells how he slew not just local water monsters but also a monster from Greece – no less – which rises up from the depths of a loch and swallows him alive. Undeterred, Finn cuts the monster open from the inside and lives to fight another day and slay numerous other monsters in watery places, hills and remote glens. At the micro end of the scale, toothache was believed to be caused by a nasty little worm which went by various names and was treated with charms or water from a 'toothache well' if there happened to be one nearby. A similar mini-beast was believed to be the cause of colic in cattle. And what are bacteria and parasites but microscopic mini-beasts, some of them water-borne?

Beware the beast

Any kind of wilderness could hold hidden terrors. When the ice was heard cracking on Loch Awe, the 'big beast' was known to be at work. Another horror, *Biast Mhòr Bhàrasdail* (big beast of Barrisdale) was supposed to have been seen a couple of times, though usually only its footprints were found. It could be heard roaring in the vicinity of Loch Hourn and Loch Nevis, causing panic in dogs and cattle and scaring people out of their wits. This was a beast of modern times, first noticed, allegedly, in 1845.

Cautionary Tales

It is easy to imagine parents making use of such beliefs to keep their children safe. 'Keep off the ice' is the clear message of the beast of Loch Awe. Stories of the water horse may well have been told to warn children against playing at the water's edge or consorting with strangers in out-of-the-way places. Water horse stories are widespread and always cautionary. In Gaeldom, the *each-uisge* could live in the depths of almost any loch and stories abound of girls who met a good-looking man by the lochside and lay down with him, only to see, as he laid his head in their lap, the tell-tale strands of water-weed in his hair. If he fell asleep, you might escape unharmed; otherwise he would make off with you into the depths of the loch, or kill you and leave your heart and lungs on the shore, like the particularly nasty water horse on Raasay. But children were not the only target audience for water horse stories. One tells of a strange horse which was harnessed and worked well with

Water bull

The *tarbh-uisge* (water bull) was less common and in most of the surviving stories, relatively harmless. There is even a story from Argyll about a water bull which saved the honour of one of the shieling girls. One winter, a young man found a black bull dying of starvation on the shores of a loch. He fed the beast and cared for him till he was strong enough to fend for himself. That summer, his girlfriend went with the other women to the shielings, to tend the cattle and make butter and cheese. She wandered off on her own one evening, hoping perhaps for a secret visit from him but instead, she found a jealous former boyfriend lying in wait. He tries to carry her off, but suddenly a black bull appears, whisks her away and returns her to her mother unharmed. This is so unlike the expected outcome that it looks like deliberate re-working, an appeal to the better nature of young men. Courage and generosity are rewarded and the bull turns out to be a spirit whose good deeds win him release 'after three hundred years of bondage'. So, lads: rescuing maidens in distress is good for the soul; skill with animals gets the girl. A darker version survives in a Travellers' tale about a 'wee white bull' who invites a lassie to mount, then makes off with her, much like a water horse.

other horses, till the ploughman whipped him. Then, he bolted into the loch, taking the whole team with him.

The kelpie was the east of Scotland equivalent of the *each-uisge*. Some say they were one and the same, others that the kelpie was different. He was located mainly in rivers and streams and would drown anyone, male or female, who dared to mount him. He too could be caught and put to work, using a bridle sealed with the sign of the cross. In an east-coast variation of the banshee myth, it was said in fishing communities that the kelpie could be heard roaring before a loss at sea.

In the early twentieth century, the Baden-Powells, founders of the scouting movement, included kelpies among the subdivisions of a Brownie pack. 'We're the little Scottish kelpies, smart and quick and ready helpers'. If you were a kelpie rather than a sprite or a fairy, you sang this at the beginning of every meeting, but even at the age of eight it sounded unconvincing and a quick look in *Chambers Dictionary* confirmed that the little figure on my Brownie uniform was about as much like a 'real' kelpie as a guide dog is like a werewolf.

The Orcadian knoggelvi (nuckelavee) lived in the sea and could appear like a whale, a horse or a man, but he too seduced his victims, usually female, in lonely places near the shore. In Shetland, the njuggle lived in fresh water like the kelpie and could easily be mistaken for an ordinary horse or pony, but mount him, and with one flick of his turbo-charged tail he would be off with you and drown you in the nearest loch. Only a steel bridle could hold him.

Be Not Afraid

Sea serpents and mermaids were sometimes depicted in an ecclesiastical context. This might seem strange, but the medieval church was just as interested in unusual natural phenomena as anybody else. Also, it understood imaginary creatures symbolically as well as literally. Mermaids were

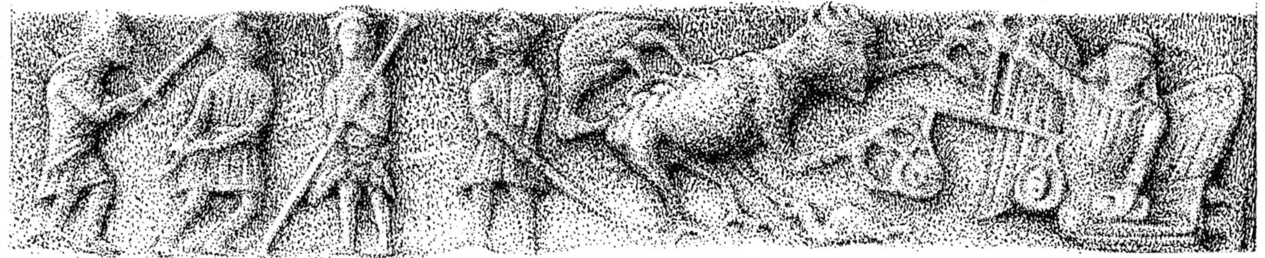

Detail of the south choir arcade at Iona Abbey (© RCAHMS. Licensor www.scran.ac.uk)

All kinds of animals appear in the margins of the Book of Kells. This stunning illuminated manuscript, now housed in Trinity College, Dublin, was probably begun on Iona before the monks moved headquarters to the relative safety of Ireland at the beginning of the ninth century. Some of the animals are naturalistic, mostly native species, but we also find creatures of the imagination. Folio 27v, for example, depicts a lion rampant with golden wings and, in the opposite quadrant, a calf or ox, with four spiky wings like a dragonfly. The lion represents St Mark, and the calf, St Luke. Together with an eagle and a winged man, they stand for the four evangelists as described by St Irenaeus of Lyon in the second century. He in turn had based them on St John's vision of the four 'living creatures' round the throne of God. Such surreal images draw the reader into a strange but half-familiar world. Winged but still earthly, they combine flesh and spirit in a way that is provocative and unsettling. We also find the occasional griffin, merman and outlandish bird as if to illustrate a world of infinite possibilities.

Trinity College Dublin, Book of Kells, f.27v

wreckers. No sailor wanted to see one. So while every cross is a reminder of the victory of life over death, the mermaid on the Campbelltown cross, for example, adds the assurance that nothing in all creation – neither in heights or depths – can separate people from the love of God. Another reason for monsters in an ecclesiastical context would be their appearance in the Bible as images for tyrannical kings and empires and for the devil himself. When an Irish stonemason carved a horrendous beast on the capital of a pillar in Iona abbey, some time during the fifteenth century, everyone would have known what that meant. They would also have recognised the winged figure of St Michael opposite him. The beast is cheating, tipping the scales of justice with an outstretched claw, but notice the bird pecking irreverently at the diel's bahookie. Nearby, a man holds another monster on a leash, and the bird appears again, tweaking the beak of a griffin many times its own size. More conventional images of sin and redemption can be

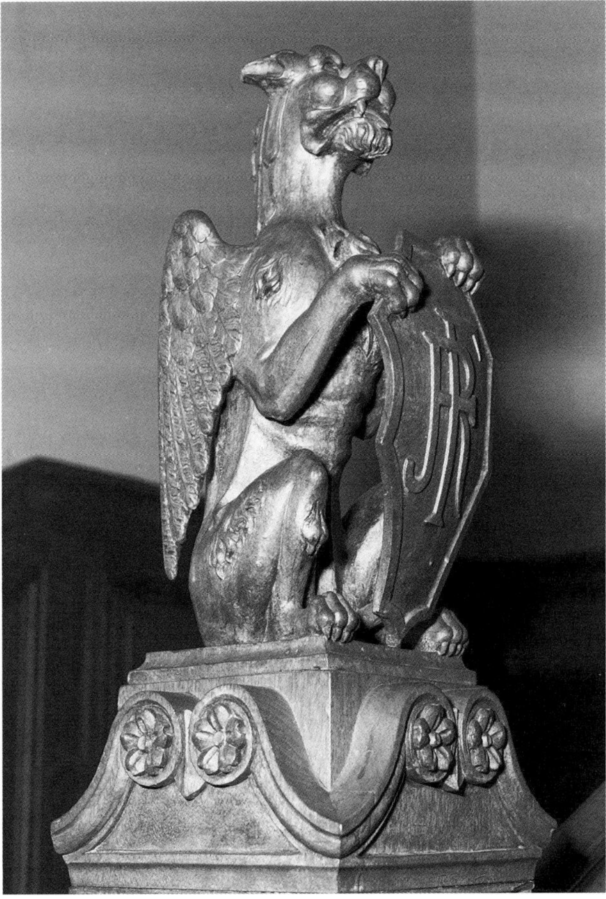

Top far left. On fire with lust? Salamanders were believed to live in fire, poison wells and destroy fruit trees. Here they infest the dreams of a recumbent figure. (Aberdeen Bestiary, University of Aberdeen, Univ. Lib. MS24, f.70r)

Left. Detail of griffin stair newel from No. 3 Rothesay Terrace, Edinburgh (© RCAHMS c/43419. Licensor www.scran.ac.uk)

Bottom left. One of the many dragons in the Murthly Hours (Trustees of the National Library of Scotland)

found alongside (the explusion from Eden, a virgin and child, a crucifixion scene) but the monster imagery also seems to say yes, there is evil in the world; no, it is not invincible. These carvings flourish only in one corner of the abbey, the rest is plain and simple, but they help to counter fear with faith and touches of humour.

Allegory and Symbol

None of the great medieval Bestiaries was compiled in Scotland, as far as I know. The splendid Aberdeen Bestiary did not arrive here till the seventeenth century; and the Murthly Hours, with its fantastic procession of dragons and monsters, was in the hands of the Stuarts of Lorne by the fifteenth century but was created in Paris some three hundred years earlier. However, scholars would have been aware of works like the *Physiologus,* an early Christian catalogue of animals and their symbolic meanings. They were certainly familiar with Isidore of Seville's *Etymologies* which contained similar material. From the thirteenth century onwards, they might also have known Aristotle's *De Animalia* (in Michael Scot's translation) and bestiaries south of the Border and abroad would have been seen and studied by travellers, along with the many fantastic beasts depicted in Roman, Greek and Middle-eastern art. These would be the most likely source for Scottish depictions of griffins, centaurs, phoenixes and unicorns. A griffin appears on the bestiary door of Dalmeny church near South Queensferry. If Isidore said there were griffins in the Hyperborean mountains, who, in Dalmeny, was in a position to argue? But it was their symbolic meaning that mattered to the medieval mind. Griffins combine the features of the eagle and the lion, with all of their powerful associations. Griffins were also believed to guard gold. Was this a warning to passing miscreants that the treasures of Dalmeny were protected by invisible forces, or was it simply a touch of grandeur on the part of artist and patron?

At times one senses the mind of a mystic at work. The tenth-century Irish text, *Tenga Bhith-Nua* (The Evernew Tongue) may or may not have been familiar in the west of Scotland, but it is too good to leave out. It begins, like some bestiaries, with a Creation story, but develops into a kind of visionary travelogue, following the journey of the sun after dark. It describes sea monsters, whales, a beast which causes the tides, and seems about to embark on a full-blown bestiary when the author becomes captivated by birds:

> Firstly, there are the birds of the island of Naboth. There has not shone on earth a colour or radiance which does not shine from their wings. They shed tears in cold and snow. They rejoice in the heat and brightness of summer. They awaken always at midnight and sing melodies as sweet as harpstrings. As for the birds of Sabes, their wings shine in the night time like lighted candles. Any affliction which is touched by their wings or by their shadow when in flight is cured. They assume a torpid inertia in the season of winter and cold, and they awaken at Mayday. In their slumbers they sing gentle music like the sound of the wind.

He or she also tells us about the birds of Naboth, Sabes and Abuad, somewhere to the east of Africa. At midnight, we are told, they sing about the 'wonderful innumerable mysteries' of Creation and, at the end of the night, about Doomsday and the life to come. Only gradually does it become apparent that we have left even Africa behind and crossed into another realm altogether, for 'if the race of Adam should hear the music of those birds, they would not be parted from the sound gladly or with pleasure, but rather with grief, longing, and sadness until they die from weeping.'

High and Mighty

Animal imagery is often used to assert identity, power and status and this is just as true of imaginary beasts as of real ones. Most of the animals on Pictish carved stones are recognisable from nature, but the 'swimming elephant' is definitely a creature of the mind. With its elongated nose and fluid limbs, it has sometimes been compared to a dolphin, but it is manifestly a 'beastie' in its own right. If bulls and horses could be associated with particular people or social groups, perhaps the beastie was too. Was it perhaps akin to water monsters and kelpies? Centaurs, two-headed animals, fish-tailed men and bird-headed men also appear on Pictish carved stones, less commonly than the beastie, but equally enigmatic.

And so to unicorns, minotaurs, bellerophonts, were-

Axe-wielding centaur from Glamis (drawn by Edith Brand Hannah)

wolves, winged horses and other members of parliament. These are the most noble lords in Henryson's 'Parliament of the Four-footed Beasts.' It tells how the fox (referred to here as 'Lawrence') was called before the highest court in the land, charged with theft. He had stolen and devoured a lamb, despite being on a vegetarian diet as a penance for raiding the henhouse. The unicorn acts as herald, summoning all the animals to court. Every creature, high and low, comes to the trial, but the most fantastic beasts represent the nobility. The lion is, of course, the king. He takes his throne and the other beasts process in, headed by the most preposterous and fantastic. Readers at the time must have loved guessing who these creatures represented. Bellerophon [sic] in *The Iliad* is the rider of Pegasus and

From 'The Parliament of Fourfouttit Beasts'

Thre leopardis come a croun off massie gold
Beirand thay brocht vnto that hillis hicht,
With iaspis ionit, and royall rubeis rold,
And mony diueris dyamontis dicht,
With pollis proud ane palzeoun doun thay picht.
And in that throne, thair sat ane wild lyoun,
In rob royall, with sceptour, swerd, and croun.

Efter the tennour off the cry befoir,
That gais on fut all beistis in the eird,
As thay commandit wer withoutin moir,
Befoir thair lord the lyoun thay appeird.
And quhat thay wer to me as lowrence leird.
I sall reheirs ane part off euerilk kynd,
Als fer as now occurris to my mynd.

The minotaur, ane monster meruelous,
Bellerophont that beist of bastardrie.
The warwolff, and the pegase perillous,
Transformit be assent of sorcerie.
The linx the tiger full off tiranie:
The elephant: and eik the dromedarie:
The cameill with his cran-nek furth can carie.

Robert Henryson

Top. Cross slab from Gask, near Perth (drawn by Edith Brand Hannah)

Bottom. The swimming elephant from the Dunfallandy Stone (© Historic Scotland)

killer of a fire-breathing monster. Here he is 'that beist of bastardrie'. But the key to Henryson's satire has been lost, so we will never know who blushed and spluttered as the *Fables* were read aloud.

A red lion rampant has figured on the royal arms of Scotland since the twelfth century. By Henryson's time, the unicorn had been adopted as well and the royal account book for the reign of James IV has several entries for items depicting unicorns: a gilded ornament, a painting, an embroidered 'covering'. One of the king's heralds was known as 'the unicorn' hence his role in 'The Parliament of the Four-footed Beasts'. King James V inherited his father's enthusiasm for unicorns. His tapestry collection included a series known as 'The Hunting of the Unicorn' which is presently being re-created in Stirling Castle.

The subject is allegorical and can be read in a number of different ways. According to the *Physiologos* and Isidore, the unicorn was an animal so fierce and strong that he could never be taken alive, except by trickery. He would grow meek, however, at the sight of a virgin's breast. Then he would lay his head quietly in her lap, and in this vulnerable state could be captured and killed. This could be presented in spiritual terms as an allegory of the Incarnation: the power and the wisdom of God, born into the world, nursed by Mary, vulnerable in his humanity, ensnared by enemies. Some unicorn tapestries emphasised the human dimension of this relationship, dwelling on the love and faithfulness of the woman, but 'The Hunt of the Unicorn' includes a scene in which the slain unicorn is clearly a prize, borne aloft by triumphant hunters. Unicorns (always male) were associated with physical as well as spiritual prowess, so perhaps the possession of such a creature, even in threads and stitches, was intended to enhance the reputation of the king by suggesting, in an audacious but suitably ambiguous way, his divine right and mastery over everything, and also his wealth. 'To the king, to offir in the Cors Kyrk of Pablis, ane vnicorn' – this from the Treasury accounts of 1488. Both James IV and V issued gold coins known as unicorns, hence this bizarre-sounding donation to the Cross Kirk, Peebles. Unicorn horn (sourced from rhinoceros or narwhal) was a precious and extremely expensive substance, believed to detect and cure poison. James VI and I had one among his treasures and either he or his translators made the most of his association with unicorns by using the word several times in the King James version of the Bible (1611) though the original languages scarcely warrant it. The animal in question, now usually translated as 'wild ox', was a byword for strength, and also for tribes and kings exalted by divine favour. What ruler could resist? Certainly not James.

We do not know where the Stirling unicorn tapestries

Unicorn bearing arms of King James V, Holyrood, Edinburgh (Mary Low)

hung in the castle originally. They are presently being re-created for the Queen's apartments, but were probably carried from place to place and used in other royal residences as well. So when the Scots lords saw the Christ-like unicorn run through with spears, did they pause in their machinations? And when the ladies of Scotland saw the unicorn, did their minds turn to theology? Perhaps, in that more religious age, but thoughts of human love and beauty can never have been far away. For all the pathos and eros of these images, the unicorn was a prize of the highest order, and the lion and the unicorn together were a claim to the highest status, as if the kings of Scotland were a sept of the court of heaven.

Just So Stories

Again, imaginary beasts were used to explain curious features of the landscape. Alexander Carmichael quotes Rona man, Angus Gunn, to the effect that deep scores in the rocks in North Rona were the marks of giant claws. In fact, they were caused by glaciation, but Carmichael preserves the story that Rona was once inhabited by griffins, lions and poisonous reptiles which scrambled backwards into the sea when St Ronan arrived there to build a hermitage. Similarly, blackened bog oak and fir in the peatlands of Caithness and Sutherland were said to be the remains of a giant forest, incinerated by the breath of the '*beisd an dubh ghiubhais*' (beast of the black firs) whose burial place ('the stone of the beast') used to be pointed out between Dornoch and Skibo.

If cattle did particularly well against expectations, or if calves were born with unusual features, this was sometimes said to be the work of the *tarbh uisge* (water bull); or they might be sea cattle which had come ashore from fairy farms under the waves, like the fine-looking cattle of Luskentyre or Bernerary. There was nothing frightening about sea

Capturing the sea cattle

There would be herdsmen with [the sea cattle] and they would be ashore until the tide turned. And when the tide turned, then whoever was in charge, or whatever herdsman there was out at sea, he would come in close to the shore and cry:

> *Donnach, Tromach, Sgiathan, Liathan!*
> *Thigeadh an crodh-laoigh*
> *Co-dhiùbh thig na dh'fhan na buachaillean.*

(Donnach, Tromach, Sgiathan, Liathan! Let the milch cows come, whether the herdsmen come or stay.) And that wasn't the end of it. That was the moment the people who were in a hide – as they called it – on the machair were waiting for, holding handfuls of earth, and when they heard this they would come down from the dunes [where they had been] waiting for this shout out at sea, and when one of the cattle passed them they would throw a handful of earth at the side or at the head of the animal, and that animal would stop in its tracks. They might well get two or three that night, and they could get as many more again as long as the period, as it were a set period, lasted during which they came ashore – a season as it were – and after that they were finished till next year again. Some of the old people 'believed ... that there was some of the stock of the sea cattle in our part of the country till the present day ... They believed ... that you could recognise them .... and they were supposed to be hornless ... they were polled.' They used to come ashore on the machair on the west side of North Uist and Benbecula. People would seriously discuss how long they would stay ashore, what they would eat etc. A plant called 'gortan or something' which grew on the machair ...

An unusual pet

Dòmhnall Gorm (Blue Donald) MacDonald kept a monster in one of his houses, Castle Tioram in Moidart. Perhaps it was troublesome, who knows, but one day he turned the key on it and set sail for his other home in South Uist, leaving the creature behind. It was not best pleased. How it got out, no one knows, but soon it was observed coming after him 'with such fury that it created a storm which almost sank the boat'. The crew hauled it on board, the waves died down and they crossed the Minch in safety. This story was collected in 1959, in Smearisary, near Castle Tioram. It is probably just a tall tale, but exotic animals were sometimes kept in private collections, then as now. Could it be that Dòmhnall Gorm was keeping an unsuitable pet?

cattle, but they did need careful handling. The story was told of a Mingulay man who found a strange cow among his herd. 'She was a good milker, better than the others, so he kept every calf that came from her and did away with all his own. The cattle at that time were kept under the same roof as the folk, and this night the old man was talking to his wife about the stray cow getting rather old, and they decided to kill it next day. In the morning, when he let them out, the old cow made for the shore, and all the rest followed her and disappeared into the sea. That night the old man was without a cow to his name.' Sea cattle only came ashore under certain conditions: 'the moon had to be in a particular phase so that it and the tide worked together that night. And it was when the tide was almost out, full ebb, that was when the sea cattle came to land, so they said.' Peter Morrison of Grimsay described how people used to lie in wait for them, although it was more than 60 years since he had heard about such matters, he said. His own scepticism shows through, but these were the thrillers and sci-fi films of their day. Of course, no one would ever 'borrow' a bull or rustle cattle on moonlit nights when the tide was exceptionally low, would they now?

Tall Tales

The desire to tell a good story is an irrepressible part of the tradition. After all, who wants to listen to a dull story, let alone remember it or pass it on? Mischief enters the equation from time to time. For example, John Francis Campbell collected various accounts of a creature called the 'boobrie', including an 'eye-witness' description from a man who swore he had waded up to his shoulders in a loch one February morning, hoping to get a shot at it. The boobrie could appear in three forms: as a water horse, a water bull or a bird. On this occasion, it was a bird. It dived as soon as he drew near, but he was able to give a 'most satisfactory account' of it, in exactly the kind of terms a Victorian naturalist might require ... Forbes and Campbell both thought the boobrie might have been a bittern, but traditions evolve with the communities that make them and earnest visitors (sportsmen and bird-watchers included) would do well to remember the wicked Highland sense of humour.

A similar mischief is at work in two new-style kelpie stories published by John Milne in the *Aberdeen Weekly Journal* in 1903. The first tells how Kelpie was in the habit of stealing from a kitchen on the banks of the Ugie. One night, the river was in flood and the woman of the house relaxed, thinking that for once, Kelpie would be stuck on

Ornithological notes

'In form and colour the Boobrie strongly resembles the Great Northern Diver, with the exception of the white on the neck and breast; the wings of both, bearing about the same proportion to the size of their bodies, appear to have been given them by nature more for the purpose of assisting them in swimming under water, than flying. In size of body he is larger than seventeen of the biggest eagles put together. His neck is two feet eleven inches long, and twenty-three inches in circumference, his bill is about seventeen inches long, black in colour, measuring round the root about eleven inches; for the first twelve inches the bill is straight, but after that assumes the shape of an eagle's, and of proportionate strength. His legs are remarkably short for his size, black in colour, but tremendously powerful, the feet are webbed till within five inches of the toes, which then terminate in immense claws of most destructive nature. The print of his foot on the mud at the east end of the lake (as accurately measured by an authority) covers the space generally contained within the span of a large wide-spreading pair of red deer's horns. The sound he utters resembles that of a large bull in his most angry humours, but much superior in strength. The favourite food of the Boobrie is the flesh of calves; failing them he feeds upon sheep or lambs, as suits him.'

the other side. Not so. He sneaked over by the newly built bridge at New Deer and stole her brose as usual. Even kelpies move with the times, it seems. Another of Milne's stories pokes gentle fun at the Horseman's Word traditions:

> Sometimes Kelpie was taken and wrought as a horse. The branks and the mystical crosses and strokes on the cheek could never be taken from his head nor the bit from his mouth. It is reported that a Kelpie from the Ugie was taken by a man in the locality and worked as a horse most of the winter. In the spring when food got dry and scarce, Kelpie got very lean. One day the man was away from home, and the wife thinking he would be better of a bite of young grass led the kelpie out, and believing that he would be better without the bit, slipped out the branks. Kelpie at once flung up his heels, and galloped away crying –
>
> 'Harrow, harrow wi' fa ye like,
> Yes'e harrow nae mair wi' me, ye tyke.'

Kelpies (Alan McGowan)

From monster of the deep to folk hero, Kelpie had come a long way. And what about the Coddy, the famous storyteller from Barra, describing his father's encounter with a 'tremendous beast' while out fishing for lobster. The Coddy describes in detail the strange bubbles breaking the surface, the enormity of the creature's back, how the men made their escape. Then, just as the story seems to be over, he adds solemnly that 'after hearing so much about monsters nowadays, it is very probable that it was a sea monster – of what nature nobody can say.' Credulity or deadpan delivery, who can say? The Coddy was famous for his dry wit.

A Multipurpose Monster

Some imaginary beasts are multi-purpose. The story of MacMhuirich's beast 'explains' remarkable features of the landscape in South Uist, showcases the wit and cunning of a famous bard, extends the range of the water monster tradition, and manages to be spooky and entertaining, all at once. It tells how MacMhuirich, bard and scholar to the Clanranald chiefs, was out on the moor one day when he found a pathetic kitten-like creature shivering beneath a rock. He brings it home. His wife is horrified and orders him to take it outside immediately, but the bard insists on keeping it for a while, to see what happens. It turns out that he has brought home 'the little whelp of the Great Beast' and pretty soon, its mother comes looking for it, threatening to fight MacMhuirich unless her 'gentle, soft, intimate, only-beloved prancing-paws (?) baby' is restored to her right away. The bard refuses and demands a ransom. First the monster must build a causeway, then another; then carry home the peats from the moor, thatch a house with feathers and many other onerous tasks. All these it does quite easily. Eventually, the bard makes a totally impossible demand and the monster gives up. At this, MacMhuirich relents and returns the little animal to its mother. She lifts her onto one shoulder and heads back into the wilderness, singing. What proof do we have of all this? The stepping stones on Loch Druidibeag are the remains of the causeway, of course.

Large as life, or even imaginary . . .

This shy denizen of the Lowlands and Southern Uplands was thought to be extinct in the wild until 1957, when a pregnant female haggis was discovered in the boiler room of Crichton Royal Psychiatric Hospital, Dumfries. Caretaker Willie B. Leavis could hardly believe his eyes. 'There she was, large as life, just looking for a wee quiet place to have her kitts.' Willie was a gentle man or the outcome could have been very different: wild haggis is a gourmet dish, far superior to the farmed variety. Indeed, it is a well-kept secret among butchers that the domestic haggis is not in fact a haggis at all, but a species of hedgehog. Following Willie's discovery, a breeding programme was established and hundreds of the sharp-clawed rough-coated creatures were released back into the wild. They did exceptionally well, though round-the-clock watches had to be maintained to protect them from poachers. Immature haggis claws are a close match for a costly ingredient in Chinese medicine where they are believed to have aphrodisiac properties. Similar beliefs in Scotland may have contributed to the collapse of the wild population following the famous exhortation of the Ayrshire bard Robert Burns to 'Gie her a haggis'.

Happily, by 2008 numbers had recovered to such an extent that the traditional winter sport of haggis hunting could be resumed under licence in a number of locations. The Selkirk Meet takes place in January and attracts visitors from as far afield as New York and Beijing. Fortified with a stirrup cup and led by pipers, the hunters, young and old alike, make their way to The Hill armed with baggie nets, bows and arrows and accompanied by dogs. In a good year, they take home fifteen or twenty. The rest are released unharmed. Haggis can now also be spotted on the internet. This innovative project has webcams trained on a variety of habitats, from traditional lek sites where the males gather to display each year, to city centres and Highland castles. Click and report your sightings. Already this has proved beyond doubt that the common haggis is extending its range. There have been reports of sightings from as far west as Berneray and visitors to St Kilda are now routinely invited to check their luggage. 'It's just a precaution' said a spokesman for Scottish Natural Heritage, 'but the lowland haggis could pose a threat to its close cousin *Maragus Niger,* a native of the Western Isles.' Local opinion is divided on the subject, but Stornoway businessman Tormod MacLeod is unconcerned. 'The Marag will hold its own,' he said. 'It's a tenacious beast.'

NOTES

INTRODUCTION

Tam Lin, p. xi
Anon., *Scottish Ballads*, ed. Emily Lyle Edinburgh, 1994, p. 13.

John Calvin, p. xii
Calvin's Commentaries: The Epistles of Paul the Apostle to The Romans and to the Thessalonians, ed. D.W. Torrance and T.F. Torrance, trans. Ross Mackenzie, London and Edinburgh, 1961, pp. 173–4.

'Life be near you, poor beast', p. xii
Alexander Carmichael, *Carmina Gadelica* II.143, pp. 52–3. Source given as Donald MacPherson, Griminish, Benbecula, ibid. p. 378; For further discussion see Mary Low, 'The spiritual status of animals in *Carmina Gadelica,*' in *Cànan &Cultar / Language & Culture, Rannsachadh na Gàidhlig* 3, ed. Wilson McLeod, James E. Fraser and Anja Gunderloch, Edinburgh, 2006, pp. 235–52.

Chronicle of Melrose, p. xii
Stevenson, Joseph., *Chronica de Mailros*, Edinburgh, 1835, year 1263.

Benedicite, p. xii
From 'The Fox, the wolf and the farmer' Daniel 3.57–88; Henryson, R., *The Complete Works*, ed. Parkinson, D., Kalamazoo, 2010, p. 82, lines 2235–44; www.lib.rochester.edu/camelot/teams/pdrhffrm.htm

The tenant of Fladda Chain, p. xiii
Martin, Martin. *Description of the Western Islands of Scotland*, second edition, Edinburgh, 1981, p. 167–8.

CHAPTER ONE: Mountain

The deer in Gaelic literature, p. 5
Kuno Meyer, *Ancient Irish Poetry*, London, 1911, p. 59, from the late twelfth century *Acallam na Senórach* (Colloquy of the Ancients).
John Frances Campbell, *Leabhar na Feinne*, London, 1872, p. 198; John Gregorson Campbell, ed. Ronald Black as *The Gaelic Otherworld,* Edinburgh, 2005, pp. 14, 65–7, 71; Alexander Carmichael, *Carmina Gadelica (CG)*, vol. II, pp. 22–3 ; Alexander Forbes, *Gaelic Names of Beasts (mammalia), Birds, Fishes, Insects, Reptiles etc*, Edinburgh, 1905, pp. 124–30; Dathi O hOgain, D., *Myth, Legend & Romance*, London, 1990, p. 350.
Margaret Faye Shaw, *Folksongs and Folklore of South Uist,* Edinburgh, 1999, pp. 152–3, 168–9; Martin Martin, *Description of the Western Islands of Scotland*, second edition, Edinburgh, 1981, p. 107; Angus MacLeod, Orain Dhonnchaidh Bhàn/*The Songs of Duncan Bàn MacIntyre*, Edinburgh, 1978, pp. 196–225; George Henderson, *Survivals in Belief among the Celts*, Glasgow, 1911, pp. 124–5, citing *The Glasgow Herald* 20 Aug. 1910 (the story came originally from Duncan Whyte, an 8th-generation descendent of the forester and ancestor of a family known to Mary Low).

Finn Mac Cumhail's Bran, p. 6
Eoin MacNeill, *Duanaire Finn / Book of the Lays of Finn*, vol. 1, Irish Texts Society 7, Dublin, 1908, pp. 38, 140; Gerard Murphy, *Duanaire Finn/Book of the Lays of Finn*, vol. 2, Irish Texts Society 28, Dublin, 1933, p. 187.
Angus MacLellan, *Stories from South Uist*, Edinburgh, 1997, pp. 3–13.
See also Forbes, *Names*, pp. 137–41.

Eagle myths, p. 8
Martin, *Description,* pp. 26, 299; *Tocher* 50, p. 397; Carmichael, *CG* I. pp. 156–7, collected from Neill Morrison, a shepherd on Pabbay. For quarter day offerings, see Thomas Pennant, *A Tour in Scotland* 1769, ed. Brian D. Osborne, Edinburgh, 2000, pp. 68–9.
Campbell, J.F., *Popular Tales of the West Highlands,* vol. I., Hounslow, 1983 [1860], pp. 168–80; William MacGillivray, *A Hebridean Naturalist's Journal*, 1817–1818, ed. Robert Ralph, Stornoway, 1996, pp. 100–1; Hull, E., 'The Hawk of Achill, or the Legend of the Oldest Animals', *Folklore,* Dec. 1932, pp. 376–409.

The falcon, the dog and the otter, p. 11
Campbell, J.F., *Tales,* vol. I pp. 1–24, from the Gaelic of James Wilson, Islay, 1859, translation by Mary Low.

The young king of Assaroe, p. 12
Campbell, J.F., *Tales,* vol. I pp. 1–24, from the Gaelic of James Wilson, Islay, 1859, translation by Mary Low.

Raven knowledge, p. 13
R.I. Best 'Prognostications of the raven and the wren' *Eriu* VIII, Dublin, 1916, pp. 120–6; *The Poetic Edda*, trans. Henry Adams Bellows, intro. by William O. Cord, Lampeter, 1991, pp. 67, 74; John Lorne Campbell and Trevor H. Hall, *Strange Things*, Edinburgh, 2006, p. 312; Forbes, *Names*, pp. 324–8.

Goat placenames, p. 14
Forbes, *Names*, pp.164–6.
Blending in, p. 17
Acts of the Parliaments of Scotland, IV 628/2, Thomson, T., Innes, C. (eds), Record Commission, Edinburgh, 1814–75.

CHAPTER TWO: Moor and Bog

Song: Composed in August, p. 22
Complete Poems and Songs of Robert Burns, ed. James Barke, Glasgow 1995, pp. 362–3.
Jock o' Hazeldean, p.31
Scottish Songs, ed. Chris Findlater and Mairi Campbell, New Lanark 2003, pp. 92–3.
Twa Corbies, p. 33
Emily Lyle, *Scottish Ballads,* Edinburgh, 1994, p. 263; Anne Ross, *Pagan Celtic Britain*, London, 1992, pp. 366–8, 281–4.
John Hewit, SSS SA 1956.141.A5. Recorded by Calum Maclean.
Cuckoo proverbs, p. 36
Crombie T206T. Campbell, J.G., *Otherworld,* p. 553; Campbell, J.L., *Rites*, pp. 35–7; Ross, 'Fil o ro' in Anne Lorne Gillies, *Songs of Gaelic Scotland*, Edinburgh, 2010, pp. 392–3; Hewit, SSS SA 1956.141.A5.
Fox and fable, p. 38
Henryson, Robert, *Moral Fables Of Aesop the Phrygian,* ed. Gopen, G.D., Notre Dame, 1987, pp. 61–81, 141–169; Campbell, J.F., *Tales*, vol. III, pp. 102–5.
Carmichael, *CG* II, pp. 128–9; Campbell, J.F., *Tales*, I, p. 276; Carmichael-Watson, *CG* IV, p. 248; *Dictionary of the Scots Language* (DSL) http://www.dsl.ac.uk/dsl/ s.v. 'tod'.
Snipe proverb, p. 44
Forbes, *Names,* p. 333.
Carmichael, *CG* II, pp. 180–1; cf. II, pp. 178–9.
Adders and serpents, p. 45
Forbes, *Names,* pp. 451–6.
Campbell, *Otherworld,* p. 379; Stewart, A., *Nether Lochaber*, p. 180; Genesis 3.15.
Stewart, W.G. *Popular Superstitions and Festive Amusements of the Highlanders of Scotland*, London, 1851, pp. 53–6; Campbell, J.F., *Popular Tales* II, pp. 377–80.
Serpent iconography, p. 46
CG I, p. 169.

CHAPTER THREE: Woods

Nuisance of the glen, p. 53
Forbes, *Names,* p. 202; Carmichael, *CG* I, pp. 208–9; Pennant, *Tour*, pp. 68–9.
The indomitable wren, p. 56
Crombie ms. T206T. Collected in Keith, Aberdeenshire.
Forbes, *Names*, pp. 347–9.
King David and the deer, p. 61
History of Croniklis of Scotland be Maister Hector Boece, translatit be Maister Johne Bellende, Edinburgh, c. 1530, book 12, fo. Lxxxiiii, trans. Mary Low.
The smelly polecat, p. 62
Carmichael, *CG* I, 66, pp. 156–7; II, 136, pp. 34–5.
Poems of Alexander Montgomerie, ed. George Stevenson, Scottish Texts Society, Edinburgh, 1910, p. 136.
The mean kite, p. 64
Crombie MS. T206 T.
Are Ye Sleepin', Maggie?, p. 69
Tannahill, *Poems and Songs, chiefly in the Scottish Dialect*, Paisley 1807, pp. 188–9.
Hoolets old and new, p. 70
Dòmhnall Mac Fhionnlaigh nan Dan, *Oran na Comhachaig / The Owl of Strone,* ed. John Mackechnie, Glasgow 1946; Meyer, K., *Poetry,* pp. 90–3; MacNeill, E., *Duanaire,* vol. I, and Murphy, G., *Duanaire,* vols.2 and 3, Irish Texts Society 28 and 43, Dublin 1933 and 1953, passim but especially vol. 2, pp. 15, 183, 187.
Robert Hay, 'The Forgotten "Forth and Clyde"', *The Scots Magazine,* January 1951.
The stone hedgehog, p. 71
Stewart, *Nether Lochaber,* p. 384; Forbes, *Names*, p. 170.
Wildcat reflections, p. 72
MacGillivray, *Journal*, p. 21.
Friar Wolf Waitskaith, D.D, p. 78
Robert Henryson, *Moral Fables*, ed. George Gopen, Indiana, 1987, pp.72–81; John Gower, *Confessio Amantis* 4.I.1167.
Campbell, J.F., *Tales* I. pp. 281–3.
The Pictish wolf, p. 79
Sally Foster, *The St Andrews Sarcophagus: a Pictish Masterpiece and its International Connection,* Dublin 1998, passim; biblical background: 1 Samuel 17.34–36; John 10.10.
The Brown Bear of the Green Glen, p. 80
Martial, *Liber Spectaculorum* VII in *Martialis Epigrammata,* ed. Heraeus, W. and Borovskij, J., Leipzig 1976/82.
Campbell, J.F., *Tales* I, pp. 168 –180. Collected in Inverary from John MacDonald, travelling tinsmith, in May 1859, trans Mary Low.
The Dunadd boar, p. 81
Sally Foster, *Picts, Gaels and Scots,* Edinburgh,1996, pp. 38–9.
The great boar of Glenshee, p. 81
Diarmaid and the boar. 'The Death of Diarmaid' from manuscript collection of James MacGregor, Dean of Lismore, The Book of the Dean of Lismore, 1512. Ascribed to Ailean mac Ruairdhri, pp.30–34, probably C15. Oral version recorded in Barra, SA 1976.190.B4

CHAPTER FOUR: Lochs and Rivers

St Cuthbert and the osprey, p. 91
Anonymous Life of Cuthbert II. 5, *Two Lives of St Cuthbert*, ed. Bertram Colgrave, Cambridge, 1940; Mary Low, *St Cuthbert's Way*, Glasgow, 2000, pp. 181–2.
Forbes, *Names*, p. 266.
The fox and the goose, p. 96
Campbell, J.F., *Tales* I, p. 275 as told by J. MacLeod, fisherman on the Laxford, Sutherland.

Cù Chulainn and the bird women, p. 97
'The Wasting Sickness of Cù Chulainn' in Jeffrey Gantz, Early *Irish Myths and Sagas*, London 1981, pp. 155–78; O hOgain, *Myth,* London 1990, pp. 271–2; Campbell, J.G., *Otherworld*, pp. 156, 213, 216.

The regal swan, p. 98
James, Viscount of Stair, *The Institutions of the Law of Scotland*: new ed. by John S. More, Edinburgh, 1832 vol.1, p. 240; Martin, *Description*, pp. 70–1; Raghnall MacilleDhuibh (Ronald Black), 'Vowing on the swan' in 'The Quern-Dust Calendar', *West Highland Free Press*, 13 July 2006; Shaw, *Folksongs*, pp. 214–5, 104–5; Carmichael, *CG* I, pp. 310–13; SSS SA 1958.88.B11 (Argyll), 1976, p. 190 (Barra).
Mary Low, 'Adomnán among the Bird Hunters', in *Adomnán of Iona,* ed. Jonathan Wooding et al., Dublin 2010, p. 232; 'Dumbaris Dirge to the King', *Poems of William Dunbar,* ed. Priscilla Bawcutt, Glasgow 1998, I, 275.

Tàladh (Lullaby of the swan), p. 100
Carmichael, *CG* II, pp. 194–201, trans Mary Low with thanks to the reciter's great nephew, Calum Laing; cf. *CG* IV, pp. 28–9.

A poaching tale, p. 105
Carmichael Watson, J, *CG,* IV, Edinburgh 1941, pp. 9–10, trans Mary Low.

Finn and the wisdom fish, p. 106
Low, *Celtic Christianity and Nature*, Edinburgh 1996, 68–9; 76–8; Campbell, J.F., *The Fians, Waifs and Strays of Celtic Tradition*, Argyllshire Series IV, London, 1891, p. 19ff; MacLellan, *Stories*, pp. 7–8.

Trout in holy wells, p. 108
Martin, *Description*, pp. 140–1; *Old Statistical Account, 1791–99*, vol.2, p. 556; Rev. D. Lamont, *Strath*, Isle of Skye, Glasgow, 1913, p. 162; Low, *Celtic Christianity,* pp. 76–78

The king frog of Morvern, p. *112*
Campbell, J.G., *Otherworld*, pp. 221–2, 486.

Deadly eel stew, p. 114
Lyle, *Ballads*, pp. 257–8.

CHAPTER FIVE: The Sea

Giant cod, p. 121
SSS SA 1953.168.6b; *Tocher* 2, pp. 83–5.

Fish or flesh?, p. 122
James Hall, *Travels in Scotland*, London, 1807, vol. I, pp. 98–9.

Dinno burn me beans, p. 123
Ernest Marwick, *The Folklore of Orkney and Shetland,* Edinburgh 2000, pp. 75–6; Gregor, 'Notes', p. 146; Anson, *Fisher*, p. 24.

Shellfish aplenty, p. 127
Martin, *Description,* p.145.

Shellfish lore, p. 129
Campbell, J.G., *Otherworld,* pp. 548, 540, 136; SSS SA 1968.88, Islay; 1969.151, Tiree; 1970.341, Jura; Shaw, *Folksongs*, p. 47.

The servant of Bride, p. 131
Campbell, J.F., *Tales*, I. 283; Carmichael Watson, *CG* IV, pp.10–11; Tom Tulloch of Yell, Shetland, SSS. SA 1974.207.A1b.

Long-tailed ducks in Tiree, p. 132
Carmichael, *CG* II, p. 312; George Seton heard this from a Mr Grey who had been listening to long-tailed ducks off Dunbar. Seton, G., *St Kilda*, Edinburgh 2000 [1878] p. 120.

The salted bishop, p. 136
Martin, *Description*, p. 158; *Curiosities of Art and Nature: the new annotated and illustrated edition of Martin Martin's Classic "A Description of the Western Islands of Scotland"*, ed. M. Robson, 2003, pp. 130, 166.

Loupers, p. 139
James Robertson, *Tour through the Western Islands*, 1768, p. 17; *The One that Got Away* (otter) SSS, RL.1476.A.3.

St Brendan and the Whale, p. 142
The Voyage of St Brendan, trans. John J. O'Meara, Gerrards Cross 1991, pp. 18–19, cf. pp. 39– 40.

Heron proverbs, p. 147
Shaw, *Songs, Folksongs and Folklore of South Uist*, Edinburgh, 1999, p. 38; Campbell, J.G., *The Celtic Otherworld*, ed. Ronald Black, pp. 132, 388–9; Gerald of Wales, *Expugnatio* I.33; Carmichael, A., CG II., 52–3 where the threat is from three 'crooked cranes' or herons; SA 1969.008.A70; SA 1976.191.A3.

Fossils and Genesis, p. 148
James H. Burns, 'Zeal, Zoology and Natural Theology', paper delivered to the Scottish Church History Society, New College, Edinburgh, 25 October 2005; Hugh Miller, *Cruise of the Betsey,* Edinburgh 1858, p. 7.

Seashell games, p. 148
An Island Shore: selected writings of Robert Rendall, ed. Neill Dickson, Kirkwall, 1990, pp. 136–152.

CHAPTER SIX: Islands and Skerries

Seal hunters, p. 154
Pennant, T., *A Tour in Scotland and Voyage to the Hebrides 1772*, ed. Simmons, A., Edinburgh, 1998, p. 564; Martin, *Description*, pp. 61–6; Campbell J.G., *Otherworld,* pp. 131, 156–7; Marwick, *Folklore*, pp. 27–9, 152–6.

The Great Selkie, p. 155
Lyle, *Ballads*, pp. 124–5; Marwick, *Folklore*, p. 28; Campbell J.G. *Otherworld,* pp. 156–7; Carmichael Watson, *CG* IV, pp. 12–17.
Tocher I, pp. 257–9, 1971.
Campbell, J.G., *Otherworld*, pp. 118/376.

The sacred goose, p. 156
Anson, *Fisher,* p. 132; C.F. Gordon Cumming, *In the Hebrides*, London 1883, p. 369; Henderson, *Survivals*, p. 121.

Fulmar, p. 158
Martin, *Description,* p. 284.

Great auk, p. 161
Wiglesworth, J., *St Kilda and its Birds,* Liverpool, 1903, p. 37; Robson, M., *St Kilda*, Port of Ness, 2005, pp. 578–9.

MacPhee's dog, p. 169
Campbell, J.G., *Otherworld,* p. 64.

Hunting shags, p. 170
Arran, SSS SA 1965.130; Mingulay, SA, 1960.95–6; Westray. SA, 1968. 195; Barra. SA, 1976.190.

Rat satire, p. 172
Frazer, *Golden Bough*, p. 530–1; Campbell, J.G., *Otherworld*, p. 122–3; *Tocher* 5.31–7, p. 333; Forbes, *Gaelic Names of Beasts*, pp. 206–7.

The territorial eagle, p. 174
Martin, *Description,* p. 26.

CHAPTER SEVEN: Farm and Croft

The Burghead bulls, p. 179
Sally Foster, *Picts, Gaels and Scots,* Edinburgh, 1996, pp. 41–3; Henderson, *Survivals,* pp. 273–5; *The Tain,* ed. Kinsella, T., Oxford, 1969; Walter Scott, *Letters on Demonology and Witchcraft,* Ware and London 2001, letter V, p. 99.

Cattle raids, p. 180
Martin, *Description,* pp. 101–2.
Edward Burt, *Letters from a Gentleman in the north of Scotland,* London 1815, vol. II, pp. 208–14; Forbes, *Names*, p. 96.
Legends of the Saints in the Scottish Dialect of the Fourteenth Century, ed. W.M. Metcalfe, Edinburgh, 1896 vol.II, pp. 316–7; cf. Forbes, *Lives,* pp. 16–17.

Charm for rutting, p. 182
Adomnán, *Life of St Columba* II.27.
Snorri Sturluson, *The Prose Edda,* ed. Jean Young, Cambridge 1954, pp. 55–6, 86–9; Walter Traill Dennison, *Orkney Folklore and Traditions,* Kirkwall, 1961, pp. 8–9; Marwick, *Folklore,* pp. 20–22, 139–44; 'The Chase of Sliabh Truim', *Duanaire* I., ed. MacNeill, p. 192.

Beltane and winter traditions, p. 183
Campbell, J.G., *Otherworld*; Campbell, J.L., *Rites,* p. 67; J.G. Fraser, *The Golden Bough*, abridged edition, London 1987, pp. 617–22; F. Marian McNeill, *The Silver Bough*, Glasgow 1959, vol.2, pp. 62–3, 543, 546, 553; Marwick, *Folklore*, pp. 117; Gregor, 'Notes', p. 159.

Fairies, witches and traditional healers, p. 184
Martin, *Description*, pp. 110, 120; Campbell, J.G., Otherworld, pp. 73, 96, 99–100.
Kirk, *The Secret Commonwealth of Elves, Fauns and Fairies*, ed. Andrew Laing, London, 1893, p.11.
Walter Mason papers WM/8/7/4, Scottish Borders Council archives, Selkirk.

Year of the sheep, p. 188
This song 'Dùthaich Mhic Aoidh' can be heard on the website *www.tobairandualchais.co.uk* and also on Kathleen MacInnes's 2006 album 'Òg-Mhadainn Shamraidh'.

Milking sheep, p. 189
Robert Burns, 'The Lea Rig', *Complete Poems and Songs of Robert Burns,* Glasgow 1995, pp. 665–6; SSS SA.1966.19.A5.

Nothing wasted, p. 191
Campbell, J.L. *Rites*, p. 59.
Shaw, *Folksongs*, p. 49; Marwick, *Folklore,* p. 130; Anson, *Fisher*, p. 147; Forbes, *Names*, p. 216.

Horseman's Word, p.193
Timothy Neat, *The Horseman's Word,* Edinburgh 2002; Hamish Henderson, 'The Horseman's Word' in *The Scots Magazine*, May 1967; Marwick, *Folklore,* pp. 66–8, 192; Colin MacDonald, *Highland Life and Lore: Croft and Ceilidh and Highland Memories,* Edinburgh 1997, pp. 44–5.

Remedies from mare's milk, p. 193
Timothy Neat, *The Summer Walkers*, Edinburgh 1996, p. 3; Shaw, *Folksongs,* p.50; Henderson, *Survivals*, p. 337.

Night riders, p. 194
Henderson, *Survivals*, pp. 109–114.

Morality and blessings, p. 195
Williamson, *Fireside Tales of the Traveller Children*, Edinburgh 1983, pp. 87–104.
Carmichael, *CG* I, pp. 208–9; 246–7.

Pig-keeping in the city, p. 196
Dictionary of the Scots Language, s.v. 'swine'; Campbell, J.G., *Otherworld,* pp. 16, 77.
Forbes, *Names*, pp. 198–202; Gregor, 'Notes', pp. 129–30.
Mark 5.1–17; *The Works of Sir David Lindsay,* ed. Hamer, D., Scottish Texts Society, Third series (2), Edinburgh, 1931, vol. II, pp. 206–7; Rogers, C., *Transactions of the Royal Historical Society,* London, 1877, vol. 5, p. 380.

Hens, p. 197
Crombie, MS T206 T.

Cockerels, p. 198
Colin MacDonald, 'Echoes of the Glen', in *Life in the Highlands and Islands of Scotland,* Edinburgh 1993, pp. 60–62; *see also* Gregor, 'Notes', p. 140; Campbell, J.G., *Otherworld*, p. 226 and Henderson, *Survivals*, pp. 266–7, 337. Cf. Anson, *Fisher*, p. 48.

Collies in the divine service, p. 200
'The Sagacity of a Shepherd's Dog,' in *Blackwood's Magazine*, January 1818, pp. 417–21. The event is dated to around 1773. Michael Robson has identified the writer as William Laidlaw.
James Russell, *Reminiscences of Yarrow,* 1894, pp. 168–71, 361.

In a hare's likeness, p. 205
Campbell, J.G., *Otherworld*, pp. 26, 175, 188; Scott, *Letters,* pp. 99–100, 169–173; Carlo Ginzburg, *Ecstasies: Deciphering the Witches' Sabbath,* London 1991, p. 11.

Mouse lore, p. 208
Carmichael Watson, *CG* IV, pp. 8–9; Campbell, J.G., *Otherworld,* pp. 119, 375.
Forbes, *Names,* pp. 206–7; Martin, *Description,* p. 380; Marwick, *Folklore*, p. 130.

Rats for evermore, p. 208
SSS SA 1972.206.A2, recorded by Sheila Scott.

The 'Teuchit Storm', p. 218
Carlyle Letters 1827 4:202–6; www.carlyleletters.dukejournals.org.
Gregor, 'Notes' p. 143; cf Forbes, *Names*, p. 299.

Skylark song, p. 220
Andy Hunter, SSS SA 1973, 174 sung by Lizzie Higgins.
Crombie MS. T206 T.

Persecution, p. 222
Robert Tannahill, *Poems,* pp. 159–60; cf. Henderson, *Survivals,* p. 96; Gregor, 'Notes', pp. 13–40.

Where does the corncrake go in winter?, p. 224
Martin, *Description,* p.71; Forbes, *Names,* p. 254.

The harvest corncrake, p. 224
Carmichael Watson, *CG* IV, pp. 22–3.

CHAPTER EIGHT: About Town

St Mungo and the robin, p. 231
Forbes, *Names,* p. 328; Jocelyn of Furness, *Life of Kentigern,* V, 552–6.

A song in May, p. 232
Forbes, *Names,* p. 304.

Magpie lore, p. 233
Campbell, J.L., *Rites,* pp. 35–7; Forbes, *Names*, p. 303; Gregor, *Notes,* pp. 137–8; Crombie MS T206 T.

Reynard in Paradise, p. 241
From the album 'Posted Sober', 2000, Inner City Sound Records.
Swans on the Nor' Loch, p. 243
Extracts from the Records of the Burgh of Edinburgh 1589–1603, Edinburgh 1927, pp. 10–11; *Extracts from the Records of the Burgh of Edinburgh 1665–1680*, ed. Marguerite Wood, Edinburgh 1950, pp. 298–9.
Faithful cohorts: milk horses, p. 244
Tocher vol. 51, 006b; SA1985.28.49–51. Recorded by Gail Christy.
Tracer horses, p. 245
James Watson Farquhar, unpublished memoirs, Edinburgh 1998, pp. 57–8.
Beyond the grave: Greyfriars Bobby, p. 246
Jan Bondeson, *Greyfriars Bobby*, Stroud 2011, pp. 112–22.

CHAPTER NINE: Wild Work

Poor Bruin, p. 252
MacGillivray, *Journal*, pp. 106–9.
It's complicated, p. 254
Colin MacDonald, Highland Journey, in *Life in the Highlands and Islands of Scotland*, Edinburgh 1999, pp. 17–18.
Whizz and dirlos, p. 256
Marwick, *Folklore*, pp. 127–8.
Sly thief, sly saint, p. 257
William Mackenzie, 'Gaelic Incantations, Charms and Blessings of the Hebrides', *Transactions of the Gaelic Society of Inverness*, XVIII, 1891–2, pp. 101–2.
Ace with Animals, p. 259
Personal communication with Mary Low, summer 2007.
The beginnings of the animal welfare movement, p. 261
David Hume, *An Enquiry Concerning the Principles of Morals*, ed. Tom L. Beauchamp, Oxford,1998, p.18; Nicolas Malebranche, *The Search for Truth*, ed. T.M. Lennon and P.J. Olscamp, Cambridge 1997, pp. 98, 494–5.
Neat, *Horseman's Word*, p. 57.
Aristotle, *Politics*, I.8; Mary Low, 'Humans and Other Animals in Alexander Carmichael's *Carmina Gadelica*', *Journal for the Study of Religion, Nature and Culture*' I.3.2007, London 2007, pp. 371–94.
Thomas Chalmers, 'On Cruelty to Animals: a Sermon, preached in Edinburgh, 5 March, 1826', published Glasgow 1826, p. 39; Proverbs 12.10.
One Hundred Years of Work for Animals 1839–1939, Scottish SPCA Report, Edinburgh 1939, pp. 9–85.

CHAPTER TEN: Creatures of the Mind

Serpents, leopards, etc., p. 263
Gray, Alasdair, *Lanark*, Edinburgh, 1991, pp. 39–69; John Barbour, *The Buik of Alexander*, Cambridge, 1992, pp. 437, line 11016. The ascription to Barbour is contested; Gilbert Hay, *The Buik of Alexander the Conqueror*, STS series IV, vol. II, passim, especially pp. 73, 84, 120, 131, 135, 161, 172.
River Ness monster, p. 264
Adomnan, *Life of St Columba*, II.27.
Water monsters, p. 264
Snorri Sturluson, *The Prose Edda*, ed. Jean Young, Cambridge, 1954, pp. 55–6, 86–9; Walter Traill Dennison, *Orkney Folklore and Traditions*, Kirkwall, 1961, pp. 8–9; Marwick, *Folklore*, pp. 20–22, 139–44; 'The Chase of Sliabh Truim', *Duanaire* I., ed. MacNeill, p. 192.
Beware the beast, p. 264
Campbell J.G. *Otherworld*, p. 117; *Tocher* 50, pp. 407–11
Toothache worm, p. 264
Alexander MacBain, 'Gaelic Incantations', *Transactions of the Gaelic Society of Inverness*, XVII 1890–91, pp. 255–7, 264–6; William Mackenzie, 'Gaelic Incantations and Charms of the Hebrides', *Transactions of the Gaelic Society of Inverness*, XVIII 1891–2, pp. 154–5, 172.
Water horses, Raasay, p. 264
Campbell, J.G., *Otherworld*, pp. 109–114; MacPherson, J., *Tales from Barra*, Edinburgh 1992 pp. 130–1; MacKay, J.G., More *West Highland Tales*, vol. II, ed. Matheson et al., Edinburgh 1960, pp. 12–13; Henderson, *Survivals*, pp. 136–8; Campbell, J.L and Thomson, Derek, *Tour of Edward Lhuyd in the Scottish Highlands, 1699–1700*, Oxford 1963, p.56.
Kelpie: loss at sea, p. 265
Crombie T206; Anson, *Fisher*, p. 106.
More water horses, N. Isles variants and water bull, p. 265
Campbell, J.G., *Otherworld*, p.115; Shaw, *Folksongs*, pp. 11, 170; Marwick, *Folklore*, p. 23–4; Henderson, *Survivals*, pp. 138–40; *Tocher* 50, 348–54.
Mermaid, p. 265
Romans 8.35–39; Psalm 104.24–26; Daniel 4.33; 7.1–8; Ezekiel 32.2. Revelation 12; 13.1–10.
Kells beasts, St Michael, p. 266
Revelation 4.7; Irenaeus of Lyon, *Adversus Haereses* 3.11.8.
Bestiaries, Michael Scot, p. 267
Mary Low, *St Cuthbert's Way*, Glasgow 2000, pp. 70, 83 n.17. Pliny's *Natural History* was also an important source.
'Evernew tongue', p. 268
Máire Herbert and Martin MacNamara, *Irish Biblical Apocrypha*, London, 2004, 116–7
Unicorn, pp. 269–70
Charles J. Burnett and Mark D. Dennis, *Scotland's Heraldic Heritage*, Edinburgh 1997, pp. 51–5; *Dictionary of the Scots Language*, s.v. unicorn; Josephine Barry, 'Weaving the Unicorn: new tapestries for Stirling Castle,' background research paper for Historic Scotland, March 2001; Robert Henryson, *Moral Fables*, ed. Gopen, pp. 86–7; Numbers 23.22; 24.8; Deuteronomy. 33.17; Job 39.9–10; Psalm 22.21; 29.6; 92.10. Isaiah 34.7.
Rona, Dornoch and Skibo, p. 271
Carmichael, *CG* I, p. 127; cf. Campbell, J.G. *Otherworld*, pp. 118, 375; Anne Dempster, 'The Folklore of Sutherlandshire' *The Folklore Journal*, vol. 6, no. 4, 1888, pp. 156–7; Forbes, *Names*, p. 403; Henderson, *Survivals*, pp. xxii–xxiii.
An unusual pet, p. 271
SSS SA.1959.27.B10; The informant may have been Sandy Gillies. For the persistence of Dòmhnall Gorm's dread reputation, see John Shaw, 'Emigrating legends and Sea Change,' *Folklore* vol. 37, pp. 52–7.
Capturing the sea cattle, pp. 271
Campbell J.G., *Otherworld*, pp. 14, 72.
Mingulay man, p. 272
This is the version told by Angus John Campbell in Shaw, *Folksongs*, p.11; cf. MacPherson, *Tales*, pp. 129–30; SA 1974/156/A2; *Tocher* 16, 1974,

pp. 308–311. Recorded by Donald A. MacDonald.

Ornithological notes, p. 272

Henderson, *Survivals,* pp. 136–8, 143–4.

Aberdeenshire kelpies, p. 272

Anon. and John Milne, *Aberdeen Weekly Journal*, 13 May 1903.

The Coddy, p. 273

MacPherson, *Tales*, p. 116.

Macmhuirich's beast, p. 273

William Gillies, 'Alexander Carmichael and the Clann Mhuirich' *Scottish Gaelic Studies,* 20, 2000, pp. 1–66; Angus Matheson, *CG* V. pp. 314–9.

BIBLIOGRAPHY

Alcock, L., 'From realism to carcicature: reflections on Insular depictions of animals and people, *Proceedings of the Society of Antiquaries of Scotland,* 128, Edinburgh, 1998

Anson, P., *Fisher Folklore,* London 1965

Armit, I., *Celtic Scotland,* London 1997

Armstrong, E. A., *The Folklore of Birds,* London 1958

Arnold, N. & Overden, D., *Reptiles & Amphibians,* London 2004

Brown, L., *British Birds of Prey,* London 1976

Barbour, J. *The Buik of Alexander,* Cambridge 1992

Barry, J., 'Weaving the Unicorn: new tapestries for Stirling Castle,' background research paper for Historic Scotland, March 2001

Bellows, H.A. (trans) *The Poetic Edda,* Lampeter 1991

Best, R.I., 'Prognostications of the raven and the wren' *Eriu* VIII, Dublin 1916

Black, G.F., 'Scottish Charms and Amulets', *Proceedings of the Society of Antiquaries of Scotland* 27, Edinburgh 1892–3.

Black, R., (Raghnall MacilleDhuibh), 'The Quern-Dust Calendar', *West Highland Free Press,* 13 July 2006

Black, R. *see also* Campbell, J.G.

Bondeson, J., *Greyfriars Bobby,* Stroud 2011

Buczacki, S, *Fauna Britannica,* London 2002

Burnett, C.J., and Dennis, M.D., *Scotland's Heraldic Heritage,* Edinburgh 1997

Burns, J.H., 'Zeal, Zoology and Natural Theology', paper delivered to the Scottish Church History Society, New College, Edinburgh, 25 October 2005

Burns, R., *Complete Poems and Songs of Robert Burns,* ed. Barke, J., Glasgow 1995

Burt, E., *Letters from a Gentleman in the north of Scotland,* London, 1815, vol. II

Campbell, J.F. *Leabhar na Feinne,* London 1872

Campbell, J.F. *The Fians, Waifs and Strays of Celtic Tradition,* Argyllshire Series IV, London 1891

Campbell, J.F., *Popular Tales of the West Highlands,* vols I–III, Hounslow 1983

Campbell, J.G., ed. Black, R., *The Gaelic Otherworld: John Gregorson Campbell's Superstitions of the Highlands and Islands of Scotland* and *Witchcraft and Second Sight in the Highlands and Islands,* Edinburgh 2005

Campbell, J.L. and Hall, T.H., *Strange Things,* Edinburgh 2006

Campbell, J.L. and Thomson, D., *Tour of Edward Lhuyd in the Scottish Highlands, 1699–1700,* Oxford 1963

Campbell, J.L., (ed.) *A Collection of Highland Rites and Customes Copied by Edward Lhuyd from the Manuscript of the Rev James Kirkwood (1650–1705) and annotated with the aid of the Rev John Beaton,* Cambridge 1975

Carmichael Watson, J., (ed.) *Carmina Gadelica* III–IV, Edinburgh, 1940–1

Carmichael, A. (ed.), *Carmina Gadelica* I–II, Edinburgh 1900

Carmina Gadelica, see Carmichael A., Carmichael Watson J., and Matheson, A.

Chalmers, T., 'On Cruelty to Animals: a Sermon, preached in Edinburgh, 5 March, 1826', Glasgow 1826

Clutton-Brock, T. and MacIntyre, N., *Red Deer,* Grantown-on-Spey 1999

Cocker, M., Mabey, R, *Birds Britannica,* London 2005

Coddy, *see* MacPherson, J.

Collier, R., *Scottish Wildlife,* Lanark 1992

Colquhoun, J., *The Moor and the Loch* volumes 1 & 2, Edinburgh & London nd

Cooper, J. Ashley, *The Great Salmon Rivers of Scotland,* London 1980

Cunningham, P., *Birds of the Outer Hebrides,* Perth 1983

Darbyshire, J. and Campbell L., *Badgers,* Grantown-on-Spey 1998

Dee, T., *The Running Sky,* London 2010

Dempster, A., 'The Folklore of Sutherlandshire' *The Folklore Journal,* vol. 6, no.4, 1888

Dennis R., *Puffins,* Lanark 1990

Dennis, R., *Ospreys,* Lanark 1991

Dennis, R., *Peregrine Falcons,* Lanark, 1991

Dennison, W.T., *Orkney Folklore and Traditions,* Kirkwall 1961

Dickson, N., (ed.) *An Island Shore: selected writings of Robert Rendall,* Kirkwall 1990

Dickson, T., (ed), *Compota thesaurariorum Regum Scotorum,* Edinburgh 1877

Durkheim, E., *The Elementary Forms of Religious Life,* ed. Fields, K., New York 1995

Eliade, M., *From Primitives to Zen,* London 1967

Extracts from the Records of the Burgh of Edinburgh 1589–1603 [editor not named], Edinburgh 1927

Extracts from the Records of the Burgh of Edinburgh 1665–1680, ed. Wood, M., Edinburgh 1950
Farquhar, J., unpublished memoirs, Edinburgh 1998
Fisher, J. and Lockley R.M., *Sea-birds,* London 1954
Fisher, J., *The Fulmar,* London 1952
Fisher, J., *The Shell Bird Book,* London 1966
Fitzgibbon T., *Traditional Scottish Cooking*, London 1991
Fletcher, J., *A Life for Deer,* London, 2000
Forbes, A., *Gaelic Names of Beasts (mammalia), Birds, Fishes, Insects, Reptiles etc,* Edinburgh 1905
Forbes, A.P. (ed.), *Lives of S. Ninian and S. Kentigern*, Edinburgh 1874
Forgan, S., *The Scottish Fishing Book*, London 2005
Foster, S., *The St Andrews Sarcophagus,* Dublin 1998
Foster, S., *Picts, Gaels and Scots,* London 1996
Fraser, A.F, *The Days of the Garron,* Midlothian 1980
Fraser-Darling, F., *A Herd of Red Deer,* Edinburgh 2008
Fraser-Darling F., *Natural History in The Highlands and Islands*, London 1947
Frazer, J., *The Golden Bough,* London 1987
Freer, A., 'More Folklore from the Hebrides', *Folklore* 13.i., London 1902
Gantz, J., *Early Irish Myths and Sagas*, London 1981
Garvie, E., *Gaelic Names of Plants, Fungi and Animals,* An Teanga 1999
Gillies, .A. L., *Songs of Gaelic Scotland*, Edinburgh 2010
Gillies, W., 'Alexander Carmichael and the Clann Mhuirich', *Scottish Gaelic Studies,* 20, 2000, Aberdeen, pp. 1–66
Ginzburg, C., *Ecstasies: Deciphering the Witches' Sabbath,* London 1991
Giraldus Cambrensis, *Expugnatio Hibernica, the Conquest of Ireland,* I.33, A. Scott and F. Martin (eds), Dublin 1978
Gordon Cumming, C., *In the Hebrides*, London 1883
Gordon, S., *Days with the Golden Eagle,* Dunbeath 2003
Graham, K., *Hares,* Grantown-on-Spey 1995
Grant, I., *Highland Folk Ways,* London, 1961
Grant, W., *The Popular Superstitions and Festive Amusements of the Highlanders of Scotland*, London 1851
Greenoak, F., *British Birds, their Folklore. Names and Literature,* London 1997
Gregor, W., 'Notes on the Folklore of the North-east of Scotland', London 1881
Gregory, J.; Goodenough, K.; Gordon, J.; Wrightman, M.; Miller, K.; Benn, S.; Raynor, R.; Owen, R.; Ralston, I.; Dugmore, A.; Kempe, N., *Hostile Habitats,* Scotland's Mountain Environment. 2006
Haldane, A.R.B., *The Drove Roads of Scotland,* Newton Abbot 1973
Hall, S. J.G. and Clutton-Brock, J., *Two Hundred Years of British Farm Livestock*, London, 1989
Hamilton James, C., *Kingfishers,* Grantown-on-Spey 1997
Hart-Davis, D., *Fauna Britannica,* London 2002
Harvey, G., *Shamanism: a reader*, London 2003
Hay, G., *The Buik of Alexander the Conqueror,* ed. Cartwright, J., Scottish Texts Society, series IV, 18, Edinburgh 1990, vol. II
Henderson, G., *Survivals in belief among the Celts*, Glasgow 1911
Henderson, H., 'The Horseman's Word' in *The Scots Magazine*, May 1967
Henderson, L., 'The Road to Elfland: fairy belief and the Childe Ballads' in *The Ballad in Scottish History,* ed. Cowan, E., East Linton 2000
Henryson, R., *Moral Fables Of Aesop the Phrygian,* ed. Gopen, G., Notre Dame 1987
Henryson, R., *The Complete Works,* ed. Parkinson, D., Kalamazoo 2010
Her Majesty's Commission of Enquiry into the Condition of Crofters and Cottars in the Highlands and Islands, London 1884
Hewer, H.R., *British Seals,* London 1974
Hull, E., 'The Hawk of Achill, or the Legend of the Oldest Animals', *Folklore*, Dec. 1932
Hume, D., *An Enquiry Concerning the Principles of Morals,* ed. Beauchamp, T., Oxford 1998
Hunter, M., *Shetland Ponies from Shetland,* Shetland 2000
Hurrell, H.G., *Pine Martens,* London 1963
Jacobsen, M., *Shamanism,* Oxford 1999
James,Viscount of Stair, *The Institutions of the Law of Scotland*, ed. More, J., vol. 1, Edinburgh 1832
Kerr Cameron, D., *The Ballad and the Plough*, London 1987
Kirk, R., *The Secret Commonwealth of Elves, Fauns and Fairies,* ed. Laing, A., London 1893
Kirkwood, J., *see* Campbell, J.L. (1975)
Laidlaw, W., The Sagacity of a Shepherd's Dog,' in *Blackwood's Magazine*, Edinburgh, January 1818
Lamont, D., *Strath, Isle of Skye*, Glasgow 1913
Lever, C., *The Naturalized Animals of the British Isles,* London 1977
Lewis, C., *The Illustrated Guide to Chickens*, London 2010
Lockley, R.M., *Grey Seal, Common Seal,* London 1891
Love, J. A., *Eagles,* London, 1989
Low, M., *Celtic Christianity and Nature,* Edinburgh, 1996
Low, M., *St Cuthbert's Way,* Glasgow, 2000
Low, M., 'Humans and Other Animals in Alexander Carmichael's *Carmina Gadelica*', *Journal for the Study of Religion, Nature and Culture*' I.3, 2007, London 2007
Low, M., 'Adomnán among the Bird Hunters', in *Adomnán of Iona,* ed. Wooding, J., et al., Dublin 2010
Lyle, E., *Scottish Ballads*, Edinburgh 1994
Mac Fhionnlaigh, D., *Oran na Comhachaig / The Owl of Strone,* ed. Mackechnie, J., Glasgow 1946
MacBain, A., 'Gaelic Incantations', *Transactions of the Gaelic Society of Inverness,* 17, Inverness 1890–91
MacDonald, C., *Highland Life and Lore* (*Croft and Ceilidh* and *Highland Memories*), Edinburgh 1997
MacDonald, C., *Life in the Highlands and Islands of Scotland* (*Echoes of the Glen* and *Highland Journey,* Edinburgh 1993
MacDonald, D., 'Righ Eilifacs' in *Scottish Studies* 16, Edinburgh 1972
MacDonald, F., *Missions to the Gaels,* Edinburgh 2006
MacDougall, J., *Folk and Hero Tales,* Waifs and Strays of Celtic Tradition, Argyllshire Series III, London 1891
MacGillivray, W., *A Hebridean Naturalist's Journal, 1817–1818*, ed. Ralph, R., Stornoway 1996
MacKay, J.G., *More West Highland Tales,* vol. 2, ed. Matheson, A., et al., Edinburgh 1960
Mackenzie, O., *A Hundred Years in the Highlands*, London 1950
Mackenzie, W., 'Gaelic Incantations and Charms of the Hebrides', *Trans-actions of the Gaelic Society of Inverness*, 18, Inverness 1891–2
Maclean, C., *Island at the edge of the world: the story of St Kilda,* Edinburgh 1972
MacLellan, D., *Stories from South Uist,* Edinburgh 1997
MacLeod, A., *The Songs of Duncan Bàn MacIntyre,* Edinburgh 1978
MacNeill, E., *Duanaire Finn / Book of the Lays of Finn,* vol. 1, Irish Texts Society 7, Dublin 1908
MacPherson, J., *Tales from Barra: told by the Coddy,* Edinburgh 1992
MacPherson, the Rev. H.A.; Lascelles, the Hon. G.; Richardson, C.,

Gibbons, J.S.; Longman, G.H.; Kenney, Col. H., *The Hare*, Southampton 1986

Maitland, P. S, *Freshwater Fishes of Britain and Europe*, London 1972

Malebranche, N., *The Search for Truth*, ed. Lennon, T. and Olscamp, P., Cambridge 1997

Martial, *Liber Spectaculum*, in *Martialis Epigrammata* ed. Heraeus, W. and Borovskij, J., Leipzig 1976/82

Martin, M., *Description of the Western Islands of Scotland*, second edition, Edinburgh 1981

Martin, B. P., *Sporting Birds of Britain and Ireland*, Newton Abbot 1992

Marwick, E., *The Folklore of Orkney and Shetland*, Edinburgh 2000

Matheson, A. (ed), *Carmina Gadelica* V–VI, Edinburgh 1971

McInerny, C.; Murray, R.; McGowan, B.; Zonfrillo, B.; Jardine, D.; Grundy, D.; Betts, M.; *The Birds of Scotland*, Vols 1 & 2, East Lothian 2007

McNeill, F., *The Silver Bough*, vol. 2, Glasgow 1959

Meyer, K., *Ancient Irish Poetry*, London 1911

Miller, D., *Seals*, Lanark 1991

Miller, H., *The Cruise of the Betsey*, Edinburgh 1858

Miller, J., *Salt in the Blood – Scotland's Fishing Communities Past and Present*, Edinburgh 1999

Milne, J., *Aberdeen Weekly Journal*, 13 May 1903

Murphy, G., *Duanaire Finn / Book of the Lays of Finn*, vol.2 and 3, Irish Texts Society 28 and 43, Dublin, 1933 and 1953

Murray, D.S., *The Guga Hunters*, Edinburgh 2008

Napier Commission, *see Her Majesty's Commission of Enquiry*

Neat, T., *The Horseman's Word*, Edinburgh 2002

Neat, T., *The Summer Walkers*, Edinburgh 1996

Nelson, B., *The Gannet*, London 2001

Nicholson, J. R., *Shetland Folklore*, London 1981

O hOgain, D., *Myth, Legend & Romance*, London 1990

O'Meara, J. (trans.), *The Voyage of St Brendan*, Gerrards Cross 1991

Pennant, T., *A Tour in Scotland 1769*, ed. Osborne, B., Edinburgh 2000

Pullar, P., *Rural Portraits, Scottish Native Farm Animals, Characters & Landscapes*, Wigtown 2003

Ralph, R., *see* MacGillivray, W.

Rendall, R., see Dickson, N.

Riddle, G., *Seasons with the Kestrel*, London 1992

Irvine Robertson, J., *Harvesting the Field*, London 1991

Irvine Robertson, J., *Random Shots*, London 1990

Robertson, J., *Tour through the Western Islands* 1768

Robson, M., *Curiosities of Art and Nature: the new annotated and illustrated edition of Martin Martin's Classic "A Description of the Western Islands of Scotland"*, Port of Ness, 2003

Robson, M., *St Kilda: church, visitors and natives*, Port of Ness 2005

Ross, A., *Pagan Celtic Britain*, London, revised edn 1992

Russell, J., *Reminiscences of Yarrow*, Edinburgh 1886

Sage, D., *Memorabilia Domestica*, second edition, Edinburgh 1975

Salvin, F. H.; & Brodrick, W., *Falconry in the British Isles*, London 1980

Scott, W., *Letters on Demonology and Witchcraft*, London 2001

Scottish Society for the Prevention of Cruelty to Animals (SSPCA), *One Hundred Years of Work for Animals 1839–1939*, Edinburgh 1939

Scrope, W., *Days and Nights of Salmon Fishing*, London 1885

Seton, G., *St Kilda past and present*, Edinburgh 1878

Shaw, J. '(E)migrating legends and Sea Change,' *Folklore: Electronic Journal of Folklore* vol. 37, Tartu 2007

Shaw, M.F., *Folksongs and Folklore of South Uist*, Edinburgh 1999

Smith, W. McCombie, *The Romance of Poaching in the Highlands of Scotland*, Stirling 1904

Snorri Sturluson, *The Prose Edda*, ed. Young, J., Cambridge 1954

St John, C., *The Wild Sports & Natural History of the Highlands*, London 1981

Statistical Account of Scotland, ed. Sinclair, J., Edinburgh, 1791–2

Steven, K., *Island*, Edinburgh 2009

Steven, M., *Parish Life in Eighteenth-Century Scotland*, Aberdeen 1995

Stewart, A., *Nether Lochaber: the Natural History, Legends and Folklore of the West Highlands*, Edinburgh 1883

Stewart, K., *Crofts and Crofting*, Edinburgh 1980

Stewart, W., *Popular Superstitions and Festive Amusements of the Highlanders of Scotland*, London 1851

Svensson, L.; Mullarney, K,; and Zetterstrom, D., *Collins Bird Guide* 2nd edition, London 2009

Tannahill, R., *Poems chiefly in the Scottish Dialect*, Paisley 1807

Thom, V.M, *Birds in Scotland*, London 1986

Thomas, K., *The Sporting Wife*, London 1962

Thompson F., *Crofting Years*, Edinburgh 1989

Thomson, T., and Innes, C., (eds), *Acts of the Parliaments of Scotland*, IV 628/2, Record Commission, Edinburgh 1814–75

School of Scottish Studies Sound Archive:

SA 1953.168 (Skye, Norman MacDonald, cod)
SA 1955.097 (Yell, Brucie Henderson, seals)
SA 1956.141.A5 (Roxburghshire, John Hewit, birds)
SA.1959.27.B10 (Smearisary, Sandy Gillies, monster)
SA, 1960.95-6 (Barra, Roderick MacNeill, cormorant)
SA 1965.130 (Arran, John Henderson, shellfish)
SA.1966.19.A5 (Berwickshire, Edwin Davidson, ewes)
SA 1968.88 (Islay, John MacEwan, shellfish)
SA 1968.195 (Westray, John Hutcheson, cormorant)
SA 1969.008.A70 (Islay, James MacArthur, heron)
SA 1969.151 (Islay, John Kennedy, whelks)
SA 1970.341 (Donald MacSween, Jura, whelks)
1972.206.A2 (Lanarkshire, Ned Robertson, rats)
SA 1973,174 (Midlothian, Lizzie Higgins sings Andy Hunter, skylark)
SA 1974.207 (Shetland, Tom Tulloch, rats)
SA 1974/156/A2 (Grimsay, Peter Morrison, sea cattle)
SA 1976.190 (Barra, Roderick MacPherson, wild boar)
SA1985.28.49-51 (Edinburgh, Willie Skedd, horses)

Tocher: Tales, Songs, Tradition, selected from the School of Scottish Studies Archives, vols 1, 50, 51, Edinburgh 1971ff

Tulloch, B., *Bobby Tulloch's Shetland*, London 1988

Tulloch, B., *Otters*, Grantown-on-Spey 1994

various authors, *Shetland Breeds*, USA 2003

Wain, B., *Vets in Kelso*, Kelso 1986

Walter Mason papers, WM/8/7/4, Scottish Borders Council Museum and Gallery Service

Watson, D., *Birds of Mountain and Moorland*, Edinburgh & London 1972

Whitehead, G.K., *Half a Century of Scottish Deer Stalking*, Shrewsbury 1992

Wiglesworth, J., *St Kilda and Its Birds*, Liverpool 1903

Williamson, D., *Fireside Tales of the Traveller Children*, Edinburgh 1983

Woolfson, E., *A Life with Birds*, London

INDEX